Baldrige Award Winning Quality

Seventeenth Edition
Covers the
2008 Award

How to Interpret the Baldrige Criteria for Performance Excellence

Baldrige Award Winning Quality

Seventeenth Edition
Covers the
2008 Award

How to Interpret the Baldrige Criteria for Performance Excellence

Mark Graham Brown

CRC Press
Taylor & Francis Group
Boca Raton   London   New York

CRC Press is an imprint of the
Taylor & Francis Group, an **informa** business

A PRODUCTIVITY PRESS BOOK

7th October, 2008
54050000 301457

Productivity Press
Taylor & Francis Group
270 Madison Avenue
New York, NY 10016

© 2008 by Mark Graham Brown
Productivity Press is an imprint of Taylor & Francis Group, an Informa business

No claim to original U.S. Government works
Printed in the United States of America on acid-free paper
10 9 8 7 6 5 4 3 2 1

International Standard Book Number-13: 978-1-4200-8014-8 (Softcover)

Visit the Taylor & Francis Web site at
http://www.taylorandfrancis.com

and the Productivity Press Web site at
http://www.productivitypress.com

CONTENTS

INTRODUCTION

Almost two decades after their initial publication, The Malcolm Baldrige Award criteria continue to be a powerful set of guidelines for running an effective organization. Originally designed for manufacturing businesses, the criteria evolved to be relevant to service companies, health care organizations, schools, and in 2006 to nonprofit and government organizations. Not only are many large and small businesses using the criteria to drive improvement, but many branches of the military use the Baldrige model to assess their units, as well as a number of federal, state, and local government organizations. Most states now have their own Baldrige-styled awards, using the same criteria and an identical or similar application and review process. Many of the Baldrige Award winners in the past five years have won state awards before becoming national winners. Appendix A of this book lists the state awards based on the Baldrige criteria. Interest in Baldrige was on the decline for about five years, but in recent years, the number of applicants was about double the average for the last few years. Applicants from healthcare, education, and non-profit organizations have dramatically increased. Interest in Baldrige is clearly on the rise again.

When this book was first published in 1990, it was the only book on the Baldrige Award and criteria. Since then, there have been more than 20 other books and hundreds of articles published on the award. The Baldrige criteria are identical to those used in Brazil, Japan, Australia, New Zealand, and a number of other countries. The European Quality Award also parallels Baldrige on most of the criteria. What we have now is a worldwide set of standards that can be employed in running any type of organization, from small to large, from business to charity, to hospital or school.

The Growth and Decline of the Quality Movement

The Malcolm Baldrige National Quality Award program was started in 1988 to promote total quality management, or TQM, as an increasingly important approach for improving the competitiveness of American companies. In the past seventeen years, what started as a major business fad has become integrated into the fabric of the way many organizations do their business. Some elements of TQM have become standard in many organizations, including the use of statistics to analyze data, documentation and improvement of key work processes, pulling together employees into teams, and investing in employee education and training. Other aspects of the TQM movement have faded away. One lesson we have learned over the years is that focusing on any one aspect of performance is an unhealthy way to run an organization. A number of companies focused too much effort on quality and too little on other such factors such as profits, new product development, or employee morale. Quality is important in any organization, but so are a number of other factors. Some early Baldrige winners later got into financial trouble even though they had excellent quality. Focusing on defect removal and customer satisfaction does not necessarily lead to improved business performance.

The Baldrige criteria have always been nonprescriptive, supposedly. In other words, the criteria do not provide a checklist or prescription indicating how to run an organization. However, in the early days, the criteria did require or prescribe a quality program that included a mission statement, quality values, quality plans, quality training, quality teams, and quality results. In 1995, the authors of the Baldrige criteria removed the word "quality" from all parts of the criteria and replaced it with "performance." This was much more than a simple word change—the entire focus of the Baldrige Award changed. The old focus was on defect-free products/services and satisfied customers. The focus for the last five years has been on balancing all aspects of organizational performance, including profitability, safety, growth, market share, employee morale, innovation, and a variety of other factors. The new focus has caused the criteria to get much tougher than they were in the early days. I have heard executives from several companies that won Baldrige Awards in the first few years say they could not come close today to earning the 750+ points generally needed to win.

The folks at NIST who revise the Baldrige criteria have done an excellent job of not including the latest business fads in the criteria. You will not find initiatives like "lean," "six-sigma," "e-commerce," or "reengineering" required in the criteria. Being immune to buzzwords has allowed the Baldrige criteria to be accepted widely across the world as the best model for assessing organizational health.

Do Big Corporations Still Follow the Baldrige Model?

Many Fortune 500 corporations in the last few years have dropped the internal Baldrige-based award programs they started in the early 1990s. IBM, AT&T, Baxter Healthcare, Westinghouse, and others have eliminated internal Baldrige Awards in recent years. The U.S. Air Force, the first branch of the military to conduct Baldrige assessments, stopped doing them in 1998. Many of these organizations found that the assessments cost millions of dollars each year, and that there was little evidence the companies improved as a result of the Baldrige assessments. I worked with a large aerospace company for seven years doing Baldrige assessments, and the company did not improve. These assessments failed to lead to improvement because the Baldrige evaluation was a sideline project conducted by a quality department, and the feedback was never incorporated into company strategic plans. Separate Baldrige improvement plans were prepared but never seemed to get executed. Other organizations found that their units became better at playing the Baldrige game; hiring consultants to help write their application and prepare for the on-site visit. Scores went up from year to year, but the organizations really did not become healthier.

The failure of many of these internal Baldrige assessments is in the implementation, not the criteria. Many of the companies that have dropped their Baldrige assessment efforts did so prior to 1997 when the focus of the criteria shifted to business results. It would be difficult to receive a high score on the 2007 criteria without a solid business plan and financial results. Many executives believe that the Baldrige award is still about TQM, and they have moved on to other approaches like Six Sigma and Lean. The Baldrige office has not done a good job of communicating this change in focus to corporate America.

Why More Big Corporations Don't Win the Award

In the early days of the Baldrige Award, the vast majority of winners were big corporations like Motorola, Xerox, Cadillac, and Milliken. In fact, there was talk that unless you had the financial and human resources required to write a good application, hire consultants for help, and prepare every employee for the site visit, you were unlikely to win. As the U.S. progressed through the 1990s, there was a mix of winners that included big and small businesses, service and manufacturing. Since 2000, there have been a declining number of applications from big city corporations and a declining number of winners in this category. Many of the former big company winners such as Xerox and IBM no longer follow the Baldrige model. Many of the others still follow the core values of he Baldrige model but don't necessarily apply for the award. Much of what is in the Baldrige criteria has evolved to become standard business practices. If you look at a company like Southwest Airlines, which has never won the award and probably never applied, you will find that they follow just about all tenets in the Baldrige model and it shows in their performance. In the early days of this award, the big company winners were pioneers and implementing more systematic processes in their organization. What was innovative in 1992 is considered commonplace today, however.

Many big corporations do not apply for the award because the Baldrige principles have become ingrained in the daily operations of most corporations. If you examined most of the Fortune 500, you would find that almost all of them have the basic components asked for in the Baldrige model:

- *Strategic plans that include mission, vision, goals and strategies.*
- *A balanced set of performance measures that go way beyond lagging financial metrics.*
- *Competitor and comparative/benchmark data are gathered to use in setting targets, developing strategies, and improving processes.*
- *Market research on the needs and desires of current and future customers.*
- *Processes for measuring customer satisfaction and product/service quality.*
- *Systematic approaches for selecting the best new employees and training them.*

- *Knowledge management systems have been implemented.*
- *Processes have been documented, analyzed, and improved using systematic approaches such as Lean and Six Sigma.*
- *Results are reviewed on a regular basis and action plans are developed when performance falls below targets.*

The Baldrige program has accomplished a very important goal: it has succeeded in integrating the model into the operational practices of most major corporations around the world. This accomplishment took about 20 years, but the Baldrige model has had major impact on the way corporations conduct their business. That impact is now just beginning to be felt in education, healthcare, and non-profit organizations. Currently, the implementation is spotty, and limited to a few shining stars like Sharp HealthCare, Richland College, and recent military winner, the U.S. Army Armament Research, Development, and Engineering Center in New Jersey. In the future, I hope that the Baldrige principles become so well integrated in these other types of organizations we will see a drop off in the number of applicants in these types of organizations as well.

Ritz-Carlton and Solectron—Two-Time Baldrige Winners

Winning one Baldrige Award is tough enough, but two companies have won the coveted award twice! The Ritz-Carlton hotel chain won the award the first time in 1992, and again in 1999. When they won the award in 1992, critics complained that the company was not profitable, and that good quality is easy when you charge $300 a night. The Ritz-Carlton was owned at the time by a company that also owned the Waffle House restaurants, which are on the other end of the economic spectrum from the Ritz-Carlton. A greater number of people can afford to eat at the Waffle House, however, and that part of the business was profitable enough to help keep the Ritz hotels going.

As the Baldrige criteria changed over the years, so did the Ritz-Carlton. Marriott bought the major share of the company some years ago, and Marriott was concerned about the lack of profitability in most properties. Management at the Ritz-Carlton convinced Marriott to leave them alone, and they continued to follow the new Baldrige model that emphasizes financial results along with customer satisfaction and quality. I spoke with one of the vice presidents from Ritz-Carlton several years ago who informed me that the Ritz- Carlton had become the most profitable division of Marriott. The Ritz-Carlton has done exactly what the new Baldrige criteria call for: demonstrate a balance between financial results and customer and employee satisfaction. Ritz-Carlton did not trade quality for financial results; it has managed to retain the exceptional service that won the award in 1992 while achieving profitability.

Solectron is another two-time Baldrige winner that has had amazing success. The company has grown from about 1,800 employees when it won its first Baldrige Award in 1991 to around 26,000 today, with manufacturing facilities all over the world. Solectron's stock has risen over 1,000% and is picked continually by analysts as a strong investment. The company, which manufactures circuit boards and electrical components, is so successful that it opened a store in the outlet mall in Milpitas, California, for recruiting new employees! Solectron has not had the profit problems that Ritz-Carlton needed to surmount to win a second Baldrige. The challenge for Solectron has been maintaining its strengths and systematic approaches as it experiences explosive growth domestically and internationally. Solectron won its second Baldrige Award in 1997 and continues to show stellar performance when compared to competitors. The company looks at the Baldrige assessment process as one of the biggest consulting bargains out there. A similar evaluation by one of the big consulting firms would cost over $25,000, compared to the few thousand dollars it costs to apply for Baldrige. Solectron uses the feedback from the Baldrige application process to improve the company each year.

Boeing—Another Two-Time Baldrige Winner

David Spong became the first executive in 16 years of Baldrige history to lead two different organizations to the trophy. Spong was the president of Boeing's Airlift and Tanker unit when it won the Baldrige Award in the Manufacturing Category in 1998. Spong then took the job of president of Boeing's Aerospace Support, a 2002 winner. The Airlift and Tanker unit was experiencing many problems with quality and very unsatisfied customers when the Baldrige effort began. Spong and his team turned things around and went on to win the Baldrige Award after about five years of effort. The unit demonstrated some dramatic improvement trends, and results were positive in just about every area of the business. Seeing the impact of the Baldrige model on one business, Spong applied the same approach in his new job in 1999, president of the Aerospace Support Program. The business maintains and upgrades military aircraft so they can fly as long as 75 years.

Costs for this maintenance work were rising, due to an aging military fleet of aircraft, but the Aerospace Support Program managed to cut costs significantly, while improving quality. Defects on the C-17, for example, fell 95 percent! Under Spong's leadership, sales in the program more than doubled from 1999 to 2003 and now account for $4 billion of Boeing's $54 billion in annual revenue. On November 26, 2003, The National Institute of Standards and Technology (NIST) announced that the Boeing Aerospace Support Program had won the Baldrige Award in the Service Category. The story of Baldrige winners was on page six of the Money section of *USA Today* and in the back pages of other papers and magazines.

A few weeks later, Phil Condit, Boeing's CEO resigned. This situation can be troublesome for the Baldrige office, although there was no evidence of ethics problems in the Aerospace Support Program that won Baldrige. Some media outlets may print provocative headlines such as "President Gives Out Baldrige Award to Company with Questionable Ethics" without thoroughly checking the facts or providing the complete details.

Can these difficult situations be prevented? Probably not completely. When asked how Boeing could win a Baldrige award after Boeing had fired several executives for ethics violations and its CEO resigned, The Baldrige office replied and clearly pointed out that:

> A division of Boeing, Boeing Aerospace Support has been named to receive the 2003 Malcolm Baldrige National Quality Award. As an applicant for the Baldrige Award, Boeing Aerospace Support was thoroughly examined by an outside board in seven different areas including leadership; corporate governance; employee and customer relations, and results. The review process took about six months and included a site visit by a team of examiners that took up to a week and a background check. The nine judges that recommended that Boeing Aerospace Support, and six other organizations, receive the Baldrige Award found all seven to be worthy of the Award. As thorough as the evaluation and background check is, no process will ever guarantee knowledge of actions taken by an applicant after completion of the background checks and judging process. We cannot comment on the activities of or the internal controls exercised by the parent, but we have not received any negative comments regarding the selection of Boeing Aerospace Division as a Baldrige Award recipient.

Do Baldrige Winners Really Perform Better?

The real test of the validity of the Baldrige Award criteria is the long-term performance of the winners. NIST conducted a study for nine years, comparing the stock market performance of the Baldrige winners with Standard & Poor's index of 500 stocks. Throughout the nine years of the study, a hypothetical mutual fund of Baldrige companies outperformed the S&P 500 by as much as six to one. During 2004, the last year of the study, the Baldrige fund underperformed the S&P for the second time in 9 years. The companies that had subsidiaries win Baldrige Awards did slightly better, with a –24 percent return, versus a 45 percent return for the S&P. Since such a small percentage of Baldrige winners are publicly traded, the government stopped doing the stock study in 2004.

Does this mean that there is now evidence that following the Baldrige criteria is a mistake? Clearly not. If you had a mutual fund that outperformed the market by a significant factor eight years out of nine, would you dump it after one year of poor performance? I doubt it.

Harry Hertz, Director of the Baldrige Awards suggests that what happened in 2003 and 2004 to the Baldrige companies was because technology stocks did very poorly. Technology stocks are a significant part of the Baldrige portfolio, suggests Hertz. He goes on to suggest that the Baldrige portfolio companies will continue to excel in their performance, and show improvements in 2006.

Patricia Escobedo, an executive at Momentum Textiles in Irvine, California, recently completed a thorough review of the literature on the impact on the performance of companies following the Baldrige model. Momentum Textiles has been following the Baldrige model for years, and has demonstrated phenomenal growth and success that they believe is at least partly due to their adherence to Baldrige principles. Escobedo found a few articles suggesting that following the Baldrige approach did not lead to greater financial success. Most of these studies, however, acknowledge that the Baldrige winners tend to outperform their peers in financial and market performance by a significant margin. What these articles (York and Miree, 2004, and Dean and Tomovic, 2004) suggest is that there is not enough evidence to indicate that following the Baldrige model actually causes the improvements in financial performance. This is certainly a valid point, and other factors are likely to contribute to the Baldrige winner's greater success. Following the Baldrige model, however, always robustly improves products and processes.

Consider the performance of two early Baldrige winners: FedEx and Solectron. When FedEx became the first service company to win the award in 1990, it had sales of $7 billion and 90,000 employees. In 2001, FedEx had revenue of $19.6 billion and 215,000 employees. Similarly, Solectron, when it won the award initially in 1991, had $265 million in revenue and 1,500 employees. It won again in 1997 and had $4 billion in revenue and 18,215 employees. By the year 2001, revenues had grown to $18 billion and Solectron had 60,000 employees! When the economic crash hit the high-tech sector at the end of 2001, Solectron suffered like many, and has shrunk in size and in revenue since 2001 levels. That sort of phenomenal growth is hard to keep going.

More Evidence That Following Baldrige Leads to Business Success

Armstrong, the Lancaster, Pennsylvania, firm that manufactures flooring, furniture, and related items, has been doing Baldrige assessments of its business units for the past several years. Former V.P. Bo McBee, who served as a senior examiner for Baldrige, reports on research in his company that shows a clear correlation between scores on Baldrige assessments and the profitability of a business. In other words, units that do well on Baldrige tend to also do well on their business results. Armstrong's Building Products Operations became one of two companies to win a Baldrige Award in 1995.

Solar Turbines of San Diego is another company that has found success by following the Baldrige criteria. The company began using the Baldrige criteria for self assessment in the early 1990s, and applied for the Baldrige-based California Quality Award several times to receive external feedback on its health as a business. Solar, which manufactures large turbine engines, has about $1 billion in sales and customers all over the world. The company, which is a division of Caterpillar, used the feedback they received from California Award Examiners each year to improve their performance. Originally, they received a Bronze Award, and went on to win Silver and Gold Awards in California. Winners of a Gold Award in California often go on to win a Baldrige the next year. 3M Dental Products was the only gold winner in 1996, and went on to win a Baldrige in 1997. Subsequently, Solar won the Baldrige in 1998. The company was hoping to be a Baldrige finalist and ended up receiving the award in 2004.

Scores were so high for Solar partly because their business results are quite impressive. The company spends 13 percent of its revenue on R&D each year, which is triple the industry average, and up 10 percent from what Solar spent in 1995. Along with impressive sales, profits, and market share growth, Solar clearly stands out as a company that treats its employees well. 86 percent of employees rate the company as a good place to work, which is 32 percentage points higher than the average U.S. business. Incentive pay for employees has also increased from 7.6 percent of salary in 1994 to 10.4 percent in 1997, as the company has become more efficient. On-the-job injuries and workers' compensation claims also show reduced levels and trends over the last four years. Solar is a prime example of how a company has used the Baldrige process to find areas for improvement, over a number of years, to go from being a good company to becoming one of the best in the world.

The Baldrige Award Has Served Its Purpose Well

In spite of all the criticism about fairness in judging, and whether or not meeting the criteria predicts financial success, the Baldrige has done more to improve the quality of U.S. products and services than anything that has come before it. Quality is now something that almost every company in America is working on. The biggest benefit of the Baldrige criteria is that we now have a common framework for making sense out of all of the theories, tools, and approaches that are part of running an effective organization. We have a common language and a common way of understanding where to apply all of these theories and techniques. Another benefit of the Baldrige has been that companies are now sharing and talking to one another to help one another get better. This sharing and helping almost never occurred five years ago—companies kept to themselves and shared only those practices that they were certain would not help a competitor. The Baldrige Award has been successful beyond the greatest expectations of its founders. It has given rise to 18 similar awards in other countries, most of which are modeled exactly on the Baldrige criteria. As of 2006, 45 out of the 50 states in the United States have either established their own quality awards or have an effort underway. Through these "baby Baldriges," the approach is being deployed even more pervasively than through the Baldrige by itself.

Interpreting the Baldrige Criteria

One problem for users of the Baldrige Award criteria is that they can be difficult to interpret. The criteria are written to be very general, because they must apply equally to all types of organizations, and they must apply to organizations ranging in size from a few hundred employees to many thousands. Because the criteria are so general, they are sometimes difficult to interpret. The other thing that makes the criteria hard to use for assessment is that they are nonprescriptive. In other words, they don't tell you how you should run your organization. In my work as a management consultant and as a Baldrige examiner, I've encountered many instances where people had difficulty interpreting the Baldrige criteria. Other examiners and quality improvement consultants I've spoken to report similar observations.

The purpose of this text, then, is to provide readers with a better understanding of the Areas to Address that make up the Baldrige Award criteria. The book is designed to aid organizations that are actually preparing an application for the Baldrige Award, as well as the many organizations that will be using the award criteria as a way of improving their quality improvement efforts.

How to Use This Book

Generally, there are two types of uses for this book:

1. As a guide for individuals who are responsible for coordinating or actually writing a Baldrige Award application or an application for a state award.

2. As a tool for individuals who wish to audit or assess their organization using the Baldrige Award criteria or who wish to apply for an internal award based upon the criteria. Individuals who are responsible for developing assessment and improvement plans based upon the Baldrige criteria will also find the book useful.

The specifics of the book are directed primarily toward the individuals of the first category, with information provided on how to write various sections of the Baldrige Award application. Chapter 1 provides general information on understanding the 2008 Award criteria. Chapter 2 explains how to write an application. Chapter 3 explains how the seven categories of criteria work together as a system, and covers the overall themes carried throughout the criteria. Chapter 4 includes information on the scoring scale. The next seven chapters cover the seven main categories in the Baldrige criteria. Each of these chapters includes an overall explanation of the main category and definitions of the examination items and the areas to address. Also provided are sections entitled "What They're Looking for Here," which describe the criteria as seen by the examiners. This section is followed by a listing of "Key Indicators," or evaluation factors, provided to further assist you with the interpretation of the criteria. Naturally, I assume that those companies seriously considering challenging for the Award have had systems in place for several years and that their use of this text is to help them best represent their systems and demonstrate compliance with the Baldrige criteria.

This information is also helpful to individuals using the criteria for the second purpose. For this second type of user, the various "indicators" that are listed for each of the 32 Areas to Address are helpful in devising Baldrige-based audit instruments and in developing plans rooted in each of the seven categories in the Baldrige criteria. Chapter 12 explains how to plan for a site visit by Baldrige examiners. The final chapter outlines alternative assessment approaches and how to use such assessments as an input to your strategic planning process.

If you are not already familiar with the criteria, I suggest that you quickly review them as a means of preparing for reading and working with this text. For the purpose of actually applying for the award, you should familiarize yourself with *all* the information in this book and the criteria booklet. A copy of the criteria is available free of charge through the Baldrige National Quality Program, National Institute of Standards and Technology, Administration Building, Room A600, 100 Bureau Drive, Stop 1020, Gaithersburg, MD 20899-1020. It is also found on the Baldrige website at: http://www.baldrige.nist.gov.

How the Information for This Book Was Compiled

The information in this book was compiled on the basis of my experience as a Baldrige Award examiner. My experience as an examiner enabled me to review actual applications, discuss the examination process and award criteria with numerous other examiners, and participate in the Examiner Training Workshop in which examiners are trained to interpret the criteria. I also served as the lead judge for the California version of the Baldrige Award from 1994 through 1996, and continue to conduct training for potential examiners in California, and for examiners in New Zealand. The text is not an official publication of the National Institute of Standards and Technology, and the suggestions and opinions in it are my own.

The information in this book also draws upon my consulting experience, in which I help companies develop their own improvement processes based upon the Baldrige criteria. I have been consulting with companies such as Ford, IBM, Motorola, Unisys, Cargill, Medtronic, Bose, Ericsson, as well as the U.S. Army, Coast Guard, Navy, and Department of Energy.

Additional Notes to the Reader

Because the Baldrige examiners are not allowed to disclose any information contained in award applications, all of the examples used in this text are fictitious. Some are based upon actual applications but are thoroughly disguised so as to protect the anonymity of the applicants. Some companies have volunteered, or have made public, specific information about their experiences in challenging for the Award. These companies have been mentioned by name.

Future Volumes

Revised and updated editions of this work are planned for each year, assuming that the Baldrige Award criteria continue to be revised and improved each year. Suggestions on how we might improve the 2009 version of this book are welcome and should be directed to:

Mark Graham Brown
c/o Productivity Press
Taylor & Francis Group
270 Madison Avenue
New York, NY 10016

Chapter

1

UNDERSTANDING THE
MALCOLM BALDRIGE
NATIONAL QUALITY AWARD

The Malcolm Baldrige Award is the highest honor any business can receive, and after 18 years has remained very difficult to win. As the criteria have changed over the years, the Baldrige has become an award for overall effectiveness of an organization, as opposed to an organization that simply has high quality products/services. The Baldrige process allows winners and nonwinners alike to receive feedback on how well they meet the criteria. The overall purpose of the Baldrige Award application and award process is to strengthen the competitiveness of U.S. companies. According to the 2008 criteria booklet, the award process plays three additional roles:

- *To help improve organizational performance practices, capabilities, and results.*
- *To facilitate communication and sharing of best practices information among U.S. organizations of all types.*
- *To serve as a working tool for understanding and managing performance, for guiding planning, and opportunities for learning. (p. 1)*

The dual goals of the Baldrige criteria are to improve value to customers, which results in marketplace success, and to improve overall financial and company performance to meet the needs of shareholders, owners, and other stakeholders. Baldrige winners have shown that it is not necessary to trade off financial results for satisfied employees or customers. Baldrige winners have demonstrated that they can achieve exemplary financial results, delight their customers, and provide their employees with a good work environment. This balance is what the 2008 Baldrige criteria are all about.

The 2008 Baldrige criteria are slightly different from earlier versions of the criteria. The Baldrige program is evolving toward an overall model of how to run a successful business. The criteria are much less detailed in prescribing particular approaches such as TQM, Six Sigma, or teamwork. More emphasis is placed on the results an organization has achieved than in the past. In the 2008 criteria, 55% of the points are linked to a company's approaches and the deployment of those approaches. The other 45% of the points are for the results the company achieves. The Baldrige model is becoming more like the European Award, where the breakdown is 50/50, between results and approaches.

The people who manage the Baldrige Award have done an excellent job over the years in listening to business leaders and looking at what has worked and not worked. Benchmarking, reengineering, problem-solving teams, quality planning, and a variety of other management programs turned out not to be the silver bullets that some of us thought they were a few years ago. The Baldrige criteria have reflected those lessons learned and tried to refrain from jumping on the bandwagon with some of these fads. However, many of the trappings of TQM programs were very much a part of the early Baldrige criteria. The word quality was first removed from the criteria in 1995, and continues to be absent in 2008. More information on the changes to Baldrige for 2008 may be found later in this chapter.

The existence of the Baldrige Award is based upon Public Law 100–107, which creates a public–private partnership designed to encourage quality from American companies. The Findings and Purposes sections of Public Law 100-107 state that:

1. The leadership of the United States in product and process quality has been challenged strongly (and sometimes successfully) by foreign competition, and our Nation's productivity growth has improved less than our competitors' over the past two decades.

2. American business and industry are beginning to understand that poor quality costs companies as much as 20 percent of sales revenues nationally and that improved quality of goods and services goes hand in hand with improved productivity, lower costs, and increased profitability.

3. Strategic planning for quality and quality improvement programs, through a commitment to excellence in manufacturing and services, are becoming more and more essential to the well-being of our Nation's economy and our ability to compete effectively in the global marketplace.

4. Improved management understanding of the factory floor, worker involvement in quality, and greater emphasis on statistical process control can lead to dramatic improvements in the cost and quality of manufactured products.

5. The concept of quality improvement is directly applicable to small companies as well as large, to service industries as well as manufacturing, and to the public sector as well as private enterprise.

6. In order to be successful, quality improvement programs must be management-led and customer-oriented, and this may require fundamental changes in the way companies and agencies do business.

7. Several major industrial nations have successfully coupled rigorous private-sector quality audits with national awards giving special recognition to those enterprises the audits identify as the very best; and

8. A national quality award program of this kind in the United States would help improve quality and productivity by:
   A. Helping to stimulate American companies to improve quality and productivity for the pride of recognition while obtaining a competitive edge through increased profits;
   B. Recognizing the achievements of those companies that improve the quality of their goods and services and providing an example to others;
   C. Establishing guidelines and criteria that can be used by business, industrial, governmental, and other organizations in evaluating their own quality improvement efforts; and
   D. Providing specific guidance for other American organizations that wish to learn how to manage for high quality by making available detailed information on how winning organizations were able to change their cultures and achieve eminence.

The Award is managed by the National Institute for Standards and Technology (NIST), which is part of the Department of Commerce and is named for Malcolm Baldrige, who served as Secretary of Commerce from 1981 until his tragic death in a rodeo accident in 1987. His managerial excellence contributed to long-term improvement in efficiency and effectiveness of government.

The actual award is quite impressive. It is a three-part Steuben Glass crystal stele, standing 14 inches tall, with a 22-karat gold-plated medal embedded in the middle of the central crystal. This prestigious award is presented to winners by the President of the United States at a special ceremony in Washington, D.C.

WHO CAN WIN THE AWARD?

In 2001, the Baldrige Award expanded from awarding only businesses to include educational institutions and healthcare organizations. In 2006, a sixth category was added for nonprofit organizations. There are now six categories of awards, and up to three winners in each category:

- *Manufacturing businesses*
- *Service businesses*

AWARD WINNERS: 1999 TO 2007

2007 Award Winners

Small Business
PRO-TEC Coating
Leipsic, OH

Health Care
Mercy Health Systems
Janesville, WI

Sharp Health Care
San Diego, CA

Nonprofit
U.S. Army Armament Research,
Development, and Engineering Center
(ARDEC)
Picatinny Arsenal, NJ

City of Coral Springs
Coral Springs, FL

2006 Award Winners

Small Business
Mesa Products, Inc.
Tulsa, OK

Service
Premier, Inc.
San Diego, CA

Health Care
North Mississippi Medical Center
Tupelo, MS

2005 Award Winners

Manufacturing
Sunny Fresh Foods, Inc.
Monticello, MN

Service
Dyn McDermott Petroleum
Operations
New Orleans, LA

Small Business
Park Place Lexus
Plano, TX

Education
Richland College
Dallas, TX

Jenks Public Schools
Jenks, OK

Health Care
Bronson Methodist Hospital
Kalamazoo, MI

2004 Award Winners

Manufacturing
Bama Companies
Tulsa, OK

Small Business
Texas Nameplate
Dallas, TX

Education
Kenneth Monfort
College of Business
Greeley, CO

Health Care
Robert Wood Johnson University
Hospital
Hamilton, NJ

2003 Award Winners

Manufacturing

Medrad
Indianola, PA

Service
Boeing Aerospace Support
St. Louis, MO

Caterpillar Financial Services
Nashville, TN

Small Business
Stoner
Quarryville, PA

Education
Community Consolidated School
District 15
Palatine, IL

Health Care
Saint Luke's Hospital of Kansas City
Kansas City, MO

Baptist Hospital
Pensacola, FL

2002 Award Winners

Manufacturing
Motorola, Inc.
Commercial Government and
Industrial Solutions Sector
Schaumburg, IL

Small Business
Branch-Smith Printing Division
Fort Worth, TX

Health Care
SSM Health Care

St. Louis, MO

2001 Award Winners

Manufacturing
Clarke American Checks, Inc.
San Antonio, TX

Small Business
Pal's Sudden Service
Kingsport, TN

Education
Chugach School District
Anchorage, AL

Pearl River School District
Pearl River, NY

University of Wisconsin – Stout
Menomonie, WI

2000 Award Winners

Manufacturing
Dana Corporation –
Spicer Driveshaft Division
Toledo, OH

Karlee Company
Garland, TX

Service
Operations Management
International, Inc.
Greenwood Village, CO

Small Business
Los Alamos National Bank
Los Alamos, NM

1999 Award Winners

Manufacturing
STMicroelectronics
Carrollton, TX

Sunny Fresh Foods
Monticello, MN

Service
Ritz-Carlton Hotel Company
Atlanta, GA

BI
Minneapolis, MN

- *Small businesses*
- *Educational organizations*
- *Healthcare organizations*
- *Nonprofit organizations*

The healthcare, education, and nonprofit categories are fairly new, and there are unique versions of the criteria for those organizations. The criteria are very close to those for businesses, but have been tailored to meet the unique features of healthcare, nonprofit organizations, and educational institutions. This book focuses on the business Baldrige Award criteria, but should also help those using the other versions. Copies of the healthcare, education, and nonprofit Baldrige criteria may be found on the Baldrige website: www.quality.nist.gov.

APPLICATION AND EVALUATION PROCESS

Applicants for the Baldrige Award must write up to a 50-page application that explains how they run their business and present the business results they have achieved. The report is divided into seven sections, corresponding to the seven categories of criteria for the award:

1. Leadership	(12%)
2. Strategic Planning	(8.5%)
3. Customer and Market Focus	(8.5%)
4. Measurement, Analysis, and Knowledge Management	(9%)
5. Workforce Focus	(8.5%)
6. Process Management	(8.5%)
7. Results	(45%)

Each category is weighted according to its importance in the overall evaluation. As you can see, Category 7 is worth almost half the points, whereas most of the other categories are only worth 8.5% each.

The seven categories are further broken down into 18 Examination Items, which are themselves broken down into 32 Areas to Address and 203 Questions. See Figure 1.1.

The application report needs to address each of the 32 Areas to Address and 203 Questions separately. All Areas to Address should be covered by all organizations.

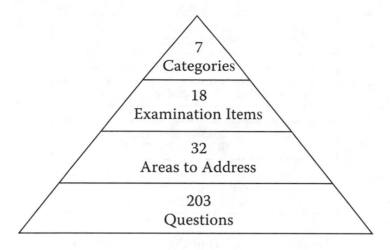

Figure 1.1:   Hierarchy of Award Criteria

However, an applicant does not lose credit if one or more Areas to Address do not pertain to his/her business. If an item is not relevant, the applicant must explain why, however. With the changes made to the criteria in 2007, it is highly unlikely that one or more of the Areas to Address will not be applicable to an organization. Chapters 5 through 12 of this book explain each of the criteria in detail, so that you can better understand what the examiners are looking for.

Evaluation

Figure 1.2 depicts the four-stage review process that occurs once an organization has submitted an application.

In Stage 1, all applications are reviewed by at least five members of the Board of Examiners. The board is composed of approximately 200 examiners selected from business, professional, and trade associations; universities; and government. All members are recognized experts in the fields of business or organizational improvement. When assigning board members to review applications, the experience and industry background of the examiner are matched to the applicant, provided that there is no conflict of interest. Examiners with manufacturing backgrounds receive applications from manufacturing companies and examiners with service industry experience receive service company applications. Board members must follow strict rules regarding the confidentiality of applications, and must agree to abide by a code of ethics, which includes nondisclosure of information from applicants. Examiners are not even allowed to reveal the names of companies that have applied for the award.

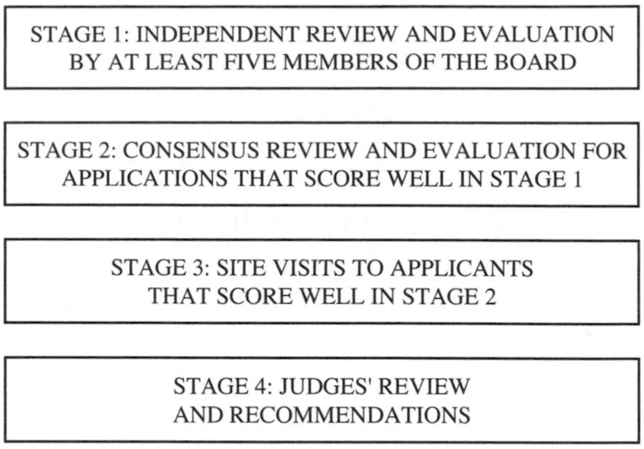

STAGE 1: INDEPENDENT REVIEW AND EVALUATION
BY AT LEAST FIVE MEMBERS OF THE BOARD

STAGE 2: CONSENSUS REVIEW AND EVALUATION FOR
APPLICATIONS THAT SCORE WELL IN STAGE 1

STAGE 3: SITE VISITS TO APPLICANTS
THAT SCORE WELL IN STAGE 2

STAGE 4: JUDGES' REVIEW
AND RECOMMENDATIONS

Figure 1.2:   **Four-Stage Review Process**

In Stage 2, the scored applications are then submitted to a senior examiner who reviews the variability in scoring, identifies major discrepancies, and schedules a consensus meeting. Much like a jury, the examiners must reach consensus on your score. A consensus meeting is held via conference call or in person, and is led by a senior examiner. Senior examiners are responsible for supervising the team of examiners assigned to review each company. A recommendation is made as to whether or not a site visit is warranted. A panel of judges decides whether or not to accept the recommendation, or to have the application reviewed by other examiners.

Of the 1,000 points possible to earn on an application, the majority of applications receive scores of less than 500 points. As a general rule, if an application receives a score of 600 or above, the organization is considered to have made it to the semifinals, and might qualify for a site visit. The 600 or above points is not a hard rule about who receives a site visit, only a general guideline based on what's happened in the past. During a site visit, Stage 3, a team of five or more examiners spends approximately three to five days in your facilities, touring, conducting interviews, and reviewing data and records. Applicants are asked to make introductory and concluding presentations. The site visit is similar to having an audit done. The purpose of the site visit is to verify and clarify the information included in your written application and to resolve any issues or uncertainties that came up in reviewing your written application. The examiners may have accepted what you said in your written application at face value, but now they want to see proof of your claims.

The findings of the site visit are summarized in a site visit report that goes to the Baldrige Award judges for the Stage 4 review. It is during this review that the judges decide which applicants they will recommend in each category to be award winners. The panel of judges makes its recommendations to the National Institute of Standards and Technology, which makes final recommendations to the U.S. Secretary of Commerce. Those serving as judges are known nationally for their expertise in the quality field and have typically served as examiners or senior examiners in the past.

At the end of the calendar year, feedback reports are sent out to all Baldrige Award applicants. Regardless of the score, each applicant receives a detailed feedback report that summarizes the strengths and weaknesses identified by the examiners in their review of the application. Feedback reports are probably the most valuable result of applying for the award because they provide very specific information on the areas in which you excel and the areas that you need to work on. In fact, the feedback report is probably the best bargain in consulting services that you could buy. It costs $6,000 for large companies to apply for the Baldrige Award and $3,000 for small businesses and most small healthcare and educational institutions. For that fee, you get five to six highly trained quality experts to review your company and prepare a detailed analysis of its strengths and weaknesses. If you wanted to purchase this service from an outside consulting firm, it may cost between $25,000 and $50,000, depending upon the size of your organization and the number of consultants involved. So, for $6,000 or less you receive a wealth of valuable information. In fact, many organizations realize that they are far from being at the level required to win the Baldrige Award, but apply anyway. That way, they can find out exactly where they need to focus their improvement efforts in the next few years.

What the Examiners Are Really Looking For

The two factors or evaluation dimensions that the Baldrige examiners look for in your application are:

- *Process*
- *Results (Category 7 only)*

Process refers to the way in which you do things or how you run your organization. In 2004, the Baldrige scoring scale was revised, as discussed in Chapter 4. Each of the items in Categories 1 through 6 are now evaluated on the *Approach, Deployment, Learning and Integration*. This is not a huge change from the old scale, which did include an assessment of all four dimensions. The four factors are now more explicit in the scoring scale so that applicants realize that they have to address all four. The *Approach* portion of the criteria basically asks how you do things, and you might also explain the logic behind your approach if it is not going to be obvious to an outsider. While there are not any approaches the Baldrige examiners favor or require, there are clearly certain themes that are looked for in your *Approach:*

- *The degree to which the approach is logical and suited to your organization*
- *The degree to which your approach is structured enough*

- *Evidence that your approach was developed with a plan, rather than through trial and error*
- *Evidence that your approach shows creativity/innovation*
- *The degree to which your approach is systematic*

Deployment refers to how well your processes or approaches have been implemented or executed. It is possible that an organization has an outstanding approach, but it has only been implemented in a few departments or segments of the organization. Some of the overall indicators for assessing *deployment* are:

- *The appropriate and effective application of the stated approach to all products and services*
- *The appropriate and effective application of the stated approach to all work units, facilities, processes, and activities*
- *The appropriate and effective application of the stated approach to all transactions and interactions with customers, suppliers, and other stakeholders*

A lousy approach that has been fully deployed is still a score of 0-5%, so the *Approach* dimension is the most important of the four.

Learning refers to the extent to which the approach has been evaluated and improved, and that lessons learned in the evaluation process have been communicated to others in the organization. The factors that examiners look for when evaluating *Learning* are:

- *Evidence of planned evaluations of the effectiveness of approaches*
- *Identification of specific metrics for evaluating approaches*
- *How many cycles of improvement there have been to your approaches over what period of time*
- *The degree of improvement that has been made to your approaches or their level of maturity*

Integration is the last of the four dimensions assessed in Categories 1 through 6. *Integration* asks about how well your approach is linked to others in the organization as opposed to being a stand-alone system. In assessing *Integration,* the examiners look for:

- *A lack of disconnects or inconsistencies with other relevant approaches/systems*
- *Evidence of an overall architectural approach that considers how each subsystem will work in the overall system of the organization*
- *Evidence of improvements in the knitting together of various approaches and systems into a comprehensive process*

Results are clearly *not* asked for in six of the seven Baldrige categories. In fact, one of the big changes made back in 1997 was that results are only asked for in Category 7: Results, which breaks out into the following items:

- *7.1 Product and Service Outcomes*
- *7.2 Customer-Focused Outcomes*
- *7.3 Financial and Marketplace Outcomes*
- *7.4 Workforce-Focused Outcomes*
- *7.5 Organizational Effectiveness Results*
- *7.6 Leadership Outcomes*

Some specific factors that are examined when evaluating results are:

- *Current and past performance levels*
- *The demonstration of sustained improvement trends or sustained high-level performance*
- *Demonstration of cause/effect between company approaches and results*
- *The rate/speed of performance improvement*
- *Comparisons to major competitors, benchmarks, and other similar organizations*
- *Significance or importance of quality improvements to the organization's overall performance*

Each of the 32 Areas to Address that are described in Chapters 5 to 12 of this book is identified as to whether it pertains to approach, deployment, or results (in brackets []).

WHAT'S NEW IN THE 2008 CRITERIA?

Since the criteria were heavily revised in 2007, they are exactly the same this year. What has changed is the scoring scale for Results. There has also been a new diagram created to show the relationship between the Core Values/Concepts, the six Categories that ask about the process, and the six items that ask for results.

Well, this is the big new diagram that is supposed to clarify how the Core Values link to the criteria. The common question I get from examiners is: "How do I assess deployment of the Core Values when I am already assessing how well the applicant answers the 200+ questions in the criteria?" The answer is that the Core Values are the foundation upon which the Baldrige model is built, and that most of the Core Values apply to multiple items, questions, and categories in the criteria. For example, one of the values is "Customer-Driven Excellence". This value might be found in the Leadership section, the section on Strategic Planning, and certainly in Category 3: Customer and Market Focus.

The Role of Core Values and Concepts

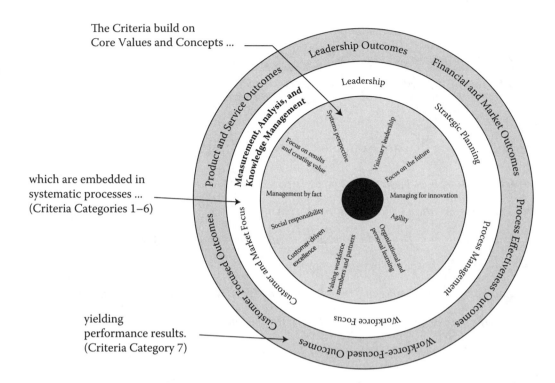

The Criteria build on
Core Values and Concepts ...

which are embedded in
systematic processes ...
(Criteria Categories 1–6)

yielding
performance results.
(Criteria Category 7)

2008 Criteria for Performance Excellence

The New Results Scoring Scale

The real change for 2008 is that the scoring scale for evaluating the results has been
made more specific. The scoring scale for Process Items asks about four dimensions:
Approach, Deployment, Learning, and Integration. These four dimensions help
examiners focus their comments on the appropriate strength of opportunity for
improvement. Similarly, the new results scoring scale now focuses on four different
aspects of performance or results:

Levels

Trends

Comparisons

Importance

This is a major improvement over the previous scoring guidelines that were not as explicit.
Examiners often gave lots of credit for strong levels and trends on performance measures
that are not critical for the organization's success. Importance as a factor was always

considered, but often not as strongly as levels and trends. Comparative data has always been asked for as well, as a way t evaluate levels and trends in an applicant's results. More Information on how to score results using the new scoring scale can be found in Chapter 4.

What is the same?

There are a lot more similarities to last year's criteria than changes. The basic architecture of the criteria is still based around seven Categories, Examination Items, Areas to Address, and Questions within the Areas to Address. The allocation of points is still the same with 45% of the points for results and 55% for process items. The focus of the seven Categories is still the same, with some changes in what is being asked for in individual Areas to Address and questions. After a fairly major change to Categories 5 and 6 and an edit of the other sections, there remain 203 questions—the same number as last year. The number of Items is now 18 versus 19, and there are now 32 Areas to Address versus 33 last year.

What's New in the Preface: Organizational Profile?

P.1a(3) has been rewritten quite a bit. Rather than ask about your employees, it asks about your workforce. This broadens the focus to include contract employees, volunteers, and others who may work in your organization but are not strictly employees. This is a good change because these groups are often ignored when developing human resource systems and programs. A new question in P.1a(3) asks about the expectations and requirements of various members of your workforce. This is similar to the information asked about customers. The danger with this new question is that it is likely to elicit a generic answer like: "Stimulating work, job security, good pay, and benefits."

P.2b now asks you to identify both your strategic challenges and competitive advantages. In other words, what key areas of advantage or expertise does your organization have that help make it successful? This is an excellent addition to the criteria and this theme can be found in other sections of the criteria as well for 2007. The theme of innovation can also be found in the new criteria, and specifically in P.2b. Innovation is a key competency in many U.S. organizations today, and the criteria for 2007 wisely ask a number of times about how your organization continues to be an innovator in your field.

The rest of the changes to the Organizational Profile section are a lot of "word-smithing" that sometimes makes the questions clearer and other times more confusing.

What's New in Category 1: Leadership?

This section is the least changed of the seven. One fairly major change is that 1.1b(2) now asks for a list of the performance measures upon which leaders review performance on a regular basis. In other words, what are the measures on your scorecard or dashboard that executives monitor on a daily, weekly, or monthly basis? Previously this information was asked for in Item 4.1 or many applicants chose to report their metrics along with relevant goals/targets in their answer to section 2 that asks about strategic plans. Because 1.1 is worth 70 points and 4.1 is only worth 45 points, this increases the importance of the scorecard or metrics in the evaluation. This is an excellent move, as a sound set of balanced performance measures is the foundation of a Baldrige effort, and often one of the first steps I take with clients looking to adopt the Baldrige model.

What's New in Category 2: Strategic Planning?

This section remains poorly written. 2.1 asks about HOW the organization does planning, but 2.2 also asks about HOW strategies or actions plans are developed as part of the strategic plan. Both Items also ask for information on WHAT the goals and plans are. The section would be much easier to follow if 2.1 focused on process or HOW and 2.2 focused on WHAT the goals and plans are and how they will be achieved.

2.1 now asks about how the organization determines both its strategic challenges and its competitive advantages. The challenges and advantages should have been listed in the Organizational Profile. This new question in 2.1 asks about how you identified these factors. Another addition to 2.1 is that it now asks about how your strategic plans address opportunities for innovation in products, services, and business processes. The innovation is usually in the strategies, not the goals or objectives. These new criteria ask about how you develop innovative strategies or products/services. Those organizations that are the innovators often lead their competition.

Item 2.2 now asks how you ensure that the organization has adequate financial resources for its overall operation and deployment of its strategic plan. This information used to be asked about in the old 6.2b. It never really fit there, and including it in the strategic plan section makes a lot of sense. Item 2.2 also asks about how the organization ensures that it has the right number of people with the right knowledge and skills to achieve the goals of objectives in the strategic plan. This is also an excellent addition. Many organizations develop strategic plans without much thought given to the personnel, knowledge, skills and competencies needed to achieve the goals and implement the strategies. There used to be a question in an older version of the criteria that asked about human resource planning, but it makes more sense to link HR plans and strategies to organizational plans.

What's New in Category 3: Customer and Market Focus?

The only thing that has really changed in this section is the addition of the phrase: "voice of the customer." Here is another instance where buzz words have crept into the Baldrige criteria that really add no value or change the meaning of what is being asked. This is nothing new and the Baldrige criteria have always asked about customers and their requirements and priorities. 3.1a(2) has had a fairly substantial rewrite, but the focus is still on market research to determine the factors that influence customer buying behavior.

What's New in Category 4: Measurement, Analysis, and Knowledge Management?

One major change is that the two Items in this category now have new names. In Item 4.1 they replaced the word review with improvement. This is more than just a title change of the Item. The criteria in 4.1 now ask about how you use reviews of performance data to identify opportunities for process improvement. In other words, there is now better linkage between 4.1 and 6.2 that asks about improving processes. In the old criteria, the focus was more on looking at performance data regularly. The new criteria for 4.1 now focus more on doing something with the data, which is a better focus.

4.2 has a new, yet more confusing title. It was Information and Knowledge Management. Now it is Management of Information, Information Technology, and Knowledge. The order of the Areas to Address has changed a little, but the criteria continue to focus on the same things as last year.

What's New in Category 5: Workforce Focus?

Basically, everything is new in this category. This section was a complete re-write, including a change in title from Human Resource Focus to Workforce Focus. The new configuration of the two Examination Items and five Areas to Address is much more confusing than the old criteria, and there is some degree of overlap in what is being asked. In the 2006 criteria this section was divided into three Items:

5.1 Work Systems – This was a broad Item that asked about all kinds of HR processes, including recruiting/selection, job design, communication, diversity, performance appraisal/management, compensation, recognition, career development, and succession planning. Of the three Items in the old criteria this was always the most confusing to people since it included so many things. What is even more confusing this year is that the phrase "work system" now means something completely different and is now found in Category 6: Process Management.

5.2 – Employee Learning and Motivation – This 2006 Item was fairly clear in its focus, unlike the previous one that included just about all HR processes. This section focused on training and developing people to give them the knowledge and skills needed to do their jobs.

5.3 – Employee Well-Being and Satisfaction – This section was the clearest and most focused of the three. It focused on employee health, safety, and satisfaction.

The new configuration of criteria for this section is not quite so clear. The 2007 criteria are now divided into two items:

5.1 Workforce Engagement – This new Item now asks for information on what is important for employees and other members of the workforce, which is an excellent addition. This makes it more parallel to 3.1 that asks about customer needs and requirements. This section also asks about the culture of the organization, including variables such as communication, diversity, goal setting, and empowerment. The second Area to Address asks about training and development, which used to have its own Examination Item (5.2). The third Area to Address asks about how you measure workforce "engagement" and satisfaction. So, there is a little of what used to be in 5.1, 5.2, and 5.3 in the new 5.1. The old 5.1 is now closely matched with the new 5.1a. The old 5.2 is now closely matched with the new 5.1b, and the old 5.3b now closely matches what is asked for in the new 5.1c.

5.2 Workforce Environment – This second new item is the more confusing of the two. The first Area to Address (5.2a) asks about "Workforce Capability and Capacity." The first question asks about how you determine the human resource needs of your organization, including headcount, and specific knowledge and skills. Most of this was asked before in the old 5.2.a that asked about how training needs analysis is done. The new criteria go beyond just training needs analysis in that it also asks how many people are needed with specific capabilities. The second question in the new criteria asks about recruiting and hiring, which used to be asked for in 5.1 c. The third question is about managing the workforce and seems to have some overlap in what is asked for in 5.1a(3) which asks about the performance management system. 5.2a(3) is broader in its focus in that it looks at your overall management approach, but it does ask about goals, measures and action plans, which are typically part of a performance management system. This is a perfect example of why I think the new section 5 criteria are poorly designed. Question 4 is a new one and it asks about how you prepare the workforce for good and bad changes such as lay-offs and new knowledge and skills they must acquire. I guess this is a good question, but it seems fairly narrow and may not apply to some organizations. Some other bigger more important things relating to human resources have been eliminated or given less emphasis than in the past.

The new 5.2b is called Workforce Climate, which is a bad title, because it is really not about climate or culture; it is about safety, security, health, and employee benefits/services. The new 5.2b(1) parallels what used to be asked in 5.3a(1) and focuses on workforce health, safety and security. The new 5.2b(2) asks about workforce policies, benefits and services, which used to be asked for in the 2006 5.3b(2).

To sum up the changes for 2007 in the Workforce Focus category: most of what is being asked for is the same as last year, but it has been configured in a less logical and harder to understand format.

What's New in Category 6: Process Management?

This category has been completely rewritten as well, and not necessarily for the better. In the old Category 6 there was a clear distinction between processes involved in producing the organization's products/services (6.1) and support processes (6.2). In the new criteria they have thankfully dropped the phrase "value-creation processes," but they have put in a new phrase: "work systems" which had a completely different meaning in previous versions of the criteria. There is also very little mention of the administrative or support processes in an organization which can take up a huge portion of a company's resources and people. There is one entire Examination Item worth 35 points that focuses on how you design your work processes or systems. This used to be an Area to Address and is now an entire Item. Most organizations designed their work processes or systems long ago.

In 2006, Process Management included the following Items:

6.1 Value Creation Processes – This first Item asked about how you design, manage and improve the major processes involved in producing your products/services.

6.2 Support Processes and Operational Planning – This second item asked about how support processes were designed, managed, and improved. The questions were almost identical to those asked about the "value creation" processes and the section had a good inherent logic. This item also asked out operational planning, which always seemed to fit better in Category 2: Strategic Planning.

The new criteria for 2007 are divided into two Examination Items with one focusing on process or work system design and the second one focusing on managing and improving work processes.

6.1 Work System Design – The first big change is the phrase "work system" that used to refer to HR programs and processes. The new definition is:

> *Work systems refers to how the work of your organization is accomplished.*
> *Work systems involve your workforce, your key suppliers and partners, your contractors,*
> *your collaborators, and other components of the supply chain needed to produce and*
> *deliver your products, services, and support processes. (p. 29)*

What this new Item is asking for is how you design what used to be called your "value-creation processes" and your "support processes." The first Area to Address asks you to identify your "core competencies," or areas of greatest expertise. This is a good question, but it seems to belong better in the Organizational Profile than here. In fact, it kind of already asks for this information in P2. The second question in the Area to Address called "Core Competencies" asks about how you decide which processes are done internally, and which ones are farmed out to contractors or other external resources. This question sounds like it will generate a generic answer that will not reveal anything of real importance about the organization. The next Area to Address is called Work Process Design and it asks most of the same questions that were asked in the 2006 version of section 6. The last question is kind of a weird add-on that asks about emergency readiness. This focus first appeared after 9/11 and Hurricane Katrina. It is not clear why Baldrige asks about this specific process, but not others that are equal in importance. Perhaps because most organizations are poorly prepared for emergencies and this puts more focus on preparedness.

6.2 Work Process Management and Improvement – This Item is about the same as what used to be asked for in Items 6.1 and 6.2. The first Area to Address asks about how you manage and control your key work processes, including measures and standards. It also asks how a prevention-based approach is used to minimize reliance on inspection and testing. The second Area to Address asks about the approach used to evaluate and improve your processes and how these improvements are shared with others in your organization that might benefit from this knowledge. This is all great stuff.

What is missing from the 2007 criteria is an analysis of the administrative or support functions or processes in the organization. As I mentioned earlier, this can make up half of an organization's people and other resources, and these processes have historically lagged way behind those in the "line" part of the organization. The questions asked in the old 6.2 about your support functions are completely gone, suggesting that these functions will not even be assessed in a 2007 Baldrige applicant. The only mention at all of these processes is in Note 3 in Item 6.1 that says key processes might include support functions.

What's New in Category 7: Results?

This section is mostly unchanged. They replaced the word results in the Item titles with the word outcomes, but then use the word results in the definition. For example, 7.2 Customer-Focused Outcomes: What are your customer-focused results? Am I missing something here or does the definition say the same thing as the heading? There have been some changes to the types of data asked for in the six items in this section. 7.3 Financial and Market Outcomes now asks for more data on the financial viability of the organization. I guess they don't want to se any more Baldrige winners file for bankruptcy or go out of business after winning the award. The types of data asked for in the new 7.4 Workforce-Focused Outcomes are very different than last year, and line up with the configuration of the new Category 5. The new 7.4 asks for three types of data:

- *Workforce engagement/satisfaction and training/development*
- *Workforce capability/capacity*
- *Safety/health/security*

The types of results asked for are similar to last year, but the questions are worded differently, and it is not clear what a measure of engagement would be other than the metrics used to assess employee satisfaction such as surveys, focus groups, turnover, absenteeism and other similar things. "Employee engagement" is a new phrase that Baldrige has become enamored with from reading books by Gallup, just like they were enamored with the word "re-engineering" back when that was in vogue.

The title of 7.5 has changed to now read: Process Effectiveness Outcomes, and it asks for mostly the same types of operational and process results as last year. The big difference: the criteria no longer ask for data on how well support or administrative functions are performing. 7.6 Leadership and Social Responsibility Results is essentially unchanged from 2006.

Summary

So there you have it. The criteria have changed, but mostly changed for the worse in my opinion. They still have not fixed the Strategic Planning section to make 2.1 focus on the "How" of planning and 2.2 to focus on "What" your plans are. The new section 5 is a convoluted mess, with too many buzz words and overlap in the areas to address. In general I like what they did to rewrite section 6, but I think it was a big mistake to leave out an analysis of support functions, and I think process design is not something that warrants being one of the 18 Examination Items. I predict we will see another major re-write of the Baldrige criteria in the next year or two, as others realize the problems and confusion of the new criteria.

Chapter

2

Preparing an Application for the Baldrige Award

GENERAL OUTLINE OF THE MAJOR COMPONENTS OF THE APPLICATION PACKAGE

Your 2008 application package must contain all required forms including (1) the Eligibility Determination Form (which must already have been approved); (2) the Application Form; and (3) the Site Listing and Descriptors Form. These forms are available in the 2008 Application Forms and Instructions booklet, as are complete instructions on how to prepare them.

Your application package must also contain an application report. The application report consists of a 5-page organizational profile of your business and a 50-page document that is generally divided into seven major sections, corresponding to the seven categories of criteria. In this document you must respond to and address all of the Examination items and Areas to Address as presented in the criteria. If you are in the small business category your written document is limited to 50 single-sided pages (the 5-page overview is not counted as part of the page limit). This 50-page limit includes charts, graphs, tables, and any supporting materials you decide to attach to your application. The examiners are very strict on this guideline. If your application report contains 60 pages, the Baldrige administrators will probably tear off the last 10 pages before sending the application to the examiners to review. It will be very difficult to respond to all of the criteria within 50 pages, so you may need to employ a ruthless editor. You may also be required to submit Supplemental Sections as a part of your application report.

According to the Award Criteria, these are required when the applicant is a unit within a company that is in many different businesses. The Award Criteria booklet (http://baldrige.nist.gov) provides more details on this.

The major components of your application package should be organized into logical and clearly defined sections, such as:

- *Application and Other Forms*
- *Organizational Profile*
- *1.0 Leadership*
- *2.0 Strategic Planning*
- *3.0 Customer and Market Focus*
- *4.0 Measurement, Analysis, and Knowledge Management*
- *5.0 Workforce Focus*
- *6.0 Process Management*
- *7.0 Results*

HOW TO WRITE THE APPLICATION

The way most internal users and award applicants approach writing the application is to form seven teams to work on each of the seven sections in the application. A project manager oversees the effort and attempts to edit the final document to make it appear as if it were written by one person. Although by far the most common approach, it is also the reason why most internal users and award applicants receive such low scores.

Using seven teams and/or individuals to work on each of the seven sections in the application is a major mistake.

The seven categories of Baldrige criteria work together as a system. They are not seven independent factors. One of the most common problems appearing in Baldrige applications is what I call "disconnects." Disconnects are inconsistencies between sections. For example, an applicant might report in section 3.2 that they collect data on three different measures of customer satisfaction, but include no goals for these measures in section 2.2 and no graphs of results in section 7.1. All seven sections need to be consistent and work together as a system.

So, how do you ensure that all sections work together effectively? One answer is to have one person write the entire application. Although this is not feasible in many large and complex organizations, it has been done. Marty Smith, of New England Telephone, was the primary author of that company's Baldrige application. Marty had a committee that assisted in gathering the information needed to write the application, but he did the majority of the project coordination and writing himself. Several small companies that have won Baldrige Awards submitted applications written primarily by the CEOs.

In most large complex organizations it simply is not practical to have a single person write the application, so some type of team must be formed. But if forming teams around each of the seven Baldrige categories is not the way to organize the effort, how should it be done? A recent client of mine put together an application for the award by forming teams as follows:

TEAM A: Section 1.0 Leadership

TEAM B: Section 5.0 Human Resource Focus

TEAM C: Sections 2.0 Strategic Planning and 4.0 Measurement, Analysis, and Knowledge Management

TEAM D: Sections 3.0 Customer and Market Focus and 6.0 Process Management

TEAM E: Section 7.0 Business Results

Sections 1.0 and 5.0 in the Baldrige system are the easiest ones to work on independently of the other sections. The approach of dividing into the five teams as listed above worked fairly well in this case, but Teams C, D, and E had to work closely with one another. Team E (results) did not write its sections until the planning and measurement team (C) finished its section.

Another organization I worked with organized two small teams and one large team to prepare their Baldrige Award application:

TEAM A: 1.0

TEAM B: 5.0

TEAM C: 2.0, 3.0, 4.0, 6.0, 7.0

This approach also worked well and helped to ensure that the seven sections flowed together well. Granted, the third team that had five sections had a lot of work to do, but it was a larger team than the other two and was prepared for the bigger effort.

MANAGING THE APPLICATION DEVELOPMENT PROJECT

Regardless of how you choose to put together teams to write the application, you will undoubtedly need a steering committee to oversee and approve the application, as well as a project manager to coordinate the effort. The steering committee should consist of 4 to 7 executives, including the CEO and his/her direct reports. These individuals may not have any involvement in writing the application, but they should provide access to any data needed by those writing each section and review the completed report. The steering committee members allocate resources to write the application and make any decisions regarding policies and the divulgence of confidential information. Steering committee members should plan on attending a minimum of two 4- to 8-hour meetings and spending an additional 6 to 8 hours reviewing various sections of the application.

Once the steering committee has been formed, select a project manager. In some organizations, the vice president of quality is chosen. In others, a function manager or director fills the position. The job this individual currently has is not important. What is important is that this individual have a good overall knowledge of the entire organization, know quality concepts, have good rapport with other managers, and pay great attention to detail. The project manager is responsible for seeing that the individuals working on various sections of the application meet their deadlines and adhere to key quality standards. The project manager serves as the liaison between the steering committee and a group of representatives from the teams who will make up an award application committee.

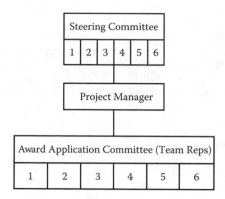

Figure 2.1: **Typical Organization Structure for Baldrige Application Committee/Team**

The number of people who participate on the award application committee will depend upon the size and complexity of your organization and how you decide to divide into teams. Figure 2.1 depicts a typical structure of the teams/committees that work on preparing the Baldrige application.

Select people to work on the award application committee who are knowledgeable of the area/category they have been assigned and possess excellent writing skills. This will consume a great deal of time over the months that it takes to polish the application, so it is important to release them from some of their other responsibilities.

It is also a good idea to form a team of individuals responsible for editing and formatting the various sections of the application, creating graphics, doing word processing, and coordinating the reproduction and binding of the application. These tasks are time-consuming, yet important. And it is important that the application look good and be error-free. The leader of the application production team should be a member of the award application committee and attend all key meetings.

The first task on the project manager's and the award application committee's agenda is to hold a meeting to create a project plan for the development and production of the application. A project plan is a detailed list of tasks, resources, estimates, and deadlines. It specifies the person(s) responsible and the amount of time allocated for performing each task. This serves as the basis from which a project can be built. The project plan can be created during a meeting facilitated by the project manager. An example of such a plan is shown in Figure 2.2. The numbers listed in the columns represent the time estimates (in days) for the various people who will work on the application. The plan presented is based upon using a seven-person award application committee. Time estimates apply to each person on the committees, and are based upon the assumption that quality assurance systems are already in place.

Project Plan
Baldridge Award Application

Tasks	Responsibilities & Time Requirements						Schedule
	PM	AAC	PROD	EDIT	SC	REV	
1. Project Planning Meeting							
a. Prepare for meeting	0.75	-	0.25	-	-	-	
b. Conduct/attend meeting	1.0	1.0	-	-	-	-	
c. Write Project Plan	1.0	-	1.0	0.25	-	-	
d. Review/Revise Project Plan	0.25	0.25	0.25	-	0.25	-	
2. Conduct Inter views and Gather Data	2.0	3.0	-	-	-	-	
3. Write First Drafts of Application Sections	2.0	2.5	5.0	4.0	-	-	
4. Review First Drafts	-	-	-	-	1.0	1.0	
5. Complete Mock Evaluations	0.5	-	-	-	-	2.0	
6. First Draft Feedback							
a. Assemble Reviewers' comments and evaluations	2.0	-	1.5	1.0	-	-	
b. Conduct/attend Feedback Meeting	2.0	2.0	-	-	-	-	
c. Document meeting outputs	1.0	-	2.0	-	-	-	
7. Write Second Drafts of Application Sections	1.5	1.5	-	3.0	-	-	
8. Production of Application Report							
a. Prepare and conduct/ attend Production Planning Meeting	1.0	-	0.5	-	-	-	
b. Produce artwork, graphics, and printing specifications	1.5	-	4.0	0.5	-	-	
c. Printing of Final Award Applications	0.5	-	1.0	-	-	-	
9. Review Final Materials, Complete Forms, Prepare Overview, and Submit Application	1.5	0.5	1.5	0.5	0.5	-	4/3
TOTALS (days)	18.5	10.75	17.0	9.25	1.75	3.0	

KEY	PM	= Project Manager	EDIT	= Editors
	AAC	= Award Application Committee	SC	= Steering Committee
	PROD	= Production/Graphics	REV	= Reviewers

Figure 2.2:   **Project Workplan**

Information/Data Needed

3.2 Customer Relationships and Satisfaction
- Focus Group Data
- Customer Requirements Survey Instruments
- Process Descriptions for Customer Requirements Data CollectionApproaches
- Comparison Data on Complaints, Customer Gains/Losses, and Performance Data
- Process for EvaluatingApproach to Defining Customer Requirements
- Customer Requirements Survey Data — Last 3 Years

Figure 2.3:   Example Flipchart From a Planning Meeting

As you can see in Figure 2.2, the plan includes a detailed list of tasks for each committee member or subcommittee. This plan is the project manager's tool for tracking the progress of the committee members. Many applicants don't bother to create such a plan and end up missing deadlines or having to race around at the last minute to complete the application in order to get it out by the May 25th deadline.

The best way to approach the application report is to look at each Examination Item and Area to Address separately. For each one, make a list of the data or resources needed for reference in order to prepare your response. For any area to address that asks for trends or data, you should also make a list of the graphs or charts you will need to prepare. This can be done in the committee meeting by listing the information on flipcharts, as demonstrated in Figure 2.3.

If you are working with several subcommittees, it may be necessary to assign information-gathering tasks to specific individuals. At the conclusion of the initial meeting, the project manager should formalize the project plan and distribute it to all award committee and steering committee members.

Gathering the information necessary to write the various sections of the Baldrige Award is the most difficult and time-consuming task. Rarely will an organization have all the data needed readily at hand. Some data may not exist anywhere in the organization and may need to be collected. A number of departments and individuals within the organization may need to be contacted to collect all of the information needed to write each section of the application. The biggest problem experienced by committees working on the Baldrige application is lack of cooperation from other employees and managers who must dig up the information or data needed. This is one of the reasons that it is important to have high-level individuals on the steering committee. If the CEO or one of the vice presidents calls a manager to ask him or her where the data are that you requested in order to write your section of the award application, you can bet that the delinquent manager will get the information quickly.

All first drafts of sections of the application report should be turned in to the project manager, who will review them for accuracy, completeness, and clarity. He or she will return the edited copy of first drafts to the committee members who wrote them. The writers will then make the corrections suggested by the project manager and resubmit the application sections. If the project manager is satisfied that all of the necessary changes have been made, the material will be turned over to an editor who will edit the grammar, consistency, headings, readability, and other factors. After the sections have been edited, they will be turned over to production for word processing and preparation of graphics.

Once the report has been produced, internal copies should be prepared and distributed to the steering committee members and other key managers and technical professionals for their review. It is also a good idea to give the application to a few relatively new employees who have industry experience but little knowledge of the organization. These individuals can review the manuscript and the practices of your organization more objectively.

In addition to having many different people review the application and provide their feedback, it is also a good idea to train a group of people to actually evaluate the application against the Baldrige criteria. This might be a group of outside consultants or a group of your own employees. Whomever you select to perform this evaluation should be familiar with the Baldrige criteria and be objective in his or her evaluation of the organiza-tion's application.

Feedback from reviewers and evaluations of the application should all be returned to the project manager by a specified date. After assembling and summarizing all of the comments, suggestions, and scores of the evaluators, the project manager should plan a two-day meeting with the award application committee to review the feedback and discuss changes and additions needed to each of their sections, as well as any overall comments that pertain to all sections. As each section is reviewed, the project manager should record the changes needed in each Area to Address to satisfy the reviewers' suggestions and to improve on the scores given during the mock evaluation.

Following the meeting, the committee members revise their assigned sections based upon the action items and suggestions outlined in the meeting. Final drafts are submitted to the project manager for review and to the editor for final editing. The entire application should then be given to production so that the layout, cover, tabs, and any other aspects of the final document can be designed. Some applicants custom design a cover and special tabs for their applications, but this is definitely not necessary. In fact, an application that looks too slick may make the examiners suspect that the applicant is perhaps substituting flash for substance. Final artwork is then done, the materials are thoroughly proofread, and the application is printed and bound.

Then, the tough part comes—the waiting. Applications are due at the latest on May 24th, and you won't receive feedback for several months. This can be very frustrating, but the review process takes a long time.

Figure 2.4 provides a graphic representation of the major steps involved in completing an application. The exact process you use will no doubt vary somewhat from this. A mock evaluation by people trained on the Baldrige criteria is an important step that you should not leave out. Many organizations don't do this because they lack time or expertise. Lack of time shouldn't be a problem if you prepare the application far enough in advance. Lack of expertise is no excuse either. Universities and professional associations such as the American Society for Quality offer workshops on how to interpret the Baldrige criteria.

HOW TO WRITE THE APPLICATION REPORT

The main reason for writing this book is that many applicants and others using the Baldrige Award criteria misinterpret what the Areas to Address are requesting. Reading Chapters 5 to 12 of this book and using them as a reference when writing your responses to the 32 Areas to Address should help you to interpret the criteria accurately. In writing your report, it is important that you don't make the same mistakes made by many of the previous Baldrige Award applicants.

Pages 51–54 of the 2008 Baldrige Award Criteria provide some fairly specific instructions and advice about the best way to write your application. Make sure that you read these pages thoroughly and understand all of the guidelines. An important guideline that bears repeating is to make sure that you reference each section with the appropriate numbers and letters. It is helpful to the examiners if you include the Examination Items in your response, for reference.

Several applicants have labeled each section with a number to correspond to the Examination Item (e.g., 4.2, 2.1, etc.). But when this is done without indicating letters for

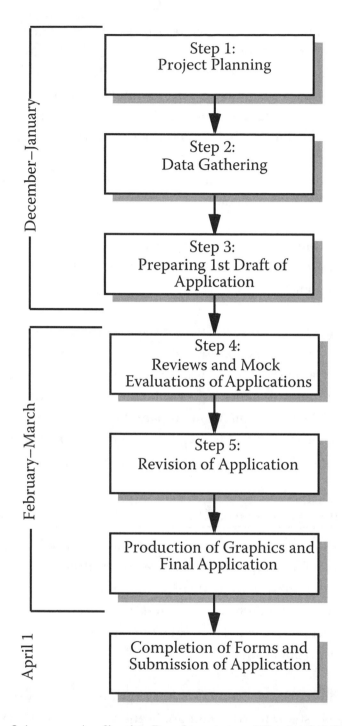

Figure 2.4:   **Application Development and Production Process**

the Areas to Address and the question number, it is difficult for the examiners to find the information that pertains to each Area question. You should denote responses to Areas by underscoring the item/Area number and letter [e.g., 2.2a(1)].

TEN COMMON MISTAKES TO AVOID WHEN WRITING YOUR APPLICATION

The general guidelines on how to write the application report are clear and well written. However, sometimes general guidelines are not enough to effectively guide performance. Judging by some of the applications received, many applicants either misunderstood the guidelines or chose not to read them. The purpose of this portion of the book is to list and explain some of the mistakes made by previous applicants. By reviewing this information, you should be able to avoid making some of the errors that others have made in the past. I have listed and discussed ten of the most common mistakes in the pages that follow. Some of these are minor errors, but most are mistakes that may cost you a large percentage of the points that otherwise might have been earned for a particular item.

Some of the information in this section is based upon the Baldrige Award Criteria. Other information is based upon my own and other examiners' experience in reviewing applications.

Mistake #1: Reiteration of Words from the Criteria

This is a technique that can enhance your score only if the examiner is not paying much attention to what he/she is reading. Examiners all have other jobs, so frequently they must review the applications in the evenings, after a long day of work. If your response includes some of the same words from the criteria, at first glance, it sounds like your response meets the criteria well. An examiner who is tired might just skim your response and give it a high score because it "sounds good." However, you must remember that up to six different examiners review each application. For every one or two who give you a higher score because your response includes words from the criteria, there will be others who will take points away for this. Repeating the criteria in your response is unnecessary.

Mistake #2: Use of Examples Rather Than Descriptions of Processes

This commonly occurs when the applicant does not have a systematic process to describe. A typical response starts out with a general statement such as: "We identify customer requirements in a variety of different ways." This is then followed by a detailed example of one situation where customer requirements have been identified. The problem with responding this way is that it doesn't tell the examiners how you identify customer requirements. If you do not describe a well-defined process in your response, chances are that you do not have a process, and customer requirements are identified in a casual and unsystematic manner. Whenever the criteria ask about processes, respond with a fairly detailed description of a step-by-step process or with a detailed flowchart.

Mistake #3: No Examples When They Will Help to Illustrate a Process

This is just the opposite of Mistake #2, using an example as your response. Including an example or two helps to clarify a flowchart or process description. Examples add interest and credibility to your process descriptions; just be certain that you have adequately described the process(es) before the example is used. When you use examples, make sure that you label them as such, and explain whether or not the situations you described are typical. Remember that the examiners have never seen your company and may not even be very familiar with your industry. Examples help to paint a picture for the examiner, making it easier for him/her to understand how your processes and approaches work.

Mistake #4: Lack of Specificity

Of all the mistakes made by applicants, this is the most common and the most severe. Answering all of the Baldrige questions thoroughly within 50 pages is tough. It is obvious that many applications have been ruthlessly edited to include only the most necessary information. Often, too much information is eliminated. A vague and general description of a process will earn few points from the examiners. An example of a nonspecific response is shown in the following box.

> **3.2a(1) How do you build relationships to acquire customers, to meet and exceed their expectations, to increase loyalty and repeat business, and to gain positive referrals?**
>
> *We pride ourselves at MGB Industries at being proactive in our approach to managing relationships with our customers. With our own sales force and our field representatives, we are in almost constant contact with our various customers to ensure that we are consistently meeting or exceeding their expectations. This sometimes daily telephone or face-to-face contact, has allowed us to forge strong bonds with our customers, making it likely that we will be their supplier of choice for years to come. One example of this is Willow Manufacturing, who has been a customer of ours for the last 21 years.*

There is nothing particularly wrong with what is said in this example. The problem is that the response is vague and nonspecific. It also includes an example of an isolated incident, rather than describing a system or process. The response is about as long as the criteria, and not enough information is provided to adequately judge how well the applicant is doing on this Area to Address. When a response is vague or nonspecific, examiners are taught to assign a low score. You don't need to provide pages and pages of information in response to each area. However, a sentence or two is usually not enough.

Mistake #5: Presenting Data on Only a Few Performance Indices/Measures

This is also a very common occurrence, and one that will cause you to lose a significant number of points. If you collect data on over 20 different indices of performance and report on only 5 or 6 of them, the examiners might assume that you have chosen to report on only the measures for which your performance is good. Data not reported are often assumed to be negative. In one case study used to train the Baldrige examiners, the applicant claims to have 160 indices that are used to measure performance. Yet, the application presents data on only three or four of these indices and says nothing about performance levels for the other 150+ measures. Although it may not be practical to present data for 160 indices, a great deal of information can be summarized in a table or chart.

Mistake #6: Too Many Cross-References to Other Sections

According to the directions in the 2006 Award Criteria, you should cross-reference when appropriate.

> *As much as possible, each item response should be self-contained. However, responses to different items might be mutually reinforcing. It is then appropriate to refer to the other responses rather than to repeat information. In such cases, key process information should be given in the item requesting this information. For example, employee education and training should be described in detail in item 5.2. Discussions about education and training elsewhere in your application would then reference but not repeat details given in your item 5.2 response. (p. 57)*

The criteria further explain that you should not repeat information included elsewhere. You can cross-reference information if it will help enhance your response to a particular area to address. Make sure that you cite the page number, the Examination Item (number), and the specific Area to Address (letter).

You should minimize the amount of cross-referencing that you do, however. It is very frustrating to the examiners to have to constantly flip back and forth from section to section. Because each of the areas to address is designed to stand on its own, it should not be necessary to cross-reference very often.

Mistake #7: Responding with Words When You Should Respond with Data

All of the Areas to Address in Category 7 ask for trends and results. Any time you see the words "trends," "results," or "data" in the criteria, this should be your clue to make sure your response includes graphs and data. It is surprising that this is misinterpreted, but applicants sometimes describe a process when the criteria specifically ask for trends (data). Or, they give a narrative summary of their results with no graphs or statistics. A narrative summary of the information included in graphs is good, but it is not a substitute for hard data. The words that appear in Section 7 should explain the performance shown on the graphs/charts.

Mistake #8: Responding with Information That Is Not Relevant to the Area to Address

This is also one of those mistakes that occurs quite frequently in the applications. It seems that either the applicants misunderstand some Areas to Address or that they understand them but have little to say in their response. Rather than admit something like: "We have not identified a process for tracking the degree to which customer requirements are met," applicants respond with some jargon that may seem good at first glance. But in reading it a second or third time one realizes that the response has nothing to do with what was asked for in the area to address.

An example of a response that is unrelated to the area to address is shown in box 3.2b(1) (following).

3.2b(1). CUSTOMERSatisfaction Determination
HOWdo you determine CUSTOMER satisfaction, dissatisfaction, and loyalty? HOW do these determination methods differ among CUSTOMER groups? HOW do you ensure that your measurements capture actionable information for use in exceeding your CUSTOMERS' expectations? HOW do you ensure that your measurements capture actionable information for use in securing your CUSTOMERS' their future business and gaining positive referrals as appropriate? HOW do you use CUSTOMER satisfaction and dissatisfaction information for improvement?

Customer satisfaction is our number one priority at Baker Industries. Every employee is expected to meet customer expectations for timely service and high quality products. We work in a collaborative fashion to systematically identify the ever-changing demands and expectations of our customers, and find ways of meeting those demands. Our quality and levels of customer satisfaction are unsurpassed in our industry, and continue to improve each year.

The Area to Address asks you to explain how the organization measures customer satisfaction. The example in the box does not discuss how customer satisfaction is measured. It only includes various "well-written" phrases, which is typical of an application submitted by an organization that does not have the data to respond to an area. A response such as the one in the example would not earn any points, because there is no information that tells the reader how the company segments its customers and measures customer satisfaction.

Mistake #9: Use of Too Many Acronyms

I was once interviewing a man from AT&T on a consulting project, and I asked him to describe a particular process he was involved with, without using acronyms in his description. He just stuttered and couldn't explain the process without including myriad acronyms. Use of acronyms is very frustrating to the Baldrige examiners. Everyone in your company may know what certain company-specific acronyms stand for, but the Baldrige examiners won't. Spelling out what an acronym stands for the first time you use it will not solve the problem either. An examiner will forget and have to refer back to previous sections to recall what the CASE or AIP programs are. Avoid acronyms entirely if you can. This is tough for many large companies that have an acronym for every process, document, and program. An example of an acronym-laden response is shown in the following.

> Our CEO, CIO, and CQO all strongly support the TQM effort at BMI through the initiation of a variety of programs such as the CCF (Customers Come First), AQP (Assessment of Quality Processes), and PTM (Participative Team Management). Our IIS and OEM Divisions have thoroughly implemented QFD using a variety of QITs (Quality Improvement Teams).

Many Baldrige applicants include a 2- to 3-page glossary of acronyms in their application. This is very frustrating to examiners. An application ought to be written in plain English without having to put a three-word title or three-letter acronym on every program and process.

Mistake #10: Use of Too Much Industry or Management Jargon

This irritates many of the Baldrige examiners because it appears as though you are trying to impress them with your vocabulary. The application should be written at a fairly low reading level, about the same level used in an annual report to shareholders. It should not be written like a college textbook or a technical paper for a professional journal. Use of complicated words and jargon should be thoroughly discouraged. The Baldrige examiners are probably as unfamiliar with your industry jargon as they are with your acronyms. To eliminate jargon, it is a good idea to have someone outside of your company, or new employees, review the application before it is finalized.

Even though the Baldrige examiners may be familiar with management jargon such as "Balanced Scorecard" or "Activity-Based Costing," it is best not to overuse these terms either. Write the application as if it were to be read by shareholders or the general public. A tenth- to twelfth-grade reading level is appropriate. This is the same level as a magazine such as U.S. News and World Report.

Similarly, you may want to avoid using trendy management words and phrases such as

- *Reengineering*
- *Intrapreneuring*
- *Cross-functional management*
- *Participative team process*
- *Delayering*
- *Outsourcing*
- *Six Sigma*

- *Value engineering*
- *Best-case scenario*
- *Competitive advantage*
- *Right-sizing*
- *Empowerment*
- *Performance-based management*
- *Balanced scorecard*

TEN RULES TO USE WHEN PREPARING GRAPHICS FOR YOUR APPLICATION

Up to this point we have been discussing the writing style of the application and common mistakes made when preparing the written response. Let's now turn our attention to graphics, which are also a big part of the application. So many of the applications contain poor and hard-to-read graphics that this subject warrants separate treatment and guidelines. I have outlined ten rules to keep in mind when preparing and discussing graphics in your application.

Rule #1: Explain Graphics in the Text

Some applicants have responded to an Area to Address that asks for data by simply including a graph, with no explanation of what the graph shows or what kind of results are shown. A graph or chart should never be included without at least some explanation or reference in the text of your application. For example, you might say something like:

> *Figure 7.1a presents a summary of our major quality results compared to our foremost competitor: DMI. As you can see, we are superior to them in each of the six measures of quality results depicted in the bar graph.*

Always explain what the graph represents and summarize the conclusions that can be drawn from the data depicted on the graph. Even though it may seem obvious, the examiner may miss the significance of certain data unless you call attention to it. For example:

> *The data in Figure 7.8 show that our levels of customer satisfaction have improved by over 80% in the last two years. We have shown steady improvements over each of the last five years.*

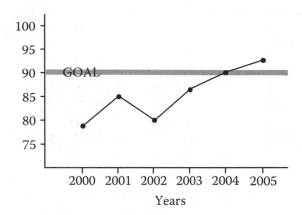

Figure 2.5: **What *Not* to Do When Explaining Graphics**

Rule #2: Don't Duplicate Information from Graphics in the Text

This is just the flip side of the first rule. Graphics should be explained and referenced, but the information contained in them need not be duplicated in the text that accompanies them. This is simply a waste of valuable space and an insult to the examiner's intelligence. Figure 2.5 shows what not to do when explaining graphics.

Rule #3: Don't Include More Than Two Lines of Data on Any One Graph

In an attempt to conserve space, some applicants have tried putting four or more lines of data on a single graph. This is also done in an attempt to show interrelationships among different quality indices. You should never include more than two lines of data on a single graph. Figure 2.6 shows the right and wrong ways to present data graphically.

Rule #4: Graphs Should Depict Goals or Targets

A graph without a line to indicate a goal or target is very difficult to interpret. Target or goal lines should be drawn on all graphs to indicate how close actual performance is to desired performance. Figure 2.7 presents an example.

Rule #5: Graphs of Performance Indices Should Show Improvement Using an Ascending Line

We are all taught that results are better when the line on a graph slopes up, representing an upward trend, and that a negative trend is indicated by a downward sloping line. Yet many applicants report positive quality results using negative indices such as number (or percent) of errors. Wherever possible, quality data should be presented in a positive fashion, so the line moves up as performance improves. Rather than graphing errors, graph the number or percentage of products without errors. Figure 2.8 shows the right way and wrong way to graph quality data.

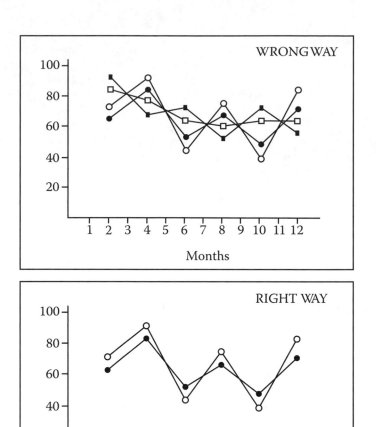

Figure 2.6:   **Put No More Than Two Lines of Data on a Graph**

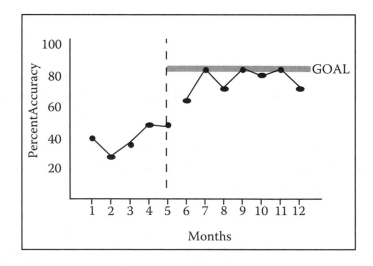

Figure 2.7:   **Goals Should Always Be Shown on Graphs**

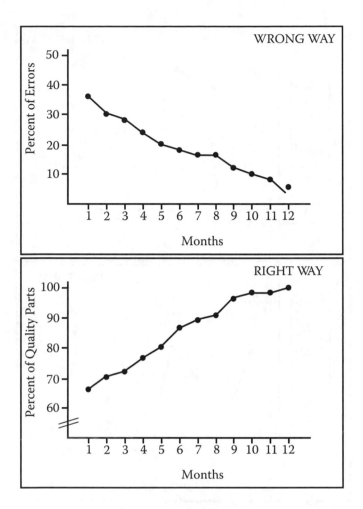

Figure 2.8: **Graph Desired Performance So Improvements Appear as an Ascending Line**

Rule #6: Scales on Graphs Should Be Set Up to Show Maximum Variability in the Data

For your own benefit, it is important that you set up performance scales on graphs to show the maximum degree of change or variability in quality performance. For example, if customer satisfaction ratings are done on a percentage scale, you would not set up the scale from 0 to 100 percent, unless there were that much variability in the data. If scores over the last five years have ranged from 80 percent to 95 percent, you might set up the graph with a scale that goes from 70 percent to 100 percent. As you can see in the "Wrong Way" example in Figure 2.9, very little variability is seen in the data scale on the graph from 0 to 100 percent. The second graph with the smaller scale, however, shows a great deal of variability.

Rule #7: Separate Baseline Data from Postimprovement Effort Data

Baseline data are those on levels of performance before a countermeasure or change has been introduced to improve performance. In many of the Areas to Address it is important

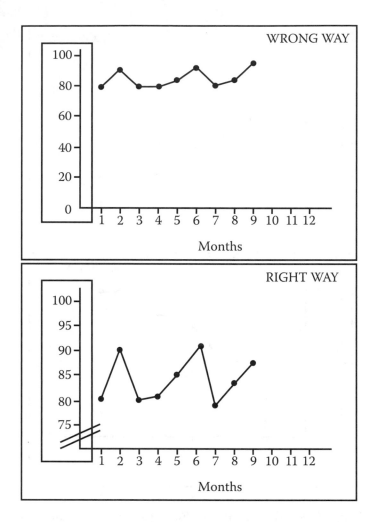

Figure 2.9:   **Setting Up the Scale for Performance on the Vertical Axis**

that you demonstrate a cause-and-effect relationship between improvements in results and the introduction of improvement efforts or programs. In order to do this, you need to show performance levels both before and after you began your improvement effort. When depicting the data on a graph, separate the two phases using a dotted vertical line, and do not connect the last baseline data point with the first postimprovement data point.

Figure 2.10 shows a sample graph that depicts the impact of goals and feedback on the percent accuracy.

Rule #8: Use Standard Graphing Formats

Use of strange or exotic graphing formats should be discouraged. Several applicants included graphics that this examiner, for one, had trouble interpreting. Almost any type of quality data can be presented using either a bar graph or a line graph. Bar graphs are most effective when comparing summary data. Line graphs are most effective for showing

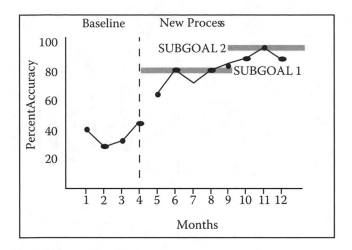

Figure 2.10:   **Graph Showing Baseline Performance and Percent Accuracy After Goals Were Set and Feedback Began**

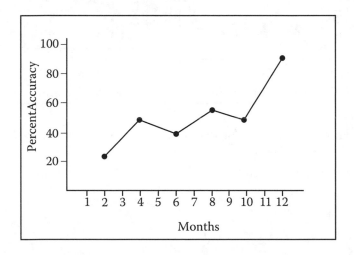

Figure 2.11:   **Line Graph Appropriately Labeled**

trends and for showing data over time. Figure 2.11 shows a line graph that has been appropriately labeled.

Other acceptable formats include pie charts, cumulative line graphs, and scatter diagrams. Examples of these formats are shown in Figure 2.12.

Rule #9: Graphs Should Be Clearly and Specifically Labeled

Every aspect of the graphs included in your application should be appropriately and completely labeled. The two axes should indicate the quality dimension that is being depicted and the measure of time. Goals and subgoals should be labeled, along with the phases in your quality improvement efforts. An example of an appropriately labeled and easily read graph is shown in Figure 2.13.

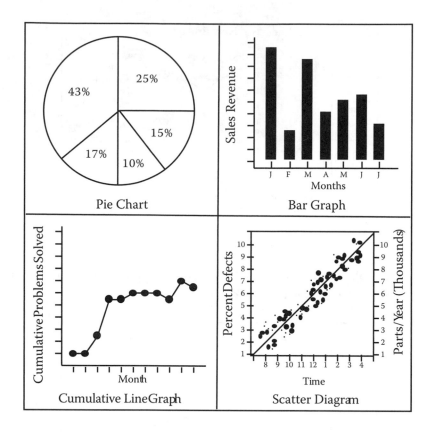

Figure 2.12:   **Various Ways of Graphing Performance**

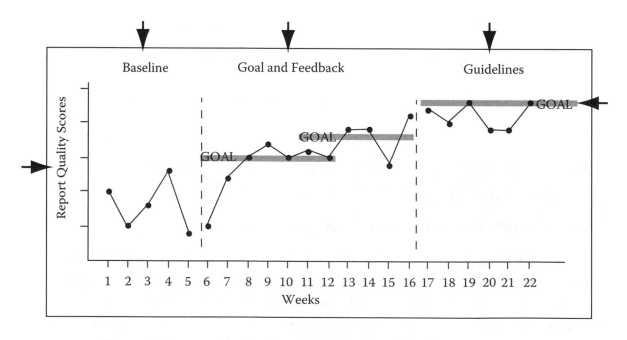

Figure 2.13:   **Graphs Should Be Clearly and Specifically Labeled**

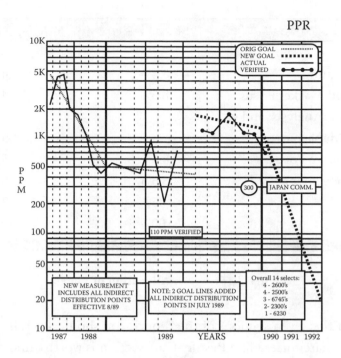

Figure 2.14:   **Graph Is Cluttered and Very Hard to Read**

Rule #10: Graphs Should Be Simple and Free of Clutter

Some people tend to make a graph as informative as possible. Pointing out significant increases or improvements, indicating where key events have occurred that have impacted the data, and including other relevant information are thought to help the reader interpret the data better. This seems good in theory, but it often results in cluttered graphics that are difficult to read. A sample graph that includes a great deal of information is shown in Figure 2.14; it is cluttered and very hard to read.

This graph includes four different lines, too many notes, and scales that are very difficult to read. The spacing between years is unequal, as is the PPM scale on the vertical axis. Furthermore, we don't know what PPM means, nor whether the scale is number of defects, ratio of defects, or something else. In general, this graph represents a perfect example of what not to do when preparing your own. It violates at least four of the ten rules we have discussed.

LENGTH OF APPLICATION REPORT SECTIONS

You are allowed a maximum of 50 single-sided pages. These limits do not include the five-page overview, the table of contents, tab dividers, and covers. Appendices and attach-ments are included in the 50-page limit, however. In deciding how much space to

CATEGORY/SECTION		% VALUE	SUGGESTED LENGTH
1.0	Leadership	12%	6 pages
2.0	Strategic Planning	8.5%	4 pages
3.0	Customer and Market Focus	8.5%	4 pages
4.0	Measurement, Analysis, and Knowledge Management	9%	4.5 pages
5.0	Human Resource Focus	8.5%	4.5 pages
6.0	Process Management	8.5%	5 pages
7.0	Results	45%	22 pages
TOTAL		100%	50 pages

Figure 2.15:   **Allocation of Pages**

allocate for each of the seven sections of the report, you should keep in mind the weight given to each of the categories. The Results (7.0) section is worth almost 50 percent of the evaluation, so it should be allocated the most pages. A suggested breakdown of the number of pages to allocate for each of the seven sections of the application report is shown in Figure 2.15.

PRODUCING THE FINAL COPY OF THE BALDRIDGE APPLICATION

The appearance of the application is not formally one of the criteria by which it is evaluated, but appearance does give the examiners an overall impression of your organization. If the application is sloppy, poorly laid out, and includes typographical and other errors, it doesn't portray a positive image about the company's level of quality. The appearance of the applications ranges from corner-stapled applications that have been typed on old typewriters, to application reports that have been typeset, printed on expensive paper, and include four-color photos and graphics throughout.

It is certainly not necessary that the application include color photos or that it be typeset. Most laser printers and desktop publishing packages can produce written materials that look as good as those that have been typeset—for a fraction of the cost. The 2006 Application Forms and Instructions provide specifics on the type style and size that must be used in the application. Be sure to review this information before writing your application.

The Baldrige officials also discourage using three-ring binders for your application. I suggest using a Cerlox plastic spiral binding. With this type of binding, the application can be opened flat on a desk and does not take up much space or hinder movement.

Be certain to include a table of contents, and to separate each of the seven main sections of the written report with tab dividers. I also suggest that pages be numbered sequentially within each tab, and that graphics and exhibits be integrated into the text and not placed at the end of each section or in appendices. Finally, material should be printed on both sides of each page to lessen the bulk and weight of the application.

WHAT IT COSTS TO APPLY FOR A BALDRIGE AWARD

During the years, there have been many rumors floating around about the true cost of applying for a Baldrige Award. Claims have been made that it costs hundreds of thousands of dollars in consulting contracts and internal labor to prepare an application and win the award. There have also been rumors that it only costs a few thousand dollars for a small company to apply and win the award. Both rumors are an exaggeration. The fees for applying for a Baldrige Award vary, depending upon the size and type of organization. A small school, business, or healthcare organization might pay as little as $2,150 to apply for the award and an additional $10,000 to $17,500 for examiner site visit expenses. Of course, most applicants do not get a site visit, so only those with a chance of winning tend to have to pay for the site visit expenses, which is the most expensive part of the process. On the other end of the spectrum, a large organization would have to pay an application fee of $5,150, plus an additional $20,000 to $35,000 in site visit expenses. As I mentioned earlier, the cost of such a thorough assessment by a team of consultants is likely to be 5 to 10 times as much, and the consultants are often inexperienced. The Baldrige Examiners tend to be older seasoned professionals who are highly regarded in their fields.

The chart in Figure 2.16 shows the breakdown of costs for 2008.

Award Category	Eligibility Fee	Application Fee*	Supplemental Section Fee (if applicable)**	Site Visit Fee Usual Range (if applicable)***
Manufacturing	$150	$6,000	$2,000	$20,000–$35,000
Service	$150	$6,000	$2,000	$20,000–$35,000
Small Business	$150	$3,000	$1,000	$10,000–$17,000
Education, nonprofit K–12	$150	$1,000	$250	$1,500
Education, nonprofit higher education	$150	$3,000	$1,000	$10,000–$17,000
Education, for-profit >500 faculty/staff	$150	$6,000	$2,000	$20,000–$35,000
Education, for-profit 500 or fewer faculty/staff	$150	$3,000	$1,000	$10,000–$17,000
Health Care >500 staff	$150	$6,000	$2,000	$20,000–$35,000
Health Care 500 or fewer staff	$150	$3,000	$1,000	$10,000–$17,000
Nonprofit >500 staff	$150	$6,000	$2,000	$20,000–$35,000
Nonprofit 500 or fewer staff	$150	$3,000	$1,000	$10,000–$17,000

*An additional processing fee of $1,250 is required for applications submitted on a CD.

** Supplemental sections are not applicable for applicants with (a) a single performance system that supports all of their product and/or service lines and (b) products or services that are essentially similar in terms of customers and/or users, technology, types of employees, and planning.

*** Site Visit Review Fee
This fee is paid only by applicants receiving site visits. The fee is set when visits are scheduled and is dependent on a number of factors, including the number of sites to be visited, the number of Examiners assigned, and the duration of the visit.

The site visit fee for applicants with more than 500 employees in the manufacturing, service, nonprofit, health care, and for-profit education sectors usually ranges between $20,000 and $35,000. The site visit fee is approximately half that rate for small businesses, nonprofit higher education organizations, and applicants in the health care, for-profit education, and nonprofit sectors with 500 or fewer employees. In 2007, the site visit fee for nonprofit K–12 education organizations is $1,500. The site visit fee for all organizations is due to ASQ two weeks after completion of the site visit.

Figure 2.16:   **Fees for the 2007 Award Cycle**

Chapter

3

KEY THEMES AND RELATIONSHIPS
AMONG THE CRITERIA

THE BALDRIGE BURGER

The diagram from the 2007 Baldrige criteria booklet, reprinted below, shows how the various parts of the criteria work together as a system.

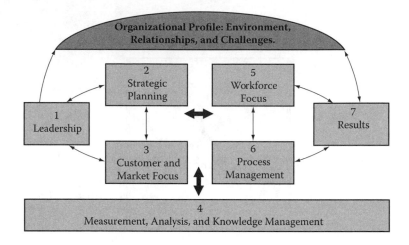

This diagram is called the "Baldrige Burger" by many because it resembles a hamburger. Parts of it make sense, and parts of it are confusing. There is one box for each of the seven Baldrige categories, which makes sense. Box number 4 is stretched out to become the bottom bun, I assume to illustrate how information and analysis are critical to the other six categories. The problem I have with the Baldrige Burger is that leadership is the first box, rather than the customer. Leaders have been known to lead their organizations off a cliff by not being attuned to the marketplace. The Baldrige model is customer driven, not leadership driven. In Figure 3.1, you will see that the customer is the first box, not the leadership. Leaders need to review market research to decide on company mission, vision, and other factors. The second problem with the Baldrige Burger involves the top bun. The words in the top bun read Organizational Profile: Environment, Relationships, and Challenges. One could put Category 2 as the top bun, since strategic planning cuts across all other categories the same way information and analysis does. However, that would leave a lopsided burger with only three boxes as the "meat" in the middle.

Figure 3.1 may appear graphically boring, but it seems to capture the system nature of the Baldrige criteria better than the Baldrige Burger. The two diagrams are mostly the same, showing inputs, processes, and outputs. The only substantive difference is that I show customers rather than leadership as the beginning of the system. Both diagrams show the importance of all seven categories working together as an organizational performance system to drive the right results.

THE BALDRIGE CRITERIA AS A SYSTEM

The Baldrige criteria are made up of seven Categories, which are further divided into 18 Examination Items and 32 Areas to Address. While each of the seven Categories is evaluated separately, there are relationships (or "linkages") between the seven and they function together as a system.

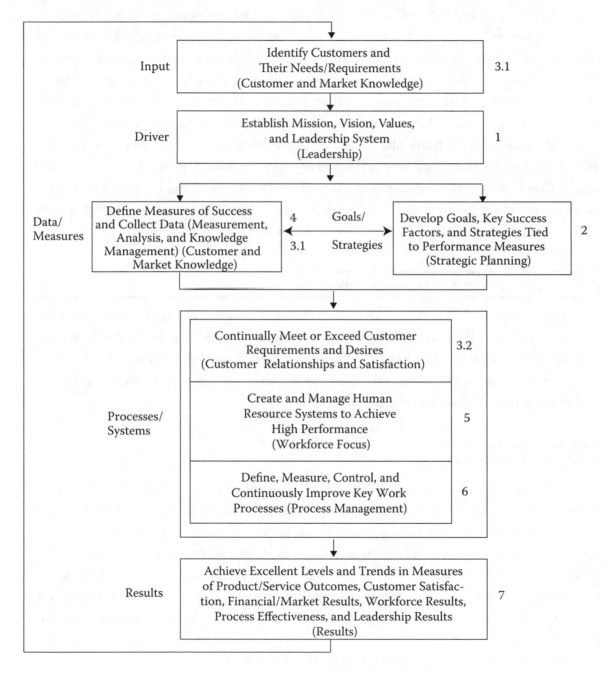

Figure 3.1:   The Baldrige Criteria as a System

As you can see from Figure 3.1, the "input," or beginning, of the Baldrige assessment is not Leadership, but customers and their requirements. Baldrige suggests that an organization first needs to define its customers and markets, and then identify what is important to each of those groups of customers. Customers and their requirements are asked for in item 3.1 of the Baldrige criteria. Once markets and needs have been identified, the company can develop its mission and direction, which is what is asked for in the Leadership (1.0) section. Once the mission and direction of the organization have been defined, you need to identify measures of success. Measures are asked for in Section 4.0, Measurement, Analysis, and Knowledge Management, and item 3.2b, Customer Satisfaction Determination. Short- and long-term goals and strategies then need to be developed, relating to each of the performance measures. Planning is asked about in Section 2.0 of Baldrige. Based upon the goals and improvement strategies outlined in the organization's plans, you need to develop systems/processes: Section 5.0 asks about human resource systems; Section 6.0 asks about work processes in the direct and indirect areas of the organization; and item 3.2a asks about the processes used to manage relationships with customers. All of these systems/processes should work together to produce results (7.0) for the organization and its customers.

CORE VALUES IN THE BALDRIGE CRITERIA

Although there are 32 Areas to Address and related individual questions in the 2007 Baldrige criteria, a few common themes or "core values" underlie many of the items and categories. This section of the book explains each of these core values. Additional information on these themes or values may be found in the criteria booklet, which is available on the NIST website: http://nist.gov.

Visionary Leadership

Every effective organization starts with a visionary leader. Herb Keleher of Southwest Airlines, Jack Welch of General Electric, Steve Jobs of Apple, Bill Gates of Microsoft, and other respected CEOs have clear visions of what they want their organizations to become, and they manage to translate that vision into strategy. Many organizations today lack a clear vision and end up with a strategy cluttered with such buzzwords and phrases as world-class, value-added, and customer-focused. These jargon-laden visions often indicate a management team that has not figured out where they want the organization to be in the future. A vision should be clear enough for employees to understand, and it should inspire them to want to help the organization achieve it.

The values of an organization that define its culture are also linked to the values of the CEO and other senior executives. Everyone watches the behaviors and decisions of the executives to learn what is considered appropriate and inappropriate behavior in the organization. One of the values of Southwest Airlines, for example, is a sense of humor. Former CEO Herb Keleher has a great sense of humor, and has been careful in selecting other executives and employees at all levels who have a sense of humor.

Executive commitment to the Baldrige process is a key criterion for success, as well. In the 17 years that I have been working with business and government organizations to use the Baldrige model to drive improvement, nearly two-thirds of those organizations have not improved much as a result of Baldrige assessments. The one-third that has dramatically improved has a common characteristic—executive commitment and involvement. Consider, for example, Don Ing, the former president of Solar Turbines of San Diego, which was the 1998 Baldrige winner. Solar made major improvements in its processes, and worked to further deploy good practices as a result of feedback from several rounds of applications for the California Baldrige Award (administered by the California Council for Excellence [CCE]). Ing used the feedback from the state award process to develop strategic plans and processes to lead his company from a score in the 300s to winning the Baldrige Award in less than five years. The entire leadership team at Solar became believers in the Baldrige process and was actively involved in the improvement efforts.

Customer-Driven Excellence

Being customer driven or customer focused is something most organizations today talk about but is something few do well. The foundation of a customer-driven organization is solid market research providing information on the factors that influence customer buying behavior. Quality used to be a differentiating factor in some industries, but not today. The car industry, for example, is one in which quality products are assumed, rather than being the competitive advantage it was 20 years ago. Market research is so difficult because customers and potential customers often have a hard time articulating what is most important to them. Leading companies today have adopted creative methods for determining the factors that most influence customer buying decisions. Daimler-Chrysler, for example, rides around with customers for hours in their cars and gets them to talk about what they like and do not like about the cars.

Part of being a customer-driven organization is determining desired customer groups. Years ago, many organizations spent huge sums of money to drive up customer satisfaction and found that it did nothing to improve sales or profits. The Baldrige criteria do not suggest that you need to build relationships with all customers. Smart organizations figure out who the most important customers are and do not worry about getting all customers to be loyal. Solectron, a two-time Baldrige winner that manufactures circuit boards and electronic components, managed to improve sales and profits dramatically while reducing its number of customers. It is hard for a growing organization to turn away business, but this is often the best strategy for ensuring profitable growth.

The frustrating part of trying to be customer driven is that customer needs and priorities seem to change constantly. A company finally figures out what customers want, and then customers change their priorities. The Internet and other new technologies have dramatically changed customer expectations and priorities for many things in life, such as how we buy books or get information from others. Part of what the Baldrige criteria look for is an organization that is flexible enough to adapt and change as customer requirements change. Ritz-Carlton, another two-time Baldrige winner, keeps an extensive database on each guest, which includes information on preferences and special requests. The process required to keep the database up-to-date is even more impressive. Ritz customizes aspects of its service to the guests' preference, such as making sure you always get fat-free milk with your cereal, or that the Ritz employees refer to you by first name, or that you have SPF 30 sun block waiting by your favorite chair at the pool. Understanding what customers want is enough of a challenge, but being able to act on those demands quickly is the mark of an exceptional organization.

Organizational and Personal Learning

This is what author Stephen Covey calls "sharpening the saw." Organizations and employees need to continually improve their knowledge and skills and have ways of sharing lessons learned with each other. The "learning organization" is another buzzword that gets talked about a great deal, but is rarely practiced well. Larger organizations have a bigger challenge to learn from one another. Big organizations get chopped up into smaller units, facilities, and departments, often having little opportunity to learn from one another. A company that does this well is Cargill. Cargill, the largest privately owned firm in the world, is the first food company to win a Baldrige Award. Its Sunny Fresh Foods egg business captured a Baldrige award in 1999 and again in 2005. Cargill has used the Baldrige criteria to drive improvement in its companies for over seven years. Each year it holds a conference that is attended by over 500 employees from around the world to share best practices. It also publishes a book of best practices each year called Cargill Gems that summarizes the best practices gleaned from the 100 or so applications for its internal Baldrige-based award. Sharing lessons learned in a company of over 100,000 employees in all parts of the world is a challenge that Cargill does well.

Along with organizational learning, the Baldrige criteria also focus on individual learning. Motorola, the first Baldrige Award winner, has always been a role model for other companies when it comes to employee education and training. The Motorola

University remains one of the best facilities of its kind in the world. However, you do not need to be a major corporation with its own university to emphasize employee learning and development. A company called Momentum Textiles, which I predict will be a Baldrige winner in a few years, has an extremely sophisticated and successful approach to training and development, and it does not even have an HR manager, let alone a corporate university. The company, a designer and manufacturer of fabrics for office furniture and commercial interiors, has less than 100 employees and is number two in market share. The company defines a curriculum for each job, and detailed development plans are prepared for each employee once a year. The company relies on outside resources such as public workshops, college courses, and technical schools to meet some of its training needs, and makes use of structured on-the-job training to satisfy other developmental needs. Motorola and Momentum have in common a focus on continually improving employee knowledge and skills. The theme of continual learning is found throughout all sections of the Baldrige criteria, not just in the human resources section. Each approach/deployment item asks for evidence of evaluation and improvement of processes and approaches showing evidence of learning.

Valuing Workforce Members

An increasing number of organizations today rely on employees and suppliers or partners for success. Organizations that depend on the latest manufacturing equipment for success are becoming fewer and fewer today. Even such capital-intensive businesses as steel mills, paper mills, and airlines are finding that employees and suppliers give them the edge over competitors. Southwest Airlines stands out as a role model for the wonderful culture it has created. The company is extremely careful about each person it hires, making sure it has the right mix of skills, ethics, and personality traits to ensure the culture is maintained. It also values its employees and treats them like they are members of a big family. The company was listed last year in *Fortune* as one of the best to work for in America, and it consistently beats most competitors in safety and on-time performance.

Companies that truly value their employees often do creative and sometimes weird things to show their devotion to their workforce. For instance, Southwest has great parties, and Baldrige finalist MBNA has a department that plans weddings for employees and another department that arranges funerals for relatives of employees. Another Baldrige finalist, Appleton Papers, teaches employees that family and personal lives always come before the job. The company has about 2 percent annual turnover, while other paper companies often have more than 30 percent annual turnover.

Suppliers and vendors also need to be valued and treated like partners. Many organizations still treat suppliers as if they cannot be trusted and foster an adversarial climate. For example, the federal government has been farming out a greater amount of its work to outside companies. However, although the outside companies do the work at a fair price, the government often employs an army of federal agents to do "program oversight." Such oversight entails watching the suppliers so they follow all the rules and do not cheat the government. Much of this oversight is not necessary, and a number of government employees I have spoken with suggest that their jobs are nothing more than white collar welfare.

Private industry has done a better job of partnering with its suppliers and vendors. Shea Homes in Phoenix has narrowed its list of contractors to about 50, using them to build several thousand homes a year in Arizona. The suppliers fill out abbreviated Baldrige applications. Shea evaluates suppliers against the Baldrige criteria and provides consulting to help them improve their businesses. Several of the suppliers have won Arizona Quality Awards, and Shea Homes has won state awards in both California and Arizona. By partnering with the contractors that build the homes, 76 percent of the homes built by Shea had zero defects—an 8 percent improvement from previous year.

Strategic alliances are important to many organizations today, as well. Forming alliances with similar companies or those that provide a related product/service often allows both companies a stronger presence in the market. United Airlines' "Star Alliance," for example, is a partnership with other airlines around the world. Aligning with the wrong partner can spell disaster for a company, however. It is important to develop specific criteria for selecting other organizations with which to partner.

Agility

The second section of the Baldrige criteria asks about strategic planning. While it is important to have a strategic plan, it is also necessary sometimes to scrap the plan two months into the year and take a different direction. Agility, a characteristic found in many Baldrige winners, means that an organization can quickly adapt to changing competitive, technological, or customer factors. One of the things that has made Nokia number one in market share in the cellular phone business is its fast new product development cycle. Nokia designs and introduces new products in about half the time it takes its major competitors. The trick is to improve cycle time for R&D and new product introduction without sacrificing quality and thoroughness. Another cellular phone manufacturer worked hard to improve its new product design timeliness and found that a large number of its phones were failing after two years.

Being the first to market something new can make all the difference in the world. A competitor can often do a lot to capture a huge share of the market just by being first with a new product or service. Barnes&Noble.com is working hard to catch Amazon. com, but Amazon remains far ahead and it is unlikely that B&N will catch up in the near future. Changing from a bricks and mortar chain of bookstores to selling books on the Internet is a drastic change, the type of change with which most companies would struggle.

Focus on the Future

Another core value in the Baldrige criteria is the focus on identifying future customers, markets, technologies, and other factors that might impact the business. Doing a good job on today's requirements and today's products may not ensure an organization's long term survival. Part of the job of senior executives is to search out new opportunities for the business. Opportunities might consist of companies to buy, others to partner with, new markets to enter, or new products or services that might expand a company's offerings. Cisco is clearly focused on the future. The company has acquired more than 40 new firms in the last five years and continues to show outstanding results. One of its core competencies appears to be finding and acquiring the right companies that allow it to become larger and stronger without distracting the company from its mission or changing its culture.

1999 and 2005 Baldrige winner Sunny Fresh Foods is another organization that does a good job focusing on the future. Sunny Fresh supplies McDonald's with all the liquid eggs used in scrambled egg products. One of the factors that helped Sunny Fresh earn the contract with McDonald's (a very demanding customer) was its record of exceeding the new food safety regulations that came out a few years back. Sunny Fresh, as well as other Cargill businesses, gained an edge on many competitors by exceeding new food safety requirements before anyone else. One might think of the egg business as one that would not change much from year to year, but Sunny Fresh has proven that a food company needs to focus on the future as much as its high tech counterparts in other industries.

Managing for Innovation

Winners of the Baldrige award are often characterized as innovative companies. 1997 winner 3M Dental Products is known for innovation. 3M is known all over the world for its innovative products in a number of fields. Innovation is not just the job of research and development, either. Employees in all functions need to be encouraged to be innovative. Risk taking and innovation are cultural values that are hard to find in many big companies today. They may have become large and successful because some creative and innovative people had a great idea at one time, but big companies tend to lose that entrepreneurial spirit as the founders retire and the size of the corporation increases.

Maintaining a culture of risk taking and innovation in a large company with thousands of employees takes work. Apple seemed to have lost its creative edge for a while but is back stronger than ever with Steve Jobs in charge, creating some of the most innovative new computing products to come along in quite a while.

Management by Fact

This is probably the most difficult of the Baldrige core values to follow. What it says is that the Baldrige criteria expect a company to put more science into how they run their organizations. Baldrige expects organizations to systematically gather data on the right variables, to analyze those data, and use them to make decisions and plan improvements. The level of analysis expected by the Baldrige examiners is much more sophisticated than one normally sees in a business. Selecting the right performance measures in the first place should be a fairly scientific process, linked to business strategy and strategies of competitors. Once an organization has developed a good balanced set of metrics, it needs to conduct research between leading and lagging indicators, and between hard and soft measures. For example, very few organizations can show a link between customer satisfaction scores and future business, or between customer satisfaction and profits. Understanding these links and using the correlational data improves the accuracy of decision making.

Social Responsibility and Citizenship

Because the Baldrige judges expect winners to be role models for the world, it is important that the company be a good corporate citizen. A well-rounded organization is not unlike a well-rounded individual who should balance the priorities of work, family, charity, and personal interests. Many big corporations donate a lot of money and time to charities and community groups. However, most are completely reactive, waiting for someone to knock on their door and ask for a check or some other donation. Writing a lot of checks is not what this value is about.

Smart organizations select a few beneficial charities to support that will help the community and also help their image. For example, Baldrige finalist Haworth, donated several million dollars to Western Michigan University to build the Haworth Business School. The company could have divided the money among 20 different charity and educational organizations, but this would not have had much impact. Haworth draws many new employees from this university's business program, because it is in nearby Kalamazoo. McDonald's is another organization that is more proactive and strategic in their approach to community support and public citizenship. Ronald McDonald House is a charity the company created to help families with children in the hospital. This doesn't hurt their image either, because McDonald's caters to families with small children.

Focus on Results and Creating Value

Baldrige used to be a prize for companies that did all the right things. Quality gurus told us in the 1980s that U.S. companies need to spend less time watching the bottom line and more time thinking about quality, customers, and employees. Just about every organization jumped on this quality bandwagon to some extent. Many found that the effort did nothing to improve bottom-line results. In fact, just the opposite occurred in some companies. Quality and customer satisfaction improved, but expenses also went up, and profits came down. The 2007 Baldrige criteria expect a balanced focus on all kinds of results, including financial performance. Emphasis now is on balance between short- and long-term performance, ensuring long-term survival and success. About half of the points in the Baldrige criteria are based on the results an organization achieves, so Baldrige is not just about doing the right things; it is about getting the results.

An orientation toward specific types of results is also important. An analysis of the market, economy, competition, and a number of other factors should help the company to decide its driving forces for success in the next 5 to 10 years. It might be increasing their market share, decreasing prices and operating expenses, or any number of things necessary to be a leader in the markets it serves. Results-oriented organizations need to show flexibility in pushing for different results from time to time, as situations change. One year profits might be the most important index, and the next year, it might be safety and environmental performance.

Systems Perspective

As I explained in the beginning of this chapter, the seven categories of the Baldrige criteria work together to form a system of organizational performance. One of the core values of the criteria is the alignment of all the pieces of the organizational systems. Large organizations typically have great difficulty in ensuring that all units and locations are properly aligned with the corporate vision and goals. I have worked with some units of large organizations that work at cross-purposes with each other or even compete against each other. It is OK that different parts of an organization have different approaches. In fact, the Baldrige criteria encourage the tailoring of approaches to the nature of the business in each unit. However, it is also important to look at all of these units or locations as part of a larger organization that has its own goals and objectives.

One of the major reasons applicants for the Baldrige Award lose points in the approach/deployment sections is that breaks or inconsistencies exist between various parts of their performance systems. The various items and areas to address in the Baldrige criteria relate in many ways to other items and areas to address. A common inconsistency involves multiple process improvement teams working on projects that in no way are connected to the company's strategic plan. Another common inconsistency is to find no connection between the overall strategic plan and various lower level activities such as the technology plan, human resource plan, marketing plans, and so forth. Finding and correcting these inconsistencies are important to winning a Baldrige Award. Read the next section of this chapter carefully, have someone evaluate your draft application to identify any of these breaks, and get them fixed before the final draft is prepared. Finding and correcting these inconsistencies are not just important for the sake of a good Baldrige assessment. These breaks waste valuable resources, and often send mixed messages to employees about the behavior the organization expects of them. Finding an organization that has all of its sub-systems aligned is quite impressive and is something one finds in all winners of the Baldrige Award.

RELATIONSHIPS BETWEEN THE CORE VALUES AND THE CRITERIA

In addition to the relationships between and across Items and Categories, there are also relationships between the Baldrige Core Values and the criteria. Some of the values are broad and can be found In many of the criteria items, whereas others are fairly specific and focus mostly on one Item or Category. The table below lists the Core Values and shows the primary and secondary relationships of the 32 items in the criteria. In other

	LINKS (ITEMS)	
CORE VALUE	PRIMARY LINKAGE	SECONDARY LINKAGE
Visionary Leadership	1.1, 7.6	2.1, 2.2
Customer-Driven Excellence	3.1, 3.2, 7.2	2.1, 2.2, 6.2
Organizational and Personal Learning	5.1, 6.2, 7.4	2.2, 4.2
Valuing Workforce Members as Partners	5.1, 5.2, 7.4	6.1, 6.2
Agility	1.1, 2.1, 2.2, 7.6	6.1, 6.2, 7.3, 7.6
Focus on the Future	1.1, 2.1	3.1, 4.1, 4.2, 7.6
Managing for Innovation	3.1, 6.1, 7.1	4.2, 6.2
Management by Fact	1.1, 4.1	7.1 to 7.6
Social Responsibility	1.2, 7.6	4.1, 5.1, 5.2
Focus on Results and Creating Value	1.1, 2.1, 2.2	7.1 to 7.6
Systems Perspective	All 7 Categories and 32 Items	

words, the primary and secondary places where an Examiner might see evidence of the organization following a particular value.

KEY RELATIONSHIPS AMONG THE SEVEN CATEGORIES

Although each of the 18 Examination Items is given a separate score and evaluated independently, performance on one item clearly affects performance on other items. Something that the Baldrige examiners routinely do is to look for what I call "disconnects" or missed linkages among items in different categories. The more of these missed linkages that are found, the more likely it is that an applicant will receive a low score. A lack of consistency across the categories and items shows a system that is flawed, or at least an application that was not well planned and written. In the next few pages I will discuss the linkages that should be addressed for each of the seven categories, and the common "disconnects" that I have found in the Baldrige Award applications I've reviewed in the last few years.

How to Check for Consistency among Baldrige Items

Although it's important to understand the major relationships among the various Baldrige items, there are so many of them that it can get confusing. In a related book by another Baldrige expert, interrelationships are defined between each of the 19 Baldrige items, using a graphic with arrows from one item to many others. This information may be interesting for Baldrige scholars, but has little practical use. Baldrige examiners simply don't have the time to check for consistency between one item and the 10 or 15 others that may relate to it when reading an application. A good application takes between 16 and 24 hours to review and score as it is, and this endless checking for consistency between most items would add many hours of time to the review process. Rather than identify how each Baldrige item may be even slightly connected with others, I have chosen to discuss only the most important interrelationships. These are the relationships that could have a major negative impact on your score if inconsistencies are found.

1. Leadership—Key Relationships with Other Criteria

The strongest link to the Leadership section is the Organizational Profile. The profile includes a lot of basic information on the organization's mission, goals, and challenges that must be further addressed in the Leadership section. Compared to other sections of the criteria, the Leadership section is probably the most independent of others. Area to Address 1.1a(2) asks about how leaders promote an environment that fosters ethical behavior. This must be consistent with the criteria in 1.2, which asks about the governance system. The questions in 1.1a(3) ask about how leaders create an environment that encourages performance improvement, agility, learning, and innovation. The answers to these questions must be consistent with those answers provided to questions in Category 5, Workforce Focus, that address employee performance management and workforce capability and capacity; and Category 6, Process Management. Processes that are too tightly controlled and managed may be barriers to innovation and agility, for example. The last question in 1.1a(3) asks about how leaders participate in succession planning. This information must be consistent with 5.1b(4), which asks about the succession planning process.

Area to Address 1.1b(1) includes a series of questions about communication and reward and recognition. The information included in your answer here must be consistent with both 5.1b, which asks about the employee performance management system and 5.1a(3), which asks about employee motivation.

Item 1.2, which asks about your efforts in the areas of social responsibility, ethics, and environmental performance, should correspond with the results you present in section 7.6, which asks for governance and social responsibility results. If you have developed metrics for environmental performance, ethics, or other measures of social responsibility, you will want to list these metrics in section 1.2, and present data on these measures in section 7.6 of your application. Similarly, you will want to set targets or goals for these social responsibility and citizenship metrics and discuss these goals in section 2.2, where you outline your strategic plan.

2. Strategic Planning—Key Relationships with Other Criteria

2.1 asks about the process you use to develop your annual and longer-term business plans. 2.1a(2) asks about how you use information on current and future customer requirements to develop appropriate goals and strategies. The information in this section should correspond exactly with the response to 3.1a, which asks about your targeted customers and their requirements. In this section, you need to explain how you use the market research data on customers and their priorities to develop plans and strategies. 2.1a(2) also asks about information on the competitive environment that is used during the planning process. Information on your competitors should be presented in section 4.1 of the application, and should be well integrated with your response here.

Your approach to strategy deployment (2.2a) should be consistent with your leadership system, described in section 1.1, as well as your overall performance management system, which would be described in section 5.1. The approach you use to track performance against plans should also closely match the approach you use to analyze performance data, which is found in item 4.1.

Section 2.2 is where you outline your goals and strategies for both the long and short term. Your goals or targets that you list in 2.2a should link directly with the performance metrics you identify in section 4.1 or 1.1. This is a common area where disconnects or inconsistencies are found. If you list something as a measure in section 4.1, you should make sure that targets and improvement strategies are presented in 2.2a. The company's overall long-term vision should also correspond with the information on the company niche or mission that might be outlined in the response to item 1.1. The improvement strategies that you discuss in 2.2a might also correspond to the processes you elect to improve in section 6.2. Many good companies use the strategic plan as the driver of process improvement activities. This helps ensure that process improvement activities are linked to the company's goals and plans.

Your human resource plans that you present in 2.2a(5) should present goals or targets that are linked to your HR strategies, which are outlined in section 5.0. The HR systems that you discuss in sections 5.1 through 5.2 should be consistent with the HR goals and targets that you outline in your response to 2.2a(5).

Area to Address 2.2b asks for information on where you project your performance to be in the next five years, relative to major competitors. Your response to this item should be consistent with the information you present on your major competitors in item 4.1a. Both responses should address the same competitors.

3. Customer and Market Focus—Key Relationships with Other Criteria

Item 3.1a(1) asks about your targeted market segments and the requirements of each group of customers. This information should be consistent with the factors that you evaluate when discussing how you measure customer satisfaction in section 3.2. If you divide customers into three distinct segments in 3.1, because of their unique requirements, then you should probably measure customer satisfaction in three different ways in section 3.2. Customer requirements outlined in 3.1a should also be consistent with internal requirements and standards described in 3.2a.

Your approach to prioritizing customer requirements and using this information to design new products and services [3.1a(3)] should link well with your process for new product/service development outlined in 6.1a. Your response to these two Areas to Address should be fairly close in content and may require some cross-referencing.

Item 3.2a asks about how you make it easy for customers to contact your organization and do business with you, and how you handle and track complaints. Service standards should be consistent with any targets or goals you set in section 2.2. Your system for tracking complaints should link to your market research processes described in 3.1a, where you discuss customer requirements.

Item 3.2b asks about the approach used to measure customer satisfaction. Your response to this section should expand upon a briefer description of customer satisfaction measures presented in section 4.1. Item 4.1 asks about your overall performance metrics, including how you measure customer satisfaction. Your response to 3.2 should go into more detail on the methods used to measure customer opinions and buying behavior as a way of gauging their overall satisfaction. The customer satisfaction measures discussed in 3.2b should also be consistent with the results you present in section 7.1. If you identify six different customer satisfaction metrics in 3.2b, you should present data on all six of these metrics in section 7.1. In discussing how you obtain information on customer satisfaction levels of competitors, you might want to reference back to 4.1, wherein you discuss approaches for gathering all types of data on competitors.

4. Measurement, Analysis, and Knowledge Management

This section is all about data. The performance metrics that you list in section 1.1 and discuss in section 4.1 should be directly linked to the company strategy, vision, and key business drivers outlined in section 2.2. In fact, you should see targets set for each metric, and strategies outlined in 2.2 to hit or exceed the targets. In section 4.1, the examiners are evaluating whether or not your performance metrics are the right measures. One way of ensuring this is to make sure that they are closely linked to your overall strategies for success, and your business plans (2.2). The measures that you identify in section 4.1 should also be the metrics on which you present data in section 7.0. The overall performance measures you identify in section 4.1 should also be linked to the process metrics identified in section 6.0. The process metrics should support the overall performance measures used on your company scorecard. The metrics you identify in section 4.1a should also be linked to the analyses you do on the data in section 4.1b.

Item 4.1 also asks about data you gather on competitors, the industry, and benchmark organizations. The types of data you gather on your competitors should be linked to your overall strategy and key success factors. For example, if you decide that having the lowest prices in the market is one of your strategies, you would want to gather data on competitors' pricing on a regular basis. The types of companies and processes that you choose to benchmark or compare yourself to would also link in to your overall business strategy (2.2) and the processes you select for improvement (6.1 to 6.2). Data on your competitors and other comparative data should be presented on the graphs you include in section 7.0. Without comparative data on the graphs, it is impossible for examiners to evaluate your levels of performance. All graphs of results should include comparative data. A low score in this item, or a lack of competitor and comparative data, will have a dramatic negative impact on your score in section 7.0.

Item 4.1b asks about the approach used to review and analyze performance data. This write-up should mesh well with 2.2a(1), which asks about the approach for deploying your plans. The focus of 4.1b should be more on how data are analyzed rather than simply how they are reviewed. Data analysis approaches should also be consistent with the company approach for analyzing and correcting problems. For example, if the company employs a particular process analysis and improvement model that is discussed in section 6.1, this analysis model should be referenced in 4.1b. Aggregation of individual metrics into an index may also be discussed in section 4.1b. If this is done, the examiners will expect to see data on this index somewhere in section 7.0. If you have established correlations between performance measures (e.g., customer satisfaction and repeat sales), graphs showing these correlations should be presented in section 7.0. Your response to section 4.1b should be consistent with your answer to 5.3b(4), which asks about how you establish correlations between measures of employee well-being and health and overall company performance. You might mention some of these correlations in 4.1b and go into more detail in 5.3b(4).

5. Workforce Focus—Key Relationships with Other Criteria

As with section 1, this section on human resource development is fairly independent. I have already mentioned the link between 2.2a(3), which asks about your human resource plans, and the HR processes described in this section of the criteria. It is also important that your leadership system described in item 1.1 links well to the overall performance or work systems described in section 5.1. Your compensation and recognition programs described in 5.1a(3) should be linked to the company strategies and goals listed in item 2.2, and the overall performance measures identified in item 4.1. The examiners will look for inconsistencies between what you measure and what you write. For example, if you write about growth in market share as a critical success factor, and a primary performance measure, and pay executive bonuses for profit rather than market share growth, this would be seen as a negative. Similarly, if you write about the importance of teamwork and cooperation as a key part of your success strategy, and have a recognition and compensation system that is strictly based on individual performance, the examiners would see this as a problem.

Also important here is the link between your work systems and your overall business strategy (2.2). It is important that the approaches you use to ensure consistent performance from your people are aligned with the company mission, vision, and values.

HR practices such as performance appraisal systems and annual raises based on seniority often contradict stated company philosophies or values.

Item 5.2(a) asks about workforce capability and capacity. What is important here is that your training and development priorities link to your overall business strategies and to the work systems you have defined in item 5.1. It is also important that your leadership training is integrated with your leadership approach described in item 1.1. Training on process analysis and improvement should link well to section 6.0, and training on customer relationship management should be consistent with your response to item 3.2.

Item 5.2 is about safety, employee engagement, and satisfaction. Safety and employee satisfaction goals and measures listed in items 2.2 and 1.1 should be referenced here. Safety and employee satisfaction results should be presented in item 7.4, and should be consistent with the measures and targets identified in this section. Any overall safety and employee satisfaction measures that are part of your company scorecard and that are mentioned in item 1.1 should also be consistent with the information presented in this item.

6. Process Management—Key Relationships with Other Criteria

Category 6 asks about how the company designs and manages its key work processes and work systems to ensure consistency in its products and services. Item 6.1 is very broad and includes most of the work done by an organization. Any activity that relates to the core mission of the organization is discussed in 6.2. The process measures and standards asked for in 6.2a should be linked to, but not the same as, the overall performance metrics listed in 1.1 and discussed in 4.1. Process measures and standards tend to support the grander outcome measures that often appear on executive scorecards. Process improvement activities are asked about in 6.2a and should link back to the improvement strategies or action plans discussed in item 2.2.

Process improvement activities are often initiated as a result of benchmarking or comparative data. Therefore, any comparative or benchmark data discussed in section 4.1 should link to 6.1.

7. Results—Key Relationships with Other Criteria

This is the most important category in the Baldrige criteria. The data you present in this section should be consistent with the performance measures you identify in items 1.1, 4.1, 3.2, 5.0, and 6.0. All of these sections ask about performance measures. It is important

SUMMARY OF KEY RELATIONSHIPS AMONG THE CRITERIA

WHEN REVIEWING THESE CRITERIA	CHECK FOR CORRESPONDENCE WITH THESE CRITERIA
1.0 Leadership	
1.1	2.1, 2.2, 3.1, 4.1, 4.2, 5.1, 5.2, 6.1, 6.2, 7.6
1.2	1.1, 2.2, 7.6
2.0 Strategic Planning	
2.1	1.1, 3.1, 4.1, 4.2, 5.1
2.2	1.1, 3.1, 4.1, 4.2, 5.1, 5.2, 5.3, 6.1, 6.2, 7.0
3.0 Customer and Market Focus	
3.1	3.2, 6.1
3.2	2.2, 3.1a, 4.1, 7.1
4.0 Measurement, Analysis, and Knowledge Management	
4.1	1.1, 2.1, 2.2, 4.2, 6.0, 7.0
4.2	2.1, 4.1, 5.2, 7.0
5.0 Human Resource Focus	
5.1	1.1, 2.2, 7.4
5.2	1.1, 3.2, 5.1, 6.0, 7.4
5.3	2.2, 4.1, 7.4
6.0 Process Management	
6.1	1.1, 3.1,
6.2	1.1, 2.1, 2.2, 3.1, 4.1
7.0 Results	
7.1	1.1, 2.2, 3.1, 3.2
7.2	1.1, 2.2, 3.1, 3.2
7.3	1.1, 2.2, 4.1
7.4	1.1, 2.2, 5.1, 5.2
7.5	1.1, 2.2, 6.1, 6.2
7.6	1.1, 1.2

that you present data on most of the measures you list in other sections. Goals or targets identified in item 2.2 should appear on the graphs and charts in section 7.0. Data on competitors, industry, and benchmark companies from item 4.1 should be presented on performance graphs to illustrate your levels of performance. This is extremely important in demonstrating how good your results are compared to others.

Chapter

4

UNDERSTANDING THE
BALDRIGE AWARD SCORING SCALE

The scoring scale comprises two parts:

- *Process*
- *Results*

The Process scoring scale is used for categories 1 through 6 of the criteria; Results correspond to category 7.

PROCESS

The Process scoring scale is now based on an examination of 4 factors: Approach, Deployment, Learning, and Integration, and coded in the scale as A, D, L, or I. The Process sections of the criteria ask about how you do things, why you do them this way, where you have implemented whatever approach is being assessed, improvements you have made to the approach based on lessons learned, and linkages of the approach to other approaches and items in the criteria.

Approach

Approach questions ask about how you do something, or the process you employ to do market research, planning, training, or whatever the focus is of the criteria being scored. In grading the approach, the examiners look for logic behind why you do something a certain way. If the approach is inherently logical, this does not need to be explained, but many approaches that seem clear and logical to you may not to an outside observer. An important factor in assessing your approach is its appropriateness to your type and size of organization. For example, in a company of 50 people, it may be very appropriate to have a number of informal systems and processes for getting things done. This would not be the case in a company of 10,000 employees, where approaches are expected to be more structured, documented, and formal. Also examined in the approach dimension is the extent to which a process is planned and repeatable or systematic, as opposed to doing something different each time with no consistency. An important factor in grading your approach is that it not be too formal and systematic as well. There are many creative work processes where a checklist approach would be counterproductive and destroy any creativity that might be important for good performance.

One of the best features of the Baldrige criteria is that there are no right answers when it comes to approach. There are an infinite number of approaches that an organization might use to perform its mission. There is no such thing as the correct approach. Everything is evaluated in context as to its appropriateness for your organization in the situation that you face. The bad news about this lack of prescribed approaches is that examiners often disagree on the ratings they give your approach. They all bring their prior experience and knowledge to the process, which leads to variability in grading approaches.

Deployment

A synonym for deployment is implementation, which is often the area where large organizations lose points. It is fairly easy to get 20 people in one location to use the same approach, but quite a challenge in an organization of 20,000 people spread across 50 locations. Keep in mind that of the four factors (A, D, L, I), approach is by far the most important. If you have a really ineffective approach that is fully deployed or implemented, you will still get an extremely low score. The key is to first have a good logical approach and then deploy it wherever it makes sense.

Deployment does not mean that every part of the organization does things the same way. However, if there are differences, there better be some sound logical reasons for those differences. For example, each business unit of a large corporation I worked with had a different set of performance measures, so there was no way to aggregate the data at the corporate level, because they all had slightly different measures. There was no logic to this in most cases. There could be common measures of areas such as sales, morale, ROI, or customer satisfaction across all business units. Several of the units had good approaches to measurement, but they lost points because the approaches were not consistently deployed.

Deployment also addresses the extent to which the applicant has answered all of the questions in the criteria. Applicants often fail to answer one of the sub-questions in an Item or Area to Address if they do not have an answer. The completeness of your descriptions or answers to the Baldrige questions will also be taken into consideration in scoring Categories 1 through 6.

Learning

No matter how logical or well planned your approach is, the Baldrige criteria ask for evidence that your approaches are periodically evaluated and improved. Many applicants fail to explain how their approaches or processes have been improved over time or how innovations and breakthroughs have resulted in dramatic improvements in results (Category 7). If you are just at the pilot stage when implementing a new approach, you obviously won't have any evidence of system maturity. Scores in the higher ranges require evidence of approaches being improved several times over a period of years. The learning dimension also considers the sharing of effective approaches across different units of the organization.

Integration

This final dimension of the Process scoring scale asks about how your approach or process is linked to other related processes and approaches in the organization. Organizations that score in the higher scoring ranges tend to show excellent linkages of many different organizational systems. For example, you might expect that the performance measures monitored on a monthly basis are also the foundation of the strategic plan, incentive compensation system, and performance appraisal system. Essentially what examiners look for in evaluating the integration dimension is a lack of disconnects between organizational systems.

As you will come to learn, there are many interactions and dependencies among the various Baldrige items. I reviewed many of these interrelationships in Chapter 3. Examiners will look for consistency in the areas identified in Chapter 3 to assess integration. Organizations that achieve scores good enough to win a Baldrige Award are not a collection of a bunch of impressive individual processes and approaches. Rather, there appears to be some overall architecture or systems model in mind that was considered when designing each subsystem and approach in the organization, so that each piece works well with the others to drive strategy, performance, and results. This sort of integration is rarely seen, as many organizational systems are barely functional on their own, let alone when they must be linked to other parts of the business. Integration is difficult to assess on an individual item, because what is considered is the integration of the processes in one item with processes in other Baldrige items.

RESULTS

Results are only assessed in Category 7 of the criteria, but they are worth 45 percent of the points, so this is the most important section. The new scoring scale for results is based on an evaluation of four different dimensions: levels of current performance, trends over time, comparisons to competitors and benchmarks, and the relative importance of the metric to the success of the enterprise. Essentially, level and trend are the two major factors being evaluated. You can't assess the level of performance without comparing it to something and usually those comparisons are to competitors, industry averages, and benchmarks. You don't get more points if you have much comparative data but you are clearly worse than any of the comparisons. If you have no comparative data, which is fairly common in new Baldrige applicants, it will be impossible to assess your level of performance. A comparison of actual performance versus some target or goal is not very meaningful, because many organizations set targets that are easy to achieve.

When grading one of the six items that ask for results, examiners look at levels and trends in the collection of charts and graphs in that section. They are not all considered equal, however. First of all, the examiners will consider whether the graph represents overall organizational performance, or is simply a unit or subset of the organization. The examiners will also consider the importance of the metric on which data is presented to your overall strategy and success. For example, market share might be considered much more important than profit, if the vision of the company is to first become one of the top three in market share and later worry about becoming profitable. Examiners are taught to go back to the Organizational Profile section and review the factors that you identified that were key to your success or challenges that must be overcome when deciding how to weigh the importance of the various graphs you present. Other sections will also be used as reference when considering the importance of an individual graph or chart. For example, if you identified on-time delivery as the most important requirement of your customers, that graph might be counted more heavily than other performance measures linked to customer requirements. In other words, be careful what you say in categories 1 through 6 because you have to prove the effectiveness of your approaches in Category 7.

How Do Baldrige Applicants and Winners Score?

When you look at a breakdown of the Baldrige applicants over the past 10 years or so, you find that most of them score less than 600 points out of a possible 1000. In fact, about 80 percent score below 600 points or 60 percent. This does not necessarily mean that applicants are poorly run operations that have no business applying for an award. What it means is that this is a tough contest with a tough scoring scale. As a general rule, it takes between 550 and 600 points to earn a site visit, or qualify as a semi-finalist for the award. A score in this range does not mean that you are an average organization. It means that a team of examiners thinks you might be good enough to be a winner and they want to spend a week or so visiting your organization. One recent winner received a score of close to 600 on their written application and their final score was closer to 800 points because of all the additional effective processes the examiners saw on the site visit.

Winners of the Baldrige Award don't receive their actual score, but find out which scoring band they fell into, and it is generally the 70 percent to 80 percent band. I have never heard of an organization receiving a score of 900 or greater, although it is possible. Over the years, the winners have probably averaged scores of around 75 percent, which would earn you a grade of "C" in most schools. What this means is that the Baldrige scoring scale is very stringent, and that even a score of 50 percent of the points should be considered a level of performance that many organizations will never achieve.

UNDERSTANDING THE NEW BALDRIGE SCORING SCALE

Each of the 18 items in the Baldrige Award criteria are given a separate percentage score from 0 percent to 100 percent, and each item is worth a different number of points, ranging from 25 points for a couple of the Human Resource or Category 5 Items, to a high of 120 points for Item 1.1 Organizational Leadership. The percentage score is multiplied by the available points to determine each item score. The 19 item scores are then added together to determine the overall score of points out a possible 1000. Percentage scores used to always be given out in multiples of 10 percent, making the math much easier. With the 2004 scoring scale, scores ending in 5 percent are now OK, which should lead to much lengthier negotiations among teams of five to six examiners trying to reach consensus on your percentage score. This change of allowing scores in the 5 percent band is a good one, because some organizations really were in between, and the policy of rounding up rather than down inflated scores slightly.

One change that I disagree with is the scoring bands have increased in range from 10 percent point bands to 15 percent point bands. There are the same descriptors in a scoring band, so it is less clear now whether an organization should receive a score ranging from a low of say 50 percent to a high of 65 percent, which could be good enough to win the award.

Point Values for Baldrige Items

1.0 LEADERSHIP

1.1 Senior Leadership	70 points
1.2 Governance and Social Responsibility	50 points

2.0 STRATEGIC PLANNING

2.1 Strategy Development	40 points
2.2 Strategy Deployment	45 points

3.0 CUSTOMER AND MARKET FOCUS

3.1 Customer and Market Knowledge	40 points
3.2 Customer Relationships and Satisfaction	45 points

4.0 MEASUREMENT, ANALYSIS, AND KNOWLEDGE MANAGEMENT

4.1 Measurement, Analysis, and Review of Organizational Performance	45 points
4.2 Management of Information, Information Technology, and Knowledge	45 points

5.0 WORKFORCE FOCUS

5.1 Workforce Engagement	35 points
5.2 Workforce Environment	50 points

6.0   PROCESS MANAGEMENT

6.1 Work Systems Design	35 points
6.2 Work Process Management and Improvement	50 points

7.0   RESULTS

7.1 Product and Service Outcomes	100 points
7.2 Customer-Focused Outcomes	70 points
7.3 Financial and Market Outcomes	70 points
7.4 Workforce-Focused Outcomes	70 points
7.5 Process Effectiveness Outcomes	70 points
7.6 Leadership Outcomes	70 points

IMPORTANT AS A SCORING DIMENSION

Along with your processes and results, an important dimension to consider when assigning scores is the relative importance of the approach or result to your overall success. In a university that has been around for 200 years and continues to prosper, a strategic plan is far less important than it might be in a company that needs to re-invent itself or die. When you are looking over the edge of the cliff, a strategic plan becomes very important. Similarly, a company that has 2 percent to 3 percent turnover might not need a sophisticated approach to training and development. Whereas, a company with 40 percent annual employee turnover better have a pretty good system of training new people. The importance of a process, approach, or result will not cause your score to go up or down, but the examiners will be expecting more or less effort if that item is important or unimportant to your success. So, a company that is barely profitable might get a fairly good score for financial results if the strategy is to forgo profits for the first few years while building brand recognition and market share. Alternatively, a company whose success rides on its ability to recruit, hire, and keep the best technical people and scientists would have section 5.1 scrutinized much more than another organization where labor and people are not a big success factor.

SCORING BAND 1

Scores of 0 Percent on Process

It is difficult to get a score of 0 on an item. You basically have to have no answer at all or one that is laughably bad. The 2006 criteria suggest that a score of 0 indicates that your approach is either not there or completely anecdotal. In other words, you tell some stories about how this and that happened, but there really is no consistent approach. An alternative way to get a 0 score is to have a completely ineffective approach that is fully implemented or deployed and has not changed in 20 years. I've seen a few of those.

SCORING GUIDELINES
For Use With Category 7

SCORE	RESULTS
0% or 5%	▪ There are no organizational PERFORMANCE RESULTS and/or poor RESULTS in areas reported. (Le) ▪ TREND data either are not reported or show mainly adverse TRENDS. (T) ▪ Comparative information is not reported. (C) ▪ RESULTS are not reported for any areas of importance to the accomplishment of your organization's MISSION. (I)
10%, 15%, 20%, or 25%	▪ A few organizational PERFORMANCE RESULTS are reported, and early good PERFORMANCE LEVEL Sare evident in a few areas. (Le) ▪ Some TREND data are reported, with some adverse TRENDS evident. (T) ▪ Little or no comparative information is reported. (C) ▪ RESULTS are reported for a few areas of importance to the accomplishment of your organization's MISSION. (I)
30%, 35%, 40%, or 45%	▪ Good organizational PERFORMANCE LEVELS are reported for some areas of importance to the Item requirements. (Le) ▪ Some TREND data are reported, and a majority of the TRENDS presented are beneficial. (T) ▪ Early stages of obtaining comparative information are evident. (C) ▪ RESULTS are reported for many areas of importance to the accomplishment of your organization's MISSION. (I)
50%, 55%, 60%, or 65%	▪ Good organizational PERFORMANCE LEVELS are reported for most areas of importance to the Item requirements. (Le) ▪ Beneficial TRENDS are evident in areas of importance to the accomplishment of your organization's MISSION. (T) ▪ Some current PERFORMANCE LEVEL Shave been evaluated against relevant comparisons and/or BENCHMARKS and show areas of good relative PERFORMANCE. (C) ▪ Organizational PERFORMANCE RESULTS are reported for most KEY CUSTOMER, market, and PROCESS requirements. (I)
70%,7 5%, 80%, or 85%	▪ Good to excellent organizational PERFORMANCELEVELS are reported for most areas of importance to the Item requirements. (Le) ▪ Beneficial TRENDS have been sustained over time in most areas of importance to the accomplishment of your organization's MISSION. (T) ▪ Many to most TRENDS and current PERFORMANCE LEVELS have been evaluated against relevant comparisons and/or BENCHMARKS and show areas of leadership and very good relative PERFORMANCE. (C) ▪ Organizational PERFORMANCE RESULTS are reported for most KEY CUSTOMER, market, PROCESS, and ACTION PLAN requirements, and they include some projections of your future performance. (I)
90%, 95%, or 100%	▪ Excellent organizational PERFORMANCE LEVELS are reported for most areas of importance to the Item requirements. (Le) ▪ Beneficial TRENDS have been sustained over time in all areas of importance to the accomplishment of your organization's MISSION. (T) ▪ Evidence of industry and BENCHMARK leadership is demonstrated in many areas. (C) ▪ Organizational PERFORMANCE RESULTS fully address KEY CUSTOMER, market, PROCESS, and ACTIONPLAN requirements, and they include PROJECTIONS of your future PERFORMANCE. (I)

SCORING GUIDELINES
For Use With Categories 1–6

SCORE	PROCESS
0% or 5%	▪ No SYSTEMATIC APPROACH to Item requirements is evident; information is ANECDOTAL. (A) ▪ Little or no DEPLOYMENT of any SYSTEMATIC APPROACH is evident. (D) ▪ An improvement orientation is not evident; improvement is achieved through reacting to problems. (L) ▪ No organizational ALIGNMENT is evident; individual areas or work units operate independently. (I)
10%, 15%, 20%, or 25%	▪ The beginning of a SYSTEMATIC APPROACH to the BASIC REQUIREMENTS of the Item is evident. (A) ▪ The APPROACH is in the early stages of DEPLOYMENT in most areas or work units, inhibiting progress in achieving the BASIC REQUIREMENTS of the Item. (D) ▪ Early stages of a transition from reacting to problems to a general improvement orientation are evident. (L) ▪ The APPROACH is ALIGNED with other areas or work units largely through joint problem solving. (I)
30%, 35%, 40%, or 45%	▪ An EFFECTIVE, SYSTEMATIC APPROACH, responsive to the BASIC REQUIREMENTS of the Item, is evident. (A) ▪ The APPROACH is DEPLOYED, although some areas or work units are in early stages of DEPLOYMENT. (D) ▪ The beginning of a SYSTEMATIC APPROACH to evaluation and improvement of KEY PROCESSES is evident. (L) ▪ The APPROACH is in the early stages of ALIGNMENT with your basic organizational needs identified in response to the Organizational Profile and other Process Items. (I)
50%, 55%, 60%, or 65%	▪ An EFFECTIVE, SYSTEMATIC APPROACH, responsive to the OVERALL REQUIREMENTS of the Item, is evident. (A) ▪ The APPROACH is well DEPLOYED, although DEPLOYMENT may vary in some areas or work units. (D) ▪ A fact-based, SYSTEMATIC evaluation and improvement PROCESS and some organizational LEARNING, including INNOVATION, are in place for improving the efficiency and EFFECTIVENESS of KEY PROCESSES. (L) ▪ The APPROACH is ALIGNED with your organizational needs identified in response to the Organizational Profile and other Process Items. (I)
70%, 75%, 80%, or 85%	▪ An EFFECTIVE, SYSTEMATIC APPROACH, responsive to the MULTIPLE REQUIREMENTS of the Item, is evident. (A) ▪ The APPROACH is well DEPLOYED, with no significant gaps. (D) ▪ Fact-based, SYSTEMATIC evaluation and improvement and organizational LEARNING, including INNOVATION, are KEY management tools; there is clear evidence of refinement as a result of organizational-level ANALYSIS and sharing. (L) ▪ The APPROACH is INTEGRATED with your organizational needs identified in response to the Organizational Profile and other Process Items. (I)
90%, 95%, or 100%	▪ An EFFECTIVE, SYSTEMATIC APPROACH, fully responsive to the MULTIPLE REQUIREMENTS of the Item, is evident. (A) ▪ The APPROACH is fully DEPLOYED without significant weaknesses or gaps in any areas or work units. (D) ▪ Fact-based, SYSTEMATIC evaluation and improvement and organizational LEARNING through INNOVATION are KEY organization-wide tools; refinement and INNOVATION, backed by ANALYSIS and sharing,are evident throughout the organization. (L) ▪ The APPROACH is well INTEGRATED with your organizational needs identified in response to the Organizational Profile and other Process Items. (I)

2008 Criteria for Performance Excellence

Full deployment of stupidity is still a 0 score. There is obviously no improvement or integration if you have no approach at all, or one that is bad and has not been improved or changed in many years.

Scores of 5 Percent on Process

This score of 5 percent is reserved for those applicants that put out some effort but truly missed the boat. They showed up to the game in uniform, but sat on the bench. They wrote down an answer to the criteria, but the answer had nothing to do with the questions. In other words, a 5 percent is a guilt score. We feel bad giving you a 0, but you are darn close. I teach people that if you can find at least one factor that is even slightly positive you have to the give the applicant a 5 percent score. The difference between 0 percent and 5 percent is that there might be a few components of an approach in place in a couple of small pockets of the organization, but mostly nothing is happening. You really have to hunt to write any positive comments for an applicant that receives a score of 5 percent. Examiners might also give a score of 5 percent if you admit you don't have a process or approach and indicate that you will be working on one next year. At 0 percent, you are probably unconsciously incompetent, or in other words, don't realize the enormity of the problem. A score of 5 percent might indicate that you are consciously incompetent. That is, you realize the need for a process or approach, but have yet to develop one.

Most of the criteria in Categories 1 through 6 ask for evidence of a system. A score of 5 percent probably indicates that you have no real system, but a few piece or parts that could someday develop into a system. A score of 5 percent might be given if a few individual managers and supervisors have started performing some improvements in their departments that are relevant to the criteria. The efforts are driven by individual versus the organization, and if the individual were to leave, the efforts would probably fall apart.

Scores of 0 Percent on Results

A score of 0 percent on one of the six items in Category 7 indicates that one or more of the following conditions are present:

- *There are no results other than anecdotes—no graphs or data.*
- *Data presented are irrelevant to the criteria/requirements of the item.*
- *Data are presented, but they show that performance has gotten worse over time or remains flat at a very low level.*
- *Performance levels are consistently below those of industry averages, competitors, and other comparative data.*
- *No comparative data is reported.*

A score of 0 percent on any of the Results Items indicates that you have consistently terrible performance. I guess you should get some credit for being honest enough to present data like this, but this section is about good performance, and the honesty will not be enough to get you out of the 0 percent score.

Scores of 5 Percent on Results

Like the score of 5 percent for Process, a 5 percent rating for your Results indicates that the examiners found at least one chart that shows one data point that shows some improvement. Examiners are taught to give a score of 5 percent if there is anything encouraging that can be said about any of the charts and graphs presented. For example, if you present 12 charts, and all of them show negative levels and trends, but two charts show a current data point that is an improvement during the past five years, that might be enough to earn a 5 percent score. Your results are clearly terrible, but you have shown a slight improvement on a couple of measures for perhaps a single year. As with the process scoring scale, scores of 5 percent are guilt scores because examiners found at least a couple of factors on which to comment positively.

SCORING BAND 2

Scores of 10 Percent on Process

This second scoring band of 10 percent to 25 percent is fairly wide and is generally considered the "off to a good start" scoring range. A score of 10 percent probably indicates that you have some parts of a system in place, but the approach is not functional yet, and could not be described as a system. If you receive a score of 10 percent, it still means that examiners had to really hunt to find anything about your approach that deserved a positive comment. A 10 percent score probably means that you have only a few components of what would be considered an effective process, little or no deployment, no evidence of learning or improvement in your process, and the approach is completely disconnected to other organizational processes. A score of 10 percent might also mean that you have an approach or process and it contains so many structural flaws that you have to go back and start over, saving the few things that might be salvageable. A score of 10 percent might also mean that a fairly good process has been designed, or is in the blueprint stage, but no real construction has begun yet, and it might be several years before it is deployed to even a portion of the organization.

Scores of 15 Percent on Process

A score of 15 percent still means that your process or approach is quite incomplete, but has a few more components to it than a process with a 10 percent score. In other words, the full skeleton or frame of the house is not built yet, but a number of major sections have been erected and they match the blueprints. A score of 15 percent might mean that you are a good way into designing and constructing a process, with a plan to pilot test it in one part of the organization. A score of 15 percent probably also means that there is some re-work needed to your process or approach before going any further, but that the whole thing is not flawed. It could mean that major components are either missing, or designed poorly, however, so a 15 percent score does not mean keep going full speed ahead. What it more likely means is that you need to take a few steps back and do some revision to your structure before you go much further. With 15 percent scores, there is probably little or no deployment, and certainly no evaluation and improvement. There are still many disconnects with other organizational processes, although a few linkages may have occurred due to luck rather than to good planning.

Scores of 20 Percent on Process

Now we are starting to see some evidence that a structure or design of the approach has most of the major components needed. There are still some big holes in the approach that will eventually need to be filled, but the approach needs less re-work before going further ahead. A score at the 20 percent level indicates that your approach is probably still more reactive, versus preventive, and there is still a great deal of "fire fighting" going on to deal with problems that arise. There is probably some deployment that has occurred in a small pocket of the organization, but it is not what one would call a full-scale pilot. The parts of the organization that have pioneered the approach, or implemented it, may have found some areas that did not work but have not yet figured out how to re-design the approach to make it better. Alignment with other organizational systems is again there by chance or luck, not by forethought. There may be parts of the criteria that have not been addressed at all with a score of 20 percent as well, but you will find that the majority of the questions asked do have an answer.

Scores of 25 Percent on Process

This is the top end score of the second band. It means that you have probably made some substantial progress during the past year or two in coming up with a systematic approach that makes sense for your organization. A score at this level would indicate that you have addressed most or all of the major questions in the criteria, but that your approach or processes would still be classified as beginning level. A score of 25 percent means that amount of re-work needed to the design of your approach is more minor than major. It could be that some parts of the approach are further along than others, and that most parts of the organization are not yet implementing the process or approach. There may be some evidence of lessons learned from the groups or units that have implemented the approach, and that they have made some minor changes to the approach in their departments based on findings or results. The approach to evaluation and improvement is still completely reactive. In other words, if something breaks or does not work, you fix it.

Integration of the process or approach with other major systems in the organization may have partially occurred due to joint planning and review, but is still there mostly due to chance. There would still be a number of disconnects between related organizational systems and processes with a score of 25 percent, but a few things are fairly consistent. A score of 25 percent should be considered an encouraging score to an applicant. What it means is that you have made some good progress in beginning to design and implement a more systematic approach to running your operation. A score in the 10 percent to 20 percent range means that you have more re-work to do to your process or approach before you go further. A score of 25 percent indicates a good start and effective plan, but you have a lot of work to do and are probably four to five years away from ever winning a Baldrige Award.

Scores of 10 Percent on Results

A score of 10 percent on Results should be considered pretty sad. How it differs from a 5 percent is that a 5 percent score means that almost all graphs or charts show incredibly bad performance, and maybe one or two show a single data point that indicates that you are better than last year, but clearly still bad. A 10 percent score still means that your performance levels are mostly bad, and there is little or no comparative data. What comparative data there is shows that you are inferior to industry averages or competitors. There either are no trends, or if there are, they are over a short period of time (e.g., two to three years), and many of them are negative or declining. A 10 percent means that you have gotten a little better on a couple of measures, or perhaps gone from terrible to just bad, or maintained mediocre performance. A 10 percent score might also indicate that there is no data on many of the important measures identified in other parts of the application. A score of 10 percent on results essentially means that most measures of performance show poor performance, many graphs are missing, and that there either are no trends, or that they are poor. On the positive side, it means that you have a couple of measures that show a data point or two of improvement.

Scores of 15 Percent on Results

Again, we see mostly negative levels of performance, little comparative data, few or no trends, and generally poor performance. The difference between a 10 and 15 percent score is in how many of the graphs are not purely negative or missing entirely. With a score of 10 percent, you might find that close to 90 percent of the data presented shows poor performance, and/or that more than half of the expected data is missing. A score of 15 percent might indicate that there is data presented in more measures that would be expected in the section, and more than one or two graphs show at least an average level of performance or one data point indicating performance is better than last year. Inconsistency characterizes the results of an organization that scores in the 10 percent to 25 percent band of the scoring scale.

Scores of 20 Percent on Results

Performance is improving due to actions and strategies implemented in the organization. Any improvements seen at the 5 percent to 15 percent level are probably due to luck or some external factor rather than due to actions your organization initiated. At the 20 percent scoring level, we might see a data point or two on three or four graphs that indicates that something you changed or did caused the needle to move on the gauge in a positive direction. Then again, it still could be luck. A score at this level probably indicates that you still have little or no comparative data, and that trends, where shown, are over a brief period of time. Organizations that receive scores of 20 percent on their results might also fail to report on many important measures. There are also at least half or more of the graphs/charts that show bad or mediocre performance. None of the charts show what would be considered good performance; it is just that not all of the measures show bad results.

Scores of 25 Percent on Results

This is the scoring band where the "beginnings of effective results" commences, and chances are that any improvements shown in performance are due to something your organization did differently, or better, rather than being due to luck. At least four to five of the graphs in the section show a data point or two that indicates improvement over baseline. You might have comparative data on one or two graphs in the section that show that you are no longer in the bottom 25 percent of the industry. Many graphs are still missing or show quite poor performance or no improvement. A score in this level might also indicate that due to a change in metrics, you only have one data point or one year's worth of data to present on a number of charts. An outsider looking at the results of a company at this level would feel that there is some evidence that the approaches described in Categories 1 through 6 are starting to drive some improvements in results, but that the results are spotty. In other words, if there are 12 graphs in this section, you might find that five still show poor performance, three show average or below performance, two show some slight improvement and average levels of performance, and two show improving trends over a year or two, and better than average performance. There is no real formula for doing the results scoring, but a score of 25 percent shows a mixed bag of performance results. An Australian client describes this as "patchy."

SCORING BAND 3

Scores of 30 Percent on Process

Now we are moving into the scoring band where many Baldrige applicants fall, their first or second year, into the application/feedback process. You now have an answer to all questions asked in the criteria, and have more than just the parts of a system, you actually have a systematic approach or process that addresses the major purposes of the criteria and fits your organization and situation. You do not have to go back to the drawing board and do any re-work to your approach or design at this point. There is still much work to do to implement your process or approach, and it is fairly basic, but it has all the major components needed, and you are clearly on the Baldrige road. Sadly, many organizations that get a score of 30 percent expect that they should be closer to 50 percent, because it often takes quite a bit of work and several years to achieve a score in the 30 percent range.

Implementation of your approach or system at the 30 percent level is probably more like a pilot, and the approach has yet to be implemented in 75 percent or more of the organization. California State University began implementing a balanced scorecard approach to performance measurement in three of its 23 campuses, which would be enough to get them to a 30 percent score, but they still have 20 of 23 campuses that do not have effective scorecards yet, so deployment is still limited. At 30 percent, there may have been some improvements to the approach based on results of a pilot test, but the approach is still mostly reactive, and the improvements are minor in nature. Some thought has been given to linkages with other organizational systems, but there are still a number of disconnects.

Scores of 35 Percent on Process

As you move from 30 percent up this band you find that the approach gets slightly more sophisticated and detailed, deployment reaches a larger percentage of the organization, or additional pilots have been done, and there is some planned evaluation and improvement, rather than waiting for something to break or not work right. An organization could easily go up a full 10 percent on process scores if it is in this third band. Improvement gets more difficult in the next scoring band, and a 5 percent improvement per year is more typical. At 35 percent, the approach is basically solid, and any comments on weaknesses are related to minor issues rather than major holes. There still will be a number of "areas for improvement" comments as examiners call them; they just won't be directed toward the larger issues as with lower scores. Perhaps there is a planned evaluation that has occurred once with a score of 35 percent, and you have made some improvements based on the evaluation of your approach. Some linkages have been established between the approach being examined, and other related systems and processes, but the approach is far from being completely integrated.

Scores of 40 Percent on Process

Now we are moving beyond the beginnings of a promising start on your journey to excellence. At 40 percent, you have come a long way since you began and show an approach that is probably version 2.0. In other words, you may have been through one major planned evaluation and improvement cycle, and done some fairly major changes to your approach in the second round. You have probably done a second round of pilot tests, or deployed the approach to a larger portion of the organization. The majority of the organization has still not yet implemented the approach with a score of 40 percent though. There may also still be several different approaches being used, where a single unified process would be better. All parts of the organizations may have at least the beginnings of a planned approach, but they have not yet settled on the best approach. More consistency is found between the process/approach being examined and others, but inconsistencies still exist. Some states such as California give out silver trophies to organizations that receive 400 points or get scores in the 40 percent range. It is still a long way from silver to gold, but 40 percent scores should be considered ones that could not be achieved by many organizations.

Scores of 45 Percent on Process

A score of 45 percent indicates that all of the requirements listed in this scoring band have been met. What this means is that you have a logical and systematic approach that fits your organization. It also means that the approach or process is in the early stages of implementation in most or at least 50 percent of the organization. The start of a planned approach to evaluating the effectiveness of the process or approach exists, and there have been some improvements made to the approach based on evaluation data. Finally, there is evidence of a plan and some progress made in linking the approach with other organizational systems. That is, the process does not stand on its own, but works in concert with other related systems and processes.

The improvement comments an applicant receives with a score of 45 percent often relate to the need for further deployment, more evaluation and improvement or process maturity, and better linkages to other systems and approaches in the organization. The basic approach is quite solid and includes all the necessary components for your type and size of enterprise.

Scores of 30 Percent on Results

The previous band of scores is reserved for spotty and mostly poor results with a few bright spots. A score of 30 percent or above on results shows that something is starting to happen in your organization. That is, improvements made to processes and approaches are starting to result in improvements in performance. One major difference between this band and the previous scoring band is that you are now expected to present data on many of the appropriate measures in the section. No more anecdotal data are presented—charts, graphs, and statistics tell the story. It is clear with a score of 30 percent that the organization has made specific effort to improve performance, rather than solely relying on luck. Levels of performance may still be quite average, but at least they can be compared to comparative data such as industry averages in some cases.

Trends are still lacking history, and may represent only a few years of data, but the improvements are fairly consistent. What trends do exist are mostly unimpressive, however. Slow steady improvement over a year or two is what we see in this scoring band. There will be some comparative data, but many graphs will lack these comparisons, making it hard to evaluate levels of performance. Performance can, at least, be measured against targets or goals on most graphs, however. There still may be a number of graphs that show declining or poor performance, but the good ones outweigh the bad ones now.

Scores of 35 Percent on Results

There are a few less graphs that show negative trends or levels of performance than at 30 percent. A score of 35 percent might be appropriate if a couple of the graphs actually show fairly good performance or an impressive improvement trend. Many charts will still show average, or slightly better, levels of performance and slow, steady improvement trends. A few more of the charts will have comparative data on them than at 30 percent, and performance against those comparisons will be fairly good.

Scores of 40 Percent on Results

At this scoring band, we are now quite certain that the organization has turned the corner and is on its way to showing impressive results. Perhaps 30-40 percent of the charts show better than average levels of performance. A few charts show trends of fairly steady improvement over 3 or more years; whereas others might show only a couple of years. There are a few more graphs showing good levels of performance compared to competitors or industry averages. Any data that is missing would be considered minor—results are presented for most major metrics. The charts showing poor performance are clearly in the minority at this scoring level. However, none of the charts indicate that the organization is close to being in the top 25 percent of its industry. A score of 40 percent is not good enough to win a Baldrige Award, but there have clearly been some improvement trends shown, and the results are stable enough to indicate that the changes in strategy or approach helped cause the improvements seen.

Scores of 45 Percent on Results

We are getting very close to 50 percent now, which is a difficult score to earn on results. A 45 percent score might require another year or two of improvement trends, a few more graphs with comparative data to which you compare favorably. At 45 percent you would not expect to see more than a couple of graphs showing declining performance, and they might only show one or two data points of poor performance. Results are not entirely positive, but mostly. At least half of the graphs should have comparative data that are considered objective, reliable, and relevant. There should probably be targets or goals on all graphs, and enough different measures of performance presented to do a fair assessment of overall organizational performance. Scores in the lower ranges often indicate that many of the graphs presented show only one unit, location, or department of the organization, and the examiners know that these specific charts were selected because they look good. The charts in an application that scores 45 percent on results should mostly represent all or most of the organization, rather than select departments or units.

SCORING BAND 4

Scores of 50 Percent on Process

A score of 50 percent is anything but average. Most organizations that are generally thought to be well run would not achieve a score of 50 percent on the Baldrige scale. We now see in the scoring scale that your process or approach must meet all of the requirements of the criteria, rather than just the basic requirements needed for scoring band 3. The approach or process will be logical, tailored to your organization rather than generic, and include all the necessary components of an effective system. Earning a score of 50 percent requires deployment to about half of the organization, which is a major challenge to most large outfits. This does not mean every group, level, and location must have the same approach. Rather, at least half of the organization needs to have implemented an approach that makes sense for them and is consistent with other parts of the organization where it makes sense. The criteria booklet suggests that while examiners expect to see widespread deployment (e.g., 50 percent or more), different parts of the organization are likely to be at different stages of implementation.

There will be a structured and planned approach for evaluating the effectiveness of the processes in place, with specific measures and standards identified. There will also be some evidence of refinement or improvement of the process or approach over the last few years. The processes would be far from being fully mature, but beyond the early stages of sophistication as well. Finally, one would expect to see no major disconnects between the process being evaluated and other related systems and processes in the organization. The overall feeling an examiner would get from reading an application that scores in the 50 percent range is that they really have their act together, and that the examiner will have to think a little bit and dig into the application to find comments on areas for improvement. All the basic things are there at 50 percent.

Scores of 55 Percent on Process

To move from 50 percent up to a score of 55 percent, you might show slightly more deployment of your processes in the organization, another cycle of improvement, with some minor changes or perhaps linkage to another organizational system. As I mentioned earlier, when you get to the 50 percent level, improvement often comes in 5 percent increments per year, rather than the 10 percent increments at lower scoring levels.

Scores of 60 Percent on Process

We are now seeing approaches good enough to be considered a Baldrige finalist in most instances. The processes you employ make perfect sense for your type of organization; they have been implemented in perhaps 60-70 percent of the organization. There have been several major improvements where you might have done a fairly extensive overhaul to the system, based on evaluation data. There will be good linkages to several major organizational systems and processes. Examiners often feel quite stumped when they read a 60 percent application and have to come up with improvement comments. Many times, the comments relate to further deployment, continued evaluation and improvement, communication of lessons learned to other parts of the organization, and so forth. There are often no improvement comments about your approach at a 60 percent score. When giving a score of 60 percent, examiners think that this organization is definitely performing well enough to receive a site visit or second look and is a possible winner either this year or next. A big corporation I worked with received scores of around 60 percent on their written application and went on to win Baldrige a few years ago, based on all the additional strengths examiners saw during the site visit.

Something else you typically see with processes that score 60 percent is a lack of originality or innovation. The approach is excellent, logical, and fits the organization, but it is also an approach you might find in many similar organizations, and nothing on which to write a newspaper story. Effective, solid approaches that have been well deployed and refined over time will get you into scoring band 4, but not 5 where most winners are.

Scores of 65 Percent on Process

This top end score in band 4 indicates that you are a hair away from winning a Baldrige Award, and may win, if you receive some 70 percent and 80 percent scores on other items. A more impressive system or approach, another cycle of improvement, more consistency across the organization, or similar characteristics of your process might be enough to boost you up to this scoring level.

Scores of 50 Percent on Results

Improving trends and average or better levels of performance on many charts and graphs characterize the previous scoring band. At 50 percent and above, you are not the leader in your industry, but demonstrate above average performance on many measures. An additional factor that differentiates band 3 from 4 is that in band 4 you don't see any negative trends or poor levels of performance on graphs of important performance measures for the organization's success. One bad data point does not make a trend— particularly if you know what caused it and have corrected performance. If you find any negative trends or poor levels of performance on important measures, this alone would be enough to knock you back to a lower scoring band.

Another factor that you see at the 50 percent and above scoring band is more data over a longer period of time. Typically, applicants who receive scores of 50 percent to 65 percent present graphs showing 4 to 6 years worth of data, and even more on some charts. Another factor that differentiates results at this scoring level is that many of the graphs include several types of comparative data and some data on competitors. An organization that receives a results score of 50 percent should have some hard evidence that it is as good as, or better than, some of its bigger competitors. It is still acceptable to have some charts showing flat trends or a lack of improvement, but no negative trends.

Scores of 55 Percent on Results

To move up 5 percent on the scoring scale you might have a few graphs that show an even more impressive level of performance than comparisons. There might also be one more data point covering another year on some of the graphs. More graphs will have comparative data that is relevant, and to which you compare favorably. Improvement trends might be slightly more dramatic in some cases, and the number of graphs showing no improvement will be fewer. Your data also are more comprehensive as you move up the scoring scale. In other words, there are more charts, covering more important performance measures, and probably no missing data.

Scores of 60 Percent on Results

An increase of 5 percent on a Result Item can have a fairly significant impact on your overall score, because each of the six Result Items is worth 75 points. A score of 60 percent indicates that your performance is effective enough for a site visit, and that you might be a Baldrige winner. Winners generally get 70 percent or better, but scores for results can increase during a site visit when you have a chance to show charts that had to be cut out of the application because of space constraints. A 60 percent score on Results would be characterized by excellent trends over 4 to 6 years, levels of performance that show that you are among one of the better organizations in your field, and even some data that compare favorably to benchmarks that might be outside of your industry. In other words, your performance has to be exceptionally impressive to get this high of a score. What it also means is that there is still some inconsistency in your data. There will be some charts that show less dramatic improvement than others. A few may still show performance that has flattened out or shows a good or slightly better than average level. An organization that achieves scores of 60 percent on their results is clearly one of the leaders, and probably in the top 25 percent of its peer group. There might be a missing chart here and there, but at 60 percent, the missing data will not be tier one or tier two performance measures. In other words, all the important results are represented with good performance data.

Scores of 65 Percent on Results

We are now on the edge of that elusive band 5 where the winners reside. Many of your graphs will show how your performance compares to many other measurements, such as industry average, competitor A, competitor B, and perhaps a benchmark. On a number of graphs, you show that you are superior to all of these comparisons. What you also might see at 65 percent is some fairly dramatic improvement trends with a steep slope, rather than slow steady improvement. Further, you will see evidence that the organization understands exactly how improvements were achieved, so they can replicate this performance in other parts of the organization. There should be few or no graphs that depict average performance, or flat trends, unless performance is already at a very high level.

Once you become outstanding, there is little room for improvement. The examiners don't expect to see improvement trends where improvement does not make sense. "Good enough" is sometimes good enough, and it is not worth the resources needed to move performance from 99.5 to 99.7 percent, or even from 80 percent to 85 percent. Levels of performance are probably more important in this scoring band, since you must do more than demonstrate that your results have improved. At this scoring level, you must demonstrate that your results make you one of the leading organizations in the USA.

SCORING BAND 5

Scores of 70 Percent on Process

We are now in the band where winners score. If you look at the differences in this scoring band from the previous one, you will see that you must respond to all of the requirements of the specific Baldrige item, versus the "overall requirements" in band 4. What this means is that each Baldrige item contains multiple questions that must be answered. You could receive a score of 50 percent to 65 percent and still not have much of a response to a couple of the more minor questions in the criteria, as long as your answer covers the overall requirements or major factors being asked about. Another difference between this band and the previous one is that the system of approach being asked about has been implemented in all major units or functions in the organizations. Deployment is a little spottier in the previous scoring band. Evaluation and improvement cycles are expected to be demonstrated in both bands 4 and 5, but a score of 70 percent should be reserved for a process that is more mature and has been improved more times over the years. Finally, there would be a greater degree of linkage between organizational systems with a score in band 5 than in band 4. Band 4 uses the word "alignment," whereas the term "integration" is used in band 5. The difference is that systems can be fairly well aligned, so that there are no inconsistencies or disconnects. An integrated system is one in which the various piece parts have all been designed with a desire to create a well functioning performance system in which each subsystem plays its own part.

Organizations that score in band 4 tend to have a bunch of individually designed processes and systems that were created by various groups and individuals who just looked at their little subsystem. Attempts are often made after these subsystems are implemented to link them together and iron out any disconnects.

An organization that scores in the 70 percent to 85 percent range is one in which an individual or group has first designed an overall strategy or system and then designed each subsystem, as opposed to trying to knit them together after the fact. A score of 70 percent on process still means that examiners might find a number of areas for improvement or weaknesses in your approach or process, but the areas for improvement are quite minor, and not all the examiners may agree that they are weaknesses. Scoring in this range implies that the process is exceptional and a benchmark for other organizations.

Scores of 75 Percent on Process

A score of 75 percent or 750 points has historically been where most Baldrige winners fall. If you were a little hesitant about giving an organization the trophy this year, but think it should work on approaches for another year, you might give a 70 percent. A score of 75 percent could mean, "Get ready to meet the President!" A characteristic of scoring band 5 that differentiates it from the previous one is that your approach should show some degree of creativity or innovation. In other words, organizations that score in this level often have approaches that are worthy of a newspaper story. Good solid approaches with no innovation get you into band 4, but not 5. This is not to say that everything you do must be unique and creative. However, there is usually something unique or different about the processes that receive scores at this level. It might be that your approach is fairly common in another industry, but has never been applied to your type of organization. It might also be that your organization created an entirely new approach.

Implementation or deployment tends to be very solid at 75 percent scores, with only very minor gaps in implementation. There should be a few less improvement comments about the approach, and they should be getting more and more nit-picky.

Scores of 80 Percent on Process

In my Baldrige training workshops, I use a case study that scores 80 percent to show people what one would look like. The case study depicts an organization that has an approach that has many (six to eight) creative aspects or features of its approach. The organization has been benchmarked by a number of others for the past few yeas. The approach has been through three major overhauls and four minor tune-ups over the past 8 years, and it is very mature. There is a structured evaluation and improvement cycle in place and it occurs on a regular basis. The approach has been deployed to more than 80 percent of the organization with only a few minor gaps. There is excellent integration of the process or system being studied and other relevant organizational systems.

The teams that grade this case study will have a long list of very strong positive comments about the approach and its implementation. They will also have two to four improvement comments relating to either the approach or the lack of deployment to all parts and levels of the organization. As with a score of 75 percent, the improvement comments will be on very minor issues, and examiners really have to hunt to find anything that might need improving.

Scores of 85 Percent on Process

We are now at a scoring level that even exceeds many Baldrige winners. An 85 percent score means that examiners find maybe one or two area for improvement comments on some very minor aspects of your approach, or find a small department or unit in the organization that is not as far along in implementing the approach than some of the rest of the organization. There will be many newspaper stories that could be written about the organization's process at this scoring level. In other words, there will be a lot of innovations or creative features of its approach. The organization is not perfect, but it is getting close. There will be excellent integration of systems, many cycles of improvements, and only the most minor comments relating to improvements that might be needed.

An organization with a score of 85 percent is like a finely tuned machine. All of the systems and subsystems work in harmony to produce balanced results for various stakeholders. An organization at this level has internalized the Baldrige criteria to such an extent that it is second nature to them. There is no need for teams or committees to work on Baldrige-related efforts. These are the types of things you find in an organization at a much lower scoring level.

Scores of 70 Percent on Results

Results that receive a score of 70 percent are very impressive and hard to attain. The scoring scale suggests that results at this level are either good or excellent on most graphs presented in the section. Trends at this scoring level will tend to show less dramatic improvement but will show sustained high levels and typically start to level off. Most graphs will show multiple points of comparisons, such as several competitors, industry averages, and benchmarks. The organization will not necessarily be the benchmark, or even the best in the industry, on some measures, but it will be on others. What will be clear is that the results put the organization at least in the top 20 percent to 25 percent of its industry. There may be some graphs that show some 1 or 2 year declines in performance, but those declines can be explained and are typically not due to anything the organization did wrong. If performance did decline because of a bad move on the organization's part, they should at least show that they are recovering and performance is starting to improve again.

A score of 70 percent on results would indicate an organization that might be good enough to win a Baldrige Award this year, or one that might be a year away.

Another differentiating factor for results that score in the fifth band is that projections are included for key results for the next few years. The credibility of these projections will be assessed by looking at actual history as well as approaches for achieving the forecasted results.

Scores of 75 Percent on Results

A score of 75 percent on results is good enough to win a Baldrige Award. Graphs might show one year of good performance more than at 70 percent. Examiners might also see fewer graphs where even slight declines in performance have occurred. Your performance should indicate that you are the best in the industry on a number of measures, and clearly ahead of your competition on most measures. It will be clear from looking at your performance that you lead the industry and beat your biggest competitors on most key measures of performance. There may be some graphs that show performance trends getting flat, and levels that are still good, but not the best. There may also be a little too much variability on a few graphs.

Achieving this level of score on your results should be considered a major accomplishment. Examiners might find a few less important measures of performance that do not show outstanding levels and trends. There might also be a few graphs or measures of importance for which data are not presented. If you read the last line of the criteria for this scoring band, it says: "RESULTS address most KEY CUSTOMER, market, PROCESS, and ACTION PLAN requirements." The key word there is "most" as opposed to all. What this means is that there may have been something you mentioned in another section of the application as important to your success, for which no data are presented. However, as I mentioned, this omissions will have to be quite minor to still get a score of 75 percent, and these omissions are often remedied during a site visit, where the applicant is allowed to show all the data that did not fit in the application.

Scores of 80 Percent on Results

If 75 percent is good enough to win a Baldrige Award, 80 percent should guarantee the prize. An 80 percent score indicates that your results are consistently positive compared to many other relevant organizations. You are probably number one or two on just about everything that is measured. Trends are presented over 7 to 10 years on many measures, and no trends show less than 5 years worth of good to excellent performance. There may be a graph or two missing, but all the important metrics are represented with performance data. There may also be clear cause-and-effect relationships shown between the actions of the organization and improvements in performance. In other words, it will be clear exactly what the organization did to achieve its current success, rather than relying on good luck or chance. There will be enough evidence to suggest that the organization is clearly the best in its industry at many things.

Scores of 85 Percent on Results

To move up from 80 percent to 85 percent, the organization must show it is in the number one position in its industry on most measures. Improvements will show the gap between your organization and competitors to be getting wider, with you gaining a bigger lead each year. Comparative data will show bigger discrepancies between your levels of performance. Your performance will indicate that you are not only the best in your field on many measures, but that you are a benchmark even outside of your industry. With a score of 85 percent there can be no doubt that you are a Baldrige winner. Examiners may find a few very minor things to write improvement comments on, but they will be very minor issues and often pertain to one or two graphs that show good, but not outstanding, performance.

SCORING BAND 6

Scores of 90 Percent on Process

When I teach workshops on the Baldrige criteria, I tell the students that a score of 90 percent or above indicates that you can't find even the slightest flaw in the approach or its implementation. Improvement comments at this scoring level are often limited to lack of maturity in the process or system, and a few very minor instances showing a lack of integration of the approach to other organizational systems. The feedback you should get with a score of 90 percent is that your approach is innovative, mature, perfect for your organization, and close to 100 percent deployed. If the examiners can point out a few minor suggestions on how your approach could be even better, you might receive a score of 90 percent. In my years of examining applications, I have never given out a score of 90 percent on anything, and I have never heard of another examiner doing so. It is very unlikely that a team of six highly trained examiners won't be able to find some flaw in your approaches or their implementation, but it is certainly possible. It might be possible that an individual examiner gives you a score of 90 percent, but getting the team of examiners to agree on a score this high would be truly remarkable.

I tried to write a 90 percent to 100 percent case study so people could see what one looked like, but every time I tried, the people who graded the case managed to find some flaws that I had not noticed. If you can't even write a fictional case to be this good, imagine how hard it would be to achieve this score in a real organization.

Scores of 95 Percent on Process

A score of 95 percent means that examiners can't find anything to comment on relating to your approach, its deployment, the amount of improvement or refinement you have done over time, the integration of your approach with other systems in the organization, or anything else. In other words, you have stumped six talented experienced examiners, but they might be intimidated to give out a score of 100 percent. Even 95 percent is a nearly impossible score to receive, and it might say that the examiners really think you are operating at 100 percent, but they give you 95 percent in case there is something that they failed to notice, or because they think that no organization is perfect. If you get a score of 95 percent, you should feel like you earned 100 percent. Keep in mind that Baldrige winners score a full 20 percent below 95 percent, so this is a miraculous score.

Scores of 100 Percent on Process

Here is what a score of 100 percent on a Process Item might look like. Your approach is flawless, and has been evaluated and improved eight or more times over the past 15 years. It has so many innovations that it has become the standard by which hundreds of other organizations judge their approach. It has been benchmarked by countless organizations over the years, and the approach has been adopted by many. There have been books and articles written in many languages about your approach. It has been fully implemented in every part of your organization and at all levels for more than five years. There is little in the way of improvement that could be done, but you continue to evaluate and fine-tune the approach each year anyway. There is 100 percent integration of the approach with all other relevant systems in the organization, and absolutely nothing that could be done to improve a perfect system.

Scores of 90 Percent on Results

You might see a score of 90 percent on Results in an organization that is so clearly ahead of its competitors that none of them are likely to overtake them in the next 20 years. Results at this level indicate that your organization is not only the performance leader, but you are significantly better than any of your competitors, and have been for many years. Trends will be presented for 10 or more years on most charts and graphs. There will be no missing data. Any variability in performance can be completely explained. Results will indicate benchmark level performance on many of the graphs. About the only thing that will knock you back from getting a score of 95 percent or 100 percent is one or two graphs show less than stellar performance. In other words, perhaps you are not number one by a huge margin on a couple of your graphs, or one or two show a slight decline in performance, even though the level remains very high.

Scores of 95 Percent on Results

Like a score of 95 percent on an item in Categories 1 to 6, a 95 percent score on Results indicates that your performance is flawless, but examiners could not agree to give you 100 percent. To move from 90 percent up to 95 percent you might show fewer graphs showing less than perfect performance; more graphs that show you lead the industry by a wide margin; more results that exceed benchmarks; broader comparative data from more reliable sources; and performance displayed over a longer period of time. A company like Microsoft, Bose, or others that are clearly the leader and pioneers in their respective fields might achieve scores of 95 percent on one or more of their results sections. What will be clear with results at this level is that the success of the organization has shown a long history of outstanding performance, with no indication that results will be any less impressive in the coming years.

Scores of 100 Percent on Results

Here is what your performance would look like if you achieved a score of 100 percent on a Results Item: Every important measures of performance are represented with data in the application. Every graph or chart includes 7 to 10 years worth of data. Trends show dramatic improvements during the first 3 to 5 years, indicating that you are gaining on major competitors and leaving them in the dust. Levels of performance during the last 4 or 5 years indicate that your organization is the number one performing company, and that you beat all of your competitors by a huge margin. Your performance is better than benchmark organizations outside of your industry, and the results are consistent across all relevant measures of performance. There is a clear link between changes in strategy or action plans and the results you have achieved. In short, examiners will be wishing they had bought stock in your company years ago, because they would probably be rich by now! With a score of 100 percent, there will be no graph or measure of performance that shows less than number one performance in the industry for a number of years.

This sort of performance may not be possible to achieve. Even great organizations are not the best at everything. It is possible that an organization might receive a 100 percent score on a single Result Item such as Financial and Market Results (7.2) but then get a score of 50 percent or less on another item, such as Human Resource Results (7.4). For an organization to receive 100 percent of the points for all six Baldrige Result Items, it would have to be truly remarkable and probably not even possible.

ADDITIONAL SCORING GUIDANCE

Reading a book cannot take the place of practice and feedback in learning the Baldrige scoring scale. If you want to really learn to understand the scoring scale, attend a training workshop on the criteria where you will practice using the scoring scale in a series of case studies. I teach public sessions of such a workshop in the State of California (calexcellence.org) and private sessions for clients all over the world. Others teach similar workshops in your own state that you can probably find out about by contacting the Baldrige website (www.baldrige.nist.gov). If you cannot attend such a workshop or volunteer to be an examiner in your own state, you can obtain a copy of the case study used to train Baldrige examiners and practice scoring it on your own.

By comparing your comments and scores to the "textbook answer" you will be able to calibrate your own scoring so that it mirrors that of experienced examiners. By performing this exercise, you will see what a score looks like at the varying percentage levels. Copies of the current and past case studies and accompanying answer keys can be purchased from the American Society for Quality (ASQ). You can contact the society at (800) 248-1946 or www.asq.org.

Chapter

5

INTERPRETING THE CRITERIA FOR THE ORGANIZATIONAL PROFILE

OVERVIEW OF THE ORGANIZATIONAL PROFILE SECTION

In the 2008 version of the criteria, specific questions are provided to give structure and consistency to the important first section of the application. According to the 2007 booklet:

The Organizational Profile is a snapshot of your organization, the key influences on how you operate, and the key challenges you face. (p. 12)

This section of your application sets the stage for evaluating how relevant certain factors are to your situation and organization and can make a huge difference in how the examiners judge your application. In previous versions of the criteria, the content of this section was, more or less, left up to the applicant. Certain facts were asked for such as the type of organization, its customers, products/services, etc. However, many applicants failed to identify the significant factors in the business environment that might impact their future success, as well as other important information, such as threats from competitors. The 2007 version of the criteria leave little to chance by providing applicants with specific questions that must be answered in this initial section. This ought to provide for more consistency in the applications and ensure that you don't lose any points by forgetting to mention some important information that could have a huge bearing on how the application is judged.

The Preface or Organizational Profile section of the criteria is divided into two Examination items:

    P.1 Organizational Description
    P.2 Organizational Challenges

This section is not given any points or scored as the seven major sections of the criteria. However, it probably has more impact on your score than any of the others because it puts both your approaches and your results into the proper context for your business situation. I recommend focusing on polishing this section and making sure it is clear to someone from outside of your own company and industry. This section is crucial because it tells examiners what to look for in the 50 pages that follow. The Baldrige criteria do not tell you how to run your business. They simply provide a framework that must be customized to fit your industry, customers, and competitive environment. The Organizational Profile section tells the examiners where to look for a sophisticated system, and where a less formal approach might be appropriate. For example, if yours is a very labor intensive organization that has struggled with hiring and keeping the best employees, your human resource strategies might be looked at more stringently than those of a company where labor might not be as crucial to success.

The material in this chapter provides a detailed explanation of what is being asked for in the questions in the criteria, and suggestions on how to respond appropriately. Within the two Examination Items there are a number of questions that must be answered in the Organizational Profile section. In some cases, there are multiple questions within a single Area to Address, so being able to answer all of these questions completely within the five page limit should be a bit of a challenge. The draft often begins much longer, and eventually gets edited down to the five pages. The material presented in bold print in the boxes in the text are the words taken from the 2007 criteria booklet. The normal text that follows is my interpretation of the criteria.

P.1 ORGANIZATIONAL DESCRIPTION: What are your key organizational characteristics?

Describe your organization's operating environment and your KEY relationships with CUSTOMERS, suppliers, PARTNERS, and STAKEHOLDERS.

AREA TO ADDRESS

P.1a. Organizational Environment

(1) What are your organization's main products and services? What are the delivery mechanisms used to provide your products and services to your CUSTOMERS?

N1. Mechanisms for product and service delivery to your end-use customers (P.1a[1]) might be direct or through dealers, distributors, collaborators, or channel partners.

N6. While some nonprofit organizations offer products and services (P.1a[1]), many might appropriately interpret this phrase as programs or projects and services.

N7. Customers (P.1a[1]) are the users and potential users of your products, programs, and services. In some nonprofit organizations, customers might include members, taxpayers, citizens, recipients, clients, and beneficiaries. Market segments might be referred to as constituencies.

What They're Looking for Here

In some organizations, this will be a simple and straightforward answer such as "we are in the hotel business," or "we manufacture electronic components and parts for the telecommunications industry." Many companies today are not in a single business, however, and even if they are, a simple one sentence explanation may not be clear. It should be clear that you are either a manufacturer or service business from the category of your application. What needs to be amplified here is exactly what you do manufacture or what service you do provide. A list is probably not a good idea unless you provide a wide variety of products/services. Even if you do, it is important to indicate your main businesses. For example, perhaps 80% of your business comes from one product you manufacture, and the remaining 20% is divided into 18 different types of products that you also manufacture. You probably don't need to provide a statistical breakdown of your sales figures by business unit or product/service line, but the examiners do need to know what your primary products/services are.

Note N5 says that for nonprofit organizations it might be OK to list projects or programs as services, but I would recommend against that. Within programs or projects you will find services. It will be hard for the examiners to understand what your organization does if you do not describe your products and services. All nonprofit, military and government organizations I have worked with can find some way of describing what they do in terms of specific services or products. Think if you were writing a sales brochure about your organization. What would you list on the cover as the 4-6 major services or products your organization provides? For the Army Corps of Engineers, services might include: Research Studies, Engineering Services, Construction Project Management, etc. If you think about the services that are within your programs or projects, this would be a clearer way of answering P.1a(1).

The second question in this Area to Address asks about how your products/services are delivered to customers. If you are a restaurant, the answer might be: "Meals are delivered by our wait staff." How you answer this question will probably be much more complicated. You need to explain how your products are sold to customers, as well as how they physically receive them. For example, some manufacturers sell through independent dealers or retail stores, whereas others sell directly to their customers, via telephone, mail, or the Internet. Similarly, you might use your own employees and trucks to deliver your products to customers, or use suppliers like Roadway Express or UPS. Service companies also have different ways of delivering service to their customers. Some rely on customers

P.1a(2) What is your organizational culture? What are your stated PURPOSE, VISION, MISSION, and VALUES?

to come to them, such as airlines and hotels, and others go directly to customer locations to perform their service, such as an equipment repair company or landscaping company.

This question is a little more challenging to answer succinctly than the previous one. All organizations have a culture or set of values, but rarely do they articulate them honestly or clearly. Most organizations claim to have a culture that focuses on providing value to customers, using teams of empowered employees. Describing your culture using trite words and phrases like "customer-focused," "value-added," "teamwork," and "integrity" will make it sound like you have put no real thought into defining the type of culture you want. Explain in plain terms what type of company you have. What is it like for employees and customers to associate with your firm? How are you different or unique compared to other similar companies? After providing a broad description of your culture, you need to list your mission, vision, and values. A mission is a statement that defines the purpose and scope of your company, and it might include a description of your key products/services and the markets you target. If you do not have a formal mission statement, simply write a few sentences that explain your purpose and business. The mark of a good mission statement is that it should be specific enough to differentiate your company from others, and not so narrow as to prevent you from looking at new opportunities.

In addition, you must include your vision statement in the Organizational Profile section. The vision statement is future focused and should describe some future state or grand goal your company is striving to achieve. A vision statement that restates your mission or purpose or is filled with buzzwords like "world-class" or "benchmark-level" will not show much thought. A vision statement should be understandable to all employees and measurable. For example, it would be tough to tell if a company had become a "customer-focused, world-class technology leader." Keep in mind that you will be elaborating on your future vision and strategic plan in section 2 of the application, so it is enough to list your vision here and refer to section 2 where additional explanation is provided. The final thing asked for here are your values. The typical list of words and phrases like "quality, trust, integrity, respect, honesty, diversity, and teamwork" will make examiners wonder what the real culture of your organization is. Almost every large organization I encounter has the same list of words in their values plaque, even though they have vastly different cultures. An organization that is honest about the type of values it wants to have would be a breath of fresh air compared to most I've seen. You will elaborate on your values/culture and how they are deployed in the Leadership (1) section of the application, so simply include a list here. For more information on developing mission, vision, and values statements, consult my book: Winning Score—How to Design and Implement Organizational Scorecards (Productivity Press, 2000).

P.1a(3) What is your WORKFORCE profile? What are your WORKFORCE or employee groups and SEGMENTS? What are their KEY requirements and expectations? What are their education levels? What are your organization's WORKFORCE and job DIVERSITY, organized bargaining units, KEY benefits, and special health and safety requirements?

N8. Many nonprofit organizations rely heavily on volunteers to accomplish their work. These organizations should include volunteers in the discussion of their workforce (P.1a[3]).

Some of this information can be presented by using a table or chart that lists numbers of employees by type, location, or rank. This is important for the examiners to get a feel for the majority of people in your company, and what their backgrounds are. Other information asked for here is better to present using a narrative. For example, if your company is heavily dependent upon powerful unions, or if you make extensive use of contract employees, this would be important to mention. If there are any unusual circumstances regarding employment at your company, this would be also good to mention here. For example, perhaps your work is very seasonal, or employees have to work under very hazardous conditions. The information in your response to this question should paint a picture of the types of people working for your company, as well as their work environment.

Many nonprofit organizations have a workforce that consists of people that are not actually employees. Doctors are an important part of the workforce for a hospital, but are usually not employees. Hospitals also often have many volunteers as part of their workforce. Make sure to include all the people who make up your workforce, even if they are not technically employees.

P.1a(4) What are your major technologies, equipment, and facilities?

This is fairly straightforward if you are a manufacturing company in some high-tech field. It might be a little more challenging for some service companies, or tough to answer for a diversified company, such as past winner Motorola, that is involved with many technologies and types of equipment. Try to keep your answer simple, even if your business is not. As with the previous question, this one might be best answered with a table or list, followed by a few sentences of narrative. The point is to try to paint a picture of what your organization looks like. Is it several large factories with huge pieces of equipment, a bunch of office workers in cubicles in one big high rise, or a small corporate headquarters with most employees working out of their homes or at customer locations?

P.1a(5)What is the regulatory environment under which your organization operates? What are the applicable occupational health and safety regulations; accreditation, certification, or registration requirements; relevant industry standards; and environmental, financial, and product regulations?

N9. For nonprofit organizations, relevant industry standards (P.1a[5]) might include industrywide codes of conduct and policy guidance. The term "industry" is used throughout the Criteria to refer to the sector in which you operate. For nonprofit organizations, this sector might be charitable organizations, professional associations and societies, religious organizations, or government entities—or a subsector of one of these.

For many organizations, regulatory factors play a crucial role in their success. Companies like utilities, airlines, chemical manufactures, and others are subject to a wide variety of stringent regulatory factors that end up consuming huge resources and can greatly impact their success, and even survival. You will get the opportunity to go into more detail on how you meet regulatory requirements in section 1.2 of the application. In this section you should describe the major regulatory factors that impact your organization. Don't assume that the reader understands the relationships between you and the organizations that regulate your company. It may not even be safe to assume that the examiners understand the mission of the regulatory groups. Identify the regulations and groups that are most crucial to your success. Try to give the examiners a clear idea of how regulated you are, and how much time you need to devote to meeting regulatory or legal requirements. I've worked with some companies where this is no big deal, and they meet the usual requirements from OSHA and a few other groups. Whereas others I've worked with want to list regulators as customers because they spend as much time and money satisfying them as they do their paying customers. The major point to get across here is who regulates your organization, and how much work it is to meet these regulations on a continual basis.

A number of government organizations like Department of Energy, EPA, FAA, etc., are actually regulatory agencies. If this is the case, do not explain the regulatory services you provide in answer to question P1a(5). Rather, talk about the regulations that your organization must adhere to as they do their work. Even regulators get regulated by some other groups. For example, people who work in the EPA must abide by their own rules relating to the environment, but must also follow standard regulations regarding employee safety, labor laws, finance/accounting regulations, etc.

Many nonprofit organizations get funded from a different group than their customers. For example, a Navy shipyard repairs ships for the fleet and the sailors that live and work on the ships, but the funding comes from a parent organization called NAVSEA. It is important to maintain a good working relationship with funding sources as well as customers.

AREA TO ADDRESS

P.1b. Organizational Relationships

(1)What are your organizational structure and GOVERNANCEsystem? What are the reporting relationships among your GOVERNANCEboard, SENIOR LEADERS,and parent organization, as appropriate?

N10. For some nonprofit organizations, governance and reporting relationships (P.1b[1]) might include relationships with major agency or foundation funding sources.

Simply showing your organizational structure, using a diagram is probably much better than trying to describe it. Just show the top couple of layers so that the chart does not take up too much space. The second part of the question is a little trickier. A governance system is an approach for ensuring that honest and ethical behavior occurs, especially when it comes to reporting performance data. Remember, there is an entire new Area to Address in section 1.1b, which asks for a description of the governance system, so there is no need to go into detail here. A few sentences should suffice, with reference to the details to be found in 1.1. This new question also asks about the relationship your organization has with its board and the parent company if there is one. This should not take more than a few sentences to explain, but please be specific. The examiners know the general role of a board and parent company. What they are interested in is how much autonomy your organization has, and what types of decisions are made by the board and/or parent company.

P.1b(2). What are your KEYCUSTOMERand STAKEHOLDERgroups and market SEGMENTS,as appropriate? What are their KEYrequirements and expectations for your products, services, and operations? What are the differences in these requirements and expectations among CUSTOMERand STAKEHOLDERgroups and market SEGMENTS?

N3. Market segments (P.1b[2]) might be based on product or service lines or features, geography, distribution channels, business volume, or other factors that areimportant to your organization to define related market characteristics.

N4. Customer and stakeholder group and market segment requirements (P.1b[2]) might include on-time delivery, low defect levels, ongoing price reductions, electronic communication, and after-sales service. For some nonprofit organizations, requirements also might include administrative cost reductions, at-home services, rapid response to emergencies, and multilingual services.

This question really parallels what is asked for in Item 3.1 for the criteria. In that section you will probably provide a table, listing different market segments and requirements, so you don't need to go into that much detail here. What you do need to do is identify your top three or four market segments, and the two or three most important requirements of each. You might find that some generic requirements are important to all customers such as competitive pricing, timely delivery, and quality, and that each market segment also has a few unique priorities that you should identify. The worst way to answer this question is to say that you have one type of customer, and all the customers care about the same generic things that everyone wants from every product/service that they buy. You need to put enough detail in your answer to make the reader believe that you really understand your markets and what drives their buying behavior. Price, quality, and timely delivery are usually just the basics that get you in the door, so be more specific in your answer.

Nonprofit organizations often struggle with the concept of customer. Make sure to read the Baldrige definition of customer in the glossary of the 2007 criteria. In most cases, taxpayers are not customers of a government organization. Customers are the specific clients that the organization serves. It helps to think of a government or nonprofit organization as if it were a private company and then ask: Who would our customers be? Who would write us a check for our product or services? Make sure that you do not include your vendors or suppliers as customers as well. City of Los Angeles Workforce Development Division delivers educational and job finding services to people all over the county via independent work source centers. These are their vendors or suppliers, not customers. Their customers are the youth and adults looking for education or work, and the organizations looking for good people to fill jobs.

> P.1b(3) What are your most important types of suppliers, PARTNERS, COLLABORATORS, and distributors? What role do these suppliers, PARTNERS, COLLABORATORS, and distributors play in your WORK SYSTEMS and the production and delivery of your KEY products and services? What role, if any, do they play in your organizational INNOVATION PROCESSES? What are your most important supply chain requirements?

Current organizations are increasingly reliant on their suppliers for their success. Most companies have figured out their core competencies and farm out the remaining work to outside companies. List the major types of both upstream (e.g., parts, raw materials) and downstream (e.g., distributors, dealers, customer service providers) suppliers whom you rely on for success. You don't need to go into detail about the requirements you put on each type of supplier—there will be space to do this in section 6. You do, however, need to do more than provide a generic list of requirements. In describing the relationships you have with both customers and suppliers you should identify which ones are true partners with you and which others you have a different type of relationship with. The last part of the second question asks about communication mechanisms. Many current companies have access to each others' performance data as well as have regular meetings and phone calls. The point you want to get across is that you communicate with important business partners as often as your own employees. Using multiple media for communication is generally considered a good thing, and the timeliness of information is often a crucial point to address here.

P.1b(4) What are your KEY supplier and CUSTOMER partnering relationships and communication mechanisms?

N5. Communication mechanisms (P.1b[4]) should be two-way and might be in person, via regular mail or e-mail, Web-based or by telephone. For many organizations, these mechanisms may change as marketplace requirements change.

This question asks about the type of relationships you have with major suppliers and customers. In the previous two questions, you identified who they are, and in this question you must explain how you work together. For example, an airline might partner with a commuter airline that uses its name, connections, and reservation service, but the commuter airline is really a separate company that has partnered with the big airline. Dealers are important downstream suppliers with whom car companies have established partnering relationships. Customers sometimes partner with companies agreeing to provide the company with all of their business for the mutual benefit of both firms. Suppliers sometimes work on-site at their customers' offices and are 100% committed to one customer. Whatever sort of arrangements you have with your major customers and suppliers, you must explain them here.

Nonprofit organizations often heavily rely on other agencies, groups, or vendors to get their work done. For example, at DOE facility Savannah River, only about 10 percent of the workforce are federal government employees. The other 5000 people work for a contractor. In a Navy shipyard, only about 5 percent of the workforce is Navy. The bulk of the workforce is made up of civilians that work for the shipyard full-time and contractors that do not. Law enforcement organizations must often depend on and work with other state, local and even national organizations to do their jobs effectively. Your answer to P.1b(3) and (4) should explain who these other organizations are and what your relationship is with them.

P.2 ORGANIZATIONAL CHALLENGES

Describe your organization's competitive environment, your KEY STRATEGIC CHALLENGES, and your system for PERFORMANCE improvement.

P.2a. Competitive Environment

(1)What is your competitive position? What is your relative size and growth in your industry or markets served? What are the numbers and types of competitors and KEY collaborators for your organization?

N4. Nonprofit organizations frequently are in a very competitive environment; they often must compete with other organizations and with alternative sources for similar services to secure financial and volunteer resources, membership, visibility in appropriate communities, and media attention.

The key here is to be honest in your response and to identify both current and potential future competitors. Often the biggest threats come from companies that might not be a threat today, but could come along and "eat your lunch" if you are not paying attention. General Motors did not see Toyota as a serious threat until it was too late, Sears ignored WalMart for too long. The point of this segment is to position yourself in the industry as a big or small player and to identify any niche that you might have. Identifying your top four to six competitors and their relative market share is part of helping the examiners understand your position in the markets you serve. If you are in a single business, the answer to this question might be quite brief, but not so if you are in a number of different markets and industries with different competitors in each. Try to concentrate on the major segments of your business. As with other questions in this overview section, there will be space later in the application to go into more detail about specific competitors.

P.2a(2)What arethe principal factors that determine your success relative to your competitors? What are any KEYchanges taking place that affect your competitive situation?, including opportunities for collaboration, as appropriate?

> N1. Principal factors (P.2a[2]) might include differentiators such as price leadership, design services, e-services, geographic proximity, and warranty and product options. For some nonprofit organizations, differentiators also might include relative influence with decision makers, ratio of administrative costs to programmatic contributions, past reputation for program or service delivery, and wait times for service.

This answer should also be written with much thought as to what makes your organization's products/services unique. You need to explain how you position yourself in the marketplace to differentiate your products/services. Often small but subtle differences can make huge differences in customer loyalty. The most commonplace answer to this question is "we differentiate ourselves with our customer-focused people." If this were really true, you might have a hard time convincing skeptical examiners. The key to answering this question correctly is honesty and specificity. What gives Northwest Airlines an edge over competitors in Minneapolis and Detroit is that they dominate the airports with the most flights and the most gates, as United does in Chicago and Denver. A lack of choice by customers can often be a major factor in your success. Government and nonprofit organizations often depend on relationships with Congress, and other government organizations that might impact their future. Elected officials and their appointees often have a big impact as well. If this is the case for your organization, explain the factors that determine your success, including politics, and describe how you manage these factors. The last part of this question asks about any current or projected changes that are going on in your industry that might change your position in the marketplace. For example, the Internet changed the way many people shop for books and music. Similarly, deregulation of the electric and gas utilities has caused many major changes in the business of those companies. There will be space to go into detail about future projections and your plans, but include some of the big factors here in the Organizational Profile.

> P.2b. Strategic Context
>
>   What are your KEY business, operational, and human resource STRATEGIC CHALLENGES? What are your KEY STRATEGIC CHALLENGES associated with organizational SUSTAINABILITY?
>
> N2. Strategic challenges and advantages (P.2b) might relate to technology, products, your operations, your industry, globalization, your value chain, and people.
>
> N5. For nonprofit organizations, the term "business" (P.2b) is used throughout the Criteria to refer to your main mission area or enterprise activity.

It might be tough to provide a single concise answer to this question for a complex organization that might have separate challenges for each market segment or product/service line. However, space is limited here, so try to concentrate on the major challenges that impact your entire business. As with the previous sections, it is important that you are honest about competitive, environmental, or other challenges you face now and in the near term. For example, many organizations today have a tough time finding and keeping qualified employees. Often the technology parts of the business are easy compared with softer issues such as human resources and managing relationships with customers. Be as specific as possible with your answer, but keep in mind that anything you mention as a challenge here will need to be addressed later in the application. Examiners will want to know about how you are addressing these challenges in your business strategy, and expect to see how well they are working by evaluating your business results.

The word "business" is used throughout the criteria to refer to the field or discipline you are in. Many nonprofit organizations do not consider themselves in the charity, military, or healthcare business. Just keep in mind that this term refers to the field or type of organization yours is as you see the word "business" throughout the criteria.

P.2c. Performance Improvement System

What arethe KEY elements of your PERFORMANCE improvement system, including your evaluation and LEARNING PROCESSES?

N3. Performance improvement (P.2c) is an assessment dimension used in the Scoring System to evaluate the maturity of organizational approaches and deployment (see pages 51–54). This question is intended to help you and the Baldrige Examiners set an overall context for your approach to performance improvement. Overall approaches to performance improvement might include implementing a Lean Enterprise System, applying Six Sigma methodology, using ISO 9000:2000 standards, or employing other process improvement tools.

This question will be difficult to answer without having your answer sound completely generic. I think what is important is not continuous improvement of all key processes but to convey that you focus on improving aspects of your organization that link back to meeting requirements that drive customer and employee loyalty, and that help differentiate you from competitors. You might mention how your vision was established, and how overall improvement goals are identified each year, as well as how you keep the organization focused on achievement of the vision, without losing sight of the mission, and watching your competitors at the same time. This is a tough balancing act that most organizations have to face each day. A thoughtful answer to this final question in the overview section will go a long way toward a favorable response from the examiners.

A sentence or two should be adequate to answer this final question in the profile. Part of it asks about your philosophy and part of it your approach. Don't bother with a trite statement about employees being your greatest asset. Rather, explain your approach to sharing lessons learned and ensuring that skills and knowledge acquired over the years by employees gets transferred to others.

Chapter

6

INTERPRETING THE CRITERIA FOR LEADERSHIP (1)

OVERVIEW OF THE LEADERSHIP CATEGORY

The 2008 Award Criteria define the Leadership category as follows:

The Leadership Category examines how your organization's senior leaders guide and sustain your organization. Also examined are your organization's governance and ethical, legal, and community responsibilities.

The Leadership Category is broken down into the following two Examination Items:

1.1 Senior Leadership (70 points)

1.2 Governance and Social Responsibilities (50 points)

As stated in the excerpt above, this category relates to the activities of the organization's senior executives as well as the management system as a whole. The term "senior executives" refers to the highest ranking official of the organization and the executives that report directly to the CEO or president. This would seem very clear, but applicants have been known to report on only the activities of their most senior executive, the CEO, with no information being provided on the activities of any of the other executives in the organization.

The sections that follow describe each of the Areas to Address, organized under each of the two Examination Items in the Leadership Category. Each section begins with a shadowed box containing the Examination item, the point value, and any applicable Notes.* Areas to Address falling under that item follow in a lighter shadowed box. In the upper right corner of each Area to Address box is an indication [brackets] of whether the area pertains to approach, deployment, or results. All definitions and information appearing within these boxes are taken directly from the Baldrige criteria. Following each Area to Address is an explanation defining what the examiners are looking for in assessing your application for each of the individual questions under the Areas to Address. Next, I have supplied a list of indicators or evaluation factors that will assist you in interpreting the criteria and in preparing your application.

---

* Item Notes that apply to a specific Area to Address are appropriately listed in the box containing that Area.

1.1 SENIOR LEADERSHIP: How do your senior leaders Lead?   PROCESS (70 PTS.)

Describe HOW SENIOR LEADERS guide and sustain your organization. Describe HOW SENIOR LEADERS communicate with your WORKFORCE and encourage HIGH PERFORMANCE.

AREA TO ADDRESS   [APPROACH, DEPLOYMENT]
1.1a. VISION and VALUES

(1) How do SENIOR LEADERS set organizational VISION and VALUES? How do SENIOR LEADERS DEPLOY your organization's VISION and VALUES through your LEADERSHIP SYSTEM to the WORKFORCE, to KEY suppliers and PARTNERS, and to CUSTOMERS and other STAKEHOLDERS, as appropriate? How do SENIOR LEADERS' personal actions reflect a commitment to the organization's VALUES?

N1. Organizational vision (1.1a[1]) should set the context for strategic objectives and action plans, which are described in Items 2.1 and 2.2.

What They're Looking for Here

Your response to this first question of the criteria should describe how the senior leaders set the vision and values for the organization. A typical and rarely useful approach is to do this in a planning meeting held at a resort or conference center with a golf course. The team of executives is led through a process of brainstorming words and phrases that might be contained in a vision statement. These jargon-laden words and phrases are then cobbled together into some awkward sentence that no one really understands, but they grow weary of arguing and eventually concede to something that sounds like the following:

> Our vision is to become a world-class leading edge producer of value-added products and services that meet the real needs of our customers using a Lean-Six Sigma approach to allow us to meet or exceed financial and operational targets and delight our shareholders, employees, and other stakeholders.

Using a team of leaders to write a vision statement almost always leads to a worthless garbled sentence. The problem with this team approach is that the vision ends up being a compromise that often becomes so generic that it fails to communicate direction or focus. For example, one of the largest banks in the United States has a vision to be the *"bank of choice for consumers, employer of choice for employees, and investment of choice for shareholders."* If I owned stock in this bank, I'd be selling it after reading this generic worthless vision statement that was undoubtedly crafted by a team of executives at a strategic planning retreat in the woods somewhere. The best approach for creating a vision statement is to have the boss do it since that is his or her job. It is important to get input from all the leaders on what they think the future of the organization should be, but it is ultimately the job and decision of the CEO or boss to decide on the future vision. I have helped many major corporations and government organizations do strategic planning, and I have never once seen a good vision statement that was created using a team of executives to craft the sentence.

The first question in the criteria also asks about how you set your values. As with defining vision, it is generally not a good idea to use a team of leaders to define the values of an organization. I can almost always spot a set of values that were identified by a team or committee because they are generic, vague, unimaginative, and are the same list that every other company has:

Trust	Perseverance	Integrity
Teamwork	Commitment	Ethics
Customer Service	Efficiency	Dedication
Loyalty	Truth	Respect
Innovation	Social Responsibility	Initiative

The values or culture of an organization are often one of its greatest assets, and careful thought and imagination are needed to identify the values and make them part of the company's DNA. A company that I have worked with for years that has a great culture is Bose. One of the real values that permeates this company is belief in research and innovation. The company spends about double what most of its competitors spend on R&D and does an excellent job of hiring creative people. For example, there are a lot of musicians working at Bose. The company has found that musicians and other types of artistic people tend to be more creative and innovative than some engineers, scientists, and business people.

In 2003, IBM used an interesting approach to help create a new set of values for the company. The company held a 3-day discussion via the Internet. The forum, called "ValuesJam," involved 50,000 employees in a discussion and debate about the company culture and values. After a number of drafts and more feedback from thousands of employees, IBM ended up with a new set of corporate values:

- *Dedication to every client's success*
- *Innovation that matters—for our company and the world*
- *Trust and personal responsibility in all relationships*

While it is certainly not necessary to use an approach as elaborate as IBM's, it does serve as a good example of a unique and comprehensive approach for setting values in an organization and getting the input of thousands of people without having a team meeting.

The values themselves should have been identified in the Organizational Profile section of the application, so you can refer the examiners back to this section, rather than restating the values here.

The second question in 1.1a(1) asks about how senior leaders communicate or *deploy* both the vision and values to employees and others, such as suppliers, partners, and perhaps even customers. A big part of communicating the vision of your organization is first ensuring it is:

- *Short and memorable*
- *Clearly written in plain English*
- *Realistic*
- *Verifiable*
- *Focused on one or two accomplishments*

Assuming you have a vision that meets all of these criteria, the next step is to determine the best approach for communicating the vision and getting everyone to help you achieve it. A current client has done an outstanding job of this, and would get high marks for this approach. The Santa Clara Valley Water District in Silicon Valley, California, provides wholesale water and flood protection services to the county's 1.8 million residents. The area continues to grow, property values are still on the rise, and budgets have been cut because of the financial crisis in the state of California. CEO Stan Williams recently drafted a new vision for the district: Getting Leaner, Getting Greener, Getting Cleaner.

The vision was unveiled at a recent all-employees meeting with about 75 percent of the district's 900 employees in attendance. There were the typical banners, table tent cards, and other media for communicating the new three-part vision. There was also a talk given by Stan about what the new vision meant and why it was important. Stan can give a speech to 700 people and make each person in the audience feel like he is having a one-on-one talk with him or her. Without using any PowerPoint slides and wandering through the audience as he talked, Stan communicated the new vision through a series of stories about the water district, its history, accomplishments, and challenges. The stories were both memorable, funny, and set the stage for the vision. At the end of Stan's talk, cards were placed at each table, asking attendees to explain what "*leaner, greener, and cleaner*" meant to them in their jobs. Most employees filled out the cards, and Stan and his staff read every one after the meeting and used the data to further craft their communication strategy for the vision. The district also recently created a new set of performance measures, which includes three strategic gauges (Lean index, Green index, and Clean index) that show progress toward the vision. The approach taken by this organization to deploy the vision shows both imagination and thoroughness.

An important dimension of how the values are communicated is your selection of new employees and decisions on promotions. Values are hard to change and tend to be established during childhood. Hiring a person with a different set of values than your own is often a problem. Organizations like Southwest Airlines that are known for a strong culture and consistent values achieve this mostly through careful selection of people who have the same values as the company. They are even more careful about promoting people into management jobs, realizing that everyone looks at managers' behavior to decide what the real values are in the organization. It is also vitally important that the behavior and decision making of senior executives be consistent with the stated company values. The most effective way of communicating and deploying the values is to make sure that executives model them in the actions.

Aside from careful selection and ensuring the leaders' behavior is consistent with the values, it is also important to use a variety of communication methods to remind people of the values and get them to recognize when their own behavior may be inconsistent with the values. Some companies simply post the values on plaques, or put them on the backs of employee ID badges. It is little wonder that most employees in these companies cannot recite the values. One company I worked with even went so far as to program every computer terminal so the values appeared each day when you signed on to the system. Even though employees saw this every day, not one person I interviewed could remember the full list of values. It is also important to vary the media and timing of communication. Values need to be communicated in speeches, newsletters, training programs, meetings, reports, plans, and through face-to-face interactions.

Your answer to question (1) in item 1.1a should also explain how senior leaders communicate a balance of financial results with other factors such as employee and customer satisfaction. Early Baldrige winner FedEx does this by teaching employees that they will have three masters:

- *Shareholders*
- *Customers*
- *Other Employees*

Every FedEx employee learns not to trade off one for the other, but to achieve the appropriate balance between all three. FedEx communicates this balanced focus through new employee orientation, ongoing training, close-circuit television broadcasts, and perhaps most importantly, through an incentive compensation system. Incentives are based on achieving good performance for all three stakeholders. You obviously need not copy FedEx's approach, but describe your own methods for leaders to communicate their priorities and expectations to all employees. In a small organization, communication methods might be informal and face-to-face. Larger organizations, where executives cannot have personal contact with all employees, would need a more formal structured approach to communication. The use of multiple media and communication methods is also encouraged, because all employees learn differently.

Indicators for Question 1.1a(1)

- *Senior leaders have defined a future vision for the company, based upon a review of market, customers and their needs, and an assessment of the company's own capabilities.*
- *The future vision is realistic, verifiable, and understandable to all employees.*
- *The vision has been clearly communicated to all employees.*
- *Employees understand how their jobs fit in and contribute to helping the company achieve its future vision.*
- *Senior leaders periodically review and revise the company's vision as the business environment changes.*
- *Use of a wide variety of media and methods to communicate the vision, values, expectations, and direction to employees.*
- *There is evidence that the effectiveness of the communication methods has been evaluated and improved.*
- *There is evidence that employees know and understand the values and expectations.*
- *Company establishes values and expectations that employees believe are clear, realistic and achievable.*
- *A systematic plan exists for teaching employees about behavior that is consistent with the values and expectations.*
- *Values are assessed as part of the selection and promotion processes.*
- *A proactive approach is used throughout the organization to reward employee behavior that is consistent with the values.*

- *The values are integrated with leadership selection/training and with performance planning and assessment processes.*
- *There is evidence that the approaches used to reinforce behavior are consistent with the values and have been evaluated and improved.*
- *Executives communicate a balance in priorities for meeting the needs of shareholders, customers, and employees.*
- *Communication is two-way between employees and senior executives.*

1.1a(2) How do SENIOR LEADERS personally promote an organizational environment that fosters, requires, and results in legal and ETHICAL BEHAVIOR?

What They're Looking for Here

This question fits better in Item 1.2 **Governance and Social Responsibility.** It probably ended up here because it focuses on the actions of senior executives to create an environment that encourages ethical behavior, whereas 1.2 focuses mostly on systems for governance and compliance. Other than establishing a set of values and creating a strong governance system, there are many actions leaders can or cannot perform that might encourage ethical behavior. One client does a good job in this area by having a policy of zero tolerance for unethical behavior. What this means is that leaders don't look the other way when one of their star performers gets caught doing something unethical. In this particular organization, a number of otherwise good performers, fairly high up in the organization, were fired for ethics violations. This sends a powerful message to the rest of the employees that no one is immune, and that there is no tolerance for unethical behavior. On the positive side, leaders can reward highly ethical individuals through promotions and other forms of recognition. Another way for executives to demonstrate their commitment to ethics is to dedicate adequate resources for activities in this area. One client created a new position: Chief Ethics Officer, hired a top person for this job, and had him report directly to the board, rather than the CEO. Another client created an entire department, whose job it is to measure and manage ethical behavior in the organization, while another uses executive coaches for all senior leaders to help provide individualized advice and feedback on how their actions and decisions are consistent or inconsistent with the company's code of ethics.

In short, there are a variety of ways that executives can create an environment that fosters ethics and good behavior from employees. What is important, regardless of approach, is consistency and adequate resources and focus given to this topic. Often companies only get serious about ethics after they have gotten into trouble.

Indicators for 1.1a(2)

- *Senior leaders model ethical principles in their behavior and decisions.*

- *Leaders take firm and decisive corrective actions when employees exhibit unethical behavior.*

- *Leaders are consistent in their treatment of all levels of employees when it comes to ethics— they don't give breaks to other executives or star performers.*

- *The organization structure is designed so that the person responsible for ethics has adequate power and autonomy.*

- *Adequate resources (financial and personnel) are provided for ethics training and other programs.*

1.1a(3) How do SENIOR LEADERS create a SUSTAINABLE organization? How do SENIOR LEADERS create an environment for organizational PERFORMANCE improvement, the accomplishment of your MISSION and STRATEGIC OBJECTIVES, INNOVATION, competitive or role model PERFORMANCE leadership, and organizational agility? How do they create an environment for organizational and WORK FORCE LEARNING? How do they personally participate in succession planning and the development of future organizational leaders?

N.2 A sustainable organization (1.1a[3]) is capable of addressing current business needs and possesses the agility and strategic management to prepare successfully for its future business and market environment. In this context, the concept of innovation includes both technological and organizational innovation to succeed in the future. A sustainable organization also ensures a safe and secure environment for the workforce and other key stakeholders.

What They're Looking for Here

This entire question is about ensuring the sustainability and continued success of the organization—an important role of leaders. The first area questioned is how leaders create the right environment to encourage success. One topic that should be addressed here is organizational structure and accountability. Many large organizations have far too many layers of management, too much bureaucracy, and unclear or overlapping accountabilities. Your answer to this question should address how leaders have structured your organization to encourage speed, agility, and performance improvement. Strategic planning is often done once a year, resulting in a nice binder that sits on the shelf until it is time to begin planning for the next year. This question asks how leaders ensure that this does not happen. Plans and objectives need to be reviewed on a regular basis against actual performance, with adjustments made as necessary.

The criteria in this question also ask how leaders encourage innovation. Baldrige winners tend to be the pioneers in their fields, not the followers. They are being benchmarked, rather than copying others. An important step leaders can take to encourage innovation is to allocate adequate resources to functions such as research and development. Bose, a pioneer in the audio industry, spends about double what any of its competitors spend on R&D. The company also actively recruits creative and innovative people from diverse fields outside of engineering. For example, many Bose employees are also musicians. Bose has pioneered a long list of products that are later adopted by competitors. Medtronic, another client, is equivalent to Bose in the medical devices industry. Medtronic is the leading company in the industry when it comes to applying technology solutions to health problems. Both companies put a big focus on patents, realizing that although many patents will not turn into marketable products, they still want to encourage employees to constantly look for new ideas and products.

Agility is difficult for a large, old organization. Your answer to this question should explain how the organization remains flexible and can change when the market or other factors require a change. Many large and successful companies have either gone bankrupt or ended up being bought by a formerly small competitor because of a lack of ability to adapt to changing customer needs and market conditions. Sears was bought by formerly bankrupt K-Mart, and AT&T was bought by Cingular and SBC. The topic of agility must be addressed more thoroughly if yours is a large organization, though it should not be dismissed if yours is a small one. Small organizations also find agility a challenge, because they often lack the resources to change and adapt quickly.

This question also asks how leaders create a climate that encourages organizational and workforce learning. Remember, knowledge management is asked about in 4.2, and workforce training and development is asked about in 5.2. Here they are asking how executives create an environment that encourages learning. Again, a big part of what executives can do is committing resources to learning. Past Baldrige winners tend to spend 5% to 7% of their payroll costs each year on training and developing their employees. Typical companies spend less than 1%. Some organizations have created their own corporate universities, which can be a strong way for leaders to demonstrate commitment to learning. Some companies actually have a "chief learning officer" that reports to the CEO, as opposed to the HR VP. None of these are required, of course, but serve as examples of how leaders in organizations can demonstrate their commitment to learning.

The final question in this long Area to Address asks about how executives participate in succession planning and leadership development. The succession planning process itself must be described in section 5.1. What is asked here is how executives or leaders are part of the process. An important piece of information to convey is whether or not a succession plan exists for all senior leaders. You should also explain how the leaders participate in identifying potential candidates to groom for their own positions, and for other jobs in the organization. You should also explain how the leaders play a role in your leadership development process. For example, one client has a good mentoring program where executives mentor one or more junior executives.

Indicators for Question 1.1.a(3)

- *The organizational structure is designed with minimal layers and clear accountability.*
- *Decisions are made quickly and with a minimum amount of review/approval cycles.*
- *Progress against goals/objectives is reviewed on a regular basis and adjustments are made as needed.*
- *Planning is not an annual event. Rather, the plan is a living document that is continually reviewed and adjusted throughout the year.*
- *Leaders encourage risk taking and innovation by allocating adequate resources to functions such as R&D.*
- *Failures are viewed as an opportunity to learn valuable lessons.*
- *Leaders try to hire people that are creative and different rather than always hiring people that look and think like them.*
- *Incentives are in place to encourage creativity and innovation.*
- *Leaders create an environment of trust.*
- *Executives spend less time reviewing and approving expenditures than they did in the past.*
- *The company has created a culture that rewards continual learning for everyone.*
- *Executives participate in important training and development courses/events.*
- *The training/education budget is one of the last things to get cut when times get tough.*
- *A succession plan exists for all senior executives.*
- *Executives play an active role in the succession planning process.*
- *Leaders participate in leadership development programs and make this a priority for all managers.*

AREA TO ADDRESS   [APPROACH, DEPLOYMENT]

1.1b. Communication and Organizational PERFORMANCE

(1) HOW do SENIOR LEADERS communicate with and engage the entire WORKFORCE? HOW do SENIOR LEADERS encourage frank, two-way communication throughout the organization? HOW do SENIOR LEADERS communicate KEY decisions? HOW do SENIOR LEADERS take an active role in reward and recognition programs to reinforce HIGH PERFORMANCE and a CUSTOMER and business focus?

N5. For nonprofit organizations that rely on volunteers to accomplish their work, responses to 1.1b(1) also should discuss your efforts to communicate with and engage the volunteer workforce.

What They're Looking For Here

This Area to Address is mostly about communication, which is often the biggest challenge to a large organization. Part of your answer to this first question should show some thought behind the strategies used by executives to communicate with employees and others. A typical approach is for executives to have everyone file into the auditorium for a scintillating presentation on the state of the company using PowerPoint slides that can only be read by those in the first two rows. Employees file out of the auditorium often with no idea of what was covered, but the executives feel like they really communicated with the troops. Research on communication indicates that this approach is one of the worst ways to communicate with people. Another common approach is to have a company website or online newsletter for communicating with employees and others. This is also a highly overrated approach. The keys to effective communication are tailoring the message to the audience, using a variety of media and methods, communicating frequently, and using one-on-one tactics as much as possible. Since most communication is not verbal, this means limiting teleconference and other similar approaches—nothing beats face-to-face.

The frequency of communication cannot be underrated. One client has a rule called "5 by 5" when it comes to communication. This means that employees must hear something five times before they really hear it, and that it is important to use at least five different communication media/methods for each message to get across to a diverse group of people with different learning styles.

The second question in this Area to Address asks about how the organization encourages open and honest two-way communication. This is not something that just happens, but must be engineered using planned approaches. Several executives I know encourage employees to e-mail questions and concerns, and provide timely and honest responses to staff queries. You might also discuss how your organization prevents the tendency to shoot the messenger of bad news, which is a common occurrence. A list of the various ways in which employees, customers, and others can communicate with the organization might be listed here, along with some information on how well these programs work.

The final question in this Area to Address asks about the role of leaders in employee reward and recognition. A CEO in one client organization made it a point to sign and put a personal message in cards sent to employees each year on the anniversary of their start date. Another client made a point of having most executives attend recognition luncheons. Whatever your organization does, it is important that leaders play an active role in the recognition and reward of employees. It is also important that all leaders participate in these activities. Often the President or CEO does all of the motivation and recognition, and the other executives don't do anything. It is also important to balance reward and recognition for nonfinancial accomplishments. Early Baldrige winner FedEx links bonuses to customer satisfaction, employee morale, and profitability. Other companies employ a similar approach to demonstrate that a balance is needed in all aspects of organizational performance, and that employee and customer satisfaction are often the drivers of good financial results.

Indicators for Question 1.1b(1)

- *Creative and effective communication techniques are used.*
- *Communication of important messages is evaluated for its effectiveness.*
- *Important messages are communicated multiple times using a variety of media.*
- *Most important messages are delivered face-to-face in small groups.*
- *Communication materials are aimed at the intended audience.*
- *Specific standards exist for effective communication within all media used.*
- *There are multiple systems used to encourage two-way communication between leaders and others in the organization.*
- *Communication systems are regularly evaluated for their effectiveness and improved when necessary.*
- *All executives take an active role in rewarding and recognizing employees.*

1.1b Communication and Organizational PERFORMANCE

(2) How do SENIOR LEADERS create a focus on action to accomplish the organization's objectives, improve PERFORMANCE, and attain its VISION? What PERFORMANCE MEASURES do SENIOR LEADERS regularly review to inform them on needed actions? How do SENIOR LEADERS include a focus on creating and balancing VALUE for CUSTOMERS and other STAKEHOLDERS in their organizational PERFORMANCE expectations?

N3. A focus on action (1.1b[2]) considers the workforce, the work systems, and the hard assets of your organization. It includes ongoing improvements in productivity that may be achieved through eliminating waste or reducing cycle time, and it might use techniques such as Six Sigma and Lean. It also includes the actions to accomplish your organization's strategic objectives.

N4. Your organizational performance results should be reported in Items 7.1–7.6.

What They're Looking for Here

Most senior executives get together once a month to review company performance. If this occurs in your company, you certainly want to describe this meeting in your answer to this question. Simply having a monthly meeting will not warrant many points unless the right people attend, and the right data are reviewed. It is important to have executives review performance on all the key metrics mentioned in the company scorecard (4.1) and the strategic plan (2.1). It is acceptable to refer to these other sections, rather than listing the metrics here. Along with reviewing how your own organization is doing, it is also important to review how and what competitors are doing. This should be done as part of the regular review meeting, rather than being a once-a-year process that is done in a planning meeting.

Reviewing performance data is also important outside of monthly executive meetings. Explain how executives receive feedback (on a daily basis) on key company statistics and how the data is reported or communicated to them. Having the performance data online or using other methods of communicating rather than paper reports will help improve your score in this area.

The answer to this question in the criteria might consist of a table that shows which executives review which data with what frequency. Another alternative is a matrix chart that shows daily measures, weekly measures, monthly measures, and quarterly metrics sorted according to the categories of metrics on the organization's scorecard (i.e., financial data, customer data, employee data, etc.).

This last set of questions in 1.1b(2) asks you to summarize what your recent performance reviews revealed as far as priorities. The answer to this question might work well in a chart with the following columns of information:

ANALYSIS FINDING	IMPACT ON BUSINESS	ACTION	RESULTS

The first column would list the problems or opportunities you identified. Next, briefly describe how this could or did impact your organization. Describe the action taken and the results of this action. You need not present actual performance data here, but describe the result in words. Following this table or chart, include a paragraph or at least a couple of sentences explaining how action items or strategies are communicated internally and externally to the appropriate personnel.

Indicators for Question 1.1b(2)

- *Executives meet on a regular basis to review and discuss company performance data.*

- *Data on all important metrics from the company scorecard (4.1) are reviewed on a regular basis by the appropriate executives.*

- *Performance is reviewed in relation to objectives or targets in the strategic plan.*

- *Performance is reviewed often enough to detect important changes so that problems can be quickly solved and opportunities may be exploited.*

- *Performance data are communicated using a variety of media and in easy to read and understand formats.*

- *Analyses of performance data are used to identify opportunities and challenges.*

- *Specific challenges have been identified relating to future organizational success.*

- *Specific accomplishments have been identified as a result of performance reviews.*

- *Scope of findings and action items is broader than simply financial issues.*

- *Actions are clearly linked back to prioritization method and data analysis.*

- *Analyses reveal that the organization is clever in detecting important trends inside and outside the company that may impact their future.*

- *Performance review findings identified here are consistent with overall strategic and operational plans discussed in section 2 of the application.*

- *Adequate evidence is presented to suggest that actions are properly communicated to the right individuals both inside and outside the organization.*

1.2 GOVERNANCE AND SOCIAL RESPONSIBILITIES: How do you govern and address your social responsibilities? (50 PTS.)

Describe your organization's GOVERNANCE system. Describe HOW your organization addresses its responsibilities to the public, ensures ETHICAL BEHAVIOR, and practices good citizenship.

N1. Societal responsibilities in areas critical to your organization's ongoing success also should be addressed in Strategy Development (Item 2.1) and in Process Management (Category 6). Key results, such as results of regulatory and legal compliance (including the results of mandated financial audits), environmental improvements through use of "green" technology or other means, or conservation activities, should be reported as Leadership Outcomes (Item 7.6).

N6. The health and safety of your workforce arenot addressed in Item 1.2; you should address these employee factors in Item 5.2.

AREA TO ADDRESS   [APPROACH, DEPLOYMENT]

1.2a Organizational GOVERNANCE

(1) HOWdoes your organization review and achieve the following KEY aspects of your GOVERNANCE system:
- accountability for management's actions
- fiscal accountability
- transparency in operations and selection of and disclosure policies for GOVERNANCE board members, as appropriate
- independence in internal and external audits
- protection of STAKEHOLDER and stockholder interests, as appropriate

N2. Transparency in operations of your governance board (1.2a[1]) should include your internal controls on governance processes. For some nonprofit organizations, an external advisory board may provide some or all of the governance board functions. For those nonprofit organizations that serve as stewards of public funds, stewardship of those funds and transparency in operations are areas of emphasis.

What They're Looking for Here

It is probably true that most companies are extremely honest and ethical. However, the public has a hard time believing any executive these days when every week a new corporation is in the news for unethical behavior. Because of this, you must over emphasize to make the examiners feel comfortable that they are not going to give the Baldrige Award to a company that is disgraced later because of legal/ethical problems.

A governance system often includes multiple components. The foundation of a good governance system is a clear set of rules that everyone understands. Secondly, there needs to be multiple sets of unbiased eyes looking over the organization's data and behavior to ensure honesty and integrity. Many government organizations have separate "Inspector General" functions that watch over the behavior of other government organizations. While this approach is certainly not foolproof, it does work most of the time. A governance system also has to include a feedback mechanism, so that when problems are found, they are communicated to the appropriate people. The final, and probably most important, aspect of a governance system is consequences. For consequences to be effective they must be personal, immediate, certain, and powerful enough to control behavior.

Your response should also include an explanation of how you ensure that the people checking on you are actually independent and objective. Many of the big accounting firms also are in the consulting business. It is tough to be an auditor and advice giver at the same time. Hiring an outside firm to do your audits is no guarantee of objectivity. Accounting firm partners are measured on two key factors—sales and customer satisfaction. A customer is not likely to buy more of your auditing services each year if your auditors keep nailing the company for recurring problems.

Finally, you must explain how you look out for the needs of your shareholders and other groups of stakeholders that are linked to your firm. Large institutional investors often get offered IPOs or other perks not offered to the small individual investors. Explain how you communicate to shareholders and others, and how you ensure they understand your communication. Many annual reports are slick sales presentations in the front, with no real meat on the company strategy, and hundreds of hard-to-read numbers in the back. Some forward-thinking companies are rethinking the way they communicate with shareholders and tailoring the communication to their audience, rather than assuming everyone who buys stock has an MBA.

The Council for Ethical Organizations has developed an assessment model for evaluating the governance systems of large organizations. The approach is very similar to the Baldrige assessment model, in that different elements are assessed, and scores are given on a 1 to 5 level, indicating an organization's level of sophistication in its approach and deployment. The six factors that are considered the basic elements of an effective governance system follow:

Oversight and Support – This section examines roles and responsibilities of leaders and external boards and advisory groups. This section of the criteria also looks at the level of management support and resources devoted to governance and ethics.

Corporate Compliance Officer and Office -- This second section of the criteria asks about the authority level of the compliance officer, responsibilities, resources, and how responsibility for ethics and governance is deployed throughout the organization.

Code and Supporting Policies – This section asks about the thoroughness and clarity of ethics rules, codes, policies, and other documents that are supposed to convey right and wrong to employees and others. The criteria look at depth, breadth, and clarity of the ethics policies and rules.

Internal Reporting – It is important that an organization have an easy and anonymous way for employees to report unethical behavior or violations of policies without fear of retribution. Such systems exist in the military, government, and most large corporations, the effectiveness of these systems and the level of trust employees place in them varies widely.

Education and Training – This fifth portion of the criteria examines the thoroughness, frequency, and effectiveness of training and education on ethics and values.

Internal Controls and Corrective Actions – This final and important section asks about audits done that relate to ethics and governance, implementation of corrective actions driven by audit findings or events, and the approach taken by the organization to discipline or dismiss employees found guilty of violating policies and ethics codes.

The Baldrige criteria here ask about some specific aspects of your governance system that overlap quite a bit with the criteria outlined above. The Baldrige criteria ask about accountability for actions and decisions in the first two bullets. This is a hot topic in today's news, with talk of holding executives personally responsible for the losses incurred by shareholders under their leadership when they are found guilty of illegal and unethical actions. In many corporations, employment agreements with executives are completely one-sided, allowing some executives to get in trouble, ruin the company, and still walk away with $10 or $20 million in severance pay. Executives sell their stock when they get early warnings of its decline, make out like bandits, and shareholders are left holding the bag as stock prices plummet to near nothing. A government executive in northern California is caught accepting bribes and still collects his $400,000 paycheck along with a severance bonus of $200,000 when he is fired. The trick to answering this question about management accountability is to be specific. For example, explain exactly how senior management is held accountable for company performance and ethical behavior. Do they get zero bonuses if targets are not hit or get fired without a golden parachute for unethical behavior? What if the company is plagued with lawsuits concerning a product that executives chose to release to the public despite the risks? What are the personal consequences to management for such decisions?

The third bullet in 1.2a(1) asks about transparency. This means: how open and honest is the organization at displaying its "real" operations to the public? Some organizations won't even share their financial results with their own employees, let alone the public. Of course, many organizations need to share their financial results with shareholders and the financial community, but rarely do these organizations share all their dirty laundry. Your response to this bullet should indicate the types of company information that is shared, with whom it is shared, and the methods of communication used. A truly transparent organization has few secrets.

The next bullet asks how you ensure independence and integrity of your external and internal auditors. Most of the large accounting/auditing firms also had consulting arms that were only too happy to come in and sell solutions to all the problems uncovered in their audits. Some of these firms have separated into different organizations, but this will not entirely solve the problem. Accounting and audit firms live on repeat business from good clients. In fact, that's how you get to become a partner in these firms—sales, not audit thoroughness. The close personal relationships that audit practice partners tend to form with their clients make it difficult for them to remain autonomous and objective. You need to explain how your organization ensures the integrity of your auditors and their findings.

The fifth and final bullet in this series of questions about your governance system asks how the organization's governance system protects stakeholder and stockholder interests. The key to making this happen is communication. Most communication to shareholders and other stakeholders is done poorly and too infrequently. Most annual reports are a mixture of slick photos, biased analysis of company results and plans, and reams of detailed financial reports that only the most diligent or bored will bother to wade through. Some organizations communicate more frequently and in a more user-focused format than others. Your answer to this bullet should describe how you keep stakeholders apprised of important events and decisions that might impact their interests.

Indicators for Question 1.2.a(1)

- *Executives and leaders are held personally accountable for their actions and decisions.*
- *Executives and leaders receive personal negative consequences for violations of ethics policies and codes.*
- *Clear and explicit rules have been defined for ethical behavior.*
- *The rules have been effectively communicated to all levels and types of employees.*
- *Policies and procedures are in place to ensure adequate fiscal resources are available to the organization to meet its obligations.*
- *There are personal consequences to executives for poor judgments and decisions regarding fiscal resources.*
- *A corporate compliance officer exists and reports directly to the board of directors or outside governing body.*
- *Accountability for ethical behavior lies with the employees and managers of the organization, not the ethics/compliance officer/department.*
- *The organization is transparent in its approach to communicating with the press, employees, shareholders, and other important stakeholders.*

- *The organization employs a systematic approach to keep auditors and reviewers honest and objective.*
- *There is no evidence found of collusion with auditors or reviewers.*
- *Employees at all levels receive regular feedback on how their behavior and decisions comply with ethics codes, laws, and policies.*
- *Communication to shareholders and other important stakeholders is frequent, honest, complete, and easy to understand.*

1.2a(2) How do you evaluate the PERFORMANCE of your SENIOR LEADERS, including the chief executive? How do you evaluate the PERFORMANCE of members of your GOVERNANCE board, as appropriate? How do SENIOR LEADERS and your GOVERNANCE board use these PERFORMANCE reviews to further develop and to improve both their personal leadership EFFECTIVENESS and that of your board and LEADERSHIP SYSTEM, as appropriate?

N3. Leadership performance evaluation (1.2a[2]) might be supported by peer reviews, formal performance management reviews (5.1b), and formal or informal workforce and other stakeholder feedback and surveys. For some nonprofit and government organizations, external advisory boards might evaluate the performance of senior leaders and the governance board.

What They're Looking for Here

This series of questions asks about how you assess the performance of all leaders of the organization, including your own executives and board members. A client I mentioned earlier, the Santa Clara Valley Water District, has defined an explicit set of outcomes that are used by the Board of Supervisors to evaluate the performance of the CEO. These "ends" policies all focus on organizational outcomes, and cover a broad range of performance areas, including fiscal, environmental, employees, community, and other factors. The CEO shares responsibility for the outcomes with his direct reports and includes these factors in their performance assessment. The most important factor to communicate about your approach is that executives and outside boards are evaluated on a balanced set of performance metrics and goals. It is also important that there are no inconsistencies in the evaluation factors of the different groups. Remember to fully explain how you ensure integrity in the evaluation. The water district does this by specifying specific outcomes that must be accomplished, so there is very little subjectivity in the assessment process. Another important point to address is who performs the evaluation of the board: If they evaluate the CEO and other executives, who evaluates them?

The criteria also ask about how the assessment/evaluation data are used by both executives and board members to improve their effectiveness. Along with an explanation of how this is done, it is crucial to include a few examples of changes that have been made based on evaluations of executives or board members.

Indicators for Question 1.2a(2)

- *Executives are evaluated on a balanced set of performance measures that are consistent with the metrics identified in section 4.1 of the application.*

- *Performance measures all include targets or goals and those targets are based on comparative and historical data, as opposed to being set arbitrarily.*

- *There is consistency in the factors used to assess the performance of all executives.*

- *Assessment of executive performance includes the viewpoints of shareholders, employees, and other stakeholders/partners.*

- *There are a clear set of performance expectations set for board members.*

- *Board members are consistently and fairly evaluated against expectations by an objective party such as an auditor or even the public.*

- *There is strong evidence that improvements have been made by both executives and board members based on the feedback from evaluations.*

AREA TO ADDRESS   [APPROACH, DEPLOYMENT]

1.2b Legal and ETHICAL BEHAVIOR

(1) HOW do you address any adverse impacts on society of your products, services, and operations? HOW do you anticipate public concerns with current and future products, services, and operations? HOW do you prepare for these concerns in a proactive manner, including using resource-sustaining PROCESSES, as appropriate? What are your KEYcompliance PROCESSES, MEASURES, and GOALS for achieving and surpassing regulatory and legal requirements, as appropriate? What are your KEY PROCESSES, MEASURES, and GOALS for addressing risks associated with your products, services, and operations?

N7. Nonprofit organizations should report in 1.2b(1), as appropriate, how they address the legal and regulatory requirements and standards that govern fundraising and lobbying activities.

What They're Looking for Here

This broad set of questions begins by asking about how you do research on your products and services to identify potential negative impacts on either the consumers of your products/services or society. Your answer is likely to sound like everyone else's, so you need to be specific in explaining how your approach is more thorough and responsible than is required by law, and is superior to your competitors. Some companies wait for a disaster to happen, and then deal with it; other companies anticipate public sentiment and risks and make changes in a proactive fashion. McDonald's, for example, has always been a pioneer in addressing these issues before any of its competitors. McDonald's was the first to offer recyclable packaging, outlaw smoking in all its restaurants, offer healthier food choices, and eliminate the super size items from menus. Cigarette companies have a more reactive approach and have only recently been trying to address the problem of children who begin smoking at age 10 or 12 and are hooked by the time they become teenagers.

The challenge in doing well at addressing public concerns is that they often have an adverse impact on company financial results. Pulling a prescription drug off the market might cost millions in sales, and waiting to release a product until you're sure it's safe might allow a competitor to gain a large market advantage. Acknowledging the impact of risk assessment on organizational results is an important part of your response. Of course, there are often much worse consequences to ignoring risks, but many organizations are driven more by short-term growth and profits than by long-term liability.

The criteria ask about processes for assuring that the organization still has resources to deal with possible adverse actions. For example, a class action lawsuit against a prescription drug company might be enough to put a company out of business, if it does not have adequate insurance and reserves to deal with such disasters.

The next part of this set of questions asks a series of more general questions about how you ensure compliance with laws and regulations. You might begin by listing the organizations that regulate your company. This should be followed by a description of processes to ensure compliance, measures, targets, and goals. This information ideally would be presented in a table that summarizes the requested data. The final question asks for the same categories of information (processes, measures, targets, goals) that depict your approach for assessing risks associated with your products and services.

Examiners will be looking for a comprehensive and systematic approach that includes valid measures, targets, and control strategies. As with all criteria that ask about approaches, it is a good idea to provide an example or two to show how well you assess product/service risks and address them with appropriate action plans.

Indicators For Question 1.2b(1)

- *Evidence exists of a thorough and objective approach for researching possible hazards associated with the organization's products/services.*

- *Amount of evidence presented suggests that the applicant leads its competitors in this effort.*

- *Outside resources, where appropriate, are used to conduct research of its products/services.*

- *There is a lack of evidence of cover-ups of important data on risks associated with the organization's products/services.*

- *Regulatory organizations that oversee the organization's performance are identified.*

- *Comprehensiveness of processes and approaches for ensuring legal and regulatory compliance is evident.*

- *A complete list of both leading and lagging metrics has been identified for measuring compliance with ethical and legal standards.*

- *Targets have been set that indicate the organization's desire to go beyond basic laws and regulations in important areas.*

- *Evidence exists of a systematic approach for evaluating processes for conducting research on products/services and related risks.*

- *Number and scope of improvements made over the last few years in approaches for ensuring legal and regulatory compliance is appropriate.*

AREA TO ADDRESS   [APPROACH, DEPLOYMENT]

1.2b Legal and ETHICAL BEHAVIOR

(1) HOWdo you address any adverse impacts on society of your products, services, and operations? HOW do you anticipate public concerns with current and future products, services, and operations? HOW do you prepare for these concerns in a proactive manner, including using resource-sustaining PROCESSES, as appropriate? What are your KEY compliance PROCESSES, MEASURES, and GOALS for achieving and surpassing regulatory and legal requirements, as appropriate? What are your KEY PROCESSES, MEASURES, and GOALS for addressing risks associated with your products, services, and operations?

N7. Nonprofit organizations should report in 1.2b(1), as appropriate, how they address the legal and regulatory requirements and standards that govern fundraising and lobbying activities.

What They're Looking for Here

This portion of the criteria asks about how your organization encourages and promotes ethical behavior from employees. Part of this might involve screening potential new employees for ethics. Ethics are kind of difficult to teach if a person coming in the door doesn't have any. Employee orientation is also the proper place to do some ethics training. Most ethics training is dry and boring, but it doesn't need to be. Sandia Laboratories hired Dilbert creator Scott Adams to create an ethics training program built around a board game. Employees were not only entertained during the training, they remembered the lessons they learned. In spite of all of your good up-front efforts to encourage ethical behavior, there need to be some monitoring and consequences in place. Ensure that your response to this question addresses both antecedents and consequences in your approach.

The criteria in this question also ask about how you measure the effectiveness of your ethics/governance system. Leading indicators might include metrics like test scores from ethics training, the percentage of employees who "passed" ethics training, or employee knowledge of rules and policies. Lagging indicators could include number of calls to a phone line to report unethical behavior, the seriousness of the violations reported, and amount of evidence supporting allegations. Other metrics might be the number of employees disciplined or fired for unethical behavior, or number receiving rewards/recognition for behavior that is consistent with ethics guidelines. The final question in this section asks how you deal with breaches of ethical behavior. In other words, what do you do when someone is caught behaving inappropriately? The typical answer will be a progressive disciplinary process starting with a verbal warning, and then a series of more severe consequences. It is important to address how this system is used for executives, who are often immune from punishment for unethical behavior.

Indicators for Question 1.2b

- *Potential new employees are screened for possible ethics problems.*
- *Current and potential suppliers/partners are evaluated based upon their ethics.*
- *New employees are exposed to a clear set of the organization's ethics as part of their orientation program.*
- *All employees receive refresher training on ethics on a periodic basis.*
- *Ethics training is made interesting and relevant for employees.*
- *Systems are in place to monitor behavior of suppliers and employees for ethics.*
- *Consequences for unethical behavior are severe and consistently implemented.*
- *There is a hotline or mechanism for reporting ethics violations.*
- *Measures assessing the effectiveness of governance programs include leading indicators such as training effectiveness, as opposed to useless metrics like attendance at ethics training.*
- *Specific targets or goals have been set for all metrics that are used to assess the performance of the ethics/governance system.*
- *Lagging indicators are identified and tracked on a regular basis, which look at factors such as number of employees being disciplined for unethical behavior, number recognized for ethical behavior, ethics problems uncovered by the media, whistle-blower events,*

and employee opinions on the extent to which executives follow the code of ethics in the organization.

AREA TO ADDRESS   [APPROACH, DEPLOYMENT]

1.2c. Support of KEY Communities

HOW does your organization actively support and strengthen your KEY communities? HOW do you identify KEY communities and determine areas of emphasis for organizational involvement and support? What are your KEY communities? How do your SENIOR LEADERS, in concert with your WORKFORCE, contribute to improving these communities?

N5. Areas of community support appropriate for inclusion in 1.2c might include your efforts to strengthen local community services, education, and health; the environment, including collaborative activities to conserve the environment or natural resources; and practices of trade, business, or professional associations.

What They're Looking for Here

This Area to Address looks at two factors. First, it asks for information on what you are doing as a company to be a leader in demonstrating your corporate citizenship and involvement in the communities in which you operate. Second, it asks how you help other organizations in their quality improvement efforts. Sometimes these efforts overlap. For example, Baxter Healthcare, the world's largest manufacturer of medical supplies, held a workshop for area high school principals to teach them about the Baldrige criteria and how they may be applied in educational institutions. Because these principals are from the community surrounding Baxter's corporate offices, it is a community outreach effort. However, because it also involved helping promote total quality, it qualifies for the second half of this Area to Address as well. It is important that you are proactive and think strategically about the causes you choose to support. Many big companies are completely reactive, waiting for charities and community groups to ask for money and time. Writing a lot of checks will not get you a good score here. Think of Ronald McDonald House—the charity that McDonald's created to help parents with sick children. The money the company spends helps parents and kids all over the world, but it also helps promote McDonald's image.

A good way of responding to this area to address is to summarize in chart form the activities you engage in that make you a good corporate citizen. A sample of a portion of such a chart is shown in the example on the next page.

In presenting information on the activities you engage in that make you a good corporate citizen, it may be helpful to provide some comparative data to help illustrate the

ORGANIZATION	DESCRIPTION	NOTEWORTHY ACCOMPLISHMENTS
OPAR	Organization that funds and promotes AIDS research	• CFO is chairman • Company donated $50,000 in 2004 • Meetings held at company facilities • Employees donated over 20,000 hours and $30,000 in 2004
Portage Works Project	Workshop run by the mentally challenged	• All major mailings done by PWP • PWP one of our certified suppliers • Work from our company pays salaries of nine individuals from PWP
Juvenile Diabetes Foundation	Charitable organization for children with diabetes	• CEO is on the board • Company sponsors fundraising banquet each year, devoting many hours and dollars • Prepare all print advertising free for JDF • Company donates over $50,000 each year to JDF

importance of your accomplishments. For example, if your company donated $80,000 per quarter in 2007 to the United Fund, through employee contributions, and you have 18,000 employees, that works out to less than $5.00 per employee. The Baldrige examiners may not know whether this is exceptional, average, or below par. Therefore, you might mention that for companies your size, it is typical for employees to average $3.20 per quarter in donations to the United Fund. This makes your performance look much better than that of the average company.

This Area to Address also asks about how you seek to enhance your leadership in corporate citizenship. Again, the worst thing to do is to present a general statement such as: "Our company continues to review and improve our approaches to corporate citizenship and promotion of community involvement, and hopes to continually enhance our leadership position in these areas in the coming years." Most examiners would read a statement like this and write a comment such as: "It is not clear how the company plans to seek and exploit opportunities for improving its leadership in the areas of corporate citizenship." You need to get specific and explain how you intend to do this, and what your specific goals for leadership are in these areas.

Indicators for Question 1.2c

- *Evidence of a planned systematic approach to charitable/community support.*

- *Breadth and scope of activities that indicate that the company is a good corporate citizen and concerned with the public welfare.*

- *Significance of the company's accomplishments in these areas.*

- *Evidence from news media and outside sources that the company is, in fact, a good corporate citizen.*

- *Comparison of the corporate citizenship and public responsibility activities of the applicant company to other companies that are similar in size.*

- *Evidence that the company has increased its efforts to be a good corporate citizen over the last few years.*

- *Awards and recognition received for efforts in this area.*

- *Lack of any "skeletons in the closet" that might prevent a company from being a good role model for the United States and the world. (If the issue is serious enough, it could completely disqualify an applicant.)*

Chapter

7

Interpreting the Criteria for Strategic Planning (2)

OVERVIEW OF THE STRATEGIC PLANNING CATEGORY

Category 2 addresses the area of strategic business planning. The criteria in Category 2 focus on how the organization develops short- and longer-term business plans. Although it is only worth 85 points, your responses to this section can help or hurt your scores in other sections. Not having a good plan will probably dramatically impact your business results in section 7, which are worth 45 percent of the points.

The 2008 Award Criteria Booklet defines this category as follows:

> *The Strategic Planning Category examines how your organization develops strategic objectives and action plans. Also examined are how your chosen strategic objectives and action plans are deployed and changed if circumstances require, and how progress is measured. (p. 18)*

This category is purposely vague about how a company needs to do strategic planning, because approaches may differ widely between a big corporation and a very small organization. The small organization is unlikely to have a formal strategic planning process and document, whereas the big corporation probably has many plan documents for its different businesses and has a much more structured approach to planning. As with any item that asks about your approach in Baldrige, what's important is that you tailor your approach to what's appropriate for your company or organization. A company with 25 employees that has a long and structured approach to planning with many levels of goals, objectives, and strategies may end up with a low score because its approach is overkill for a business of its size.

This Category is divided into Examination Items:

    2.1 Strategy Development (40 points)

    2.2 Strategy Deployment (45 points)

Following are the descriptions of each of the two Examination Items and the Areas to Address that fall under them. As before, each section here begins with a shadowed box, containing the Examination Item, the point value, and any applicable Notes.* Areas to Address falling under that item follow in a lighter shadowed box. In the upper right corner of each Area to Address box is an indication [in brackets] of whether the Area pertains to approach, deployment, or results. All definitions and information appearing within these boxes are taken directly from the Baldrige criteria. Following each area to address is an explanation defining what the examiners are looking for in assessing your application. Next, I have supplied a list of indicators or evaluation factors that will assist you in interpreting the criteria and in preparing your application.

---

* Item Notes that apply to a specific Area to Address are appropriately listed in the box containing that Area.

2.1 STRATEGY DEVELOPMENT: PROCESS
How do you develop your strategy?(40 PTS.)

Describe HOW your organization determines its STRATEGIC CHALLENGES and advantages. Describe HOW your organization establishes its strategy and STRATEGIC OBJECTIVES to address these CHALLENGES and enhance its advantages. Summarize your organization's KEY STRATEGIC OBJECTIVES and their related GOALS.

N1. "Strategy development" refers to your organization's approach (formal or informal) to preparing for the future. Strategy development might utilize various types of forecasts, projections, options, scenarios, knowledge (see 4.2b for relevant organizational knowledge), or other approaches to envisioning the future for purposes of decision making and resource allocation. Strategy development might involve participation by key suppliers, distributors, partners, and customers. For some nonprofit organizations, strategy development might involve participation by organizations providing similar services or drawing from the same donor population or volunteer workforce.

N2. "Strategy" should be interpreted broadly. Strategy might be built around or lead to any or all of the following: new products, services, and markets; revenue growth via various approaches, including acquisitions, grants, and endowments; divestitures; new partnerships and alliances; and new employee or volunteer relationships. Strategy might be directed towardbecoming a preferred supplier, a local supplier in each of your major customers' or partners' markets, a low-cost producer, a market innovator, or a high-end or customized product or service provider. It also might be directed toward meeting a community or public need.

N6. Item 2.1 addresses your overall organizational strategy, which might include changes in services, products, and product lines. However, the Item does not address product or service design; you should address these factors in Item 6.1, as appropriate.

AREA TO ADDRESS   [APPROACH, DEPLOYMENT]
2.1a Strategy Development Process

(1)Howdoes your organization conduct its strategic planning? What arethe KEY PROCESS steps? Who are the KEY participants? HOW does your PROCESS identify potential blind spots? HOW do you determine your STRATEGIC CHALLENGES and advantages, as identified in response to P.2 in your Organizational Profile? What are your short- and longer-term planning time horizons? HOW are these time horizons set? HOW does your strategic planning PROCESS address these time horizons?

What They're Looking for Here

How you answer this question should be fairly obvious. A graphic or flowchart that shows four to six major phases in your planning process is an effective first step. I've seen some with so many arrows, boxes, and feedback loops that it only conveys confusion. Make sure your diagram is simple and logical. Although there are certainly variations, most good planning models I've seen contain the following phases in the following sequence:

A simple and logical process like the one above will win more points than one that looks like an electrical diagram. Following the planning process graphic, you might want to describe each planning phase in a few sentences. Keep in mind that there are other questions to be answered in this section, so don't spend four pages describing the planning process. The process is not nearly as important as the plan itself.

It is important that you show that you have a systematic approach, but also that your planning process is efficient. Many large corporations have systematic approaches to strategic and annual operating plan development. However, most of these same companies spend far too much time and money developing and rewriting plans, and far too little time using them for managing. Plans go through seven or eight drafts until they are finally approved by senior management and then they are put away in file drawers until it becomes time to begin writing next year's plans. I heard a story about the new CEO of Kodak who was horrified when he first took over the company, and found out that it took about 24 weeks each year to write the company's annual business plans. He set a goal that the plans had to be written and approved in 12 weeks the next year, and 4 weeks the following year. Four weeks is a reasonable amount of time to spend writing an annual business plan.

In your application, you need to get across the idea that your planning process is very thorough but also very efficient. I worked with a small shipping company in Long Beach,

California, that won the California version of the Baldrige Award a few years ago and received a site visit from Baldrige the following year. A couple of years ago they did not do strategic planning, even though they were an amazingly successful company. They had figured out a good market niche for themselves and did an outstanding job on all measures of performance, including both profits and customer satisfaction. They simply had never bothered writing a formal strategic plan. Even a small company like this needs to do some planning, which they did. However, you can bet they don't spend six months writing the plan, and they actually use it to manage with.

A new question for 2007 asks about how your organization identifies its strategic challenges and competitive advantages. The difficult part of identifying strategic challenges is acknowledging your own weaknesses. Most organizations I've worked with are much better at identifying their strengths than their weaknesses or challenges. Your answer to this question should include an explanation of how you ensure objectivity and realism in this process. You might also explain how you begin with a long list of challenges and narrow the list down to a reasonable number of three to five factors that could have a major impact on your business. For example, a strategic challenge faced by some major corporations today is obligations to retired employees for pensions and healthcare benefits. It is also important that you explain the process used to identify your major competencies or strategic advantages. These are factors that are major strengths of the organization that are typically hard for competitors to copy. For example, a major strength of a company like Southwest Airlines is its culture of engaged employees who enjoy their jobs. Other airlines have struggled trying to create the Southwest culture.

Indicators for Question 2.1a(1)

- *Evidence exists of a planning process that is systematic and appropriate for the organization's size and complexity.*

- *There is evidence that the planning process is efficient and done over several weeks rather than many months.*

- *Planning covers a wide variety of functions besides financials: customers/markets, products/services, human resources, research and development, etc.*

- *The process for identifying competitive advantages and strategic challenges or weaknesses is the objective.*

- *There is evidence that the process is free from politics.*

- *Each year the plan focuses on a few (three to five) strategic challenges rather than a long list.*

- *Valid evidence exists to support strategic advantages.*

- *Goal or target setting is done in a scientific fashion.*
- *Potential blind spots in the planning process are identified and eliminated.*
- *The planning process is flexible, allowing for changes to be made throughout the year as the business environment changes.*

2.1a(2) HOW do you ensure that strategic planning addresses the KEY factors listed below? HOW do you collect and analyze relevant data and information pertaining to these factors as part of your strategic planning PROCESS:
  - your organization's strengths, weaknesses, opportunities, and threats
  - early indications of major shifts in technology, markets, Customer preferences, competition, or the regulatory environment
  - long-term organizational Sustainability
  - your ability to execute the strategic plan

N3. Your organization's strengths, weaknesses, opportunities, and threats (2.1a[2]) should address all factors that are key to your organization's future success, including the following, as appropriate: your customer and market needs, expectations, and opportunities; your opportunities for innovation and role model performance; your core competencies; your competitive environment and your performance relative to competitors and comparable organizations; your product life cycle; technological and other key innovations or changes that might affect your products and services and how you operate, as well as the rate of that innovation; your human and other resource needs; your ability to capitalize on diversity; your opportunities to redirect resources to higher-priority products, services, or areas; financial, societal, ethical, regulatory, technological, security, and other potential risks; your ability to prevent and respond to emergencies, including natural or other disasters; changes in the national or global economy; partner and supply chain needs, strengths, and weaknesses; changes in your parent organization; and other factors unique to your organization.

N4. Your ability to execute the strategic plan (2.1a[2]) should address your ability to mobilize the necessary resources and knowledge. It also should address your organizational agility based on contingency plans or if circumstances require a shift in plans and rapid execution of new or changed plans.

What They're Looking for Here

Once you have defined your overall planning process, you need to go into some detail on the specific types of data that are collected in the situation analysis phase of the planning process, and talk about how these data are used to set goals and develop strategies.

The first bullet asks about how you evaluate and consider your own strengths and weaknesses as part of the planning process. Many applicants use the Baldrige model as the template for assessing their strengths and weaknesses. In fact, many companies today use the Baldrige assessment process to identify their own strengths and weaknesses, and they make this one of the steps in their overall strategic planning process. It is important that the Baldrige evaluation not be a separate evaluation, but that it is integrated into the way the company does its planning. This bullet also asks about how you assess your human resource strengths and weaknesses. Section 5 of the Baldrige model provides a good set of criteria for assessing your human resources. Assessment of other resources is also addressed in this bullet. Other resources might include capital, facilities, equipment, or even data/information. In discussing your approach to analyzing your own capabilities, you might want to identify what you think your core competencies or strengths are. Your write-up might also benefit from an example or two that illustrate(s) how understanding your own capabilities has helped you make the right decisions in deciding on business strategies or growth opportunities.

A thorough situation analysis also includes an assessment of risks or threats. Financial risks could include factors such as rising interest rates, poor stock market performance, tightening of credit restrictions, increased expectations from owners/shareholders, or other factors that could have a huge impact on your success. Simply getting access to the capital needed to deploy your new strategy can be a major factor in your success. Other types of risks also need to be discussed. Regulatory or societal risks can play a huge role in a company's success. Public sentiment toward retailers that sell fur coats has made it difficult for some companies to do business. Tobacco companies are facing not only an image problem, but massive lawsuits that could even put them out of business. So far, there is no definitive evidence that cell phone use is linked to brain cancer, but if there ever was such a link found, it could forever change the cell phone business, and cell phones might become the new cigarettes. They are already banned in many restaurants and airport lounges. Other types of risks should also be discussed, as appropriate for your industry.

The second bullet asks about how you assess what is happening externally, and how it might impact your organization and its ability to achieve its goals. Technology can have a major impact on even low-tech organizations, and can make a big difference in your strategy. The entire telecommunications industry is still going through a major shake-up because of changes in technology that allow people to use the Internet and cell phones, rather than traditional land lines, to make phone calls. The ability of individuals to download music from the Internet is having a major impact on the music industry. Leading organizations do a good job of looking at trends in technology and anticipate how new technologies might help or hurt their business. Your answer should explain how you keep tabs on technological trends and how this information is communicated to the right people to ensure that it is considered during planning.

This second bullet also asks about how you keep up with changes in customer or market demands and competitor strategies. You might refer to section 3.1 where you discuss methods of doing market research on customer needs and market trends and explain how this data is fed into the planning process. It is also important to have an ongoing process for gathering competitive intelligence. My experience is that the smaller and medium-sized organizations do a better job than the market leaders. The medium or small company is always watching their big competitors and keeping track of their strategies. The market leaders tend to be less concerned with smaller competitors who come along and take away their market share. Sears is a great example of a company that did not do enough to keep up with competitors such as Wal-Mart and Target. In 1992, Sears was a $50 billion company. Fourteen years later they were bought by K-Mart for $11.5 billion. Often the most important competitors to watch are the new smaller organizations, not the big two or three with whom you always compete.

The final topic in this bullet asks about how you keep up with changes in regulations and laws that might impact your organization. This factor might actually give you a strategic advantage. Cargill's Sunny Fresh Eggs, a former Baldrige winner, was one of the first companies to meet the new more stringent food safety regulations that came out some years ago. This strategy helped Cargill win a contract to supply McDonald's with eggs.

The third bullet in 2.1a(2) asks about how your planning process addresses the long-term sustainability of the organization. In other words, how are you going to ensure that your company or organization is around and still successful 10 or 20 years from now? Keep in mind that the criteria in 2.1a do not ask what your strategies are for sustainability, but how you do this kind of planning.

The fourth and final bullet in this question asks about how you accurately and honestly assess your ability to achieve your goals and strategies. This is probably the part of the planning process that is done most poorly—especially in large successful corporations and other big organizations. The culture of most of these organizations is often one of arrogance and infallibility, and it is a rare individual that would challenge the ability of the organization to pull off one of its chosen strategies. We've seen many large organizations embark on new business ventures and strategies that clearly appear destined for failure to outsiders, but no one inside the company is willing to acknowledge the organization's slim chance of success. Everyone is taught to remain upbeat, positive, and optimistic. Money and other resources are dumped into the new strategy even though many employees have a strong feeling that the strategy will fail. Your answer to this final bullet in 2.1a(2) should address both the formal processes you have in place for doing risk assessments and capability analyses of your strategies, and also the cultural aspects. In other words, how do you encourage people to be critical and challenge new ideas and strategies, and balance this with a need to take risks and be innovative? This is one of the most difficult parts of the planning process.

Indicators for Question 2.1a(2)

- *The Baldrige model is used to assess and categorize strengths and weaknesses as part of the planning process.*

- *Degree to which quality and customer satisfaction goals, strategies, and issues are addressed in the long-term strategic business plan for the company/organization.*

- *Evidence that customer requirements are thoroughly identified and that this information is used in developing goals and plans for the organization.*

- *Quality and customer satisfaction goals are based upon current and future quality requirements of customers in key markets, as well as projections of changes in customer requirements.*

- *Goals and strategies are developed based upon performance of major competitors in target markets.*

- *Credibility of evidence that economic and market trends are considered as part of the planning process.*

- *A logical and systematic process is used to make decisions on strategies and allocate resources appropriately.*

- *Availability of data on the capabilities of all important processes and technologies in the organization.*

- *Evidence that process and technology capabilities/limitations are taken into consideration when developing long- and short-term plans and goals.*

- *Extent to which supplier data are used as an input to the planning process.*

- *Degree to which the future competitive environment is addressed in the plan.*

- *Evidence that financial, market, and societal risks are considered in the development of goals and strategies.*

- *Evidence that technology is thoroughly reviewed and that technological issues are considered during the development of strategies.*

- *Evidence of systemic risk analysis being done as part of the planning process.*

- *Evidence that changes in laws and regulations are thoroughly researched and fed into the planning process.*

- *A systematic process exists that addresses the long-term sustainability of the organization, as well as shorter-term goals.*
- *The planning process includes contingency planning for emergencies and disasters.*
- *There are systematic processes in place for objectively evaluating the ability of the organization to achieve its chosen strategies—especially new products, services, or business ventures.*
- *Review processes are in place to assess the feasibility of selected strategies.*
- *Processes are in place to ensure objectivity in assessments of the organization's ability to achieve goals and strategies.*

AREA TO ADDRESS   [APPROACH, DEPLOYMENT]
2.1b Strategic Objectives

(1) What are your KEY STRATEGIC OBJECTIVES and your timetable for accomplishing them? What are your most important GOALS for these STRATEGIC OBJECTIVES?

What They're Looking for Here

This portion of the criteria does not ask about how you do planning; it asks what your plans are. In the Organizational Profile section, you should have identified your vision. It might bear repeating it here, or simply referring the reader back to the appropriate page. Following a discussion of your overall vision, you need to specify the key success factors or goals that will need to be achieved to accomplish your vision. When Continental Airlines wrote their vision: "Worst to First," they also identified some key success factors to help them achieve this vision: 1. fly to win, 2. fund the future, 3. make reliability a reality, and 4. work together. These might sound vague to the reader, but each one was explicitly defined, and performance measures and targets were set for each key success factor. By the time the year 2000 came and went, Continental had achieved its vision, and was rated as the number one airline in the United States for customer satisfaction by J.D. Power. Continental's stock price more than triple what it was six years before, profits were healthy, and the company was listed as one of the 25 best companies to work for in America by Fortune Magazine in 2000. After September 11, 2001, Continental and most other U.S. airlines had to rethink their plans and focus more on staying in business.

In explaining your key success factors, strategic objectives, or whatever you call them, make sure that they are not too generic. I review a lot of strategic plans of big corporations and government organizations and I see a lot of strategic objectives such as: become employer of choice, provide value-added products/services to customers, growth in market share, building relationships with important customers, partnering with suppliers, etc. These are some of the basic elements of any successful organization, and they sound very generic. Examiners want to know exactly what you must concentrate on to achieve your vision. The criteria also ask about specific goals or targets you might have set. These goals and targets should be measurable, linked back to the key performance metrics listed in 1.1 or 4.1 of the application, and show evidence that they were set in a scientific fashion. Targets should never be set arbitrarily. These are easy to spot because they are often nice round numbers like 10 percent improvement, or 90 percent customer satisfaction. Targets should be based on past performance, resource constraints, competitor/benchmark performance, and customer requirements. I've seen other applications where the annual and longer-term targets were listed in a chart along with the performance metrics in item 4.1 of the application. You could also put this chart in either 2.1 here, or in 2.2 where you identify your strategies/action plans. It probably makes the most sense to include it in section 2.2. Several example formats are presented in the section that follows. It is a mystery to me why the authors of the criteria chose to separate the targets from the action plans, but that does not mean that you can't put the answers in one section. Wherever you choose to put it, I think it is wise to put the metrics, annual targets, and longer term targets all on one chart.

Indicators for Question 2.1b(1)

- *Specific key success factors or strategic objectives have been identified and they link back to the vision.*

- *The strategic objectives are specific to your organization and its future vision, as opposed to being generic.*

- *Metrics have been identified for the strategic objectives or key success factors.*

- *There is evidence that a variety of information was considered in selecting key success factors or strategic objectives.*

- *There are no more than five key success factors or strategic objectives.*

- *Focus on the key success factors or objectives identified here will likely lead to the achievement of the vision.*

- *Specific measurable targets have been set for all performance measures identified in either items 1.1 or 4.1.*

- *Targets show evidence of being based on research rather than arbitrary numbers.*

- *Annual and longer-term targets are set for all performance metrics.*

- *Metrics and targets are linked back to overall mission and strategic objectives/vision.*

- *Strategic objectives or success factors show evidence of refinement or change as the business environment or company strategy has changed over the past few years.*

2.1b(2) How do your STRATEGIC objectives address your STRATEGIC CHALLENGES and strategic advantages? How do your STRATEGIC OBJECTIVES address your opportunities for INNOVATION in products and services, operations, and the business model? How do you ensure that your STRATEGIC OBJECTIVES balance short- and longer-term challenges and opportunities? How do you ensure that your STRATEGIC OBJECTIVES balance the needs of all KEY STAKEHOLDERS?

N5. Strategic objectives that address key challenges and advantages (2.1b[2]) might include rapid response, customization, co-location with major customers or partners, workforce capability and capacity, specific joint ventures, virtual manufacturing, rapid innovation, ISO 9000:2000 or ISO 14000 registration, Web-based supplier and customer relationship management, and product and service quality enhancements. Responses to Item 2.1 should focus on your specific challenges and advantages—those most important to your ongoing success and to strengthening your organization's overall performance.

What They're Looking for Here

This question is mostly about linkages to other sections. First of all, it asks how your plan links to the challenges faced by your organization. This is often a disconnect. Challenges and advantages described in the Organizational Profile section need to be linked to goals and strategies in your plan. In other words, you need to explain how you propose to deal with these threats and challenges as well as further capitalize on your strengths or competitive advantages. The third question asks about the balance between short and longer-term plans, and how goals and strategies are developed for both. Finally, the last question asks for evidence that your plans are balanced across the needs of your various stakeholders. If your scorecard or list of metrics from section 1.1 is well balanced, there should be a balanced set of goals and strategies in this section. The link here is to make sure that for each measure listed in 1.1, there are appropriate goals and strategies or action plans in this section. Many companies have unbalanced strategic plans, with the majority of the focus on financial results, and very little on customers, employees, suppliers, and other stakeholders.

Indicators for Question 2.1b(2)

- *All of the challenges and advantages described in the Organizational Profile section are covered by objectives and strategies/action plans.*

- *The strategies/action plans to address the threats/challenges and competitive advantages sound like they would be successful.*
- *There are about an equal number of objectives and strategies for the various stakeholders (e.g., shareholders, customers, employees, and others).*
- *There is very tight linkage between the metrics or scorecard described in item 1.1 and the objectives and strategies in the plan.*

2.2 STRATEGY DEPLOYMENT   PROCESS
How do you deploy your strategy? (45 PTS.)

Describe HOW your organization converts its STRATEGIC OBJECTIVES into ACTION plans. Summarize your organization's ACTION PLANS and related KEY PERFORMANCE MEASURES or INDICATORS. Project your organization's future PERFORMANCE relative to KEY comparisons on these PERFORMANCE MEASURES or INDICATORS.

N1. Strategy and action plan development and deployment are closely linked to other Items in the Criteria. The following are examples of key linkages:
- Item 1.1 for how your senior leaders set and communicate organizational direction;
- Category 3 for gathering customer and market knowledge as input to your strategy and action plans and for deploying action plans;
- Category 4 for measurement, analysis, and knowledge management to support your key information needs, to support your development of strategy, to provide an effective basis for your performance measurements, and to track progress relative to your strategic objectives and action plans;
- Category 5 for meeting your workforce capability and capacity needs, for workforce development and learning system design and needs, and for implementing workforce-related changes resulting from action plans;
- Category 6 for changes to work systems and work process requirements resulting from your action plans; and
- Item 7.6 for specific accomplishments relative to your organizational strategy and action plans.

AREA TO ADDRESS   [APPROACH, DEPLOYMENT]

2.2a ACTION PLAN Development and DEPLOYMENT

(1) HOW do you develop and DEPLOY ACTION PLANS throughout the organization to achieve your KEY STRATEGIC OBJECTIVES? HOW do you ensure that the KEY outcomes of your ACTION PLANS can be sustained?

N2. Deployment of action plans (2.2a[1]) might include key partners, collaborators, and suppliers.

What They're Looking for Here

This question in the criteria asks how you figure out the strategies that will be used to achieve your objectives. Often there are many different approaches that can and should be considered in developing a strategic plan. This is actually the most difficult part of the planning process, because you have to figure out exactly how you are going to accomplish all these lofty goals or objectives you have set for yourself. It is important that you describe some sort of systematic decision-making process for generating ideas and evaluating them against specific criteria like cost, risk, and likelihood for success. Explain how you evaluate each alternative and make a decision on the best course of action, and provide a few examples, if possible, of actions that were considered before deciding on the final strategy. Your answer to this initial question in 2.2a should not require much more than a paragraph or two to answer.

This question also asks how plans are deployed. In other words, how do you take the overall goals for the company and cascade them down to different units, functions, and areas of the organization? Again, a graphic might help show this cascading process. The key is to illustrate that plans at all levels are linked, so that every employee is working toward the common goals of the entire organization. Every employee needs to understand how his or her job contributes to the company's vision and strategic plan.

If appropriate, you might also write about how plans and goals are communicated to suppliers, so they can help you achieve your own goals. Often this is an area where disconnects are found. Not only should you explain how goals are linked to the formation of supplier requirements, but you might want to provide a few examples.

It is also important that you explain how process reengineering or process improvement efforts are linked to the overall goals in the business plan. One way that former Baldrige winner AT&T Transmission Systems does this is by identifying what they call: "The 10 Most Wanted." These are the 10 process improvement efforts that are underway in the company at any one time. Each of the 10 most wanted is linked to strategic business goals, and only 10 projects are going at any one time, to help ensure that process improvement efforts are not too disjointed. Companies that tell every employee to go off and improve their processes frequently find that this leads to chaos, and the improvements in one area cause problems in others. Process improvement efforts need to be prioritized and channeled. Linking them to the strategic business plan is the way to do this.

Many organizations do a commendable job creating strategic business plans, but few do a good job translating those plans into actions throughout the year. The plans are written, reviewed, and often end up in a file drawer until the end of the year or until a periodic review meeting occurs. This section of the application should describe the mechanisms and systems you have in place to ensure that plans do not remain in file drawers but are actually implemented. Explain how plans are reviewed by various levels of employees and translated into individual performance plans. All levels of goals and objectives should be based upon and contribute to the overall plans of the organization.

Your response should explain how plans drive regular and ongoing work activities. Explain how major projects as well as recurring work tasks relate to major business and quality goals. Be as specific as possible, citing an example or two to illustrate that plans really do drive day-to-day activities in your company.

There should be regular review meetings that occur among various levels of employees to review plans, discuss progress toward meeting the goals outlined in the plans, and change/update the plans as necessary. Describe when these meetings occur and who attends. Explain how plans have been revised based upon changing business conditions, changing customer requirements, or other factors. Also, explain what you do when performance is not reaching projected goal levels. Be specific. The examiners are looking for a positive approach rather than a punitive approach. One applicant who received a low score said, "Individuals who are not meeting their goals are talked to and reminded of the consequences to them of not meeting their goals." The mechanism for implementing strategies outlined in organizational plans may consist of projects, priority initiatives, task forces, teams, or other approaches. The specific approach you use is not important. What is important is that you have a clear and workable approach for translating your plans into actions and results. The leadership of the senior executives is critical to the success of implementing the plans.

A question in this Area to Address asks how the improvements that result from your action plans can be sustained. The first part of your answer should explain how frequent monitoring of performance is used to evaluate the success of the action plans. If the data show that the strategy or action plan is able to sustain positive results, no changes are made. If, on the other hand, performance has begun to deteriorate, changes are made to the strategies or action plans to bring performance back in line with targeted levels. This is why it is so important to have performance measures linked to each of the action plans or strategies. It is also important that performance is measured frequently to determine if the desired results are being achieved.

Indicators for Question 2.2a(1)

- *A systematic decision-making process is used to review and select appropriate strategies/action plans.*

- *Approach for deciding on action plan/strategies involves all appropriate personnel.*

- *Action plans are communicated and deployed through the organization to the appropriate personnel in a timely fashion.*

- *Action plans are deployed to suppliers/partners as necessary in a quick and efficient manner.*

- *Strategy/action plan development is done in a timely and efficient manner.*

- *Existence of a well-defined and workable process for deployment of long- and short-term plans in the organization to achieve quality and customer-satisfaction leadership.*

- *Scope of deployment includes all functions and levels of employees in the development of individual improvement plans that support overall plans for the company.*

- *Amount and objectivity of data to suggest that the plan implementation/deployment process is successful in the organization.*

- *Manner of assigning and deploying resources is consistent with long- and short-term goals and priorities.*

- *Evidence that plans are used to direct and control day-to-day work activity in the organization, with management involvement to ensure implementation and follow-up.*

- *Plans are used to make decisions and control actions and priorities in the organization.*

- *Goals and plans are communicated to suppliers and linked to supplier/partner requirements, if appropriate.*

- *Productivity, cycle time, and other process improvement efforts are all linked to the goals and strategies outlined in the strategic plan.*

- *Performance against targets or objectives is frequently monitored.*

- *Changes are made to action plans as necessary to sustain positive results.*

2.2.a(2) HOW do you ensure that adequate financial and other resources are available to support the accomplishment of your ACTION PLANS? HOW do you allocate these resources to support the accomplishment of the plans? HOW do you assess the financial and other risks associated with the plans? HOW do you balance resources to ensure adequate resources to meet current obligations?

What They're Looking for Here

This long series of questions basically asks how you make sure you have enough money, people, and other resources to achieve the goals outlined in your plan. This is a very common reason why goals are not achieved and strategies are not implemented—management fails to provide adequate resources. Organizations often expect that strategies will be carried out by forming committees or teams of people that are already overworked. At the next year's planning meeting, everyone wonders why so few goals or objectives were accomplished when everyone has spent a year working 70-hour weeks. Your answer to this series of questions should explain how the budgeting and planning processes are integrated. Often these are completely separate processes and budgets are established and set in stone before plans and strategies are developed. If there is a separate process for allocating resources for the achievement of strategic goals/objectives, you need to explain how that process works. There should be a feedback loop in the process whereby those responsible for the achievement of the goal can provide feedback to management on the adequacy of the resources provided.

A factor often ignored in the planning process is an assessment of the risks involved in implementing certain strategies or working on major goals. For every goal achieved or strategy implemented, there is some risk or cost that is often not even discussed. A systematic planning process should involve a thorough risk analysis that looks at factors other than financial risks. For example, cutting costs to satisfy a big customer who wants to double his order for next year might result in a decrease in product quality that destroys your company's reputation for premium products.

Your answer to the questions in 2.2a(2) should also address how your organization balances the resources needed for ongoing operations with those needed to achieve the goals and objectives in the strategic plan. What often happens is that operational budgets are cut to find new strategies or initiatives. This may result in poor performance from the bread and butter part of your operation that made you successful in the first place.

Indicators for Question 2.2a(3)

- *Evidence exists that the budgeting and human resource/workforce planning processes are integrated with the strategic planning process.*
- *The process for allocating resources for achievement of goals/strategic objectives is quick and efficient.*
- *The resource allocation process includes a feedback loop.*
- *Major strategies are achieved by allocating dedicated resources rather than by forming teams or committees of people that are already busy with other work.*
- *Each objective or goal is assigned a single owner or person responsible for its accomplishment.*
- *A thorough risk analysis is conducted for each major goal and strategy in the strategic plan before resources are allocated and work is begun.*
- *There is evidence that risk assessments have resulted in changes to the goals or strategies where appropriate.*

> 2.2a(3) HOW do you establish and deploy modified ACTION PLANS if circumstances require a shift in plans and rapid execution of new plans?

What They're Looking for Here

This third question asks about your process for modifying your action plans or strategies when it is clear that they are either not working, or that external events caused a change in your approach. Planning in many large organizations is an annual event. By the time the plan is finally approved, it basically is set for the remainder of the year, regardless of events. No one wants to fish out the plan and bother revising it—especially if it took five drafts and three months to get it approved in the first place. **Planning should not be an annual event.** Planning should be an ongoing process that allows plans to be easily adapted and changed as the situation dictates. Your answer to this question should explain the processes you have in place to make it easy for people to adjust goals and strategies throughout the year, rather than just during an annual planning cycle. Include some examples of changes you have made to goals, targets, strategies, or actions plans over the last few years to provide evidence that planning really is a fluid process, subject to change as needed.

Indicators for Question 2.2a(3)

- *Evidence of a systematic, yet simple, process for modifying goals, targets, and action plans when the need arises.*

- *Controls are still in place to ensure there are proper reviews and approvals before changes are made to plans.*

- *The review/change process is efficient and done quickly.*

- *Revised plans are communicated to all appropriate individuals in a timely manner.*

- *Evidence that the organization has modified its plans throughout the last few years, and that the changes were warranted and appropriate.*

2.2a(4) What are your KEY short- and longer-term ACTION PLANS? What are the KEY planned changes, if any, in your products and services, your CUSTOMERS and markets, and how you will operate?

2.2a(6) What are your KEY PERFORMANCE MEASURES or INDICATORS for tracking progress on your ACTION PLANS? How do you ensure that your overall ACTION PLAN measurement system reinforces organizational ALIGNMENT? How do you ensure that the measurement system covers all KEY DEPLOYMENT areas and STAKEHOLDERS?

What They're Looking for Here

I have combined questions (4) and (6) in one answer because I think it makes sense to discuss them together. This section is essentially asking what your strategic plan is. In the previous item (2.1) you were asked about your overall strategic objectives or key success factors and targets. These two questions ask about how you will measure the success of your strategies, and what the specific action plans are that you plan to use to achieve your vision. All of this information asks about what your plan is, not how you developed it. In the early years of the Baldrige Award, applicants would get a good score if they had what looked like a good plan with the right hierarchy of goals, objectives, measures, and strategies. Not any more. Examiners now look at your plans like a venture capitalist might look at a potential investment. In other words, the substance of your plan is evaluated for the likelihood of success, not for whether you have a plan that looks good on paper, but is unlikely to fly in the real world. Many of the Internet firms that went bankrupt in 2000 had shaky business plans that were based on some very optimistic assumptions. It is important that you convey the right hierarchy of goals, measures, and strategies, but the substance of the plan and the likelihood that your strategies will be successful is more important than anything else.

An easy way to answer these two questions is to use charts or tables to summarize your plans rather than try to describe them in narrative terms. Several examples follow of effective formats I have seen in response to this section.

You would fill out the table or chart with all of your key objectives or success factors, and list the associated measures/metrics and strategies. You will not have the space to go into detail on the strategies, so simply listing them and showing a good link back to the objectives is all that is necessary.

GOAL	METRICS	STRATEGIES/ACTIONS
International Market Growth	• $ in sales from international customers	• Acquire new distributors
	• % international revenue	• Sales offices
	• # of international proposals submitted	• Targeted proposals to select prospects
Customized Products	• Increased loyalty from targeted customers	• Small batches
		• Improved knowledge of customer requests
	• $ in revenue from customized products	• Joint R&D with customer

Another approach to creating a chart that summarizes your strategic plan is to also include specific short- and longer-term targets or goals for each of your performance metrics linked to your overall objectives. A chart like this might take up an entire page, and have the following headings:

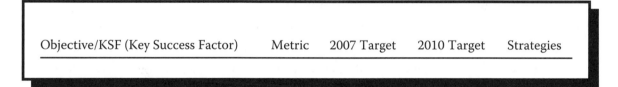

Objective/KSF (Key Success Factor)	Metric	2007 Target	2010 Target	Strategies

How much detail you put into this section will depend upon the level of detail in your strategic plan, and the space limitations of a couple of pages for each item in section 2, Strategic Planning.

Another approach to writing this section is to also include your overall performance metrics and appropriate long- and short-term targets and strategies in this section. In many organizations, there is not a separate set of organizational measures and targets. I realize that information on your organizational scorecard is asked for in Item 4.1, but it may be practical to put all of this information here because the planning and metrics sections are so closely linked. Somehow, you need to make the distinction between strategic metrics and targets, and those that cover business fundamentals like customer satisfaction, employee morale, or profits. One applicant simply used an asterisk and a number to code the metrics/targets that link back to specific key success factors or strategic objectives. An example of a portion of such a chart is shown below.

EXAMPLE STRATEGIC PLAN SUMMARY				
METRICS	KSF (Key Success Factor) LINK	'07 TARGET	'10 TARGET	STRATEGIES
CUSTOMER				
Cust. Sat. Index	No	78/100	86/100	• Key account selling
$ in Lost Accounts	No	<6%	<4%	• Improved communication • Better selection of targeted customers
Loyalty Index	KSF # 3	56/100	72/100	• Customized products/ standards
FINANCIAL				
Sales	No	$ 1.8 billion	$ 2.4 billion	• Market demand + Improved products
International $	KSF # 1	8%	21%	• Distributor partners • Acquisitions • Targeted proposals

As you can see from the example, some of the measures and targets are basic fundamentals that might be found in many companies. Others are linked to specific key success factors (KSF) such as building increased loyalty from key accounts (KSF # 3) and growth in international sales (KSF # 1). By including a chart with the information shown above, you will summarize on one page much of the information that is asked for in Items 2.2 and 4.1. Any time you can combine answers to multiple items like this is generally beneficial because it saves you space, and it makes the job of the examiners easy by giving them some key charts that summarize a lot of information. You might notice that the Strategies column in the chart is a little vague in defining exactly how the organization will achieve its targets. You might use the text in section 2.2 to expand upon a few of the strategies. You will not have the space to go into much detail, but you want to provide the examiners with enough detail to let them know that you have a well-thought-out strategic plan. They can see all the detail by reviewing your plan in the site visit. Your goal is to convince them that you warrant a site visit.

Indicators for Questions 2.2a(4) and (6)

- *Strategies or action plans sound like they will help to achieve the overall vision and key objectives.*

- *Consistency is shown between business strategies identified here and information on analysis of current and future customers' needs (3.1), leadership vision and direction of the company (1.1), and analysis of the competitive environment (2.1 and 4.1).*

- *Annual goals/targets have been developed for each major performance measure from section 4.1, and performance measures are linked back to key success factors or strategic objectives.*

- *Longer-term goals/targets are developed for each major performance measure from section 4.1, and performance measures are linked back to key success factors or strategic objectives.*

- *Goals/targets are measurable and are not confused with projects or activities—goals must be linked to result measures.*

- *Goals/targets will cause the company to stretch to achieve them, and help propel them to world-class levels of performance.*

- *Goals/targets are based on research of what is possible (i.e., through benchmarking and other means), rather than just being arbitrarily picked out of the air.*

- *Goals/targets and strategies are cascaded down throughout all units and levels of the company.*

> 2.2a(5) What are your KEY human resource plans to accomplish your short- and longer-term STRATEGIC OBJECTIVES and ACTION PLANS? HOW do the plans address potential impacts on people in your WORKFORCE and any potential changes to WORKFORCE CAPBILITY and CAPACITY needs?

What They're Looking for Here

This question asks about your human resource plans. The examiners want to see that your human resource goals are driven by the goals in your overall business plans. In some organizations the HR plan is developed by individuals who have no knowledge of the company's overall business goals. In order to receive a good score for this area, you need to demonstrate that there is a clear and logical relationship between your business plans and your HR plans. For example, if one of your business goals is to increase your market share in the telecommunications industry with more new products, this fact might lead to an HR goal that calls for increasing the levels of knowledge and skills among employees who design, manufacture, and market telecommunications-based products. You might also have a goal for recruiting more telecommunications experts into the company over the next few years. Examples will help the Baldrige examiners see the relationship between human resources and overall business planning. Simply making a statement that "Our human resource planning is based upon our goals for quality and operational performance outlined in our business plan" is obviously vague and will not elicit favorable comments from the examiners. In order to make your response more credible, you need to use illustrations and examples that are specific. Generalizing your response does not enable the examiner to get a true picture of how well you really meet the criterion.

Indicators for Question 2.2a(5)

- *Demonstration that human resource plans and strategies are determined based upon long- and short-term quality and operational performance goals of the organization.*

- *Amount and credibility of evidence presented suggests that business and HR planning are linked/integrated.*

- *Human resource plans are developed as part of the overall strategic business planning process, rather than as a separate planning activity.*

- *There are no arbitrary HR goals such as "Reduce head count by 10 percent" and "Every employee will receive 80 hours of training."*

- *Specific goals and plans exist for educating, training, and empowering employees.*

- *Specific goals and plans exist for improving mobility, flexibility, and workforce organization.*

- *Specific goals and plans exist for improving reward, recognition, compensation, and benefits.*

- *Specific goals and plans exist for improving recruiting and selection.*

- *Goals and objectives are measurable and specific.*

- *Both long- and short-term plans are presented for all of the four major HR areas asked about in the criterion.*

- *Clear relationship exists between long- and short-term plans for each of the four major HR areas asked about in the criterion.*

AREA TO ADDRESS   [APPROACH, DEPLOYMENT]

2.2b Performance Projection

For the KEY PERFORMANCE MEASURES or INDICATORS identified in 2.2a(6), what are your PERFORMANCE PROJECTIONS for both your short- and longer-term planning time horizons? HOW are these PROJECTIONS determined? How does your projected PERFORMANCE compare with the projected PERFORMANCE of your competitors or comparable organizations? How does it compare with KEY BENCHMARKS, GOALS, and past PERFORMANCE, as appropriate? HOW do you ensure progress so that you will meet your PROJECTIONS? If there are current or projected gaps in PERFORMANCE against your competitors or comparable organizations, HOW will you address them?

N3. Measures and indicators of projected performance (2.2b) might include changes resulting from new ventures; organizational acquisitions or mergers; new value creation; market entry and shifts; new legislative mandates, legal requirements, or industry standards; and significant anticipated innovations in products, services, and technology.

What They're Looking for Here

This Area to Address asks for short-term and long-term specific targets or goals for key performance metrics. I recommend that you include this information in the charts discussed for your answer to 2.2a(4) and (6). It simply does not make sense to have separate answers that relate to action plans [2.1a(4)], performance metrics or indicators [2.1a(6)], and targets or projections for desired levels of performance on each metric [2.2b]. All of this information should be presented together in a single chart to show the relationships among the various factors.

As I mentioned earlier, when discussing targets or goals, it is important to convince the examiners that they are set on the basis of thorough research. The factors used to set good targets or goals include: past performance, customer requirements, resource constraints, competitor performance, and performance of benchmark organizations who may not be competitors.

The third question in this Area to Address requires more of a narrative answer. Your answer to this third question should read like an annual report to shareholders. Your task is to convince the examiners that you know exactly where your business will be in the future, relative to your competitors. Avoid the term "world class" in your response. This is an overused, meaningless phrase that I often see in this section. It adds no value. "We're projecting that we will become the world-class supplier of . . ." does not say anything. Examiners are looking for specifics. Some examples of statements that are specific enough are as follows:

- *By 2009, we will have at least 300 of the Fortune 500 companies as our clients.*
- *We will become the #4 supplier (in market share) of any company in our industry by the year 2010.*

I saw a credit card company that had a projection to put American Express out of business by the end of the century. (They obviously did not achieve this projection.) These statements are specific. It is in this section that you are allowed to write about what you want to do. In every other Baldrige category, you are only given credit for what you have already done. The key is to be realistic and specific. Explain where you think your company will be in the market, and how you will be performing on key measures. Talk about major factors such as the quality of your products and services, customer satisfaction, financial results, and operational measures.

You also need to explain where you think you will be relative to your major competitors. Keep in mind what the note to this Area to Address says. Your competition is getting better also, and they will be trying to take business away from you. Acknowledge the fact that competitors will not be standing still, and project what will happen to them as well. Will they be bigger, smaller, more profitable, etc.?

Along with projections of how your performance will compare to direct competitors, you need to explain how your organization will compare to benchmark companies that may not be in your industry. Again, avoid empty statements like: "By the end of the century, companies will be benchmarking us, rather than us going to them." If you are projecting benchmark-level performance for your company, specify on what measures and on what processes or products. If you can get specific about areas where you are expecting to show benchmark-level performance, examiners will be less likely to find fault with your response. Referring to the results sections of the application (7.2, 7.4, 7.5, and particularly 7.6) may also be appropriate to show the progress you have already made in achieving your longer-term projections.

Indicators for Question 2.2b [Refer to 2.1a(4) and (6) Indicators for assessing goals and targets questioned in 2.2b]

- *Breadth and scope of projections cover major business areas and products/services.*
- *Projections are specific and show that a thorough analysis has been done.*

- *Projections are consistent with long-term goals and strategies outlined in response to 2.2a.*

- *Level of specificity of projections is appropriate.*

- *Comparisons are projected between applicant and major competitors.*

- *Information is presented on how key competitors are expected to improve and change over the next two to five years.*

- *Validity of sources of information used to make projections regarding company's position relative to competition in the future.*

- *How realistic projections are, given current results and the business environment.*

Chapter

8

INTERPRETING THE CRITERIA FOR CUSTOMER AND MARKET FOCUS (3)

OVERVIEW OF THE CUSTOMER AND MARKET FOCUS CATEGORY

The third category in the Baldrige Award Criteria is Customer and Market Focus. The model I outlined in Chapter 3 indicates that Item 3.1 is the major input to the Baldrige system. Well-run organizations target specific groups of customers or markets, learn everything they can about what is important to those groups of customers, and measure their satisfaction. This section asks about all of these points. It also focuses on your approach to building loyalty through strong relationships with preferred customers. Increasing loyalty from select customers can have a dramatic effect on profits. According to the 2008 Award Criteria, Category 3, Customer and Market Focus, is defined as follows:

> *Customer and Market Focus addresses how your organization seeks to understand the voices of customers and of the marketplace with a focus on meeting customers' expectations and requirements, delighting customers, and building loyalty. The Category stresses relationships as an important part of an overall listening, learning, and performance excellence strategy. Your customer satisfaction and dissatisfaction results provide vital information for understanding your customers and the marketplace. In many cases, such results and trends provide the most meaningful information, not only on your customers' views but also on their marketplace behaviors—repeat business and positive referrals—and how these views and behaviors may contribute to the sustainability of your organization in the marketplace. (p. 41)*

Figure 8.1 is a macro process model of an organization that shows where customers and their satisfaction are assessed. Customer satisfaction is measured after the external customers have purchased the products or services produced by the organization. As you can see in the figure, this occurs at point 8, and this information is then fed back to the organization to aid them in producing better performing products and services.

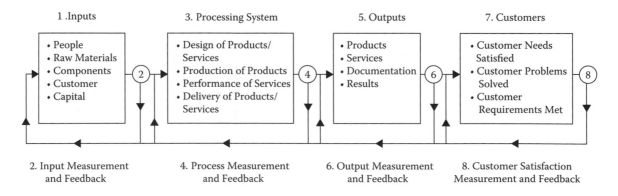

Figure 8.1:   **Macro Process Model of an Organization**

The satisfaction level of internal customers is not addressed in Category 3. This category relates only to external customer satisfaction.

This chapter describes each of the two Examination Items in this category of the Award Criteria. As in previous chapters, each section begins with a shadowed box, containing the Examination Item, the point value, and any applicable Notes,* Areas to Address falling under that item follow in a lighter shadowed box. In the upper right corner of each Area to Address box is an indication [in brackets] of whether the Area pertains to approach, deployment, or results. All definitions and information appearing within these boxes are taken directly from the Baldrige criteria. Following each Area to Address is an explanation defining what the examiners are looking for in assessing your application. Next, I have supplied a list of indicators or evaluation factors that will assist you in interpreting the criteria and in preparing your application.

3.1 CUSTOMER AND MARKET KNOWLEDGE   PROCESS
How do you obtain and use customer and market knowledge?   (40 PTS.)

Describe HOW your organization determines requirements, needs, expectations, and preferences of CUSTOMERS and markets to ensure the continuing relevance of your products and services and to develop new business opportunities.

AREA TO ADDRESS   [APPROACH, DEPLOYMENT]

3.1a Customer and Market Knowledge

(1) HOW do you identify CUSTOMERS, CUSTOMER groups, and market SEGMENTS? HOW do you determine which CUSTOMERS, CUSTOMER groups, and market SEGMENTS to pursue for current and future products and services? HOW do you include CUSTOMERS of competitors and other potential CUSTOMERS and markets in this determination?

N1. Your responses to this Item should include the customer groups and market segments identified in P.1b(2).

N2. If your products and services are sold or delivered to end-use customers via other businesses or organizations (e.g., those that are part of your "value chain," such as retail stores, dealers, or local distributors), customer groups (3.1a[1]) should include both the end users and these intermediate organizations.

---

* Item Notes that apply to a specific Area to Address are appropriately listed in the box containing that Area.

What They're Looking for Here

Many organizations fall into their current marketplaces by accident. They don't proactively sit down and figure out who they should be selling to—they divide up their existing customers into groups. The problem with this approach is that you may end up with the wrong customers. Continental Airlines found out almost too late that it had too many low price customers, which the airline calls the sandals and knapsack market segment. AT&T Universal Card, a former Baldrige winner, does not exist as a company today because it did a poor job of deciding which customers they wanted to have their credit card. The company made the mistake of selecting too many customers with great credit ratings who pay off their bills in full each month. Credit card companies make most of their money on customers they call "revolvers," those who pay only the minimum balance each month. AT&T Universal Card went out of business not long after winning the Baldrige Award, and the company's portfolio of customers now belongs to Citibank.

The lesson to be learned from both of these companies is that you need to be very careful about the types of customers from whom you solicit business. This question in the criteria asks about your market or customer segments, why you picked them, and what criteria you use to separate them. There is no right or wrong way to separate your customer into groups, but there needs to be some logic in your approach. For example, if half of your business comes from the automotive industry, it might make sense to segment your customers into two groups:

- *Automotive*
- *Nonautomotive*

A manufacturer of printing equipment uses the following market segments to categorize its customers:

- *Service companies*
- *Educational institutions*
- *Manufacturing companies*
- *Government*
- *Printers*

Along with a list of your various market segments, you need to explain the criteria for their selection. Certain characteristics of an industry might make it attractive or unattractive to your organization, so document what those characteristics are.

Indicators for Question 3.1a(1)

- *Customers are segmented logically according to common needs.*
- *Your organization has been deliberate in deciding what types of customers and market segments it wants to work with.*
- *Amount of evidence suggests that the organization has been proactive in selecting particular markets or customer types.*
- *Customers are segmented into logical groups based upon common characteristics.*
- *New and potential market segments are evaluated periodically for growth opportunities.*
- *Customer segments are selected to reduce the organization's vulnerability to economic trends in a particular customer or industry.*

3.1a(2) HOW do you use the voice of the CUSTOMER to determine KEY CUSTOMER requirements, needs, and changing expectations (including product and service features) and their relative importance to CUSTOMERS' purchasing or relationship decisions? How do your listening methods varyfor different CUSTOMERS, CUSTOMER groups, or market SEGMENTS? HOWdo you use relevant information and feedback from current and former CUSTOMERS, including marketing and sales information, CUSTOMER loyalty and retention data, CUSTOMER referrals, win/loss ANALYSIS, and complaint data for PURPOSESof planning products and services, marketing, making WORK SYSTEM and work PROCESS improvements, and developing new business opportunities?

N3. The "voice of the customer" (3.1a[2]) is your process for capturing customer-related information. Voice-of-the-customer processes are intended to be proactive and continuously innovative to capture stated, unstated, and anticipated customer requirements, needs, and desires. The goal is to achieve customer loyalty and build customer relationships, as appropriate. The voice of the customer might include gathering and integrating survey data, focus group findings, Web-based data, warranty data, complaint logs and field reports, and other data and information that affect customers' purchasing and relationship decisions.

What They're Looking for Here

Your response to this question should include an explanation of what the common requirements for all your customers are and what the requirements for customers in the different market segments you serve are. A common way to respond to this area is to make the following statement: "We have identified all of the requirements and expectations unique to each of the different market segments we serve." But as you have learned by now, using broad statements such as this will not earn many points. Listing the requirements and expectations of your different groups of customers will earn points in this area. A matrix with customer requirements and expectations listed along the left side and market segments listed horizontally along the top is a great way to show common and unique customer requirements.

You also need to explain how you gather data on customer requirements. Your response will be evaluated according to the objectivity and reliability of your research methodologies and instruments. The examiners will also be looking at factors such as sample size, frequency of data collection, and use of a variety of different methods to gather data on customer requirements. Your own market research should be supplemented with data collected by outside firms to increase the objectivity of your data.

A great many customers may not be included in your efforts to gather data on customer requirements, and you may not hear from them when they have a service or product complaint. In fact, for every eight customers who are unhappy with a product or service, only one complains. Rather than complain, most unhappy customers simply take their business elsewhere. Two valuable sources of data on customer requirements are complaint data and an analysis of lost customers to determine why they leave. The examiners are looking for evidence that you gather data from customers who decide to buy their product/service elsewhere and that you use both this and customer complaint data to identify customer requirements that may not be apparent from the other market research you do.

Another good source of data is new customers. Surveying new customers to find out why they selected your product or service can provide valuable information. In your response, explain how data on lost and new customers is gathered and directed back through the appropriate channels to serve as input to the product/service design process.

Your response for this Area to Address should also explain how you use complaints and performance data as a way of identifying possible customer requirements. For example, a car company may look at the number of warranty repairs that customers have done on their cars during the first year as a set of performance data relevant to customer requirements for reliability.

The criteria in 3.1a(2) also suggest that companies need to focus on determining what customers are likely to want and expect in the future. This may seem a difficult task, but being able to predict future customer demands is what separates the leading companies from the followers. Many large manufacturing companies are designing products now that won't be on the market for several years. These companies need to be aware of how tastes and expectations of customers are likely to change in the future so that their new products will meet or exceed those expectations.

You should explain the time horizon for determination of future customer requirements. The time horizon should be based upon the trends and frequency of changes in your industry and a reasonable time frame within which you can predict trends. The amount of time you need to develop and test new products also should be considered in determining the time frame for your predictions. Some pharmaceutical companies are working on drugs that may not be on the market for more than 5 years. Clothing designers, on the other hand, come up with their product designs about a year or so before they hit the stores. In a fashion-oriented business, it is much more difficult to predict trends and customer tastes more than a couple of years in advance. Your response should explain the logic behind your selection of a particular time frame for predicting future customer expectations.

Your response should explain how needs of current and potential new customers are likely to change. You should also explain how you are in touch with the current and future expectations of competitors' customers. Explain how you predict your existing and potential customers' buying behavior. If you do market research, explain how you ensure that predictions made by this research have turned out to be valid.

This portion of the Area to Address asks how you take the information on high-priority customer requirements (current and future) and use these data to design new products and services. Good companies not only spend a lot of time listening to customers, they find out what requirements or needs might really make a difference in customers' buying behavior. Understanding these priorities helps companies to make wise business decisions about how to invest their money. Often customers will express a desire for a particular feature or product/service characteristic but are unwilling to pay for it when it is offered.

This section asks for information on how you determine the relative importance of current and future customer requirements and get customers to assign a value to the things that they want to see in your products/services. The trick to doing this well is finding out information that allows you to predict customer buying behavior with a fair degree of certainty. Focus groups and surveys tend to produce unreliable results because customers are often not good predictors of their own buying behavior. They may tell you something is important, and that they would buy your product if it had a particular feature, and then not buy it for some reason. Explain the methodologies you employ to conduct research on customer priorities, and how this information serves as an input to the product/service design process you will discuss in more detail in 6.1a.

This portion of 3.1a also asks about how data on gains and losses of customers and complaints are used to determine future product/service features. Customers cannot often articulate what they want until they don't get it. Therefore, complaints are a rich source of data for new product/service development. Customers might complain about how hard it is to find the on/off switch on a fax machine, but would never list the location of the on/off switch as one of their most important requirements.

Indicators for Question 3.1a(2)

- *Data on requirements collected from your own and competitors' customers.*
- *Degree to which customer requirements have been identified for each market segment your company serves.*
- *Identification of the common and unique requirements and expectations for each market segment.*
- *Objectivity of data collection methods used to identify customer requirements and expectations.*
- *Frequency of data collection on each market segment.*
- *Sample sizes are large enough to be adequate representation of customer populations.*
- *How the company provides information to customers to help ensure that their expectations are realistic.*
- *Evidence of a proactive approach to identifying targeted customer markets.*
- *Use of multiple methodologies (e.g., telephone interviews, mail surveys, focus groups, etc.) to gather data on customer requirements.*
- *Use of comparative data for such areas as product/service performance, complaints, and gains/losses of customers to help determine customer requirements.*
- *Use of outside sources of data to supplement the applicant's own data on customer requirements.*
- *How the role of and logistical support for customer contact personnel are determined.*
- *Use of a systematic process for gathering customer requirement data.*
- *Evidence that customer complaint data are summarized and used as input for design or enhancement of products/services.*
- *Tracking of lost customers and follow-up to determine their reasons for buying products/services elsewhere and why they were dissatisfied with your products/services.*
- *Thoroughness of a system for following up with lost customers.*

- *Data gathered from new customers to determine why they selected the product/services offered by your company.*
- *Use of performance data on products/services to identify customer requirements.*
- *Evidence that data from new or lost customers are used to design, enhance, or change products and/or services.*
- *Extent to which requirements have been identified for all dealers or distributors if appropriate.*
- *Explanation of a time horizon for determination of how future customer requirements match applicant's business, products/services, and technology.*
- *Time frame for determination of future requirements is far enough in the future to allow the organization to capitalize on trends by designing and introducing products and services to meet future customer expectations.*
- *Extent to which projections are made about requirements of existing customers in the future and requirements of potential customers who currently do not buy the organization's products or services.*
- *Identification of important trends in technology, competition, society, economy, demographics, and other factors that may impact the business.*
- *Extent to which the company has identified how each of these trends will impact its business.*
- *Identification of specific strategies the company will use to capitalize on future trends in all areas listed above.*
- *Evidence of a systematic approach being used to link high-priority customer requirements to the product/service design process.*
- *Use of a variety of different sources of data to identify customer priorities.*
- *Use of a systematic process to evaluate the importance of various future customer requirements.*
- *Demonstration that only the most important future customer requirements are translated into new product/service features.*
- *Clarity and completeness of explanation of how future trends are translated into customer requirements leading to design of new or enhanced products/services.*
- *Thoroughness of data collection process used to determine customer priorities.*
- *Deployment of customer requirements research to all customer market segments and product/services.*
- *Use of complaint data as input to the product/service design process.*
- *Use of gains and losses of customer referrals, and other similar data as input to the product/service design process.*
- *Use of data on future customer requirements to design new or enhanced products/services.*

> 3.1a(3) How do you use voice-of-the-CUSTOMER information and feedback to become more CUSTOMER-focused, to better satisfy CUSTOMER needs and desires, and to identify opportunities for INNOVATION?

What They're Looking for Here

Translated into English, this question asks what you do with the customer feedback you collect. It is not enough to gather this sort of data if nothing is done with it. Customer feedback should be a key input to the process improvement and goal setting process for an organization. For example, if a hospital found out that a major source of customer aggravation is the issuing of confusing hospital bills, they might change the billing and coding process and billing format so that is easier to understand. Customer feedback and complains can be a rich source of data that drives innovations you might not have otherwise thought of. Your answer to this question should include a few examples of major changes, innovations, or process improvements that were introduced as a result of customer feedback. These examples will help lend credibility to your claims of really listening to customers and taking action based on their feedback. You might also want to reference any results in section 7.2 that support your claims that the change or innovation really made a difference in improving customer satisfaction or loyalty. Organizations often make changes that are supposed to improve the experience for customers but often result in further aggravating them.

Indicators for Question 3.1a(3)

- *There is evidence of a systematic process for analyzing customer feedback for trends and opportunities for improvement.*

- *Results of customer feedback is provided to individual and departments who are able to make changes and improvements.*

- *Links between customer feedback and the strategic planning process are clearly delineated.*

- *Customer feedback is one of the inputs to process improvement initiatives and new product/service development.*

- *Credibility and number of examples provided to illustrate improvements or innovations implemented based on customer feedback.*

- *Results in Item 7.2 clearly support the claims that the changes or innovations actually resulted in improved customer satisfaction and/or loyalty.*

3.1a(4) HOW do you keep your listening and LEARNING methods current with business needs and directions, including changes in your marketplace?

What They're Looking for Here

If you've come this far in the book, this portion of the Area to Address should look very familiar to you. The last question in a sequence typically calls for evidence that you systematically evaluate and improve a process. This is exactly what is being asked for here. The Baldrige examiners are looking for evidence that you employ a systematic process to evaluate your market research and other investigations to determine future customer expectations. Begin your response with a list of the various types of research you do to determine customer requirements in the future. Along with a list of the various types of research, you might also mention who does the research, indicating whether you use outside firms or do it all using your own internal resources. For each type of research that is done, list the type of evaluation factors or measures used for assessment. Next, describe the methodology used to gather the evaluation data. Explain how the evaluation data are compiled and how conclusions are drawn.

Following your description of the methods used to evaluate your research approaches, you should explain how you use these evaluation data to improve your research methodology or expand the time horizon for your research. One area you should work on improving is the accuracy of your predictions and the length of your time horizons. The best companies in the future will be those that accurately predict long-range trends. You might end your response with an example or two of how you have used evaluation data to improve your research methodology, leading to improvements in the accuracy of your predictions or in the time horizons of your research.

Indicators for Question 3.1a(4)

- *Evidence that a systematic process is used to evaluate the approaches used to determine future customer requirements.*
- *Extent to which evaluations are done on all methodologies employed to conduct research on future customer requirements.*
- *Degree to which evaluation methods are appropriate for the research methods used.*
- *Validity of measurement indices used for evaluation.*
- *Validity of evaluation approaches used.*

- *Clear description of a system to compile evaluation results and follow up on them.*
- *Evidence that evaluation results are acted upon and result in improvements in research approaches.*
- *Evidence to indicate that improvements have been made in the last few years in the accuracy and/or time frames of predictions about future customer requirements.*
- *Evidence of a number of improvements being made in approaches for determining customer needs and priorities.*

3.2 CUSTOMER RELATIONSHIPS AND SATISFACTION PROCESS
How do you build relationships and grow customer satisfaction and loyalty? (45 PTS.)

Describe HOW your organization builds relationships to acquire, satisfy, and retain CUSTOMERS to increase CUSTOMER loyalty. Describe also HOW your organization determines CUSTOMER satisfaction.

AREA TO ADDRESS [APPROACH, DEPLOYMENT]

3.2a CUSTOMER Relationship Building

 (1) HOW do you build relationships to acquire CUSTOMERS, to meet and exceed their expectations, to increase loyalty and repeat business, and to gain positive referrals?

N1. Customer relationship building (3.2a) might include the development of partnerships or alliances with customers.

N6. For some nonprofit organizations (e.g., some government agencies or charitable organizations), customers may be assigned or may be required to use your organization, and relationships may be short term. For those organizations, relationship building (3.2a[1]) might be focused on meeting and exceeding expectations during the short-term relationship, resulting in positive comments to other people, including key stakeholders of your organization.

What They're Looking for Here

In the previous section you should have identified your target markets and customer groups. In this section, you need to explain how you build loyalty from these customers. Building customer loyalty is difficult. Often loyalty is determined by unnoticed factors. Part of the key to building loyalty is how well you understand what drives buying behavior. The other part is consistently delivering on those important requirements.

Two-time Baldrige winner Ritz-Carlton does an outstanding job of building loyalty from their customers by learning as much as possible about what is important to each guest, documenting that information in the database, and communicating it to all Ritz employees.

In answering this question, you must explain how you take the information on customer requirements that was defined in 3.1 and perform those requirements consistently for customers to create loyalty. Part of building loyalty is performing operational processes consistently. Loyal airline customers can become very frustrated after a few cancelled flights or lost pieces of luggage and may, finally, avoid your airline at all costs if they are inconvenienced enough times. Your approach for ensuring consistent quality in your products and services should probably be discussed in section 6, Process Management. In this section, you want to describe specific efforts that build loyalty and delight your customers beyond just the basics. It is important to convince the reader that these techniques actually work to build loyalty. Many companies miss the point and spend money on extraneous perks to try to build loyalty, when they should have concentrated on other factors, such as accessibility and customer service.

Account management contributes to building customer loyalty as well. If we really like the people from your organization that we interact with on a regular basis, we will tend to be more loyal. Companies don't realize the real price of turnover among their customer contact staff. Customers get comfortable dealing with the same people, and it is very disturbing when someone you liked dealing with leaves and a new person comes in who does not know you or your needs. Another part of building loyalty is creating exit barriers. If it will be expensive or simply a major aggravation to switch suppliers, customers may be more loyal. Banks have had high degrees of loyalty from customers often because it is so much trouble for customers to switch banks—new forms to fill out, waiting for checks to be printed, etc. A smart bank in California offers to switch you over from another bank with one brief phone call. This removes the exit barrier that keeps customers at a bank even though they were unhappy with the service. Forming a partnership or alliance with customers is another way of increasing their loyalty. Companies like Cisco and Solectron have done an excellent job of forming partnerships with their major customers.

Indicators for Question 3.2a(1)

- *Important customer requirements are communicated to customer contact personnel.*
- *Great care is taken in selecting customer contact personnel, and effort is put into minimizing turnover of the good ones.*

- *A systematic approach is used to get to know customers as individuals where possible, and to build trust and rapport with them.*
- *Exit barriers are used where possible to make it more difficult for customers to switch suppliers.*
- *Efforts to delight customers and build loyalty through extra features/services are evaluated for their effectiveness.*
- *Efforts to reward customers for their loyalty through entertainment events (e.g. golf outings, trips) or by providing them with special privileges are benefits customers want and enjoy.*
- *Efforts are made to form partnerships or alliances with key accounts where possible.*

AREA TO ADDRESS [APPROACH, DEPLOYMENT]

3.2a Customer Relationships

(2) How do your KEY access mechanisms enable CUSTOMERS to seek information, conduct business, and make complaints? What areyour KEY access mechanisms? How do you determine KEY CUSTOMER contact requirements for each mode of CUSTOMER access? How do you ensure that these contact requirements are deployed to all people and PROCESSES involved in the CUSTOMER response chain?

What They're Looking for Here

This is one area in which many otherwise well-run companies have difficulty. Probably the best way of ensuring easy access for customers to comment on an organization's products or services is to have a company representative visit each customer frequently. In some organizations this may not be feasible, so other methods must be used. The key here is to make it easy for the customer. Most organizations place the burden upon the customer to exert the effort and take the initiative to comment on service or product quality. If, however, you take the initiative to determine customer comments rather than waiting for a complaint, you will excel in this section.

Another aspect of your response for this area is to describe the ease with which customers can take the initiative to comment or complain about your products or services. Many organizations have customer service 800 numbers or hotlines. Although this is a great idea, many of the companies I've dealt with don't adequately staff their customer service phone lines, so that the lines are either busy for hours or you're put on hold forever while waiting for the "next available customer service representative." If you have an 800 number or hotline for customer comments and questions, your response here should include data that indicate the prompt and efficient handling of incoming calls by your staff.

Comment cards are another common technique for allowing customers to voice their opinions. These are frequently used by hotels, restaurants, car dealers, and others. If you make use of these cards or a similar instrument, explain how customers receive or obtain the cards, how much time it takes to fill them out, and what the customers need to do to turn them in. If you simply leave the cards lying out in your place of business for the customer to choose to fill out—in their hotel room, on the seat of a new car, on the restaurant table—only people who are very upset about poor service will take the time to fill them out. If the customer needs to put a stamp on the card and mail it, even fewer of them will bother to fill out and send in the comment card. The same is true of product comment cards that are included with the owner's manual of many consumer products. Only people who fill out the cards are part of the sample, so the sample is not representative of all customers.

To receive a high score for your response to this area, you must first have a well-designed and simple system for customers to comment on your products or services, and second, a set of data from customer surveys and interviews that suggest how truly easy it is to comment, complain, or get a question answered. If 98 percent of your customers say that your customer service department answers the phones in three rings or less and is able to answer questions or resolve problems adequately almost every time, the Baldrige examiners will take notice.

In your response, define the major customer requirements or needs for each major point of interaction with customer contact employees. Finally, explain how you track or measure whether or not you meet the requirements. What do you measure to determine your performance levels in meeting the customer requirements? Once again, this is a situation where a chart might be a good way of presenting all of the information called for. An example is shown below for an accounting firm that presents all three types of information asked for in this part of this Area to Address.

MAJOR INTERACTION POINTS	KEY CUSTOMER REQUIREMENTS	INDICATORS/ MEASURES
Audit planning meeting	• All key players in attendance	Attendance log
	• Major milestones defined	Project plan
	• Labor budget established	Project plan
	• Efficiency of meeting	Customer satisfaction survey

As mentioned in other sections of this book, measures are meaningless without standards or goals. A customer service standard should always have two parts. The first part is the behavior or action the employee should perform, and the second is the standard or criterion that specifies how well the action must be done. Some examples are as follows:

> "Approach customers *within three minutes of the time they enter the department.*"
>
> "End the transaction *by thanking the customer for using AT&T.*"
>
> "Greet members *using their names when they walk into the club.*"

The italicized parts of the statements are the criteria or standards that specify how a task should be done or how well it should be done.

Standards should always be stated in a manner that allows conformance to be reliably and objectively measured. Many applicants list standards that include words and phrases such as "in a friendly manner," "showing empathy for the customer's situation," "promptly," or "in an efficient manner." Although these may all be good adverbs to describe service, they are neither precise nor objectively measurable. My definition of "promptness" may be quite different from yours. Standards need to be very specific and quantified whenever possible.

After listing your customer service standards, the second half of your response to this area should concentrate on how the standards are based upon customer requirements. Many organizations base their standards upon either past performance or industry standards. For example, a medical insurance company uses a standard of 30 days for the time that it should take to process a customer's claim. The 30 days is based upon industry standards. If, on the other hand, the company asked customers how long it should take (which it hasn't), customers would probably say one week or so. Your score in this area will be partially based upon how well you demonstrate that your major customer service standards are derived from customer requirements and expectations.

In almost all companies, it is impossible for customer contact employees to meet customer service standards by themselves. In a restaurant, the waiter must rely upon the host/hostess, food buyer, restaurant manager, cooks, chef and others to help meet customer service standards. In a manufacturing plant, the sales representatives must rely upon production, quality assurance, procurement, accounting, production control, and other departments to help meet customer service standards. In any organization, the people who have the face-to-face contact with the customers must count on the cooperation of many others to help them deliver services and products that meet all of the customers' expectations and needs.

INTERPRETING THE CRITERIA FOR CUSTOMER AND MARKET FOCUS (3)   179

For this to happen, it is essential that all the employees who help the customer contact people to achieve their goals are knowledgeable of the customer service standards and are held accountable for completing the tasks necessary to enable the customer contact people to meet those standards. One applicant who received a high score in this area presented a list of customer service standards along the left side of a chart, and a list of the various functions in the organization horizontally along the top of the chart. Codes were used to indicate the degree of influence each support department had in helping to achieve the customer service standard. A portion of such a chart is shown below.

ACCOUNTABILITIES—CUSTOMER SERVICE STANDARDS					
STANDARDS	ACCOUNTING	PROCUREMENT	ENGINEERING	PRODUCTION	HRD
Deliver all orders by customer deadline	4	3	4	1	3
Provide appropriate prints and documentation with orders	4	4	1	3	3
Answer technical questions within 24 hours	4	4	1	2	3
Key: 1 = Primary Responsibility 3 = Support Responsibility 2 = Secondary Responsibility 4 = No Responsibility					

This chart is only one way of depicting the level of responsibility each function has in assisting customer contact employees in meeting customer service standards. Your response needs to explain how support departments and others are made aware of the customer service standards and how they are held accountable for helping to achieve them.

Simply setting customer service standards and communicating them to all employees will not ensure that the standards are met. The expression "you get what you measure" is very true. If you do not track and measure the degree to which standards are met, you can almost guarantee that they will not be met on a consistent basis. Performance improvement is a matter of selecting measurement indices, setting standards, measuring performance against those standards, and sending performance feedback to employees who have influence or control over the indices.

Performance of customer contact employees compared to established standards needs to be measured and the data fed back to employees in a timely and consistent manner. A great many service and manufacturing companies receive low scores for this area because they do not measure performance against the customer service standards, other than by surveying customers. Surveying customers is a very imprecise way to measure performance against standards. It is important to gather customer opinion about how well you meet satisfaction standards, but you should also do your own internal measurement.

As customers, the expectations and standards we have for the products and services we buy are constantly changing. Because of the poor on-time performance of airlines in recent years, many of us have lowered our expectations. Other standards have been raised. We expect our cars to be more trouble-free, to need less maintenance, and to run more efficiently than in the past.

Your response for this Area to Address should also briefly explain a process for periodically evaluating the validity of your customer service standards and your process for ensuring they are met. This should be done through ongoing research into customer requirements and expectations. The requirements and expectations should then be translated into new or revised customer service standards. After describing your approach to evaluating customer service standards, present information on how the standards have evolved or changed over the last several years. A trend indicating that the changes have resulted in more stringent standards will earn you points in this section of your application.

Indicators for Question 3.2a(2)

- *Amount of effort and trouble customers must go through to comment or complain, or seek assistance.*
- *Use of frequent personal contact with customers where appropriate.*
- *Staffing levels and expertise of personnel operating toll-free lines designed to help customers are adequate to ensure minimal waiting and accurate answers to questions.*
- *How many times customers receive a busy signal when trying to call your toll-free lines (blocked calls) and how long they must wait on hold.*
- *Evidence of a proactive approach to get customers to comment and complain.*
- *Definition of key customer contact points with customers, and most important requirements for each transaction.*
- *Identification of specific performance measures for each major interaction with customers.*
- *Extent to which measures have been identified for each customer interaction point.*
- *Evidence that measures are clearly related to customer requirements.*
- *Definition of standards for each measure associated with customer service levels.*
- *Standards exist for all measures.*

- *Standards are set based upon requirements and desires of customers and upon what competitors and benchmark organizations do.*
- *Evidence that data are collected on each major service measure.*
- *Data on extent to which standards are met is fed back to appropriate employees and used to improve performance.*
- *Processes for meeting or exceeding customer requirements are continually improved.*

> 3.2a(3) How do you manage CUSTOMER complaints? How do you ensure that complaints are resolved EFFECTIVELY and promptly? How do you minimize CUSTOMER dissatisfaction and, as appropriate, loss of repeat business? How are complaints aggregated and analyzed for use in improvement throughout your organization and by your PARTNERS?

What They're Looking for Here

Most companies have systems for filing and summarizing complaint letters and phone complaints made to customer service departments. However, the majority of customers who have comments on the services and products they buy don't bother writing a letter or calling a customer service department. Many organizations we buy from don't even have customer service departments. The Baldrige examiners are looking for methods and procedures you have in place to capture formal and informal customer comments or complaints. Most of the informal data get lost in many organizations, creating an unrealistic picture of actual levels of customer satisfaction. For example, the comments you make to the copier machine repair person or the field support representative from the computer company may never be recorded anywhere. Comments made to salespeople, or even customer-contact employees, are often heard and then forgotten.

In order to receive a high score for this area, you need to demonstrate that you have a comprehensive, yet simple, system for documenting all written and/or verbal comments made by customers about the quality of your products and services. You also need to have a system for summarizing and reporting all formal and informal complaints/comments received from customers.

Your response should include a combination of process description and results. A flowchart, algorithm, or list of steps should be included that depicts the process for responding to and correcting customer complaints. You should also explain the escalation process that occurs when a customer feels that his/her complaint has not been resolved satisfactorily.

Your process will be assessed for its logic, thoroughness, and the degree to which it fits your type of business and the size of your company.

The second part of your response for this area should include data, covering a variety of different indices that show you are timely in resolving customer complaints, and that complaints are resolved completely and with a minimum of inconvenience to the customer. Data on the number of complaints received is not really relevant to this Area to Address. The number of complaints received is a measure of the quality of services and/or products offered by the organization. This section should focus on how well you handle and resolve the complaints that do come in. Preventing complaints in the first place is addressed elsewhere.

One of the most common mistakes that applicants make in responding to these "process" items is to write a brief and very general description of how they deal with a particular issue or input. A typical response is as follows:

> *Each complaint received is analyzed by customer service representatives to determine its root cause. The cause of the complaint must be recorded on the Complaint Log form. Once a month, a summary report is prepared that lists the causes of complaints and provides statistics on the number of complaints tied to specific causes. Reports are sent to the department managers who have responsibility for correcting the causes of the complaints.*

The problem with a response such as this is that it is too vague and the process described does not explain:

- *The steps a customer service representative follows to analyze the cause(s) of a problem.*
- *The knowledge customer service representatives have to analyze the cause(s) of customer complaints.*
- *How the organization follows up on corrective actions that need to be taken to correct problem situations.*
- *Evidence that the company has a system for recording all customer comments and complaints.*
- *Evidence that data on customer comments and complaints from all areas of the organization are aggregated and analyzed to identify trends that may help identify opportunities for improvement.*

Sending a report to managers once a month is not an effective system for resolving problems.

The criteria also ask how you summarize complaints and comments from throughout the company and use these data to better manage relationships with customers. Many companies do not do this. Complaints or comments are received by individual units or facilities, logged, and resolved. Many comments or minor complaints are never even logged, because they are resolved before they get worse. The only overall data on complaints that the company has are complaint letters or phone calls that made it to some corporate officer. These are few and far between in most companies. Baldrige is suggesting that companies have a tracking system to enable all complaint and comment data to be summarized. The key is to learn as much about customers and their needs as possible. Failure to aggregate these data and look at them across the entire company may handicap the company in making good decisions about how to improve relationships with customers.

Your response for this Area to Address should also explain how you use your analyses of the causes of customer complaints to improve processes, products, and services in the organization. Describe the process, and perhaps give an example or two of how you have used customer-complaint analyses to modify processes or a product/service.

Indicators for Question 3.2a(3)

- *Comprehensiveness of system for tracking customer comments and complaints.*
- *Objectivity of the approach for gathering and documenting data on customer comments and/or complaints.*
- *All employees who have telephone or personal contact with customers have a simple but thorough way of documenting any incidental comments or complaints heard about the company's products or services.*
- *Data on customer comments/complaints from a variety of sources are aggregated for overall evaluation and comparison.*
- *Data on customer comments/complaints are fed back to appropriate personnel in a timely fashion.*
- *Customers believe that the comments/complaints they make to any of the organization's employees will get documented and reported.*
- *A formal and logical process exists for resolving customer complaints.*
- *Clearly defined escalation procedures are in place for situations in which customers do not feel their complaint has been resolved by lower-level personnel.*
- *Improvements have been made showing reductions in the amount of time needed to resolve customer complaints over the past few years.*

- *Objectivity and reliability of data on levels of customer satisfaction with the handling of complaints are established.*
- *Evidence is presented on the thoroughness with which complaints are handled.*
- *Organized and systematic process is used for analyzing the causes of customer complaints.*
- *Those analyzing the causes of customer complaints have the knowledge and skills to do so.*
- *Information on the causes of customer complaints is fed back to employees who can correct the problems.*
- *Evidence that complaint data are used to initiate improvement projects that prevent future complaints and potential loss of customers.*
- *Evidence that analyses of causes of customer complaints are used to make changes in processes, products, and/or services.*
- *Complaint data is communicated to suppliers/partners as necessary.*

3.2a(4) HOW do you keep your APPROACHES to building relationships and providing CUSTOMER access current with business needs and directions?

What They're Looking for Here

This portion of the criteria asks about how you evaluate and improve your approaches for all of 3.2a. To receive a score of 40% or above on the Baldrige scale, you need to provide evidence that your approaches have been continually improved. Make sure that you address all of the variables covered in this broad item:

- *Channels for customers to access information on products/services.*
- *Customer comment and complaint tracking.*
- *Complaint resolution process.*
- *Customer satisfaction measurement.*
- *Customer relationship building strategies/techniques.*

A good way of answering this Area to Address is to list the variables on which you evaluate your approaches, describe the frequency and approach to evaluation in a sentence or two, and provide a laundry list of changes and improvements that have been made over the past few years. This will provide examiners with enough information to see that your approaches are mature and subject to continual evaluation and improvement. You won't have space to go into a lot of detail, but it might also be important to explain how some of the changes or improvements you've made are linked into key business strategies or plans, described in section 2.

Indicators for Question 3.2a(4)

- *Evidence of a planned systematic approach to evaluating approaches outlined in this section.*
- *Identification of specific measurement indices for evaluating customer satisfaction and relationship building approaches.*
- *Formal evaluation and improvement is done at least once a year.*
- *Mechanisms exist for ongoing continual refinement or improvement to approaches, along with more formal periodic evaluation and improvement.*
- *Major overhauls have been done to systems, along with minor tune-ups.*
- *Changes and improvements to approaches are consistent with business plans and strategies.*
- *Number and scope of changes and improvements that have been listed or described in the application.*
- *Evidence that approaches to customer satisfaction and relationship building are based upon the best practices of leading companies where appropriate.*

AREA TO ADDRESS   [APPROACH, DEPLOYMENT]

(1) How do you determine CUSTOMER satisfaction, dissatisfaction, and loyalty? How do these determination methods differ among CUSTOMER groups? How do you ensure that your measurements capture actionable information for use in exceeding your CUSTOMERS' expectations? How do you ensure that your measurements capture actionable information for use in securing your CUSTOMERS' future business and gaining positive referrals, as appropriate? How do you use CUSTOMER satisfaction and dissatisfaction information for improvement?

N2. Determining customer satisfaction and dissatisfaction (3.2b) might include use of any or all of the following: surveys, formal and informal feedback, customer account histories, complaints, win/loss analysis, and transaction completion rates. Information might be gathered on the Internet, through personal contact or a third party, or by mail.

N3. Customer satisfaction measurements (3.2b[1]) might include both a numerical rating scale and descriptors for each unit in the scale. Actionable customer satisfaction measurements provide useful information about specific product and service features, delivery, relationships, and transactions that affect the customers' future actions—repeat business and positive referral.

Continued

N4. Other organizations providing similar products or services (3.2b[3]) might include other organizations with whom you don't compete but provide similar products and services in other geographic areas or to different populations of people.

N5. Your customer satisfaction and dissatisfaction results should be reported in Item 7.2.

N6. For some nonprofit organizations (e.g., some government agencies or charitable organizations), customers may be assigned or may be required to use your organization, and relationships may be short-term. For those organizations, relationship building (3.2a[1]) might be focused on meeting and exceeding expectations during the short-term relationship, resulting in positive comments to other people, including key stakeholders of your organization.

What They're Looking for Here

Currently, it's rare to find an organization that does a great job of measuring customer satisfaction. While it's true that most organizations survey their customers to determine their satisfaction, most surveys miss the mark and often provide misleading data. For example, survey data show that about 90 percent of customers of one major car company are either satisfied or very satisfied with the car they purchased. Yet, only about 40 percent of those satisfied customers trade their car in for another one of the same make several years later. This suggests that there may be little correlation between customer satisfaction and buying behavior. Facts like this are causing many leading companies today to rethink their whole approach to customer satisfaction measurement. Most traditional surveys provide data that are not reflective of customers' true opinions and do little to predict their future buying behavior.

There are many ways to measure customer satisfaction. Most companies rely upon only two methods:

- *Comment/feedback cards*
- *Annual mail survey sent to all or a sample of customers*

Although these two approaches are certainly valid, if this is all you do, it is not likely that you are obtaining a clear view of the degree to which customers are satisfied with your products/services. The problem with comment cards and surveys is that most customers can't be bothered to take the time to fill them out. Or if they do fill them out, they do so quickly and carelessly, rating everything average or above average. As consumers of numerous goods and services, we are inundated with requests for our opinions and feedback. Most of us respond to a few of these requests and ignore the rest, unless we are extremely unhappy with the level of service or product quality. And when we are very unhappy, we usually don't bother with filling out a comment card or waiting for the annual survey—we write a letter or make a phone call right away.

The most objective way to measure customer satisfaction is by examining customers' behavior, not their opinions. The fact that Mr. Green traded in his 2002 Ford Taurus for a 2006 model from the same dealership says more about Mr. Green's level of satisfaction than any survey could. In fact, if you surveyed Mr. Green, you might find that there are a number of things he didn't like about his Taurus. The bottom line, though, is that he bought another one. The amount of repeat business an organization receives is one of the best indicators of customer satisfaction. (Unless you're the only game in town. If you live in Butte, Montana, for example, there may be only one car dealer who exclusively sells or services Mercedes.)

Market share can be an indicator of customer satisfaction, but it is not a good one. Market share is influenced by too many extraneous factors such as competition, advertising, and pricing. In this Area to Address, the examiners are looking for an approach to measuring customer satisfaction that takes into account a variety of different sources of data. Opinion data should be gathered using several approaches and large representative samples of all the organization's customers. Other measures, such as repeat business, need to be used to supplement opinion data. The specific measures you utilize will depend upon the nature of your products/services. A single measure can be misleading, so the use of multiple indices and data-gathering methodologies adds a great deal of objectivity and reliability to your approach.

If you are a large corporation with many products and/or services, chances are that you serve a variety of customers with differing needs and levels of satisfaction with your products/services. For example, a large service company might have hotels, restaurants, and amusement parks, each catering to different types of customers. A company that makes only personal computers may have many different types of customers for this single product. Customers may be segmented based upon how they will use their personal computers.

In this Area to Address, the Baldrige examiners are also looking for evidence that you segment your customers in a logical manner and that your customer satisfaction efforts address the various segments. In some cases, it won't make sense to segment them at all. However, even if you are a small business you probably should be categorizing your customers somehow. If 60 percent of your business is conducted with AT&T, for example, and the rest is with miscellaneous small companies, you might segment your customers into two groups: (1) AT&T and (2) all others.

Indicators for Question 3.2b(1)

- *Measures of loyalty of important customers are used as part of overall approach to customer satisfaction measurement.*
- *Company measures customer-perceived value as well as satisfaction.*
- *Number of different sources of data on customer satisfaction.*
- *Use of objective measures such as repeat business along with opinion data.*
- *Frequency with which customer satisfaction is measured.*
- *Adequate sample sizes used when measuring customer satisfaction.*
- *Extent to which customers in all segments/markets are included in customer satisfaction data.*
- *Validation done with customer satisfaction instruments prior to their use.*
- *Reliability of instruments used to measure customer satisfaction.*
- *Use of multiple approaches to gather customer opinion data, such as surveys, focus groups, etc.*
- *Logical approach for segmenting customers and customer satisfaction data.*
- *Use of measurement indices and instruments that are unique to each customer group's expectations and needs regarding your products/services.*
- *Separate sets of data collected on levels of customer satisfaction for each major market group or segment.*
- *Use of data collection instruments and methods that minimize the time customers must spend providing you with feedback.*
- *Evidence that approach to measuring customer satisfaction has been refined and improved.*
- *Evidence that soft measures of customer satisfaction (surveys, complaints, feedback) correlate with hard measures of customer buying behavior.*

3.2b(2) How do you follow up with CUSTOMERS on the quality of products, services, and transactions to receive prompt and actionable feedback?

What They're Looking for Here

The frequency, thoroughness, and objectivity of the data you gather on how satisfied current customers are with your products and services are important in this Area to Address. A typical response for this Area is to explain, "We survey our customers once a year to determine their level of satisfaction with our products/services." Conducting a survey once a year represents a very weak follow-up approach. The examiners look for frequent contact with customers (e.g., quarterly or monthly) to determine how satisfied they are with your products and services. They also want to see that you use a variety of different follow-up methods, such as phone calls, mail surveys, etc. Although the approach should be comprehensive, it is also very important that it minimizes the amount of time the customer must spend giving you feedback. Too much follow-up can be an aggravation to the customer and end up doing more to turn him/her off than anything else. Explain how your approach to follow-up is sensitive to these issues and back it up with any data that indicate customers' opinion of your follow-up system. It is also important that you do informal follow-up with customers—not to collect customer satisfaction data, but simply to build a more positive relationship.

Indicators for Question 3.2b(2)

- *Percentage of customers surveyed during follow-up to determine their levels of satisfaction with your products and/or services.*
- *Frequent informal contact is done to build strong relationships with customers.*
- *Use of a variety of different data collection methods as follow-up on customer transactions.*
- *Follow-up approach demonstrates concern for minimizing customer time and hassle.*
- *Proactive follow-up is done for all types of customers and all of the organization's products and services.*

> 3.2b(3) HOW do you obtain and use information on your CUSTOMERS' satisfaction relative to their satisfaction with your competitors, other organizations providing similar products or services, and/or industry BENCHMARKS?

What They're Looking for Here

This part refers to how you determine how your levels of customer satisfaction compare with those of your competitors. We are not looking for data here; the criteria ask how you determine comparative levels of customer satisfaction. Including a question or two on your customer surveys, to ask your customers what they think of your competition, is a common way of doing this. This is certainly not the most objective way, however. You are surveying your own customers, and they may never have bought the competition's products/services, even though they may have an opinion about them. A more complete approach is to use an outside research firm to measure customer satisfaction among your own and your competitors' customers. J. D. Power, the market research firm used by the automotive industry, uses the same instruments to measure customer satisfaction among customers of all car companies. This way, the data are objective and can be easily compared. Your approach need not be as comprehensive as that used by the automotive industry, but you need to demonstrate that you gather reliable data on the levels of customer satisfaction your competitors achieve relative to your own levels.

Indicators for Question 3.2b(3)

- *Use of a variety of sources of data on competitors' levels of customer satisfaction.*
- *Objectivity of data gathered on how your customer satisfaction levels compare with competitors.*
- *Amount of data collected on comparison of customer satisfaction levels to those of competitors.*
- *Reliability of data-gathering methods used to assess competitors' levels of customer satisfaction.*

> 3.2b(4) HOW do you keep your APPROACHES to determining satisfaction current with business needs and directions?

What They're Looking for Here

You should begin your response here by listing the indices you use to measure and evaluate the organization's approach to determining customer satisfaction. Explain why these indices have been selected as the best measures of the effectiveness of your customer satisfaction measurement system. Next, list the steps or phases involved in your evaluation process, along with the outputs of each phase. Describe how evaluation data are summarized and reported, and explain who receives the reports. Finally, explain the process you use to review the evaluation results and develop an action plan for improving your approach to measuring customer satisfaction. A description of some of the changes you've made over the years to the customer satisfaction measurement system will help demonstrate that you do, in fact, take action based upon the evaluation data. The Baldrige examiners are looking for a trend of continuous improvements.

Indicators for Question 3.2b(4)

- *Explanation of a well-defined and systematic approach to evaluate a customer satisfaction measurement system.*
- *Objectivity and reliability of methodology and instruments used to evaluate customer satisfaction measurement system.*
- *Evaluation data are summarized and sent to appropriate managers and other employees.*

- *Action plans based upon evaluation data are created to identify improvements needed in customer satisfaction measurement system.*

- *Evidence that actions plans are actually implemented and that changes have been made in measurement instruments and/or methodologies based upon evaluation data.*

- *Trends showing continual improvements/enhancements in the approach to measuring customer satisfaction over the last several years.*

- *Evidence that improvements have been made in measurement of customer dissatisfaction indicators.*

Chapter

9

INTERPRETING THE CRITERIA FOR MEASUREMENT, ANALYSIS, AND KNOWLEDGE MANAGEMENT (4)

OVERVIEW OF THE INFORMATION AND ANALYSIS CATEGORY

The 2007 Baldrige Award Criteria define the Information and Analysis category as follows:

> *The 2007 Measurement, Analysis, and Knowledge Management Category examines how your organization selects, gathers, analyzes, manages, and improves its data, information, and knowledge assets. Also examined is how your organization reviews performance (p.29).*

The Measurement, Analysis, and Knowledge Management Category is worth a total of 90 points and is broken down into the following Examination Items:

4.1 Measurement, Analysis, and Improvement of Organizational Performance (45 points)

4.2 Management of Information, Information Technology, and Knowledge (45 points)

The purpose of this category is to assess the types of data you collect relating to company performance and to examine the process by which you analyze those data in order to make decisions. This chapter describes the two Examination Items and two Areas to Address that fall under this category. Again, each section begins with a shadowed box containing the Examination Item, the point value, and any applicable Notes.* Areas to Address falling under that item follow in a more lightly shadowed box. In the upper right corner of each Area to Address box is an indication [in brackets] of whether the Area pertains to approach, deployment, or results. All definitions and information appearing within these boxes are taken directly from the Baldrige criteria. Following each Area to Address is an explanation defining what the examiners are looking for in assessing your application. Next, I have supplied a list of indicators or evaluation factors that will assist you in interpreting the criteria and in preparing your application.

This category forms the foundation of a sound performance system. If you have a poor information and analysis system, this will lead to a low score in the sections that deal with planning (2), workforce focus (5), management of processes (6), and results (7). If you select the wrong indices to measure, this will lead to low scores in a number of different areas that ask for results. Even if your graphs look great, you won't end up with a good score for results if the performance indices on the graphs are inappropriate.

Category 4 in the 2007 Baldrige Award Criteria is a central part of a company's strategy, outlined in section 2.1, and its results, presented in section 7 of the application. Even though this category is only worth a possible 90 points out of 1,000, it is critical to high

---

* Item Notes that apply to a specific Area to Address are appropriately listed in the box containing that Area.

scores in other sections. In fact, if you do a poor job on this section, it will have a negative impact on section 7, which asks for results. Thus, section 4 actually impacts 90 points on its own, and another 450 points relating to results in section 7.

Some of the metrics that a company selects to measure its performance are directly related to the strategy and goals outlined in section 2.1 of the application. The measures are probably also the same ones reviewed by senior management, as discussed in 1.1. The measures that are discussed in section 4 will also be those on which results data are presented later in the application.

4.1 MEASUREMENT, ANALYSIS, AND IMPROVMENT OF ORGANIZATIONAL PERFORMANCE: How do you measure, analyze, and then improve organizational performance? (45 PTS.)   PROCESS

Describe HOW your organization measures, analyzes, aligns, reviews, and improves its PERFORMANCE through the use of data and information at all levels and in all parts of your organization. Describe HOW you SYSTEMATICALLY use the results of reviews to evaluate and improve PROCESSES.

N1. Performance measurement (4.1a) is used in fact-based decision making for setting and aligning organizational directions and resource use at the work unit, key process, departmental, and whole organization levels.

AREA TO ADDRESS   [APPROACH, DEPLOYMENT]

4.1a PERFORMANCE MEASUREMENT

(1) HOW do you select, collect, align, and integrate data and information for tracking daily operations and for tracking overall organizational PERFORMANCE, including progress relative to STRATEGIC OBJECTIVES and ACTIONPLANS? What are your KEY organizational PERFORMANCE MEASURES? HOWdo you use these data and information to support organizational decision making and INNOVATION?

What They're Looking For Here

This Area to Address asks about how you select your performance measures, as well as what they are. The real focus of the first question in this Area to Address is how you gather data on the metrics, and aggregate or summarize the data so that it can be used to monitor operations and make better business decisions. The frequency with which you gather the data and the methods used should be described. You should also indicate which measures are leading and lagging indicators. Leading indicators predict future organizational performance on key outcomes such as sales, profits, and loyalty from customers or employees. Lagging indicators are measures of previous events: sales, accidents, turnover, lost proposals/bids, etc. A well-balanced set of performance metrics includes both leading and lagging indicators.

Because the data collection methods, frequency, and method for consolidating or summarizing the data probably vary with each metric, it might make sense to include a table in your response:

METRIC	TYPE	FREQUENCY	DATACOLLECTION METHOD
Customer Loyalty	Lagging	Monthly	Counting of lost $ and accounts
Customer Sat. Index	Leading	Quarterly	Interviews, surveys, & Operational measures
$ in Proposals	Leading	Monthly	Total $ in proposals + % likelihood of award

An important point to include in this section is how you ensure consistency and reliability of your data collection. It is important that measurement instruments be calibrated as necessary and that controls are in place to ensure that things are measured the same way throughout your organization. This is particularly important in large complex organizations that may be spread across many locations and often different types of businesses. There need to be common definitions and methods used to gather data on high level performance. This way, the data from different parts of the business can be properly aggregated for analysis. Another factor you might want to address in this section is who gathers the data. Many companies make use of outside firms to measure performance of market share and customer or employee satisfaction. Not only does this help ensure more objectivity, but these companies tend to be specialists in measurement and data collection and may have more sophisticated instruments and comparative data than you would have if you collected the data yourself. While it is not necessary to use outside firms to gather data, you must have a method for ensuring objectivity. Many employees will tend to be less honest on an employee survey that gets sent to the HR department where people might even know their handwriting.

This question also asks about:

- *How do you measure performance in your organization?*
- *Why were these measures selected?*
- *Which metrics do you look at to evaluate daily operational performance and which metrics look at overall organizational performance?*

Question 4.1a(1) asks you to list the performance measures on your organization's scorecard and to explain how each relates to the operation of your organization, or to your overall business strategy. What is important here is that you collect data on a reasonable number of performance measures, and that you have good balance in your metrics. If your CEO or president regularly looks at more than 20 performance measures, you may receive a lower score. Many companies have scorecards that include 10 to 15 measures, which is also reasonable. The problem with recording too many measures is that it clouds your focus and ends up distracting you from the vital few performance metrics. The best indicator of a balanced scorecard approach to measurement is a relatively equal number of measures in each of the categories in your database. This is an area where many organizations have problems. Seventy to ninety percent of the data they collect and review on a regular basis are financial and operational. They prepare 50 pounds of financial reports each month, and maybe 1 pound of customer related or employee satisfaction data. Financial performance is measured a hundred different ways every single day, and employee satisfaction is measured once a year with a single survey. It is this imbalance of data that often causes applicants to receive low scores in this section.

Along with a reasonable number of performance measures, the concept of balancing the time perspective of your data is also important. Performance measures in many organizations focus almost exclusively on measuring the past. A good balanced scorecard includes measures from three perspectives: past, present, and future. Another aspect of balance that is important is that measures focus on the needs of more than just your shareholders or owners. Measures should focus on how well you satisfy customers, employees, and stakeholders, such as the community in which you operate.

In responding to this question, an effective format might be to list your performance measures down the left side of a table, grouped by category of data. For example, a common set of categories that correspond to the Baldrige criteria include:

- *Product and service measures*
- *Customer focused measures*
- *Financial and market measures*

- *Product and service quality measures*
- *Human resource measures*
- *Process effectiveness measures*
- *Leadership outcome measures*

Along the top of your table, you could list key goals or key success factors, and an additional column labeled "Business Fundamentals." Business fundamentals are used to indicate the measures that may not relate specifically to your key success factors or business drivers, but are important for running the business. For example, you will probably want to have some measure of profit, and perhaps safety in your scorecard, even though these might not be key business drivers for the organization right now. Using Xs in the boxes in your matrix, indicate which of the performance measures relate to which of the key business drivers or to business fundamentals. Assigning a percentage weight to each of the measures based on its importance in your overall business strategy is another good way of showing the linkage between your measures and your strategy.

Indicators for Question 4.1a(1)

- *Both leading and lagging indicators are included in the list of company performance measures.*
- *Data are collected frequently enough so that appropriate action may be taken to deal with problems and exploit opportunities.*
- *Methods used to collect data are appropriate for the type of metrics described.*
- *Appropriate internal or external personnel are used to gather data.*
- *Methods are used to ensure that data collection is reliable and consistent.*
- *Data are collected consistently across the organization.*
- *Data are appropriately and simply summarized for analysis and decision making.*
- *Evidence that the database was built with a plan, rather than being something that just evolved over time.*
- *CEO or president looks at not more than 20 measures every month to evaluate the organization's overall performance.*
- *Degree to which some macro measures have been derived from strategic objectives/goals or analysis of future success factors for the company.*
- *Extent to which measures have been developed for all strategic objectives or goals.*
- *Consistency of performance measures with mission, vision, and values.*
- *Consistency of measures across business units and/or locations.*
- *Evidence that the organization has a well-balanced set of metrics, with approximately equal amounts of data in each of the following categories: financial performance,*

operational/process measures, customer satisfaction, employee satisfaction, product/service quality, supplier performance, and safety/environmental performance.

- *Inclusion of both hard (customer buying behavior) and soft (customer opinions) measures of customer satisfaction in overall measures.*
- *Use of multiple measures of workforce engagement/satisfaction.*
- *Selection of 3 to 6 key financial metrics that are a good mix of short- and long-term indicators of success.*
- *Operational/process measures are related to customer or stakeholder requirements.*
- *Company database includes measures of cycle time and productivity or efficiency, as appropriate.*
- *Several overall measures of safety and environmental performance are included in the overall database.*
- *Metrics include a good mix of measures of past, present, and future performance.*

4.1a(2) How do you select and ensure the EFFECTIVE use of KEY comparative data and information to support operational and strategic decision making and INNOVATION?

N2. Comparative data and information (4.1a[2]) are obtained by benchmarking and by seeking competitive comparisons. "Benchmarking" refers to identifying processes and results that represent best practices and performance for similar activities, inside or outside your organization's industry. Competitive comparisons relate your organization's performance to that of competitors and other organizations providing similar products and services.

What They're Looking for Here

This portion of the criteria asks about how you identify the types of competitor and comparative data needed to evaluate your own performance and to develop appropriate strategies. You might begin your response to this section by identifying your major competitors, explaining the data you have to indicate that these organizations are, in fact, your most important competitors. For example, you might cite some industry data that outline the major players in your business or marketplace. Next, you should explain how you identify the types of data you need on your competitors. There will obviously be many sources of data on many competitors that you could gather. What the Baldrige examiners want to see is that you are very selective in deciding what data to gather on which competitors.

Following a description of how needs for competitor data are determined, present the same sorts of information regarding comparative data. Comparative data might consist of information on other locations or business units within your own company. Comparative data might also consist of industry performance, or information on similar companies that are in a related business. For example, a hotel might compare its reservations function to the reservations function in an airline or car rental company.

What the examiners also want to hear about in your response for this Area to Address is how you select those organizations to which you compare your own performance and practices. It is important to do both competitive comparisons and benchmarks. You might select your direct competitors as the companies you use for benchmarking purposes, or you might select companies that are totally outside your industry. A good approach employed by many exemplary organizations is to collect comparison data on all major competitors and to benchmark yourself against a variety of different functions in a variety of different organizations. In this section, you need to explain the process by which you select comparative organizations or "benchmarking partners."

One factor on which your response for this item will be evaluated is the number of different functions or indices used to compare yourself to competitors and benchmark organizations. If you compare your company with one other competitor who is also one you benchmark yourself against, you won't receive a very high score for this Area to Address. Many organizations select one or two past Baldrige winners and compare every function in their organization to them. This approach will not necessarily be effective because being a Baldrige winner does not mean that every function in the company is world-class. If, on the other hand, you have identified a dozen or more functions and compare yourself to world-class benchmarks on each function, you might end up with a perfect score in this Area to Address.

What is also considered important here is that the functions or processes you select as benchmarking and comparison targets must relate to your own goals and priorities for performance improvement, as outlined in the company's strategic and annual plans. Benchmarking is often done independently of the organization's performance improvement goals and plans. You should explain how the benchmarking and competitive comparison activities you engaged in during the past few years have supported your long-term and annual performance goals and priorities.

Within your response to this Area to Address, you should also explain how you determined which organizations were the best at performing a particular function. Some organizations do a much better job of self-promotion than others. It may be that the best organizations get overlooked in benchmarking studies because no one knows that they are the best. Explain what type and how thorough a job you did in identifying the world-class organizations used for benchmarking purposes. The more thorough your research the better. Use of benchmarking databases has received mixed reviews, so don't use this as your only source of data.

What the Baldrige people want to see in this section is that you actually use the competitive and benchmark data as stimuli to encourage improvements. Many companies conduct benchmarking studies, review the findings, and go about business as usual. You need to have some sort of process in place for using the benchmarking studies and competitive comparisons as a way to improve processes in your company. Your response for this section should begin with an explanation of what happens to benchmarking studies and competitive analyses. Explain how studies are reviewed, who reviews them, and how action plans are developed to use the data to capitalize on improvement opportunities.

Indicators for Question 4.1a(2)

- *A systematic process is used to identify the needs and types of competitor data that are collected.*
- *Needs for competitor data are consistent with the company's chosen mission, vision, and goals for the future.*
- *Various types of competitor data are prioritized so that those gathering and reporting the data understand which information is most critical to the business.*
- *A systematic approach is used to review and decide on the types of comparative data that might be most useful to the organization.*
- *The company has a systematic process for deciding which processes to benchmark or compare to others.*
- *Evidence exists of a systematic process for selecting competitive organizations for comparison purposes.*
- *Scope and breadth of data collected on competitors are appropriate.*
- *There is a strong relationship between process/functions selected for competitive comparisons and benchmarking and quality goals and plans for the organization.*
- *Thoroughness of research done to identify organizations that are the best at particular functions or processes.*
- *Comparisons to both competitors and benchmarks are used for setting improvement goals.*

- *Number and appropriateness of criteria used for selecting competitors with which to compare your organization.*
- *Number and appropriateness of criteria used for selecting benchmark organizations with which to compare your organization.*
- *Objectivity and clarity of the criteria for selecting competitors and benchmarks for comparison purposes.*
- *Linkage of competitor/benchmark data with strategic plan.*
- *Number of different sources of data on competitors.*
- *Objectivity and reliability of sources of data on competitors.*

> 4.1a(3) HOW do you keep your performance measurement system current with business needs and directions? HOW do you ensure that your PERFORMANCE measurement system is sensitive to rapid or unexpected organizational or external changes?

What They're Looking for Here

Your response for this Area to Address should explain how you systematically evaluate your metrics, data collection systems, and instruments. Describe how the evaluation is done, the procedures used, instruments, etc. Don't respond with a statement such as: "We regularly evaluate and improve the scope and accuracy of our measures and data collection." Be specific. Explain exactly how you evaluate the data collection system. Your approach will be assessed based upon its thoroughness, objectivity, validity, and use of accepted evaluation methodologies. You should begin by listing the specific indices you use to measure the effectiveness of your database. The measurement indices should include internal customer satisfaction, process, and output measures. Follow this list with a flowchart or list of steps involved in the evaluation process.

In this section you might also write about any actions you have taken to get business units and/or facilities to work together to develop common measures. If you have employed any objectives or incentives to encourage sharing of data it would also be appropriate to mention this here.

The Baldrige examiners are also looking for evidence that you have taken actions to streamline the information processing cycle and to implement countermeasures to improve quality. Even more important is an explanation of how your performance metrics have been evaluated and improved. Measures are often added and deleted as problems arise and go away and strategy changes. For example, one company measured how well it handled phone calls from customers until performance exceeded standards for several years. The metric is still tracked but it is not given the importance rating it was when this area was a problem for the company.

Indicators for Question 4.1a(3)

- *Evidence that measures or metrics have been improved to be more closely linked to business drivers or goals.*
- *Existence of a systematic approach for evaluating data collection systems.*
- *Evaluation measurement indices include measures of internal customer satisfaction, process, and output quality.*
- *Evidence that the company has increased employees' access to data and information.*
- *Validity and objectivity of evaluation instruments and methodologies.*
- *Number of years during which evaluation has been done.*
- *Evidence of improvements in data collection system based upon evaluation.*
- *Evidence that data gathering, analysis, and reporting process has been streamlined over the last several years.*
- *Amount of data indicating that cycle time of data collection and dissemination has been reduced.*
- *Description of specific strategies and tactics that have been employed to reduce cycle time of collecting, summarizing, and disseminating data.*
- *Evidence of steps taken to closely align the company's performance measures with process improvement efforts.*

AREA TO ADDRESS   [APPROACH, DEPLOYMENT]
4.1b PERFORMANCE ANALYSIS and Review

(1) HOWdo you review organizational PERFORMANCE and capabilities? HOW do your SENIOR LEADERS participate in these reviews? What ANALYSES do you perform to support these reviews and to ensure that conclusions are valid? HOW do you use these reviews to assess organizational success, competitive PERFORMANCE, and progress relative to STRATEGIC OBJECTIVES and ACTION PLANS? HOW do you use these reviews to assess your organization's ability to rapidly respond to changing organizational needs and challenges in your operating environment?

Continued...

N3. Organizational performance reviews (4.1b[1]) should be informed by organizational performance measurement and guided by the strategic objectives and action plans described in Items 2.1 and 2.2. The reviews also might be informed by internal or external Baldrige assessments.

N4. Analysis includes examining trends; organizational, industry, and technology projections; and comparisons, cause-effect relationships, and correlations intended to support your performance reviews, help determine root causes, and help set priorities for resource use. Accordingly, analysis draws upon all types of data: customer related, financial and market, operational, and competitive.

What They're Looking for Here

This section asks about what you do with all the data you collect that are described in section 2, 4.1, 5, and 6. Many organizations collect a great deal of data that they do not actually use.

As I have mentioned several times already, the key to success in the new Baldrige criteria is balance. Quality has to be balanced with financial results, process improvements and improvements in productivity need to be balanced with employee satisfaction, and so forth. To receive a high score, 2007 Baldrige applicants will need to show world-class levels of both financial and quality-related results. One way of achieving good results in all areas is to understand the relationships between individual measures on the company's scorecard. For example, how much will a 5-point improvement in customer satisfaction impact profits or repeat business? Some leading companies today have conducted the research to identify and understand these correlations. For example, IBM recently completed research that shows the correlation between their Net Satisfaction Index (NSI), which is an overall measure of customer satisfaction, and future revenue for the corporation. IBM has found that even a 1-point improvement on the overall NSI translates into several million dollars in future revenue. Satisfied customers not only stay with IBM, but they are more likely to spend more on IBM products and services in the future. By understanding the relationships between these measures, IBM can make intelligent business decisions regarding investments that are supposed to increase their NSI score.

Another organization that has attempted to analyze their performance data and find links is Sears. In 1992, Sears had the worst year in its long history—the company lost almost $4 billion on $52 billion in sales. Part of the turnaround strategy was to sell off all nonretail businesses such as Budget Rental Car, Allstate Insurance, Coldwell Banker Real Estate, and Discover Card. By 1995, the company had a new vision, a new strategy, and what looked like a balanced scorecard of performance metrics. Sears began collecting regular data on employee morale, customer satisfaction, and other variables besides traditional financial measures. The company sought the help of Dr. Thomas Buzas in analyzing the data to find links or correlations between leading and lagging indicators. Sears' hypothesis was that there should be a strong link between employee satisfaction and customer satisfaction, and between customer satisfaction and future revenue. Based on the analyses that were done, Sears found that the links were so weak, that it did not make a lot of sense to invest huge sums of money to drive either employee satisfaction or customer satisfaction. The correlations found were:

$$\begin{array}{ccc} \text{5 point increase} & & \text{0.05\% increase in} \\ \text{in employee morale} & \rightarrow & \text{customer satisfaction} \end{array} \rightarrow \quad \text{1.3\% revenue growth}$$

Dr. Buzas suggested that Sears take a look at the metrics and data collection instruments used to collect data on customer and employee satisfaction, because most companies find that there is a stronger link. Having this analysis told Sears that it would not be wise to invest millions of dollars to improve employee morale, because the data show that there is a weak link between morale and other results like revenue. It appeared Sears was going to turn the corner to financial success again early in 1998, but the end of the year's results were quite disappointing. In late 2004, Sears was bought by formerly bankrupt K-Mart for about $11.5 billion. My analysis of what happened to Sears is that they never had a clear vision for the future. The vision that Art Martinez crafted envisioned Sears becoming a compelling place to:

- *Shop*
- *Work*
- *Invest*

While this might be a catchy set of phrases, it really says nothing about the kind of organization Sears wanted to become. When a company is in trouble, creating a viable vision is one of the most important activities because it might mean success or failure. Being bought by K-Mart had to have been a huge disappointment to Sears. Their balanced scorecard has been written up in *Harvard Business Review* and other publications, but there are many serious problems in their strategic plan, and it works better as an example of what not to do when designing a measurement system.

I would begin my answer to this first question with an overall description of how various types of data are analyzed and compared in your organization. You might want to indicate which measures you believe are leading indicators of success and which ones are lagging indicators. For example, customer satisfaction survey data might be a leading indicator that is linked to and predicts customer buying behavior or loyalty, which links to future revenue. After explaining your overall approach to analyzing performance data, list some of the correlations or links you have found, and summarize the actions or plans you have implemented based upon that knowledge. Summarizing these correlations in a table or chart might be a good idea. The headings on such a chart might be as follows:

LEADING INDICATORS	LAGGING INDICATORS	CORRELATION	ACTION PLANS

The metrics or indicators listed in this chart might come from your overall scorecard (4.1), from your strategic plan (2.2), or from sections of the application that look at processes such as 5 Human Resource Focus or 6 Process Management.

The reason that the relationships between different performance measures are so important to understand is that you can then make scientific business decisions. This removes much of the guesswork of running a business. When decisions are made with data, and those data are well understood, there are no, or at least few, surprises. If you want to be a leader rather than a follower, it is imperative that you measure the right things, and understand how those measures impact each other. This is the essence of what 4.2 is all about, and why it is so important in Baldrige.

This Area to Address asks about how you translate improvements in customer satisfaction or the quality of products or services into financial measures. What the examiners want to see here is an explanation of how you measure the return on investment in your quality efforts. Let's say, for example, that you reduced the percentage of defects in your products from 2% down to .03%. The examiners will want to know how improvements in defect rates translate into financial benefits for the company. You also need to explain the relationship between key operational measures and key financial measures. A good way of presenting this data would be a matrix that lists your key financial measures along the top and the key quality and operational measures along the left side. The matrix should indicate which quality and operational measures have a strong degree of impact upon the key financial measures. An example of such a matrix chart is shown below.

KEY MEASURES	PROFITS	MARKET SHARE	SALES	ROA
Customer Satisfaction Index	M	H	H	M
Product Defects	H	M	M	H
Design Cycle Time	L	M	M	L

A chart such as this should be supplemented with an explanation of how and why key measures of quality and operational indices lead to financial measures. You need to explain, for example, how your customer satisfaction index has a high degree of impact on both market share and sales.

Following the explanation of the review and data-analysis processes, you need to provide some examples of how analysis of financial information has led to decisions or the initiation of changes that resulted in improved levels of operational results or improvements in customer satisfaction. The examples will add credibility to your process description. One of the major factors that the Baldrige examiners look for, once they have determined that you have a sound systematic approach, is deployment. A good way of giving them information on deployment is through a series of examples that include various functions and levels of employees in your organization. Space limitations will prevent you from listing as many examples as you might like, but matrices and charts are a good way of presenting a number of examples in a limited amount of space. You might create a four-column chart that looks like the following.

EXAMPLES—FINANCIAL ANALYSIS AND ACTION PLANS			
FINANCIAL DATA	ANALYSIS	DECISION/ACTION	RESULTS
Loss of market share in Midwest region	11 new Wal-Mart stores open in 2005	Increased newspaper and direct mail advertising More competitive pricing Increased staffing Additional ser vice training	1st quarter results show improvements

Indicators for Question 4.1b(1)

- *Evidence that the company has conducted research to identify correlations between customer satisfaction measures and financial performance.*
- *Evidence of research being conducted to identify correlations between measures of product/service quality and customer satisfaction.*
- *Evidence of research being conducted to identify correlations between measures of supplier performance, product/service, quality, and other performance measures.*
- *Analysis of relationships between individual performance measures is used to make key business decisions.*

- *Understanding of relationships between different performance measures has been documented for all key areas of the business.*
- *Continued monitoring of trends and correlations is done to identify changes in correlations and possible new ones.*
- *Validity/rigor of research done to demonstrate correlations between measures.*
- *Deployment of correlations across all key performance measures identified in 4.1a and 2.1/2.2.*
- *Evidence that major business decisions are based upon analysis of data and an understanding of how each measure relates to others.*

4.1b(2) HOW do you translate organizational PERFORMANCE review findings into priorities for continuous and breakthrough improvement and into opportunities for INNOVATION? HOW are these priorities and opportunities deployed to work group- and functional-level operations throughout your organization to enable EFFECTIVE support for their decision making? When appropriate, HOW are the priorities and opportunities deployed to your suppliers, PARTNERS, and collaborators to ensure organizational ALIGNMENT?

N5. The results of organizational performance analysis should contribute to your organizational strategic planning in Category 2.

N6. Your organizational performance results should be reported in Items 7.1–7.6.

What They're Looking for Here

This was a new question in 2004 and it is a very good one. In plain English, what this question asks is how do you communicate the analyses you discussed in 4.2b(1), and how do you ensure that actions and plans throughout the organization are in concert with these analyses? This tends to be very difficult in large diverse organizations that might be spread across numerous locations. This is one area where Sears has done a fine job. Sears uses a mural to depict their vision, and shows employees how their jobs can impact the company vision, and how they can prevent Sears from falling into the "retail graveyard" wherein lie Montgomery Ward, W. T. Grant, Woolworth, and many other former retail giants. Every new and existing Sears employee is taken through a several-hour training session to teach them about their role in helping the company make the right decisions and achieve the right results.

On site visits, examiners often find a number of projects, programs, and initiatives in a large organization that overlap, contradict each other, and often are directly contrary to the company's overall strategic plan. For example, one company had a large quality organization consisting of teams, team leaders, quality improvement projects, meetings, etc. Hundreds of thousands of dollars were being spent to improve product and service quality, with literally hundreds of "continuous improvement" projects going on at any one time. The problem was that company-level analyses had revealed that both product and service quality were fine, and that previous improvements had not led to increases in either customer satisfaction, or more importantly, increased revenue. Yet the company had not communicated this message to employees and it let them continue their quality improvement projects. This sort of disconnect between actions of lower-level employees and analysis done by executives is actually quite typical.

A good way of impressing the examiners in this section is to first explain how you communicate the results of your analyses to employees. Stress how you make this information understandable to all, and how you make it relevant for all levels of employees and job functions. For example, why would a systems analyst in the I.T. department care about the link you have found between external customer satisfaction and future loyalty? After describing what you communicate and the methods used for communication, you need to explain how you ensure that organizational initiatives are consistent with your analyses. This is another situation where a table or chart might be appropriate. Such a chart might include the information outlined in the example below.

INITIATIVE/PROGRAM	DESIRED RESULTS	LINK TO ANALYSES
Process Reengineering	Improved efficiency Decreased costs	• Low cost provider study • Growth in operating expenses/revenue • Western Region Pilot Studies
New Hire Assessment Center	Reduced 1st year turnover of new hires	• HR study by WMJ Associates • Analysis of cost of turnover in 1st year
Customer Intimacy Program	Increased loyalty Increased profits	• Market analysis • Internal data on sources of profitability

The format of your chart need not follow the one above exactly, but you want to convey the idea that your current initiative or programs are based upon thorough analyses that show that each one will lead to the overall success of your organization.

Indicators for Question 4.1b(2)

- *Evidence that organizational analyses are well communicated to all appropriate employees and stakeholders.*

- *Percentage of employees who can correctly explain impact of analyses of their jobs/functions.*

- *Evidence that the organization cancels initiatives or programs when they are inconsistent with current plans and analyses.*

- *No disconnects exist between initiatives/programs and analyses of data discussed in 4.2a(1).*

- *Company vision, key success factors, and strategic plans are consistent with analyses discussed in this section.*

- *Deployment of organization-level analyses to business units, facilities, and other portions of the organization.*

- *Evidence that key analysis data are used to guide decision making in the organization at all levels that are appropriate.*

---

(3) How do you incorporate the results of organizational PERFORMANCE reviews into the SYSTEMATIC evaluation and improvement of KEY PROCESSES?

What They're Looking for Here

This is a new question for 2007 and a good addition. Reviews of trends and levels in key measures of performance are a good way to identify opportunities for improving processes. This data-based approach to identifying process improvement opportunities is very consistent with a Six Sigma or Lean approach that many organizations use today. Your answer to this question should explain how results are analyzed to determine the causes of performance problems, and how the opportunities identified are reviewed and prioritized and then assigned to teams for process improvement. You will probably have to reference information in Item 6.2 of the application, which asks for more detail on how processes are analyzed and improved. The results of performance reviews should also be a key input to the planning process, and negative trends or poor levels of performance may require an extremely new strategy rather than simply an improvement in existing work processes. Your task in answering this question is to convince the Examiners that you do much more than look at performance data—you use it to identify opportunities for improving the organization. If you have room, adding a few examples that may be detailed more in section 6 would be a good idea.

Indicators for Question 4.1b(3)

- *Evidence that a systematic process is used to evaluate levels and trends in performance data to identify opportunities or problems.*

- *Deployment of this systematic analysis approach throughout all levels and units in the organization.*

- *Reviews are conducted often enough (e.g., at least monthly) to detect trends or drops in performance early on.*

- *Results of data analyses are an input to the strategic planning process.*

- *Results of data analyses are used as a starting point for process improvement efforts.*

- *All process improvement initiatives can be linked back to performance on one or more of the performance metrics in the organization scorecard.*

- *Process improvement initiatives are prioritized so that the processes selected for improvement are most likely to have a positive impact on major outcomes for the organization.*

4.2 MANAGEMENT OF INFORMATION, INFORMATION TECHNOLOGY, AND KNOWLEDGE

PROCESS

How do you manage your information, information technology, and organizational knowledge?   (45 PTS.)

Describe HOW your organization ensures the quality and availability of needed data, information, software, and hardware for your WORKFORCE, suppliers, PARTNERS, COLLABORATORS and CUSTOMERS. Describe HOW your organization builds and manages its KNOWLEDGE ASSETS.

AREA TO ADDRESS   [APPROACH, DEPLOYMENT]

4.2a Data and Information Availability

(1) HOW do you make needed data and information available? How do you make them accessible to WORKFORCE, PARTNERS, COLLABORATORS, and CUSTOMERS, as appropriate?

N1. Data and information access (4.2a[1]) might be via electronic or other means.

What They're Looking for Here

From the notes in this Area to Address, it appears that you need to have your own intranet site for communicating information to employees and partners. This is certainly not the case. However, many public and private sector organizations have developed their own intranet sites for communicating performance data to employees and partners. Many of my own clients have found that this is an efficient way to communicate real-time performance data to various personnel, without waiting for voluminous reports or monthly management meetings to check on company performance.

Many of my clients have also purchased balanced scorecard software to use in presenting performance data on their intranet sites. Programs such as Performance Softs, manufactured by a company in Toronto, provide users with easy-to-read color-coded graphics for viewing performance data, and allow unlimited "drill-downs" to analyze performance or determine the root causes of problems. These software programs provide managers, employees, and partners with important performance data whenever they want to see it. For reviews of some of the top balanced scorecard software programs, consult my recent book: Winning Score: How to Design and Implement Organizational Scorecards (Productivity Press, 2000). A smaller organization, or one without the need for an intranet site, also needs to communicate performance data in a clear and timely manner. A company called Australia New Zealand Direct Line in Santa Ana, California, uses a large bulletin board that looks like the dashboard of a car. The needles on each gauge are moved each day to reflect the previous day's performance in the company. Employees pay very close attention to the dashboard because their bonus is linked to some of the dashboard gauges.

Regardless of whether you use electronic or less sophisticated means of communicating performance data, clarity is one of the keys. Communicating performance data using monthly 100-page spreadsheet reports is a thing of the past in most forward-thinking companies today. Consistency of data reporting is also important. All performance data must be communicated using consistent formats, so time is not wasted trying to figure out what the charts say. This Area to Address also asks about data availability. If you have it all on your intranet site and half of your employees do not have computers, accessibility is rather limited. The same goes for information that you need to communicate to suppliers, partners, or others outside of the organization. It might be that your organization also communicates with customers using the Internet or other electronic means. If you have your own website for customers to place orders or seek information on your firm, you need to explain how you ensure that it is accessible and easy to use.

I recently tried to buy a laptop computer on Sony's website and gave up after about 30 minutes of being sent from one irrelevant screen and menu to another. If you do business with customers via your website, examiners will certainly check it out during a site visit, but make sure to mention here what you have done to make it accessible and easy to use.

Indicators for Question 4.2a(1)

- *Use of consistent formats for communicating performance data.*
- *Methods used to report/communicate data are easy to understand and interpret.*
- *If software is used to communicate performance data electronically, it includes easy to understand graphics/charts, and allows online analysis of data.*

> 4.2a(2) How do you ensure that hardware and software are reliable, secure, and user friendly?

What They're Looking for Here

It is tempting to answer this question with one or two sentences that explain that you have a systematic approach for evaluating the purchase of hardware and software and evaluating them for reliability and user-friendliness. This, however, will not suffice. The other option is to go into great detail with flowcharts and detailed descriptions of your processes for evaluating off-the-shelf hardware and software, and for building your own. This would be great if you had room, but you do not. You have about a half a page to explain the general procedures you have in place for ensuring reliability in your systems, and for evaluating usability of the systems. After providing an explanation of these approaches, you might want to present a few examples, illustrating how you have improved data reliability, or user-friendliness of some of your hardware and/or software. The answer you give in this section will vary depending on the size and nature of your organization as well. A small bakery with 20 employees might rely on exclusively off-the-shelf hardware and software, and rely on the manufacturers to ensure that these systems work reliably and are easy to use. Certainly, user-friendliness should be a factor in deciding which systems to purchase, however. A large high-tech firm with 10,000 employees would be expected to have a much more sophisticated approach for ensuring reliability and user-friendliness, and may develop many of the hardware configurations themselves, and design some of their own software.

Indicators for Question 4.2a(2)

- *A systematic approach is used to evaluate potential hardware and software purchases for reliability and user-friendliness.*

- *New hardware and/or software is pilot-tested in a portion of the organization, if appropriate, prior to full-scale implementation.*

- *Systems are monitored on an ongoing basis for reliability.*

- *New versions of software are implemented with appropriate user training/directions.*

- *Users of information technology hardware/software have major input in purchasing decisions regarding systems that they will use.*

- *There is no evidence that the company has deliberately purchased systems that are not the most user-friendly because of politics or relations with certain vendors.*

4.2a(3) In the event of an emergency, HOW do you ensure the continued availability of hardware and software systems and the continued availability of data and information?

What They're Looking for Here

This question asks about your back-up plans for hardware and software in the event of an emergency. With all of the disasters we've had in the past few years around the world, contingency planning has become more important than it was in the past. Your answer to this question should address how your organization would continue to operate in an emergency. Even a low-tech organization such as a restaurant or school is dependent on electricity, gas, and other resources. There are many businesses and organizations today that are almost completely dependent upon their information systems for operational performance: Call centers, airlines, hotels, and insurance firms are dependent on access to electronically-stored data to function. Your answer to this question should address how your organization would continue to function if information technology fails.

Indicators for Question 4.2a(3)

- *The organization has a comprehensive contingency plan in place to deal with interruptions in information systems (hardware and software).*

- *The system has been tested on a regular basis using drills, and it performs up to expectations.*

- *Back-up plans are in place for all facilities and categories of employees.*

4.2a(4) HOW do you keep your data and information availability mechanisms, including your software and hardware systems, current with business needs and directions and with technological changes in your operating environment?

What They're Looking for Here

First, you must understand what is meant by "data availability mechanism." I can't say I have heard that phrase used by any of my clients. What they are asking about is the method you use to report data or communicate it to your employees/partners. Previously, this consisted of a paper report, with graphs and tables of company performance figures. Today, that data is often reported online, rather than in a paper report. Companies still often have monthly executive management meetings wherein performance is reviewed via a series of PowerPoint charts and handouts. If this is the method used in your organization to communicate performance data, you must convince examiners that this is the best way to communicate data, and that the approach still makes sense and is workable in your current business situation.

Some of my government clients report and review performance data once a year in a long boring multiday meeting. Each part of the organization gets up with their set of 20 to 30 overheads and presents data on his or her organization's accomplishments for the year. This is obviously not the best way to report and communicate performance data, but some government organizations just started measuring performance, so it is a start. Whatever methods you use to communicate performance data (meetings, reports, intranet sites, etc.), you need to explain why these methods are appropriate for your organization, and how you have evaluated and improved them over the past few years. As with all approach/deployment items, the examiners look for system maturity by judging how many times you have evaluated and improved your approaches for communicating performance data. A short list of some of the most important changes and improvements you have made in this area should be included in your application.

If you use hardware and software as the primary means for communicating performance data, you can probably combine your answer to the two questions. If you use more of a system of meetings and written reports to communicate performance data, you will need a separate answer for the two questions. The answer to this final question in Category 4 might be somewhat vague if you have a wide variety of hardware and software in your organization. Try to be as specific as possible, without taking up too much space. Essentially what the examiners want to see is that you are not stuck with antiquated hardware and software that no longer works well in the current business environment. You need to convince the examiners that you buy the best and most up-to-date systems that you can afford, and that they are the right level of sophistication for your business today. Some examples of upgrades or new systems you have recently purchased or installed should be included. You might even discuss the hardware/software situation of your biggest competitors as well. Baldrige winners tend to be leaders in technology rather than followers. This does not mean that you always have to have the latest and greatest, however. It is important that you show how the information technology systems fit your current business situation.

Indicators for Question 4.1a(4)

- *Employees and suppliers/partners have adequate access to performance data all the time they need it.*
- *Data are updated often enough so that users may see the most current performance.*
- *If the company has an intranet or Internet site, it is easy to access and use.*
- *Improvements have been made over the last few years in the methods used to communicate performance data.*
- *Employees and other users frequently look at and are able to understand performance data.*
- *Colored graphics or other methods are used to creatively and simply communicate performance data.*
- *Approaches used to communicate performance data are appropriate for the type of organization and level of sophistication.*
- *Evidence that frequency of communication is related to the frequency of data collection and level of volatility in performance on some key measures.*
- *Methods used to communicate maximize use of existing tools and technology.*
- *Methods used to communicate performance data are efficient and minimize the amount of time employees, managers, and partners must spend reviewing data.*
- *Meetings are not used to present performance data that could be presented prior to meetings.*
- *Systems for communicating performance data have been evaluated and improved several times over the last few years.*
- *Evidence that hardware and software are periodically and systematically evaluated for appropriateness and usefulness.*
- *Number and scope of changes/improvements made to hardware/software based on evaluation data.*
- *Evidence that the organization buys the best and most ideally suited hardware and software systems that they can afford.*
- *Evidence that the organization is ahead of its competitors in the area of information technology.*
- *Number of evaluation and improvement cycles employed on major hardware/software systems used in the organization.*

AREA TO ADDRESS   [APPROACH, DEPLOYMENT]

4.2b(1). Data, Information, and Knowledge Management

(1) How do you ensure the following properties of your organizational data, information, and knowledge:

- accuracy
- integrity and reliability
- timeliness
- security and confidentiality

What They're Looking for Here

This bullet asks how you ensure the integrity and reliability of your data. One common way of doing this is using an outside party to collect the data for you. This is often done to obtain data on customer or employee satisfaction, because comparative data is available for assessing levels of performance. Using an outside firm does not guarantee reliability, but a good mix of inside and outside data is probably preferable to all internally collected data. Another topic that might be discussed here is data collection techniques. Sample size selection, item analyses on surveys, survey design methodology, and topics such as these are good subjects to discuss in this section. You don't need to go overboard here and list the methods used to ensure reliability and data integrity for each metric on your corporate scorecard. Nor do you just want to make a blanket statement like: "We use a variety of techniques to test and ensure the reliability of our data." Something in between is appropriate.

Indicators for Question 4.2b(1)

- *A variety of methods are used to ensure reliability of performance data.*
- *Automated measurement devices are used where possible to increase reliability.*
- *Regularly scheduled reliability checks of measurement and data collection instruments are done.*
- *Automated data collection instruments are calibrated regularly according to established standards and methods.*
- *Outside data is used where appropriate to ensure objectivity of data.*
- *There is evidence that appropriate sampling techniques are used.*
- *Data are reported in a timely fashion.*
- *Appropriate controls are in place to ensure data integrity and confidentiality.*
- *Secure information is properly safeguarded.*
- *Consistency of metrics and data collection methods across units and facilities, if appropriate.*

AREA TO ADDRESS   [APPROACH, DEPLOYMENT]
4.2b(2). Data, Information, and Knowledge Management

HOW do you manage organizational knowledge to accomplish the following:
- the collection and transfer of EMPLOYEE knowledge
- the transfer of relevant knowledge from and to CUSTOMERS, suppliers, PARTNERS, and COLLABORATORS
- the rapid identification, sharing, and implementation of best practices
- the assembly and transfer of relevant knowledge for use in your strategic planning Process

---

What They're Looking for Here

Organizational knowledge is becoming an increasingly important asset to be collected and managed systematically. Some companies call it "intellectual capital." Whatever you call it, the criteria are asking for evidence of a systematic approach to collecting employee knowledge and communicating it to those who might benefit from it. In the past, this was done by having senior people mentor young people to pass on their wisdom. This might still be an appropriate system for a small organization. In most medium to large organizations, a more formal and structured approach would be necessary. The approach used to document employee knowledge or lessons learned should be both comprehensive and easy to use. I have seen several companies that had systems that were so time consuming and complicated that employees rarely used them. Several of the big management consulting firms I'm familiar with have outstanding databases with lessons learned on client projects. A new team of consultants can then benefit from the lessons learned by their more seasoned counterparts.

The knowledge an organization collects does not just come from its employees, but from those contacts on the outside. Customers can provide a wealth of knowledge on the strengths and weaknesses of your organization and the lessons they have learned when dealing with your company. Complaints, focus groups, discussions, and hard data on the application of your product/service by customers and valuable information that must be documented and communicated to appropriate personnel. Often this information remains in the customer service area.

The bigger the organization, the harder it is to document and share best practices. In a company of ten people, this is easy because everyone talks to everyone else and sees what has been tried and what has not worked. Best practices quickly become standard procedure. In large organizations, the left hand often does not know what the right hand is doing. Most big companies do have an approach for documenting and sharing best practices, but the effectiveness of these approaches varies considerably. Cargill, whose Sunny Fresh Foods won a Baldrige Award a few years ago, publishes a book called *Gems* that documents best practices. Cargill also arranges a huge conference each year, with their employees from around the globe sharing best practices and lessons learned in almost a trade-show-like atmosphere. These are both effective approaches, but often the people who should see these best practices do not look at the database or come to the meeting. In discussing your approach to documenting and sharing best practices, make sure to mention how widely deployed the system is, and perhaps give a few examples of how the sharing of best practices has improved performance.

Indicators for Question 4.2b(2)

- *A structured approach exists for documenting employee knowledge.*
- *The documentation system is easy to use for employees and captures appropriate details to make it useful.*
- *Accessing the knowledge database is easy and finding what you need is simple.*
- *The database is continually kept up to date.*
- *There is evidence that a wide variety of types and levels of employees document their own knowledge and access others'.*
- *Systems exist for documenting and storing information learned from customers that is relevant to organizational performance or products/services.*
- *Supplier/partner knowledge is also collected and stored in a database.*
- *The system that includes supplier and customer lessons learned or knowledge is easy to access and contains details and content useful to others.*
- *There is evidence that the database of customer/supplier knowledge is accessed often and by the appropriate personnel.*
- *The organization has a systematic approach for documenting best practices and lessons learned from failures.*
- *The best practices database is comprehensive and kept current.*
- *There is evidence of wide use/deployment of the best practices database.*
- *There is evidence that the database of organizational knowledge is used as part of the planning process to set targets and develop strategies.*
- *Senior management have contributed to the knowledge database and access it on a regular basis for planning and decision making.*
- *Knowledge and lessons learned are an input to the planning process.*

Chapter

10

INTERPRETING THE CRITERIA FOR WORKFORCE FOCUS (5)

OVERVIEW OF THE WORKFORCE FOCUS CATEGORY

The fifth category in the 2007 Baldrige criteria is defined as follows:

The Workforce Focus Category examines how your organization engages, manages, and develops your workforce to utilize its fullest potential in alignment with your organization's overall mission, strategy and action plans. The Category examiners your ability to assess workforce capability and capacity and to build a workforce environment conducive to high performance. (p. 26)

This category is divided into two Examination Items:

    5.1 Workforce Engagement (45 points)

    5.2 Workforce Environment (40 points)

This category examines how you select, develop, and motivate the employees and other members of your workforce in order to achieve high performance. As with other Baldrige categories that ask about your approaches, there is not a single preferred approach. Rather, the examiners are expecting that your human resource (HR) processes match your culture, size and type of organization. What is important is that your systems for managing people are logical, efficient, and based on an analysis of real needs, rather than tradition. It is important that you demonstrate how your HR processes have been designed to drive the right behavior from your people, and encourage them to consistently achieve high levels of performance.

Innovation may help improve your score, if you demonstrate novel approaches to job design, feedback, or training, but is certainly not necessary. An organization with very traditional HR processes may end up with a high score, if it can show the logic behind the approach, and that the HR processes have been evaluated and improved many times over the last few years. Evidence of teams, empowerment, and other trappings of TQM programs of the past is certainly no longer a requirement, but may still be a plus if an organization finds these approaches effective.

The pages that follow include detailed explanations of how to interpret the individual Areas to Address and questions in this category. As before, the information on the overall item is found in a shadowed box and the explanation of the Areas to Address appears in another box below that. In some cases, there is a separate explanation of individual subpoints [e.g., 5.2a(1)] when this is the best way of presenting the material. Following each explanation of the Areas to Address and subpoints, there is a list of indicators of what the examiners might expect to see when evaluating your response to this Area to

Address. As in the previous chapter, these indicators are not requirements, or a checklist, but simply suggestions of the type of performance an examiner might see in a company that received a high score.

5.1 WORKFORCE ENGAGEMENT: How do you engage achieve your workforce to organizational and personal success? (35 PTS.)   PROCESS

Describe HOW your organization engages, compensates, and rewards your WORKFORCE to achieve HIGH PERFORMANCE. Describe HOW members of your WORKFORCE, including leaders, are developed to achieve HIGH PERFORMANCE. Describe HOW you assess WORKFORCE ENGAGEMENT and use the results to achieve higher PERFORMANCE.

AREA TO ADDRESS   [APPROACH, DEPLOYMENT]

5.1a. Workforce Enrichment

(1) HOW do you determine the KEY factors that affect WORKFORCE ENGAGEMENT? HOW do you determine the KEY factors that affect WORKFORCE satisfaction? HOW are these factors determined for different WORKFORCE groups and SEGMENTS?

N1. "Workforce" refers to the people actively involved in accomplishing the work of your organization. It includes your organization's permanent, temporary, and part-time personnel, as well as any contract employees supervised by your organization. It includes team leaders, supervisors, and managers at all levels. People supervised by a contractor should be addressed in Category 6 as part of your larger work systems. For nonprofit organizations that also rely on volunteers, "workforce" includes these volunteers.

N2. "Workforce engagement" refers to the extent of workforce commitment, both emotional and intellectual, to accomplishing the work, mission, and vision of the organization. Organizations with high levels of workforce engagement are often characterized by high-performing work environments in which people are motivated to do their utmost for the benefit of their customers and for the success of the organization.

What They're Looking for Here

This excellent question was added to the 1999 criteria and revised again in 2007. It is similar to the logic in section 3 wherein 3.1 asks how you segment customers and determine their requirements and needs. This question asks you to do the same for employees. You might start out your answer by explaining how and why you segment employees into different groups. Be careful how you do this, so as not to be implicitly offensive. Although there are some cultural differences, it might not be a good idea to explain that you have two types of employees: white and non-white. Separating employees into professionals and workers might also be offensive. The employee segments you define should be based upon important differences in what they want from the job and work environment, and not necessarily their ethnic background, or level in the company.

After listing the different segments or groups of employees, explain how you determine what's important to them. Remember the discussion from 3.1 about how traditional market research methods like surveys and focus groups tend to be very unreliable. Examiners will be impressed if you come up with some creative ways of determining what's really important to your employees. Part of your answer might be data you have collected on the success of things you have tried to make the workplace more enjoyable. For example, one company found out that employees did not like to have after work social events because they were boring, but they felt obligated to attend for fear of not being seen as a "team player." Often employees never think to analyze what they like and don't like at the place they work, so it is hard to get them to articulate those feelings in a survey.

After describing the approaches you employ to determine the needs and preferences of your employees, you must explain what your research revealed. These factors might be listed in priority order from most to least important. The list of employee needs and desires should be consistent with the services and programs you describe in 5.1.a(2).

Essentially what the examiners want to see is that your initiatives and employee support programs are tailored to the diversity of your workforce. What we often see is a traditional list of benefits and services that might have made sense 25 years ago. As the employee population has changed, we want to see that the programs and services have changed to meet the needs of the population. Government organizations I've worked with actually tend to do a better job in this area than many big corporations.

I would answer this question by presenting a list of programs and initiatives that have been designed or tailored to different groups of employees in your organization. You might want to refer the reader back to the overview, wherein you describe the composition of your employee population. The examiner might have forgotten that your workforce is 32 percent Asian, for example. If there are unique features about your efforts in this area, or if your programs have been benchmarked by other organizations, you should definitely discuss this. What will impress the examiners is the creativity of your approaches, and how far they go in making employees feel comfortable in the work environment. Gestures that look like a token effort could be viewed as a cop-out.

Indicators for Question 5.1a(1)

- *Employees are segmented into logical groups based on common characteristics or priorities.*

- *Research is conducted to determine what is most important to each group of employees about their jobs and work environment.*

- *Use of creative approaches to find out what engages employees and makes them like or dislike their job and workplace.*

- *Employee needs and priorities are researched often to determine if preferences and priorities have changed.*

- *Extent to which employee needs and priorities are generic or very specific to the organization and its people.*

- *Evidence that the organization learns from its mistakes by not continuing or repeating initiatives to improve employee engagement that have had the opposite result.*

- *Deployment of employee market research methods across all locations and levels of employees.*

- *Evidence that the organization understands the cultural issues that might impact the success of its employee support programs.*

- *Number of different employee support programs that have been designed for specific groups of employees, based on their unique needs and preferences.*

- *Appropriate allocation of resources toward unique employee support programs tailored to different groups.*

- *Deployment of good approaches to employee support programs across all locations and facilities.*

- *Evidence that employee support programs are different and tailored to the employee base in each facility, where appropriate.*

- *Number of organizations that have benchmarked your diversity and/or employee support programs.*

- *Evidence that employee support programs have evolved and changed as the workforce make-up has changed.*

- *Evidence of a planned evaluation and refinement of methods used to gather data on employee needs and priorities.*

5.1a. (2) How do you foster an organizational culture conducive to HIGH PERFORMANCE and a motivated WORKFORCE to accomplish the following:

- cooperation, EFFECTIVE communication, and skill sharing within and across work units, operating units, and locations, as appropriate
- EFFECTIVE information flow and two-way communication with supervisors and managers
- individual goal setting, EMPOWERMENT, and initiative
- INNOVATIONin the work environment
- the ability to benefit from the diverse ideas, cultures, and thinking of your WORKFORCE

What They're Looking for Here

This is a new area to address for 2007 even though it combines some of the elements from the previous criteria. The criteria ask about the culture of your organization. Culture is much more than your values, but values are certainly part of it. I have worked with many large organizations where the culture is designed to punish people for good performance and reward them for slacking off. I have worked with others where the culture is definitely about high performance, but people are so competitive with one another and so overworked, that most hate their jobs. The key here when answering this series of questions is to convince examiners that the real culture of your organization promotes both employee engagement and high performance. The fist bullet asks about systems for communicating across departments and work units. This might involve committees, teams, meetings, joint projects, newsletters e-mails, blogs, or a variety of other methods. In many large organizations separate departments and units function independently and do not have systems for collaborating and sharing lessons learned.

The second bullet asks about two-way communication with leaders and management. Most of the communication done by leaders is one way. In other words, they do a lot more talking than listening, and often have no way of measuring whether or not their messages get heard. Leaders also rarely have ways of listening and learning about employee opinions or ideas. It is important that your answer focuses more on ways leaders listen than talk. Typical approaches like an employee newsletter and meetings listening to managers drone on using PowerPoint is likely to end up with a low score.

The third bullet asks about approaches for setting individual goals, and for empowering employees at various levels to initiate improvements when necessary. For example, two-time Baldrige winner Ritz Carlton has a policy that says" "If you hear about a problem or notice it, you are responsible for solving it, regardless of your job." This means that if a groundskeeper hears about a problem in the restaurant, he will follow up with the appropriate personnel in the restaurant to see that the problem is resolved and that the guest is happy.

Innovation is something most organizations claim to value, but most only reward it when innovation is successful. Most great innovations are the result of many failures. In fact, one company I work with believes in rewarding failures because failures indicate risk taking, and with each failure a lesson is learned. Explain how your organizational culture rewards innovation and creativity, even when it does not directly contribute to the bottom line. The final bullet in this area to address asks about how the culture of your organization really rewards diversity and has mechanisms for encouraging diverse ideas and thinking. As with innovation, diversity is something most organizations claim to value, but in reality, they value people who look, think, and act like senior leaders. A well-known high-tech firm hires only Ivy-league graduates and almost everyone in the workforce is under 35 years old. Other organizations have a very diverse workforce, but don't have good systems for capturing a diversity of ideas and different ways of thinking. Many school systems, for example have not changed much in 50 years, and those in the field sometimes have a hard time thinking out of the traditional education model. Bringing in people from outside of your own industry can be a great way of introducing new thinking in an organization.

Indicators for Question 5.1a(2)

- *The organization has a variety of different methods for encouraging sharing and cooperation between department, location, and units.*
- *There is evidence that these systems for encouraging sharing are effective and well deployed.*
- *Steps have been taken to break down organizational "silos" and get the organization to function more as a large team.*
- *Many different methods and media are used for communication.*
- *Communication methods are based on an analysis of the audience and their communication styles and preferences.*
- *Leaders do more listening than talking.*
- *There are easy-to-use mechanisms in place for employees to communicate with management.*
- *Leader communication is clear, honest, and timely.*

- *The organization has ways of measuring the effectiveness of its communication on a regular basis.*
- *The structure and authority levels in the organization are designed to encourage empowerment and initiative, rather than the opposite.*
- *Evidence that the organization actually rewards innovation and diverse thinking as opposed to just talking about these things.*
- *Systems exist for gathering innovative ideas and approaches from all levels and types of employees and other members of the workforce.*

5.1a(3) HOW does your WORKFORCE PERFORMANCE management system support HIGH-PERFORMANCE WORK and WORKFORCE ENGAGEMENT? HOW does your WORKFORCE PERFORMANCE management system consider WORKFORCE compensation, reward, recognition, and incentive practices? HOW does your WORKFORCE PERFORMANCE management system reinforce a CUSTOMER and business focus and achievement of your ACTION PLANS?

What They're Looking for Here

This first question is fairly straightforward in asking about your employee performance planning and assessment program or your performance management system. Having a formal system is certainly not a requirement. In fact, if you follow Dr. Deming's philosophies, you would not have a performance appraisal system because it wastes a great deal of time and only makes most people feel bad. What would impress Baldrige examiners is that you have designed a performance management system that actually promotes better performance and requires a minimum of meetings and forms to fill out. In my 25 years of consulting experience, I have never seen an impressive performance management system. I've seen some good features and creative approaches, but each program also had its share of flaws.

One innovative approach that has been developed in the federal government is the system being used today at the Department of Energy's Savannah River facility. Terry Frizzell and Brent Armstrong convinced the office of personnel management to let them pilot a system that does not have numerical ratings or grades. Inflation had caused almost everyone at the site to receive the highest ratings over the years, so the ratings had become fairly meaningless. The new system is a pass/fail rating. The emphasis in the new program is on feedback and development, rather than on assigning a rating. The forms associated with the new approach are also much simplified, so managers and supervisors at the site are providing positive feedback.

An approach that has become popular in human resource circles over the last few years is 360 degree appraisals. In other words, employee performance is assessed by his or her peers, customers, boss, and perhaps suppliers. While this seems like an interesting idea, most systems that I've reviewed have three to five times more meetings and forms to fill out than traditional appraisal systems, and the ratings are no more valid. As one employee I talked to explained: "It was inaccurate when only my boss subjectively graded my performance based on her memory. Now I have five people who get to make a subjective judgment about me and my performance and give me a rating."

The point here is that newer approaches are not necessarily better. You need to describe your performance planning and appraisal system, and stress why and how your approach is effective and better than what the examiners might find in a typical company. You would probably get more points from some examiners for not having a performance management system than keeping one that adds no value. If you use different approaches for different levels of employees and managers, you need to point out those distinctions in your answer.

A high-performance work system includes mechanisms for rewarding the desired behavior and results from employees. One of the big disconnects in many companies is compensation systems that don't reward anything except sticking around for another year, or that exclusively reward short-term financial results.

Many organizations claim to be committed to quality and customer satisfaction, but they compensate employees based upon seniority, level, or job function. Few of the companies that have performance-based pay plans base the pay that employees receive upon quality. Performance-based pay is most often based upon sales, profits, and other financial measures. Some past Baldrige applicants have explained that they've implemented a gainsharing plan as a way of promoting improved quality. However, gainsharing in many cases is nothing more than profit sharing.

Based upon my own experience consulting with large companies, the ideal situation is to have a large percentage of all employees' compensation upon individual and group performance against quality goals and standards. Many organizations have bonus programs for executives and upper management, but not for other levels of employees. Three criteria are important in assessing the compensation systems in a company. First, a portion of employees' compensation should be based upon the degree to which individual and group performance goals have been met. The second criterion is that all levels and categories of employees should participate in performance-based compensation programs. Third and last, a large enough percentage of income should be based upon quality results to make a difference in motivating employees. Allowing employees who earn an average of $30,000 to earn an annual bonus of up to $500 for exceeding their goals is not going to do much to motivate them.

Your task in this section is to convince the examiners that your compensation plan drives performance excellence from teams and individual employees. Many former Baldrige winners have very traditional compensation systems. The new criteria ask for evidence of a compensation program that rewards performance that is critical to organization performance. For example, the key business drivers and performance measures and goals that you discussed in sections 2 and 4 might be the foundation of your compensation or bonus plan. In some leading edge companies, all employees earn a bonus, and that bonus is based upon achieving a balance between all of their measures on their own scorecards. For example, at Federal Express, employee bonuses are based on how well you satisfy internal and/or external customers (Service), how well you satisfy your employees or teammates/peers (People), and how well you achieve or control financial results (Profit). All employees from the CEO to the package sorter are on this bonus plan, and it keeps everyone focused on their three priorities.

Another aspect of your high-performance work system that is evaluated here is how you recognize employees in nonfinancial ways. Everyone likes money, but motivating employees and influencing their behavior through compensation alone is very limiting. Nonfinancial recognition is probably more important and more powerful if it is done right. Some of the important factors that will be assessed regarding your approach to recognition are:

- *How much of it do you do?*
- *How well have you analyzed the needs and preferences of employees in designing recognition programs?*
- *How much creativity has been put into recognition programs to make them interesting and fun for employees?*
- *To what extent are the behaviors and accomplishments that are recognized consistent with organizational values, goals, and key performance measures?*

Most companies and organizations pay very little attention to employee recognition, other than a few unimaginative, mostly useless, programs like "Employee of the Month." No imagination is put into the effort, very few employees receive any kind of recognition, and the items and privileges that are given out for recognition are often perceived by employees as insulting or at best small "thank yous." Certificates, hats, T-shirts, and coffee cups may not be too rewarding if you and your team just saved the company $15,000. Future Baldrige winners will need to put a great deal of emphasis on the approaches they use to motivate and recognize individuals and teams of employees. Companies like 1997 winner 3M Dental Products and 1998 winner Solar Turbines put a great deal of effort into recognizing employees.

The most important factor in a successful recognition program is to have senior management that believes in the importance of recognition and positive reinforcement, and is willing to make this a priority that does not get delegated down to an HR clerk who updates the employee-of-the-month bulletin board once a month. Your approach to recognition should also be consistent with your organizational structure and job design. If you have organized your organization around teams, for example, you wouldn't want all of your recognition to be based on individual performance.

Noncontingent recognition, such as periodic parties or celebrations that everyone attends regardless of their performance, may help build morale, but it is not relevant here. Write about things you do to boost overall morale in section 5.3, not here.

Indicators for Question 5.1a(3)

- *Amount of creativity shown in performance management system.*
- *Consistent implementation of the performance management system across levels and units in the organization.*
- *Evidence that managers and employees think that the performance management system is valuable and worth the time investment.*
- *Methods are in place to ensure reliability/consistency in ratings if any are used.*
- *Emphasis is on development and performance improvement rather than giving a rating to past performance.*
- *The performance management system requires minimal time and hassle to administer for managers and employees.*
- *The performance management system is not designed to take the place of good supervisory practices.*
- *Percentage of employees who have pay at risk, and percentage of overall compensation that is at risk—percentage is large enough to properly motivate desired performance.*
- *At-risk compensation is tied to overall performance measures over which employees have strong influence or control.*
- *Compensation system is consistent with organizational structure, job, and work design.*

- *Compensation system is considered fair by employees.*

- *Compensation system rewards exceptional levels of performance from individuals and groups of employees.*

- *Evidence of creativity and use of leading-edge approaches to compensation.*

- *Percentage of employees who receive recognition of some sort each year.*

- *Involvement of employees in the design of recognition programs.*

- *Recognition is based upon performance on key measures from 2.1, rather than separate factors.*

- *Creativity in approaches to recognition.*

- *Good mix of team and individual recognition efforts.*

- *Items and/or privileges used for recognition of employees promote peer reinforcement.*

- *Evidence of constant evaluation and improvement of approaches to compensation and recognition.*

5.1b. Workforce and Leader Development

(1) HOW does your Workforce development and LEARNING system address the following:
  - needs and desires for LEARNING and development identified by your WORKFORCE, including supervisors and managers
  - your CORE COMPETENCIES, STRATEGIC CHALLENGES, and accomplishment of your ACTIONPLANS, both short-termand long-term
  - organizational PERFORMANCE improvement, technological change, and INNOVATION
  - the breadth of development opportunities, including education, training, coaching, mentoring, and work-related experiences, as appropriate
  - the transfer of knowledge from departing or retiring workers
  - the reinforcement of new knowledge and skills on the job

What They're Looking for Here

The first three bullets in this area to address ask about how you determine training and development needs for your workforce. A thorough training needs analysis includes feedback from employees and managers and other members of the workforce on what topics or types of training and development they most need for the future. It is important that organizations regularly assess training and development needs to make sure that their offerings are in synch with what people want and need. However, what they want and what they need are often quite different. Engineers and technical employees may ask for lots of technical training, but what they really need is more training on softer topics like leadership or interpersonal skills. Employees also sometimes ask for training that is not really linked to the organization's goals, but links to their personal goals. Consequently, the majority of your training needs should be based on an analysis of gaps in organizational performance that are caused by a lack of knowledge and/or skill. Gaps may be identified by seeing declines in performance, or by a decision to embark on a new strategy, implement new technology, get into a new market, or develop a new service. The two major factors that are inputs to a training needs analysis are company performance data and the strategic plan. Training and developmental needs should be assessed for all levels and types of employees and other members of the workforce, and analyses need to be regularly updated as the organization changes and personnel come and go.

It is important to identify potential training and development issues for each major strategy or action plan that is part of the organization's strategic plan. For example, a client's decision to have more of its product manufactured in China last year required training for many of their staff on Chinese culture, language, and business ethics. When performing training-needs analysis, it is also important to identify performance problems that are not caused by a lack of knowledge/skill. Most performance problems are caused by factors other than a lack of training. The test for determining if training/development is needed is: offer the employees a strong incentive to do the job right, or threaten to fire them. If performance improves and they do the job/task correctly, they don't need training — they have a motivation problem.

The fourth bullet in this question asks about the breadth of your training and development strategies. A nice table might be a great way to demonstrate this, with various activities (e.g., classroom training, self-study, university courses, structured OJT, mentoring, job assignments, etc.) down one side of the chart, and topics or knowledge/skill types (e.g., technical, interpersonal, technology, tools, leadership, etc.) on the top of the chart. Codes can then be used to indicate what types and levels of employees participate in each of these types of training and development activities. The point is to show how comprehensive your approach is, and that it is deployed to all types and members of your workforce.

The fifth bullet in this question asks how you capture the knowledge in the heads of employees who quit or retire before they are gone. This is a major challenge in many large organizations today, particularly in government, education, and health care. The most common answer to this question is to build knowledge databases, or at least write stuff down. The problem I've seen in many organizations is that no one bothers to consult this documentation when it might help them perform better. Often retiring managers and others end up being hired back as consultants because the less experienced people can't do what they can as well or as quickly. The answer is to begin passing on this knowledge and skill early on via mentoring programs or other similar approaches so that by the time the senior employee leaves, the junior employee is ready to take over the reins.

The final bullet in this question asks about how the organization reinforces use of the knowledge and skills acquired in training back on the job. Few organizations effectively follow up on the training they do to make sure it is being applied on the job. Employees often report learning new tools or techniques in training and are told by their bosses to do things the old way and to forget what they learned in training. A lack of systematic follow-up and positive reinforcement is the number one reason why training of any sort fails to change behavior or improve organizational performance. As much or more money and effort needs to be spent on what happens after the course or workshop as is spent preparing and conducting the training. For example, a major aerospace company I worked with evaluates individual leaders' strengths and weaknesses by surveying subordinates before their boss attends leadership training. Then 3-6 months after the leadership program is completed, the same survey is conducted to see if the boss has improved. Individual coaching sessions are held with each leader to help them apply what they learned in class back on the job. By using such an approach, the company has had great success with the leadership program actually making people better managers.

Indicators for Question 5.1.b (1)

- *Evidence that training is linked to the company vision and corresponding action plans.*
- *Breadth and depth of types of training identified are appropriate for the organization.*
- *Competencies needed to achieve the strategic plan are well addressed in training plan.*
- *An effective balance exists in allocating resources to short-term needs such as new hire training and longer-term training needs such as development of employees or leadership training.*
- *Training addresses both organizational and personal needs of employees.*
- *Development of a strategic training plan or similar approach for linking training and education to business goals.*
- *Evidence that all training and education can be directly linked to one or more key business drivers or long-term business goals.*
- *An ongoing process exists for ensuring that training and education are closely tied to business goals and success factors.*
- *Linkage between training/education activities and HR goals outlined in Item 2.2.*

- *A career development plan exists for each employee, with an identification of education and training needs for potential future assignments.*

- *Depth and breadth of developmental plans and related training/education needs is appropriate.*

- *The organization has conducted systematic needs analyses to identify the knowledge and skills needed by employees to function in the work systems and organizational structures used in the company.*

- *Training on generic topics like leadership and safety has been designed based upon a thorough needs analysis.*

- *Curriculums have been designed that organize courses into logical sequences.*

- *Curriculums have been defined for most key positions in the organization.*

- *Leadership training is well integrated with the company's approach to job and work design.*

- *Employees at various levels and from various functions provide input to aid in designing and developing training.*

5.1b(2) HOW does your development and LEARNING system for leaders address the following:

- development of personal leadership attributes
- development of organizational knowledge
- ethical business practices
- your CORE COMPETENCIES, STRATEGIC CHALLENGES, and accomplishment of your ACTION PLANS, both short-term and long-term
- organizational PERFORMANCE improvement, change, and INNOVATION
- the breadth of leadership development opportunities, including education, training, coaching, mentoring, and work-related experiences, as appropriate

---

What They're Looking for Here

This is a whole new set of questions for 2007 that go into great depth in asking how you develop leaders in your organization. Most leadership development programs I've reviewed are a colossal waste of time, as far as providing skills and knowledge that really make attendees better bosses. Participants learn about the latest trendy management book, listen to some guest speakers, complete some pop-psychology assessment tool like Myers-Briggs or a clone, engage in some team building events and complete a team business case study. In the end, everyone has a good time, worked hard and most feel like they really learned a lot. Fast forward a few weeks back on the job and nothing has changed. If Jim was bad at listening before the leadership program, he's still a poor listener. If Kathy was a micro manager before the training, chances are she still micro-manages her people. In short, most leadership programs are an expensive waste of time and money that really do little to make people better leaders.

What you need to do in answering this series of questions is to convince examiners that your approach is different and that it really works to make better bosses. The first thing you should talk about is how you identified the training needs upon which your leadership program is based. The best needs analyses are done by studying your master performers or great leaders and identifying how their competencies or skills are different than more typical or mediocre leaders. This sort of gap analysis makes sure you do not waste time teaching basics that everyone already knows or that will not make them a better manager. Other inputs to the leadership needs analysis should be the strategic plan of the organization that outlines challenges, and the company's core competencies. The program should also address business ethics in general and specific topics germane to your industry and your organization. The program should also teach leaders which attributes needed to be selected, and which ones can be trained. There are great many leadership competencies or attributes that are not really trainable. For example, a recent client identified mechanical comprehension as a leadership trait important for supervisors and managers. Another one identified verbal communication skills. It is much easier to find people who already possess many of the traits needed to be a successful leader in your organization than to try to teach people who may never be proficient, no matter how much training they receive.

This question is actually quite prescriptive in suggesting that your leadership development programs should include training on personal leadership attributes, organizational knowledge, ethics, performance improvement, and specific topics derived from your strategic plan. While this is a fairly generic list of topics that might go into a leadership program, there are many others that are not listed that could be even more important. Aside from the content, the last bullet in this question asks about the variety of approaches used to develop good leaders in your organization. The most effective programs include all of the approaches listed in this bullet, whereas the least effective programs are simply a 2-4 day classroom workshops. Often the best way of learning to become a great leader is to work for one.

Indicators for Question 5.1.b (2)

- *The organization has conducted a systematic needs analysis to determine the content of their leadership development program.*
- *The needs analysis is based on a variety of data such as studying master performers, reviewing performance data, and the strategic plan.*

- *The organization separates leadership attributes and competencies that are not really trainable, but are part of the selection/promotion process.*

- *Leadership development is tailored to different levels and types of leaders rather than a one-size-fits-all approach.*

- *The program covers personal leadership attributes, organizational knowledge, products/services, ethics, and new knowledge/skills needed to accomplish strategic plan goals/objectives.*

- *The approach to leadership development is varied and comprehensive, including classroom training, external educational programs, coaching/mentoring, and work assignments.*

- *Leaders are held accountable for deploying the knowledge/skills acquired in the leadership programs on the job.*

- *The organization follows up on the leadership development programs to make sure that skills acquired are being used.*

- *Follow-up coaching is provided to individual leaders as necessary.*

- *Leadership development programs are modified and improved as needs dictate.*

5.1b(3) HOW do you evaluate the EFFECTIVENESS of your WORKFORCE and leader development and LEARNING systems?

What They're Looking for Here

This question also asks how you evaluate the effectiveness of your education and training. This education and training should be evaluated on four dimensions:

- *Reaction*
- *Learning*
- *Behavior change*
- *Results*

Reaction data are the most common and are collected via questionnaires or surveys filled out by participants at the end of a class. The typical questionnaire asks the participants to rate the course, the instructor, the content, and the relevancy of the material on a five-point scale, and includes a few open-ended questions.

The second education/training evaluation dimension is *learning*. This is another index that provides data on the effectiveness of the training delivery. This set of data should not simply report what the trainees/participants thought of the courses, but rather should indicate whether or not employees have mastered the material covered. Testing is the only appropriate means of measuring learning in an education/training program. Many large organizations do no testing in any of their courses, and hence have no data to demonstrate that participants learned any of the material. Testing does not have to consist of a paper-and-pencil, multiple-choice test. In any course in which skills are taught, performance tests are much better than written tests. A performance test might be a case study, a simulation, a role play, a demonstration, or any other situation where the trainee must demonstrate that he/she has mastered the skills taught in the course. Tests should be developed based upon the objectives of the courses, and should simulate how the trainees will use the skills in the job environment.

The third dimension of training/education evaluation is *behavior change*. This dimension considers whether trainees' behavior on the job has changed as a result of the training/education they received. Many large and small organizations do not have data on behavior change. This type of data, however, is even more important than data on what was learned. If skills learned in training are not used on the job, performance will not improve, and the money and time spent on the training will have been wasted. The degree to which employees apply and use the knowledge and skills they have learned in training is usually a direct result of the strategies employed in doing follow-up coaching and reinforcement. Data on behavior change are often collected via follow-up surveys of the trainees, their bosses, and their peers. An even more objective way of gathering such data is a measurement or audit of the actual products of people's behaviors and/or behavior changes. For example, an auditor might count the number of correctly prepared control charts posted in offices and work areas, or the number of quality improvement project reports that have been completed according to the criteria outlined in the training. A combination of process (behavior) and output (accomplishments/products) measures will earn high marks from the Baldrige examiners in this area.

The final type of evaluation data that should be collected on training/education programs and courses is data on quality *results*. Employees might like the course, master the tests, and apply the skills on the job, but results may not improve. The major reason an organization invests in training and education is to produce better results from its employees' performance. If courses on quality improvement tools and techniques don't result in improved quality, something is wrong. The examiners want to see that you identify and measure key dimensions of performance that will be impacted by each course in your education/training curriculum. You should compare performance results data both before and after the training to see whether the training has made any difference. Of course, various other activities occurring in the organization will also impact performance, so it is important that you use a sound, applied research/experimental design in your evaluation effort to rule out alternative explanations for the improvements seen in quality results. Results might also relate to costs. If you can show how improved training saved the company money, allowed it to grow, or be more profitable, these types of findings would be important to discuss here.

In summary, the examiners are looking for several types or dimensions of evaluation data here. They are also looking to see that you can demonstrate clear cause-effect relationships between the education/training and improvements in both employee performance and overall company/work unit performance.

Indicators for Question 5.1b(3)

- *Evaluation methods are deployed across all types of education and training.*
- *Data on trainee reactions or satisfaction levels with courses are collected.*
- *Learning or mastery of material is tested in courses designed to teach specific knowledge and skills.*
- *Where appropriate, employee use of skills learned in training on the job is measured.*
- *Training process measures such as the quality of instruction or delivery are measured as part of the education/training evaluation approach.*
- *The company measures the impact of certain courses on performance results such as customer satisfaction, financial results, productivity, or product/service quality.*
- *Evidence of continuous improvement in training and education as a result of evaluation data.*

5.1b(4) HOW do you manage EFFECTIVE career progression for your entire WORKFORCE? HOW do you accomplish EFFECTIVE succession planning for management and leadership positions?

N4. Your organization may have unique considerations relative to workforce development, learning, and career progression. If this is the case, your response to 5.1b should include how you address these considerations.

What They're Looking for Here

This question has been reworked a number of times in a number of ways, and now asks about career development and succession planning. What is important about a career development system is that there are career ladders for both managers and for those not wishing to be managers. Many organizations also have a technical career ladder, but the levels of compensation for professionals are often below those for an equivalent rung on a management ladder. This inequality often causes individuals to seek management positions when they would be happier and more successful in an individual contributor position. Deployment is also a major factor assessed in this question. Career ladders often exist for a small minority of employees. The question suggests that career development is important for all parts of your workforce, even some individual who may not be employees.

This final question in 5.1.b also asks about succession planning for leaders and managers. It is surprising how many large and otherwise successful organizations don't do this. It must be human nature not to want to plan for death, retirement, and turnover. We want to pretend these things don't happen so we won't have to do the unpleasant task of planning for them. Successful organizations have succession plans for all of their leaders, not just the big boss and her direct reports. It is important that several candidates are identified for each position, even though they may be at different levels of readiness. The succession planning process should also be linked in with the training needs analysis process as well as individual development plans.

Indicators for Question 5.1. b (4)

- *A career path exists for all categories and types of employees and members of the workforce.*
- *Technical and other career ladders exist for individuals who do not wish to become managers.*
- *Rungs on nonmanagement career ladders are equivalent to those on management ladders in compensation and status.*
- *Employees are aware of the career ladder system and believe it is fairly administered.*
- *There are explicit and objective criteria or standards for advancing from one rung to another on career ladders.*
- *Leadership ethics and behavior consistent with organizational values are assessed for upward moves on the management ladder.*
- *Standards or criteria for moving up from one rung to another are based on solid evidence of job requirements rather than being set arbitrarily.*
- *Succession plans exist for all senior leaders and mid managers.*
- *Plans are kept up to date each year.*
- *Succession plans are linked to strategic plans, training needs analyses, performance appraisal and individual development plans.*
- *Several candidates are identified as possible replacements for each leader, even thought they may be at different stages of readiness.*

5.1c. Assessment of WORKFORCE ENGAGEMENT

(1) How do you assess WORKFORCE ENGAGEMENT? What formal and informal assessment methods and MEASURES do you use to determine WORKFORCE ENGAGEMENT and WORKFORCE satisfaction? How do these methods and MEASURES differ across WORKFORCE groups and SEGMENTS? How do you use other INDICATORS, such as WORKFORCE retention, absenteeism, grievances, safety, and PRODUCTIVITY to assess and improve WORKFORCE ENGAGEMENT?

What They're Looking for Here

The big change here from last year is the term "engagement," coined by the Gallup organization and their excellent books on employee morale and involvement. According to the notes in the criteria engagement simply means commitment, and is related to but different from employee satisfaction. I guess an employee could be highly committed to the organization and highly dissatisfied, but it is unlikely. The Gallup Q-12 engagement survey is basically an employee morale survey that asks questions about how you feel about your boss and if you have close friends at work. Regardless of whether you are talking about engagement, satisfaction or both, this question asks about how you measure this factor.

A typical approach is to measure engagement/satisfaction once a year with a survey. A recent trend is to not even do a full survey, but to ask only one question: "On a scale of 1-10 to what extent would you rate our organization as a great place to work?" See my latest book: *Beyond the Balanced Scorecard* (Productivity Press, 2007) for more on the dangers of singular infrequent measures like this. What the examiners are looking for is that you have multiple ways of measuring employee satisfaction and engagement, and that measurement is done frequently to detect trends and drops in performance before too much time passes. A table or chart might be a good way to summarize your measures of workforce engagement. The table might list the metrics, and include columns for "Purpose" "Frequency" and "Data Collection Method." If you used such a chart or table you could also reference the appropriate chart in section 7 that includes performance data on the measure. If you measure both engagement and satisfaction make sure to indicate which measures relate to which factor, and that data are presented on all measures in section 7 of the application.

Indicators for Question 5.1.c (1)

- *A wide variety of data are collected in different measures of workforce engagement and/or satisfaction.*

- *Workforce engagement/satisfaction are measured at least once a month.*

- *It is possible to drill down into data to determine what levels, types and locations of employees are showing low levels of engagement.*

- *Data are reviewed regularly by senior management and regarded with as much importance as financial result data.*

- *Measures are in place to ensure the integrity of the data.*

- *Softer measures like surveys and focus groups are used in combination with harder measures such as turnover and absenteeism.*

- *Instruments used to measure workforce satisfaction or engagement are well researched.*

- *Use of innovative or creative measures of employee engagement/satisfaction rather than the typical surveys and turnover.*

5.1c(2) How do you relate assessment findings to KEY business RESULTS reported in Category 7 to identify opportunities for improvement in both WORKFORCE ENGAGEMENT and business RESULTS?

N5. Identifying improvement opportunities (5.1c[2]) might draw on your workforce-focused results presented in Item 7.4 and might involve addressing workforce-related problems based on their impact on your business results reported in response to other Category 7 Items.

What They're Looking for Here

This question asks what you do with the data on employee engagement and satisfaction. Often it goes into a black hole, never to be seen again until they dust of the survey for the next year. What the examiners are looking for is evidence of correlations between measures of employee engagement and other key outcome measures like sales, profits, quality, productivity, or other factors. Enough research has been conducted that shows links between a disengaged workforce and poor performance on basic outcome/business measures, but it would be important to demonstrate any links your own organization has discovered. For example, I worked with one major corporation that found that no further gains were realized in financial performance measures once employee satisfaction was between 76 and 80%. The organization worked hard to stay within this band of acceptable performance, but also learned that improvement for the sake of improvement is a waste of valuable resources that might be better spent elsewhere. Several examples would be good to include in your answer to this question. The examples might explain how you made some improvements that resulted in an improvement in workforce engagement scores, and that there were several side benefits that occurred in other important measures of organizational performance. Or, you could present an example of a problem that occurred that you traced to a root cause of a disengaged workforce and what you did to turn the situation around.

Indicators for Question 5.1.c (2)

- *Evidence that a systematic process is used to regularly review workforce engagement/satisfaction data.*

- *The organization has an approach for analyzing the root causes of poor levels and trends in measures of employee engagement/satisfaction.*

- *Research has been done to show links or correlations between measures of workforce engagement/satisfaction and important outcome measures/business results.*

- *The organization has identified targets bands of good performance for measures of workforce engagement/satisfaction rather than setting arbitrary targets or continually raising targets each year.*

- *Use of external benchmarks and comparative data to set appropriate targets and analyze performance on measures of workforce engagement.*

- *Credibility and importance of any examples presented illustrating how workforce engagement findings are analyzed and how action plans are developed to improve performance.*

5.2 WORKFORCE ENVIRONMENT: Process
How do you build an effective and supportive workforce environment?   (40 points)

Describe HOW your organization manages WORKFORCE CAPABILITY and CAPACITY to accomplish the work of the organization. Describe HOW your organization maintains a safe, secure, and supportive work climate.

AREA TO ADDRESS   [APPROACH, DEPLOYMENT]
5.2a. Workforce capability and capacity

(1) How do you assess your WORKFORCE CAPABILITY and CAPACITY needs, including skills, competencies, and staffing levels?

N1. "Workforce capability" refers to your organization's ability to accomplish its work processes through the knowledge, skills, abilities, and competencies of its people. Capability may include the ability to build and sustain relationships with your customers; to innovate and transition to new technologies; to develop new products, services, and work processes; and to meet changing business, market, and regulatory demands.

"Workforce capacity" refers to your organization's ability to ensure sufficient staffing levels to accomplish its work processes and successfully deliver your products and services to your customers, including the ability to meet seasonal or varying demand levels.

N2. Workforce capability and capacity should consider not only current needs but also future requirements based on your strategic objectives and action plans reported in Category 2.

What They're Looking for Here

If you read the notes that go along with this question, you will see that it asks how you determine if you have enough people (capacity) with the right skills and abilities (capability) to do today and tomorrow's work. This question is likely to evoke a generic response that says something about having a systematic approach for determining the existing knowledge skills, and workload of the organization mapped against current and future workload. You need to get very specific in explaining how you determine future workload and types of work that will come your way in the future. This is fairly easy in some organizations like a school district that know what their future workload looks like for the next 15 years, but most do not have the luxury of predicting their future workload with much accuracy. Many organizations have a hard time predicting what next month will look like, let alone the next 5-10 years.

The first part of your answer should be an explanation of how you do future workload planning. List the factors assesses, sources of data, and the certainty of these factors.

You might also explain what external variables you monitor on an ongoing basis that could have a bearing on your future workload and mix of work. Factors might include politics, funding, economic factors, competition, consumer trends, news stories/press, regulations/laws, and the prices for raw materials used in your organization.

After explaining your approach for determining future workload and for monitoring the factors that impact your predictions, you need to explain how you evaluate your own capabilities and capacity. Identify the specific factors that are assessed as well as the methods used to conduct the assessments. The analysis should go beyond simply identifying how many people are needed in a given job category for an upcoming project or assignment, but also look at the levels of expertise needed within specific skill areas. For example, not just identifying that you will need 12 welders and 28 pipe fitters for a job, but that of those 12 welders, 2 need to be master welders and able to weld underwater, 6 need to be experienced on this type of project, and no more than 2 of them can have less that 5 years experience or be classified as a level 4.

Following an explanation of how you determine knowledge and skill needs for future workload, explain how you determine how many people you need. For example, a military organization I worked with knows that out of a 40 hour week, only about 22 hours of that time is actually productive. The rest of the time is allocated to breaks, waiting, going to the bathroom, getting interrupted, attending to administrative requirements, and going to training. When doing workforce capacity planning they figure that each person is only productive about 50% of the time. This type of data will ensure that your capacity plans are realistic.

Indicators for Question 5.2. a. (1)

- *The organization does a thorough job of planning its future workload.*
- *Workload forecasts are based on historical data, current workload, and an assessment of a variety of external factors rather than just a sales forecast.*
- *External factors that could impact future workload are monitored on a daily or weekly basis and adjustments are made to forecasts as necessary.*
- *Evidence that past forecasts have been accurate.*
- *Evidence that the workload forecasting process has been evaluated and improved.*
- *Thoroughness of assessments done to identify knowledge, skills, and capabilities required for current and future work.*
- *Level of detail with which capability assessments are done.*

- *Deployment of capability assessments across all types and classifications/levels of staff.*
- *Evidence that staffing plans are linked to workload assessments not arbitrary budgeting guidelines.*
- *Evidence that staffing and HR plans are linked to strategic plans and associated initiatives.*
- *Ease with which staffing plans can be changed as workload changes.*
- *The organization has determined how much actual productive work they get from each category of employee and uses this information when doing HR/capacity planning.*

> 5.2.a(2) HOW do you recruit, hire, place, and retain new employees? HOW do you ensure that your WORKFORCE represents the diverse ideas, cultures, and thinking of your hiring community?

What They're Looking for Here

This crucial question should have been included in this section years ago. The caliber of people an organization hires is one of the most important determinants of its success. In fact, Ritz-Carlton Hotels, a former Baldrige winner, regards their recruitment and selection process to be their most closely guarded corporate secret. Competing hotel chains swear that Ritz has a machine that creates new employees! They can't understand how Ritz finds so many employees that are all perfectly groomed, with impeccable appearance and manners. You need to start your answer to this question by listing the generic traits or competencies that you look for in employees. Maintaining a consistent corporate culture depends on your ability to hire people with the same sets of values. Characteristics such as values or work ethic are not trainable.

Some organizations have some unique requirements and unique ways of assessing potential new employees. Southwest Airlines believes that its employees must have a good sense of humor if they are to fit into the corporate culture. This is especially true of customer-contact employees. They assess for this dimension by having each candidate get up in front of the selection committee and tell three jokes. While they don't have an applause meter, they do grade candidates on their sense of humor. A generic list of employee competencies that you assess in potential new hires will not earn you a lot of points.

Another important point to make in this section is the different approaches you use to evaluate potential new employees. Some organizations test to see if the candidate is breathing and that's about it, whereas others put candidates through rigorous tests and assessments before they hire them. I worked for a small consulting firm that put me through a grueling assessment process before I was hired. After being interviewed individually by everyone in the office—as well as a few group interviews—and spending a day being tested by a psychologist, I had to work a week for them for free to see how I would perform with clients in actual work situations.

Another point that needs to be addressed here is your approach for ensuring the diversity of your communities is reflected in your selection practices. In a desire to maintain a unified culture, many organizations hire people that all look and think like them. The key is to balance diversity with a need for common values and personality traits. One company that does this better than any I've seen is agricultural giant Cargill of Minneapolis. I have worked with Cargill employees all over the world and from all different cultures. Yet, they all have the same values and ethics. Cargill is often benchmarked for its ethics and corporate culture and its wonderful job of balancing diversity with common values.

Indicators for Question 5.2a(2)

- *Use of creative/innovative approaches for recruiting and selecting new employees.*
- *Identification of specific competencies and/or traits needed for all new employees.*
- *Thoroughness and reliability of assessment methods used.*
- *Evidence of an approach to selection that balances the need for diversity with the need for a consistent corporate culture.*
- *Evidence that characteristics that are assessed in potential new hires are actually correlated with success.*
- *Use of innovative/diverse sources for finding potential employees.*
- *Efficiency and speed of the recruiting and selection process.*
- *Validity of tests or instruments used to assess candidates.*
- *Evidence that characteristics assessed in potential new hires are actually correlated with success on the job.*

5.2a(3) HOW do you manage and organize your WORKFORCE to accomplish the work of your organization, capitalize on the organization's CORE COMPETENICES, reinforce a CUSTOMER and business focus, exceed PERFORMANCE expectations, address your STRATEGIC CHALLENGESand ACTION PLANS, and achieve the agility to address changing business needs?

What They're Looking for Here

That's a long sentence! What they are basically asking is two things: How are you organized or structured, and how do you manage your workforce so as to achieve high levels of performance. You probably included some type of chart in the Organizational Profile section that shows the hierarchy of people and unit in your organization. In this section you need to explain why this is the ideal structure and the logic behind why your organization is designed this way. This is a tough question because often there is no logic behind current organizational structures. Rather, they are based on tradition, convenience, or are standard within the field or industry. For example, why are schools based around grouping 15-40 kids with one teacher in one classroom for an entire day? Why don't most hospitals make doctors their employees? Why are there so many vice presidents in a bank?

An aerospace company I worked with for many years always seemed to have a weird structure, but later I learned that this structure was based around how its military customers were structured. Since many of the leaders were former military officers, this structure made sense to them, and it also made it easier for the customer to communicate with the company because they understood how each department operated.

In the last 15 years many organizations have experimented with alternative structures and approaches for getting work done. Job sharing, telecommuting, flex time, and similar approaches were revolutionary 10 years ago, but are commonplace today. Some of today's organizations are experimenting with alternative structures that are even more revolutionary. For example, Best Buy, the Minneapolis-based big box retailer, is experimenting with an approach that does not require employees to come to work at any specific time, or even come in at all, if they can get their work done from home, or at the local park. The key to making such a program work is having an excellent scorecard or set of performance measures for each employee. The approach seems to be working for Best Buy, since turnover has dropped significantly (between 52 and 90%), and productivity is up an average of 35 in one year! Of course, some consultants had to come up with an acronym for this new approach so they can start selling it to others. The approach, pioneered by a group of passionate employees at Best Buy is called ROWE: Results-Only Work Environment.

Business Week and other national magazines have presented feature or cover stories recently on the changing nature of jobs and work. In case you haven't noticed, the traditional job, office, and organizational structures are disappearing. IBM eliminated several floors of offices in its 590 Madison Avenue building in New York City by eliminating offices for salespeople and others. IBMers are given laptop computers, cellular phones, and told to spend work time at customer locations or at home. If they need an office, they can rent one for the day at IBM's facilities, plug in a phone and computer, and go to work. When employees complained that they missed the personal touches of their own office, IBM scanned pictures of their husbands, wives, kids, and even dogs into their laptop computers to take with them wherever they go. Desert Hospital in Palm Springs, California, has practically eliminated separate departments such as radiology. Employees work on cross-functional teams to provide a variety of different services to patients. Examples like these can be found all over America in all different industries. These are exactly the types of things that will earn you a good score in 5.1.

The first part of your answer to this Area to Address should explain how you have designed jobs and work flow. This explanation should refer back to and build upon the explanation of your organizational structure that appeared in section 1.1. Begin by explaining your approach to job and work design. Expand upon this explanation with examples of how jobs and work have changed over the years. This information will help examiners assess the degree of deployment. Keep in mind that if you have an innovative approach to design of jobs for your salespeople, but salespeople only make up seven percent of your workforce, you may still end up with a fairly low score because of a lack of deployment.

It is important that you explain how job designs make it easier for employees to contribute to improving the organization. Empowerment is not specifically asked for in the criteria this year, but it is still hidden in there. Self-directed work teams that are given authority to monitor their own performance are not a requirement, but are an approach that would likely earn you some positive comments from the examiners. If you still form teams to work on problems or projects, this is not necessarily a negative. Problem-solving teams and cross-functional teams do serve a purpose. Baldrige is asking that you go beyond simply adding some teams to traditional jobs and work methods. Although the Baldrige criteria for 2007 are much less prescriptive than they used to be, they still promote concepts like:

- *Teamwork*
- *Empowerment*
- *Flexibility*
- *Employee involvement*

Question 5.2a(3) asks how your approach to jobs and work design encourages employees to contribute ideas for improving the company, and how you have empowered employees or given them more authority than they had in the past. With traditional departments and jobs, employees are often more concerned with their own department's needs than the needs of their customers. Departments that should work together and talk to each other often don't. Hopefully, your approach to jobs, departments, and the assignment of tasks eliminates these barriers and makes it easy and necessary for employees to talk and work together. Organizing work around key processes is one way some companies I've seen help encourage this communication and teamwork.

In order to get a high score for this Area to Address, you also need to show how your approaches to job and work design have been evaluated and improved over the last few years. Explain the factors that are used to measure effectiveness, describe your evaluation methodology, and tell the examiners what you have changed or improved over the last few years based on this analysis. If the measures that you use to evaluate job designs and organizational structure are not tied back to overall performance measures, this will end up hurting your score. Having a lot of empowerment or teamwork is not how to get a good score. You need to show the link between approaches like self-directed teams and flexible job designs and business results like profits, productivity, and customer satisfaction.

Indicators for Question 5.2a(3)

- *Significance of changes to work and job design compared to traditional approaches.*
- *Evidence that jobs are more flexible than they used to be.*
- *Extent to which the organizational structure and job designs allow employees many different opportunities to suggest and implement ideas for improving the company's practices and performance.*
- *Innovation in creativity in job/work design.*
- *Evidence that employees in various positions have more authority than they did in the past—empowerment.*
- *Employee opinions on the effectiveness of new approaches to job and work design.*
- *Deployment of new approaches to job and work design across all functions, levels, and locations in the company.*
- *Evidence that new approaches to job and work design promote more open communication and more cooperation between department units and locations that need to work together.*
- *Evidence that all employees are evaluated on how well they satisfy their internal and/or external customers.*
- *Job performance measures are consistent with overall performance measures defined in section 4.1 of the application.*
- *Evidence of the effectiveness of new approaches to job and work design.*

- *Employee opinions on empowerment or levels of authority that exist today versus the past.*
- *Evidence that company management listens to employees and adopts their suggestions, or allows employees to implement their own ideas/suggestions.*
- *Evidence that motivation for redesign of jobs and work flow goes beyond saving money and getting more work out of employees.*
- *Identification of specific measurement indices for evaluating the effectiveness of new approaches to job and work design.*
- *Evidence of continuous improvement in job and work design approaches.*
- *Systems exist for promoting teamwork and sharing across units, levels, and locations.*

5.2a(4) HOW do you prepare your WORKFORCE for changing CAPABILITY and CAPACITY needs? HOW do you manage your WORKFORCE, its needs, and your needs to ensure continuity, to prevent WORKFORCE reductions, and to minimize the impact of WORKFORCE reductions, if they do become necessary?

N2. Workforce capability and capacity should consider not only current needs but also future requirements based on your strategic objectives and action plans reported in Category 2.

N3. Preparing your workforce for changing capability and capacity needs (5.2a[4]) might include training, education, frequent communication, considerations of workforce employment and employability, career counseling, and outplacement and other services.

What They're Looking for Here

This is a new question for 2007 and is a good addition. At first glance it may look similar to the questions in 5.1b that ask about determining of training needs, but this question has a different focus. It is basically asking how well prepared are you for a disaster, like a major downturn in business or the economy. The airline business was hit hard by 911 and an increase in fuel prices and had to lay off thousands of workers. The auto industry has always had its ups and downs, but is now experiencing financial problems due to pension and health insurance costs for current and retired employees. Even schools experience ups and downs in enrollments and budgets that they must deal with.

Up and down cycles invariably occur in almost every field. What this question is asking is how well prepared is your organization to weather the storm. A practice used by many organizations today is to staff up with contract workers when times are good, and let them go when things slow down. This eliminates the need to do lay-offs and continue paying for idle employees. While great in theory, the approach has a couple of drawbacks. First of all, the IRS has been cracking down on contract workers for the last 10 years or so, since it also reduced the amount of taxes and social security employers have to pay. These individuals are really employees that have a boss and show up for work each day to do the same thing, but the company does not pay social security or benefits, and can let them go with virtually no notice. Many new firms have cropped up in recent years that do the contracting and provide the people, often taking a 100 to 200% markup on the rates they pay the people. A second problem with a contract workforce is that these individual are often treated like second class citizens. They seem like employees, do the same work as employees, have the same types of workspaces and tools, but are not employees and don't get the same security and benefits as employees.

Along with having a contingent workforce, another factor that you might address here is how you prepare people for changes in workload or the nature of the work. For example, an aircraft service company I worked with has all employees trained to do at least one other job, so they can move people around when one part of the business is slow and another part is busy. Another company I worked with had a no lay-offs policy. When business goes slow, everyone goes on reduced hours and reduced pay, including executives. These are just some ideas of good practices. You need to explain your organization's approach and perhaps refer to some of your result charts that demonstrate your ability to maintain high levels of employee engagement/satisfaction during up and down business cycles.

Indicators for Question 5.2.a (4)

- *Evidence of a comprehensive plan for dealing with ups and downs in workload.*
- *Degree to which the plan for dealing with ups and downs in business is ethical and fair to all members of the workforce.*
- *Degree of innovation/creativity demonstrated by approach.*
- *Deployment of the approach for dealing with ups and downs in workload across all locations and units in the organization.*
- *Evidence that the approach has worked where it has been implemented.*
- *Workforce feedback regarding approach for dealing with ups and downs in workload.*
- *Legality of approach.*

AREA TO ADDRESS   [APPROACH, DEPLOYMENT]
5.2b. WORKFORCE Climate

> (1) HOW do you ensure and improve workplace health, safety, and security? What are your PERFORMANCE MEASURES and improvement GOALS for each of these workplace factors? What are any significant differences in these factors and PERFORMANCE MEASURES or targets for different workplace environments?

What They're Looking for Here

This Examination Item is about what you do to make your organization a safe and enjoyable place to work. Something that examiners will look for in your response to this Area to Address is that you approach safety and employee health with the same systematic prevention-based approach as you employ for ensuring the production and delivery of high-quality products and services. Most organizations and virtually all manufacturing companies have some type of safety program. Having a decent safety program may not earn you many points, but you will certainly lose some if you don't have one. What examiners will need to see to give you a good score is a preventive approach to safety. Most safety programs are not preventive. Companies approach safety in much the same manner that fire departments approach fire prevention. Fire departments spend about 10 percent of their time on prevention-oriented activities, and the rest of the time fighting fires. One key indicator of a detection approach to safety is in how the organization measures safety. Most companies measure safety in lost time accidents or incident rates. This is like measuring quality by counting the number of defects found in products after they are made. Once an accident has occurred, it's too late to do anything about it. We can learn from the accident and correct the situation that allowed it to occur, but this is a detection approach to safety.

Safety boils down to employee behavior. If you can get employees to always follow safety rules and practices, you will not have safety problems. One organization I worked with measures employee behavior and inspects the work environment on a regular basis as a major safety procedure. This company monitors employee behavior for safe practices on almost a daily basis. Inspectors measure defects such as incidents, near misses, and lost time related to accidents, and the companies safety record is near benchmark level for the industry.

Having a proactive approach to preventing safety problems would tend to earn you a very good score from examiners. If your approach is characterized by safety audits conducted a few times a year, some safety training, and a few posters placed throughout the facility, you will probably end up with a very low score. Meeting OSHA or other regulatory requirements will also not earn you many points. You have no choice but to do this. Baldrige is looking for organizations that go way beyond minimum requirements.

The criteria in 5.2b(1) asks about how health, safety, and ergonomics (human factors, engineering) are improved. The approach you use to achieve good performance in these areas is the same as the approach you employ to achieve good results in other areas, such as quality or customer satisfaction. You need to identify good measures of health, safety, and ergonomics, benchmark other organizations to identify world-class levels of performance, set stretch goals or targets based on benchmarks, assign resources, and improve processes to achieve excellent levels of performance on these measures.

Also, 5.2b(1) asks for specific information on your safety/health measures and goals or targets. This information is probably best presented in a chart that lists measures along the left side, followed by annual targets and longer-term targets or goals. As I mentioned earlier, what is important is that all of your measures are not defect-detection oriented. You need to have a good mix of prevention-based measures and detection-based measures. A good prevention-based measure is not the number of safety training programs conducted or posters put up on the wall, either. The frequency with which you collect data on safety, health, and ergonomic factors is also important. To have a prevention-based approach, you need to collect data more often than once every few months.

Measures of employee health need to be preventive as well. Tracking employee health problems or sickness and absenteeism/sick leave by themselves are detection-oriented measures. You need to be careful with preventive measures to ensure that you drive the right behavior. One organization that had an on-site gym/health club used to measure the percentage of employees who used the gym, and the average amount of time spent in the gym per employee. Many used the gym as a social activity, however. They'd go to the gym, do 10 minutes on the StairMaster, do a couple of sit-ups, and spend 45 minutes talking with coworkers, or sitting at the juice bar reading the newspaper. After realizing that hours spent in the gym was not a good measure, the company started measuring cardiovascular fitness, body fat percentage, blood pressure, and other health-related factors that were really important in maintaining employee health.

A forward-thinking company in Michigan and South Carolina has an excellent approach for encouraging employees to get healthier, and for measuring their progress. Each year, all employees must complete a detailed lifestyle questionnaire and submit to a comprehensive physical, both administered by an on-site nurse. Based on the results of the questionnaire and survey, employees are graded as:

- *Marginal*
- *Average*
- *Superior*

Typically fewer than 10% of people receive "superior" ratings, indicating that they are extremely healthy. Employees who receive "marginal" ratings get little or no money for health insurance since they are big risk to the company. Those in the "average" rating group get a reasonable stipend for insurance, and those in the "superior" group get full coverage with dental, vision, doctor visits, etc. So, there is a huge incentive to improve your health—you get much better insurance and pay next to nothing out of your pocket. The company also sponsors many programs to help people lose weight, quit smoking, and adopt other healthy habits. This small company's approach to employee health is more sophisticated than those I have seen in major hospitals and corporations.

The last part of 5.2b(1) asks you to note any significant differences in approaches based on different facilities or work groups. Often the company corporate headquarters will have a health club, medical clinic, smoking cessation, weight loss, and any number of other programs to promote employee health. However, only 20 percent of the company's employees might work at headquarters. The rest are in plants or offices in remote locations that have none of these facilities or services. In assessing deployment on this Area to Address, examiners are interested in what you are doing for all of your employees in all of your facilities. This last sentence in the criteria also asks about different approaches you might have for different employee groups—read diversity. If you do business in different locations, including international facilities, you may need to use different approaches to employee health safety and ergonomics. Examiners will look for evidence that you do not adopt a one-size-fits-all approach, but that you tailor your approaches to the culture and demographics of the employees in different locations if appropriate.

Indicators for Question 5.2b(1)

- *Absence of citations from health/safety regulatory agencies, or lawsuits relating to health/safety issues.*
- *Identification of a good set of measures for employee safety that is a combination of prevention and detection types of metrics.*

- *Benchmarking and other comparative information are used to set stretch goals for safety performance.*
- *Specific goals and targets have been set for all measures of employee safety.*
- *How employees feel about the degree to which the company promotes health and safety.*
- *Evidence of process changes and improvements that will promote better employee safety performance.*
- *Evidence of a preventive approach to employee health, safety, and ergonomics.*
- *Level of attention given to safety and employee well-being by senior management.*
- *Evidence that the company goes way beyond regulatory requirements in this area and strives to be a role model for others.*
- *Frequency with which data are collected on health and safety issues.*
- *Levels of resources devoted to health and safety efforts compared to companies of similar size in the same industry.*
- *Scope and breadth of improvements made in ergonomics.*
- *Programs the company has in place to promote the health of their employees (e.g., weight loss, smoking cessation programs, health club, smoke-free environment, etc.).*
- *Existence of a systematic process for analyzing the causes of accidents when they do occur.*
- *Evidence that employee health and safety initiatives are tailored to different cultures, locations, and employee groups if appropriate.*

5.2b(2) How do you support your WORKFORCE via policies, services, and benefits? How are these tailored to the needs of a diverse WORKFORCE and different WORKFORCE groups and SEGMENTS?

What They're Looking for Here

Almost all companies do something in this area. What the examiners are looking for is the breadth and depth of the special services you provide to employees, and the degree to which these services have been tailored to the special needs of the organization's employees. For example, in an organization populated largely by women, child care might be an appropriate and appreciated special service. In a situation in which an organization's surrounding community education system is poor, remedial reading or other similar programs may be needed. If you have done a thorough analysis of your employees, have identified their special needs, and have tailored your employee assistance programs to those needs, you will do well in this area.

Most organizations approach this area either by offering what other companies offer in the way of employee services, or waiting until a problem occurs and then developing a program to deal with the problem (e.g., drugs or alcohol). If, however, you take a proactive/preventive approach to employee assistance, this will be noticed more by the examiners. If you can demonstrate that you offer more than your competitors do in the area of employee services, this too will be of interest to examiners. Your response might consist of a table that lists all employee assistance programs on the left side of the page, and the name of your organization and a few of its competitors along the top. A matrix, like the one that follows, then could be created to illustrate which employee assistance programs you offer, as compared to your competition.

EMPLOYEE ASSISTANCE PROGRAMS			
	Your Organization	Competitor A	Competitor B
Child Care	X	X	
Home Financing Assistance	X		X
Health Club Membership	X		
Weight Control Program	X		
Stop Smoking Program	X		
Drug/Alcohol Program	X		
Discount Symphony Tickets	X		
Annual Family Picnic	X	X	X
Counseling	X	X	
Outplacement Assistance	X	X	

What is important in this section is that you get creative in offering programs and services that meet the real needs of your workforce. These serve to attract potential employees to your organization. For example, a software development firm offers free coffee for employees. Another firm has an on-site dry cleaner and hair salon that both offer discounted prices. MBNA, the credit card giant, has a separate department that plans for funerals for relatives of employees. MBNA's bereavement department does all the arrangements and pays most of the bills associated with the funeral so as to relieve employee stress. This program does a lot to build loyalty from employees because the company helped them through a very difficult time. MBNA also has a department that plans marriages and honeymoons for employees. If two employees get married to each other (which happens a lot when most of your workforce is under 30), they receive additional time off for the honeymoon.

Indicators for Question 5.2b(2)

- *Whether or not a needs analysis has been completed to determine the employee assistance programs that may be needed in the organization.*
- *Number of different employee assistance programs offered.*
- *Breadth/variety of employee assistance and special services offered.*
- *How the organization's employee assistance programs compare to major competitors'.*
- *Employee opinion on the assistance programs offered.*
- *Evidence that services and programs are offered to all employees in all locations.*

Chapter

11

INTERPRETING THE CRITERIA FOR PROCESS MANAGEMENT (6)

OVERVIEW OF THE PROCESS MANAGEMENT CATEGORY

Category 6 covers Process Management. The category addresses how you assure and improve the quality and reliability of the products and services you offer to customers through process management strategies. Emphasis should be placed on the word how. This category deals with processes, not results. Results are assessed in Category 7, Results. The Baldrige Award Criteria (p. 46-47) define Category 6 as follows:

> *Process Management is the focal point within the Criteria for your key work systems and work processes. Built into the Category are the central requirements for identification and management of your core competencies to achieve efficient and effective work process management: effective design; a prevention orientation; linkage to customers, suppliers, partners, and collaborators and a focus on value creation for all key stakeholders; operational performance; cycle time; emergency readiness; and evaluation, continuous improvement, and organizational learning.*
>
> *Agility, cost reduction, and cycle time reduction are increasingly important in all aspects of process management and organizational design. In the simplest terms, "agility" refers to your ability to adapt quickly, flexibly, and effectively to changing requirements. Depending on the nature of your organization's strategy and markets, agility might mean rapid change from one product to another, rapid response to changing demands, or the ability to produce a wide range of customized services. Agility also increasingly involves decisions to outsource, agreements with key suppliers, and novel partnering arrangements. Flexibility might demand special strategies, such as implementing modular designs, sharing components, sharing manufacturing lines, or providing specialized training. Cost and cycle time reduction often involve Lean process management strategies. It is crucial to utilize key measures for tracking all aspects of your overall process management.*

In this chapter we'll discuss the two Examination Items and the two different Areas to Address that fall within this category. As in previous chapters, each section begins with a shadowed box containing the Examination Item, the point value, and any applicable Notes.* Areas to Address falling under that item follow in a lighter shadowed box. In the upper right corner of each Area to Address box is an indication [brackets] of whether the Area pertains to approach, deployment, or results. All definitions and information appearing within these boxes is taken directly from the Baldrige criteria. Following each Area to Address is an explanation defining what the examiners are looking for in assessing your application. Next, I have supplied a list of indicators or evaluation factors that will assist you in interpreting the criteria in preparing your application.

---

* Item Notes that apply to a specific Area to Address are appropriately listed in the box containing that Area.

6.1 WORK SYSTEMS DESIGN: PROCESS
How do you design your work systems? (35 PTS.)

Describe HOW your organization determines its CORE COMPETENCIES and designs its WORK SYSTEMS and KEY PROCESSES to deliver CUSTOMER VALUE, prepare for potential emergencies, and achieve organizational success and SUSTAINABILITY.

AREA TO ADDRESS   [APPROACH, DEPLOYMENT]
6.1a CORE COMPETENCIES

(1) HOW does your organization determine its CORE COMPETENCIES? What are your organization's CORE COMPETENCIES and how do they relate to your MISSION, competitive environment, and ACTION PLANS?

N1. "Core competencies" (6.1a) refers to your organization's areas of greatest expertise. Your organization's core competencies are those strategically important capabilities that provide an advantage in your marketplace or service environment. Core competencies frequently are challenging for competitors or suppliers and partners to imitate and provide a sustainable competitive advantage.

N2. "Work systems" refers to how the work of your organization is accomplished. Work systems involve your workforce, your key suppliers and partners, your contractors, your collaborators, and other components of the supply chain needed to produce and deliver your products, services, and business and support processes. Your work systems coordinate the internal work processes and the external resources necessary for you to develop, produce, and deliver your products and services to your customers and to succeed in your marketplace.

What They're Looking for Here

Ok, now this is confusing. In 2006 the term "work systems" could be found in Item 5.1, which asked about your human resource systems. Now in 2007 the same term "work systems" is used to describe the major processes the organization uses to do its core job or mission. You no longer find the phrase in section 5 where it was last year, but find it used many times in the newly revised section 6. Oh well, if the Baldrige criteria were easy to understand, you would not be reading this book, so I guess I should be grateful for the confusion.

The first question asked here is how you go about determining your core competencies, or greatest areas of expertise. No organization is great at everything. Identifying your greatest areas of expertise often involves using outsiders or at least reading what others say about your organization. Some good sources of this information are ratings by professional groups or associations, awards/recognition, organizations wanting to benchmark some of your processes, books and articles about your organization, and consultant feedback. For example, most people would describe Ikea as a company that is good at operational excellence and supply chain management. Most people would describe Toyota as a company that excels in the area of product quality and manufacturing efficiency. Most people would describe Starbucks as a company that is good at marketing. You need to explain how you determine your own core competencies, and the second question asks you what they are. What is important about the process for identifying your core competencies is the objectivity and thoroughness of the process, and the amount of evidence supporting your claims to be great at doing something. Many organizations are legends in their own minds, and others see them far differently than they see themselves. Your answer to the first question should identify the sources of data you use to identify your core competencies, and how you ensure objectivity of this data and your own reviews of the data.

When listing or describing your core competencies it is important to list only a handful of processes or areas of expertise, rather than listing 15-20 things. What might be difficult is coming up with a general list if your organization is in a variety of businesses. An effective number of core competencies is 4 to 6. They should be things that have historically helped to make you successful and that competitors have had a hard time copying from you. For example, a core competency of Bose is innovation. Bose has pioneered a number of products and technologies that competitors end up ripping off after a few years. However, by the time a competitor has knocked off a Bose product, Bose already has two new products that are even more innovative. The company spends about twice what any of their competitors spend on R&D and this is clearly one of their core competencies. A similar company in a different field is Medtronic. The Minneapolis-based medical devices company has pioneered most of the medical devices in common use today, (such as pacemakers), and continues to be a leader in their field.

After identifying each of your major areas of expertise or competencies, you need to explain how and why these competencies relate to the mission of the organization and your position in the marketplace. Often there is a disconnect between what an organization claims is a core competency and their position in the market. An example this might be a big box retailer claiming that customer service is one of its core competencies, or a chain of bland low-priced restaurants claiming that serving gourmet food is one of its competencies. The factors that you pick as core competencies should be consistent with the type of organization yours is and how others view you in the marketplace. Sometimes public opinion and reality are vastly different, however. For example, most people would not think that quality medical care would be a core competency of VA hospitals. Yet, in the last 10 years or so, VA hospitals have dramatically improved patient care and the quality of service provided to patients, have won numerous awards, and they even have their own version of the Baldrige Award that they give out to their best hospitals each year. Quality medical treatment and patient care really are core competencies of many VA hospitals today, but you might need to convince examiners of this if you were writing an application.

It is also important that you core competencies are consistent with your strategic plan or action plans. If, for example, your organization is looking to expand its manufacturing operations to China and other countries in Asia, it might be important to have expertise in manufacturing using remote sites. If your plan is to grow by 200% this year, recruiting and selecting the right employees might need to become a core competency.

Indicators for Question 6.1a(1)

- *The organization uses a variety of external data to help them identify their core competencies.*
- *Objectivity and reliability of data sources used to help determine core competencies.*
- *The organization has identified 4-6 major core competencies as opposed to a long list.*
- *The 4-6 core competencies identified appear consistent with the organization's reputation, position in the market, and past performance.*
- *The core competencies are consistent with the organization's mission and core business.*
- *Several major processes are not identified as core competencies and these are farmed out to contractors/suppliers or partners, as appropriate.*
- *The organization periodically reviews its list of core competencies to determine if they are still valid or need to be revised.*
- *Core competencies identified make it likely that the organization will be able to accomplish its major action plans or strategies outlined in the strategic plan.*

6.1a(2) HOW do you design and innovate your overall WORK SYSTEMS? HOW do you decide which PROCESSES within your overall WORK SYSTEMS will be internal to your organization (your KEY WORK PROCESSES) and which will use external resources?

N3. Your key work processes (6.1b[1]) are the processes that involve the majority of your organization's workforce and produce customer, stakeholder, and stockholder value. Your key work processes are your most important product and service design and delivery, business, and support processes.

What They're Looking for Here

This question makes a lot of sense if one were building an organization from scratch, but rarely is that going to be the case for a Baldrige applicant. Most applicants' processes were designed long ago, and the people that designed them may be long dead. If yours is an organization that has been around for a while, you might explain how the original processes were designed and if the original approach is still being used today. There are some things that are better left unchanged. Your answer to the first part of this question should include a description of some systematic process for determining process requirements, and designing an approach for getting the work done most efficiently. Make sure that customer requirements data from Item 3.1 are part of the inputs used, along with information on process constraints or limits, raw material quality, and other key factors. It is probably a good idea to use a graphic that depicts the major steps that you go through when designing a work process. It is also a good idea to present a couple of example processes that were designed using this approach, and possibly to reference results from section 7 that indicate that the process is functioning properly.

The second part of this question asks about how you make decisions on what work processes get done internally and which ones are done by outside suppliers/partners. This is a great opportunity for a decision tree or "if'–then" flowchart that depicts the factors involved in making these internal/external decisions

Indicators for Question 6.1a(2)

- *Evidence of a systematic approach for process design.*
- *All important groups and stakeholders have input to the design process.*
- *Customer requirement/needs are an input to the design process.*
- *The design process is quick and efficient and a good balance of focus on both cycle time and thoroughness.*
- *Evidence of innovation in the design process.*
- *Clear decision-making criteria for deciding on what work processes are done internally and externally.*

- *Evidence that the organization actually followed this model in the past when making decisions about what work to farm out and what processes to perform internally.*
- *The decisions about what work processes to do internally are linked to the identification of core competencies.*

AREA TO ADDRESS   [APPROACH, DEPLOYMENT]
6.1b. Work Process Design

(1) What are your organization's KEY WORK PROCESSES? How do these KEY WORK PROCESSES relate to your CORE COMPETENCIES? How do these PROCESSES contribute to delivering CUSTOMER VALUE, profitability, organizational success, and SUSTAINABILITY?

What They're Looking for Here

Your answer should begin with a list of your organization's major products and/or services, along with the associated work processes.

Once you have identified your key products and services, and identified the three to six major processes associated with the production and delivery of each one, you need to prepare a second matrix that indicates how you measure and control your processes. This matrix chart might look like the one below.

KEY PROCESSES	REQUIRE-MENTS	CORE COMPETENCIES	MEASURES	STANDARDS	CONTROL STRATEGIES

The key processes are taken from the first chart in this section, where you indicated which processes are associated with which products and services. Chances are there will be a number of generic processes that cut across all products and/or services, like delivery or distribution. Make sure that processes have verbs in them, and that you don't go too deeply into subprocesses. Requirements are important dimensions of the processes that directly relate to important customer requirements. For example, at Alcoa plants that manufacture aluminum that is used for beverage cans, one of the customers' key requirements is the thickness of the aluminum. In a hotel, if we were looking at delivery of room service as a process, one of the key customer requirements is how long it takes to get the meal delivered. Requirements sometimes translate directly into measures; sometimes they do not. In the room service example, a good measure obviously would be cycle time from the time the customer calls in the order until it is delivered to her room. In the Alcoa example, some of the measures are not so obvious. One of Alcoa's key manufacturing processes is rolling. Alcoa starts off with a big hunk of aluminum called an ingot that is about 2 feet thick and 10 feet long. This ingot is rolled until it becomes longer and thinner. One of Alcoa's key process measures is the temperature of the aluminum as it is being rolled. Do customers care about the temperature of the finished product? No. If it is cold outside when it is delivered, the aluminum is cold. Customers do care about thickness and strength though, which are two product dimensions that are influenced by the temperature of the aluminum as it is being rolled.

After identifying several key measures for process that are tied back to requirements, you need to identify the targets, standards, or control limits for each measure. Measures are meaningless without standards or goals. You might have a band consisting of an upper and lower control limit, or simply one standard. In the hotel example, the standard for the delivery of room service might be 45 minutes or less. If the meal is delivered in 30 minutes that is not a problem, so we don't need an upper and lower standard or control limit. Standards or targets for process measures should tie back to customer requirements that are identified in section 3.1 of your application. As you will come to learn, almost everything ties back to 3.1 eventually. This is why I advise applicants to write 3.1 first to help ensure that everything else is consistent with it.

The final column in your matrix chart is used to identify the control strategies that are used to keep the process performance within the standards or levels that have been set. In the Alcoa example, the control strategy is easy. Everything is automated. If you go into an Alcoa plant, there are almost no people. The place almost runs by remote control. In most service businesses, and many manufacturing businesses such as aerospace, most processes have human behavior as a major component. If this is the case, the Baldrige examiners want to know what control strategies you have in place to ensure that employee behavior stays within acceptable limits or standards. Procedures are not a control technique because they are usually not looked at. McDonald's is a company that is a master at controlling processes dependent upon human behavior. The chain has automated where it can, but some things just can't be automated yet. McDonald's control strategies consist of thorough training, clear and precise procedures and work rules, constant monitoring, feedback, and consequences. Employees are rewarded for desired behavior and following process rules, and punished for failure to conform to standards.

Your response to this item should explain the various methods you employ to ensure that your product and/or services meet the standards outlined in the design specifications. These approaches might include in-process inspection of components, products, or services as they are delivered, as well as an inspection of the final products or accomplishments. An accomplishment produced by a service might be a repaired car, a served meal, or a completed set of architectural drawings. The examiners will also assess the degree to which your approach is prevention-based. In other words, do you have systems in place for preventing the occurrence of defects, or are your systems focused on the detection and correction of defects?

Within this Area to Address you also need to explain how process deviations are corrected and the corrections verified. Once single or multiple causes have been identified, there are usually several different alternatives for countermeasures. Your response to this area should explain how you decide on the most appropriate countermeasure, how you implement it, and how you verify that the change produced the desired result. As in most other areas, the examiners are looking for evidence of a systematic process.

This area should address your follow-up after the implementation of countermeasures designed to improve quality. Many organizations do not do follow-up. For example, a large bank conducted an experiment that showed that if clerks in the operations area were put on incentive pay, their productivity and quality would improve. Upon implementation of the pay system, they found that the incentive pay worked well only for about three months. After that time, productivity stayed up but quality began to deteriorate. If the bank had not conducted a thorough follow-up evaluation, it might have left the incentive system intact for quite some time before realizing that it was no longer producing the desired results.

One important criterion regarding your follow-up approach is the scope of your follow-up activities. Do you conduct follow-up of all changes implemented to improve quality, or only the major ones that impact the whole organization? Do you conduct follow-up assessments in the support organizations as well as in the line organization? Another important criterion is the objectivity of the approach and instruments you use to conduct follow-up evaluations. Conducting a survey of employees' bosses 6 months after the employees have been through quality training is a poor way of evaluating the impact of training, for example. It's analogous to "the emperor's new clothes." People expect to see a change after the training, so that's how they respond to the survey. Surveys should never be used when it is possible to obtain "hard" data on quality measures.

The duration of your follow-up is also considered important. Some side effects don't appear immediately. If your evaluation occurs only a couple of months following implementation of a countermeasure, you won't know what happens after 6 months or a year. The effectiveness of countermeasures may deteriorate significantly after the first few months.

The only part of this question that you have not answered already is the final one that asks about the connection between the processes and customer value, and financial success of the organization. For some key processes this connection will be obvious. The processes of cooking and serving food in a restaurant obviously link to what customers are paying for, and to the restaurant's financial results. In some organizations the link between key processes and customer value is very cloudy. Here again is an opportunity to present a lot of information in a table or chart. An example format is shown below:

KEY PROCESS	CUSTOMER REQUIRMENTS	COMPANY REQUIREMENTS

Through the use of a coding system you might indicate whether the process is directly linked to a customer or internal requirement or if it is indirectly linked. The big question you want to answer with this table is: Why are you doing this and how does it add value to either the organization or its customers? Some support processes, such as information technology, or procurement, may provide little direct benefit to customers, but provide service to line employees that produce the company's product/service.

Indicators for Questions 6.1b(1)

- *All major Value Creation Processes are listed, and verbs are included in each.*
- *Measures are listed for each process.*
- *Measures are a mix of input, output, or outcome measures and process metrics.*
- *There are clear and obvious links between process and output/outcome measures.*
- *Standards or control limits are identified for all metrics.*
- *Standards appear to be set based on research and linked to process capabilities, resource constraints, customer requirements, and other factors.*
- *Control strategies have been identified for meeting standards or targets.*
- *Control strategies appear to be appropriate and effective.*
- *Processes are clearly linked to one or more core competencies of the organization.*
- *Links between key processes and important customer requirements are clearly delineated.*
- *How the key processes help the organization achieve financial result targets and other outcomes is clearly explained.*

> 6.1b(2) HOW do you determine KEY work PROCESS requirements, incorporating input from CUSTOMERS, suppliers, PARTNERS, and COLLABORATORS, as appropriate? What are the KEY requirements for these PROCESSES?

What They're Looking for Here

Your answer to this question should come partially from section 3.1, which asks you to identify the most important requirements of customers. These requirements should help you identify the standards and targets for process measures, and link back to meeting customer requirements. This question asks about how you do research to scientifically determine process requirements. A call center I worked with determined the appropriate standard for call hold time was 90 seconds. This was determined by monitoring when customers gave up and hung up the phone while waiting on hold. The research revealed that if customers waited more than 120 seconds, some would start hanging up. Developing the 90-second standard helped ensure that customers were happy with the timeliness of the call handling process, or at least the wait time portion of it.

Your answer to this question should indicate that you use a wide variety of data to determine process requirements and standards. Market research on customer requirements is one type of data. Other sources of information on process requirements might include process capability analyses, analyses of resource constraints, technology constraints, competitor performance, link between one process and others, supplier capabilities, and other factors. Essentially, you must convince examiners that you employ a thorough and scientific approach to defining process requirements and standards. An example or two might help add credibility to your description.

Indicators for Questions 6.1b(2)

- *Requirements are identified for all key Value Creation Processes.*
- *Requirements come from research on customer or other stakeholder needs.*
- *A systematic process is used to define requirements for each process.*
- *Requirements are checked periodically to see if customer/stakeholder needs and priorities have changed.*
- *Requirements research is thorough and appears valid.*
- *Requirements are specific versus generic.*
- *Requirements appear to drive customer buying behavior and loyalty when met.*
- *Requirements for processes clearly link to important outcomes or output measures.*

6.1b(3) HOW do you design and innovate your work PROCESSES to meet all the KEY requirements? HOW do you incorporate new technology, organizational knowledge, and the potential need for agility into the design of these PROCESSES? HOW do you incorporate CYCLE TIME, PRODUCTIVITY, cost control, and other efficiency and EFFECTIVENESS factors into the design of these PROCESSES?

What They're Looking for Here

What they're asking here is how information from various parts of the organization gets fed into the process design and management processes. This is often very difficult in large organizations that do not have the mechanisms in place to communicate relevant information to the appropriate personnel in the design processes. I've seen a few Baldrige applications that attempt to convey this transfer of information in a complicated graphic, with too many boxes and arrows. I think this is a situation where a table or even a list might be better. The examiners will look for evidence of both simplicity and thoroughness. It is important that it be easy for employees and managers from different functions to communicate data to the design folks or it will probably never happen.

One way of bringing in lessons learned and other appropriate data to the design process is to ensure that the design team is made up of a diverse group of people. Many years ago, R&D was responsible for new product and process designs. In today's organizations, most new product/service and process design teams include folks from marketing, production, operations, finance, HR, IT, and R&D. A cross-functional design team helps ensure that different viewpoints and data are considered. Another approach to making sure the design process teams have considered all appropriate data is to involve a wide variety of people in the review process. These individuals may not be members of the design teams, but they play an important role in ensuring the success of new products/services.

It is also important to explain how you involve operational or production folks in the design process for new products/services. One obvious way of ensuring this is to make sure that production/operational people are on the design teams. Alternatively, they could at least be involved in reviewing major outputs of each phase in the design process. Whatever your approach, the point you want to make in your answer is that all important operational variables and capabilities are considered before you get too far along in the design process. Your answer to this question might refer back to research you've done on customer requirements (3.1) and on competitor's products/services (4.2) and how this information is used to derive appropriate process measures and standards for production/delivery processes associated with new products/services.

Indicators for Questions 6.1b(3)

- *Evidence of systems for communicating relevant information to product/service design personnel.*

- *Extent to which such systems are actually used and have helped improve the design process on specific products/services.*

- *Use of cross-functional product/service design and review teams.*

- *Evidence that input is sought from diverse sources in the organization early in the design process when the input will be most valuable.*

- *Involvement of operations/production personnel on design teams.*

- *Thoroughness of design reviews so as to include all appropriate production/operational variables.*

- *Link between customer requirements, process metrics, and standards for production/delivery processes associated with new products/services.*

AREA TO ADDRESS   [APPROACH, DEPLOYMENT]
6.1c Emergency Readiness

How do you ensure WORK SYSTEM and workplace preparedness for disasters or emergencies? How does your disaster and emergency preparedness system consider prevention, management, continuity of operations, and recovery?

N4. Disasters and emergencies (6.1c) might be weather-related, utility-related, security-related, or due to a local or national emergency, including potential pandemics such as an avian flu outbreak. Emergency considerations related to information technology should be addressed in Item 4.2.

What They're Looking for Here

If you recall, there was already a question in 4.2 that asks about how you prepare your information technology systems for emergency. This question is much broader and asks about how the organization as a whole prepares for various types of emergencies or disasters that could occur, such as fires, floods, snow/wind storms, power outages, strikes, sickness, shortages of raw materials, dramatic price increases in raw materials, dramatic changes in laws or regulations, and other types of situations or events that could have a devastating impact on your organization A great way of answering this final question in 6.1 is to prepare a table that looks similar to the one below:

EVENT/ SITUATION	LIKELIHOOD	IMPACT	PREVENTIVE ACTIONS	RESTORATIVE ACTIONS

The table would list the various types of events that could happen to your organization. There is no need to list every possible disaster, but if your company is in Florida, hurricanes would probably be on the list (tornados if you are in Kansas or Illinois). The next column is where you rate the likelihood of this even occurring on a 1-3 or 1-5 scale, ranging from remote to almost certain. The third column is used to indicate the degree of impact this might have on your organization. The scale might go from 1=minimal to 5=major devastation. In the forth column you list all the preventive actions or programs you have implemented to prepare for possible disaster or emergency. The final column is used to list the elements of your plan to restore order once an event occurs. Your goal with your answer is to convince examiners that you are doing everything you can afford to do to be prepared for the most likely and most devastating events that could hit your organization.

Indicators for Question 6.1.c

- *Degree to which the applicant has identified all major types of emergencies or disasters that could occur.*

- *Disaster/emergency planning is done more thoroughly for events that are more likely and more devastating.*

- *Appropriate resources are devoted to emergency planning and trained personnel are involved in developing and implementing these programs.*

- *Plans and programs are periodically reviewed by outside experts to validate their potential effectiveness.*

- *More focus is on prevention than on restoration.*

- *Frequent drills or simulations are conducted to test the effectiveness of emergency plans.*

- *Improvements have been made in emergency preparedness based on performance on these exercises or drills.*

- *Comprehensive plans are in place to restore the organization to being functional in the event of high likelihood emergencies or disasters.*

- *Employees at all levels and locations are aware of emergency plans and their role in carrying them out.*

- *Employees receive skill-building emergency preparedness training on a regular basis.*

- *Tests are used in the training to measure their effectiveness.*

- *Back-up plans exist for dealing with financial emergencies.*

- *Systematic risk analyses are done to determine the appropriate resources to allocate to various types of emergency plans.*

6.2 WORK PROCESS MANAGEMENT AND IMPROVEMENT: PROCESS

How do you manage and improve your key organizational work processes? (50 points)

Describe HOW your organization implements, manages, and improves its KEY work PROCESSES to deliver CUSTOMER VALUE and achieve organizational success and SUSTAINABILITY.

AREA TO ADDRESS   [APPROACH, DEPLOYMENT]
6.2a WORK PROCESS Management

(1) HOW do you implement your work PROCESSES to ensure that they meet design requirements? HOW does your subsequent day-to-day operation of these PROCESSES ensure that they meet KEYPROCESS requirements? HOW is CUSTOMER, supplier, PARTNER, and COLLABORATOR input used in managing these PROCESSES, as appropriate? What are your KEY PERFORMANCE MEASURES or INDICATORS and in-process MEASURES used for the control and improvement of your work PROCESSES?

What They're Looking for Here

This question asks once you have determined the process requirements or standards, how do you ensure they are consistently met? Baldrige is asking about control. If your organization is a paper mill, process control is simply a matter of ensuring quality raw materials, calibrating the equipment for the appropriate settings, and monitoring key process variables and making adjustments when the performance falls outside of normal ranges. The work processes in most organizations today are not that simple, however. The more human behavior you have in your processes, the more difficult it will be to ensure process requirements are met. Control strategies for behavior-dependent processes include selection of appropriate personnel, documentation, training, feedback, and appropriate consequences for good and bad performance. Variability in human behavior is often not due to a lack of training, but a lack of feedback and consequences. In other words, employees often don't realize when they have not performed to standard, and there are no consequences for not performing to standard.

How you answer this initial question has a lot to do with how much automation is in your processes and how much human behavior. If your organization makes use of techniques such as "lean enterprise" or "six sigma" approaches, it would be appropriate to explain that in this section. These approaches are certainly not required, but can be excellent methods for ensuring that process standards are met. Both approaches stress analysis and improvement of processes, which is asked about in 6.2.

You should also explain how "in-process" measures are used in managing processes. This is a much misunderstood concept. An in-process measure occurs while a process is taking place, not after the fact. Inspecting the workmanship of a product or part after it has been repaired is not an in-process measure; it is an outcome measure. Similarly, on-time deliveries or landings are outcome measures, as are sales for a salesperson. In--process measures are process variables, such as time and temperature in a bakery, that link back to important outcome measures like golden brown crust or fully cooked bread. In many service organizations, these in-process measures are measures of human behavior. you must convince the examiners that your in-process measures are actually linked to important outcomes through research. I have encountered many superstitious in-process measures in organizations. In other words, there is no real evidence that effective performance on the process measure links to effective performance on some outcome. Salespeople get measured on call frequency or reports completed, manufacturing employees get measured on safety meetings attended, and senior executives get measured on leadership courses attended. In-process measures are vital, but they must be linked to outcomes. The in-process measures themselves should be listed in the chart or table I described in how to answer the "What" questions in this section. What you need to explain here is how the in-process measures are identified and verified.

This question is also about how input from customers, suppliers, and other outsiders is used to help manage processes. These outsiders are often valuable sources of objective feedback that might be difficult to obtain from your own employees. Of course, you hire the suppliers, so their input might be a little biased as well, but customers are usually brutally honest. This question asks about how you use feedback from customers and partners/suppliers to manage work processes. You might get data on the sales process used by an account team by interviewing the customer and asking him or her questions about the process that was followed. Similarly, you might ask suppliers for feedback on what it is like to do business with your firm. Many companies I have worked for make it very hard to get the contract and to get paid once the work is completed. Suppliers/partners are often hired to do much of the real work or "value creation processes" in organizations. For example, most state transportation departments hire outside contractors to build new roads and bridges. These partners can provide valuable feedback on how well or poorly your defined work processes work. These people know because they are doing the work following the processes. Some examples of how customer and supplier feedback is used to manage processes would help your write-up.

Indicators for "How" Questions 6.2a(1)

- *Evidence that controls are in place to ensure that process requirements are met.*
- *Existence of documentation for key processes where it is required.*
- *Scope and deployment of training on meeting process requirements.*
- *Use of the best technology affordable to ensure process compliance.*
- *Deployment of approaches like "lean enterprise" or "six sigma" where appropriate.*
- *In-process measures are tracked on a real-time or frequent basis and fed back to appropriate personnel.*
- *In-process measures are linked to output or outcome measures via research.*
- *Standards or limits set for in-process metrics are based on research relating to process capabilities, customer requirements, resource constraints, and other factors.*
- *Adequacy and thoroughness of control strategies.*
- *Evidence that information from suppliers/partners is considered where appropriate to set process standards and develop controls.*
- *Evidence that customer requirements and desires are reflected in process measures and standards and linked to important outcomes for customers.*
- *Evidence that interactions between various processes are considered when setting standards and developing controls.*
- *Prevention-based approaches are appropriate for size and type of organization and focus on the appropriate variables.*
- *Relationships are identified between individual products/services and processes.*
- *Approach to process control is preventive in nature.*
- *Process owners and/or accountabilities are identified, if appropriate.*
- *Degree to which process control is automated where appropriate and possible.*
- *Frequency of measurement of key process variables.*
- *Thoroughness of control mechanisms used to ensure that processes stay within specified tolerances or guidelines.*
- *Control mechanisms for ensuring that processes based upon employee behavior are systematic and thorough.*
- *Adequate sample sizes used to collect data on end-of-process measures.*
- *Adequacy of in-process measures.*
- *Use of valid statistical procedures for analyzing process data.*

- *Number of different process measures for which data are collected.*
- *Use of established and acceptable model for cause analysis.*
- *Use of different processes for analyzing common-cause and special-cause problems.*
- *Thoroughness and rigor of cause-analysis process.*
- *Examples or evidence to suggest that the analysis process is successful for discerning the root causes of process upsets and other quality-related problems.*
- *Clear linkages between customer requirements, process measures, and standards.*

6.2a(2) HOW do you minimize overall costs associated with inspections, tests, and PROCESS or PERFORMANCE audits, as appropriate? HOW do you prevent defects, service errors, and rework and minimize warranty costs or CUSTOMERS' PRODUCTIVITY losses, as appropriate?

What They're Looking for Here

Although a prevention-based approach is the preferred method of ensuring quality goods and services, many organizations still rely on testing, inspections, and audits. This question asks about the approaches used to perform these processes. Some of the factors that might be important to address would be sample size and frequency, types of variables inspected, instrumentation used for evaluation/judgment, and how standards are determined. Thoroughness is one important dimension for which examiners will be looking. Rolls Royce is famous for thoroughly testing to destruction each component of a car before deciding to install it in an actual Rolls. Of course, when you are charging $400,000 for a car, you can be this thorough. Now that the company is owned by BMW, I wonder if they still conduct such extensive testing? The Toyota Camry or Ford Taurus are exceptional cars as well, but cost less than 10% of the price of a Rolls Royce—we would not, therefore, expect the level of testing to be the same as for a Rolls Royce. Thus, it is important to explain how your testing and inspection approach is geared to the customer expectations and pricing factors in the marketplace.

You should also mention the types of tests that you conduct, and who conducts them. Some industries have dedicated quality inspectors that pull samples of products and perform inspections and tests on them. Service companies often make use of mystery shoppers or inspectors who pose as customers to evaluate service delivery as it happens on airlines or in restaurants/stores. Inspections and testing tend to be expensive both in labor and in finding problems that are often difficult or expensive to repair. You need to do your best to convince examiners that your inspection approaches are thorough enough to catch and prevent major disasters like product recalls or other tragedies associated with your product/service. A fast food restaurant chain I worked with performed "announced" inspections. The restaurant manager and employees would spend weeks cleaning and preparing for the inspection and, miraculously, everyone passed with flying colors!

This question also asks about prevention-based approaches you employ to ensure high quality goods/services. In some manufacturing companies, automation is used to control production processes and keep process measures within acceptable control limits. Organizations that have a lot of human behavior in their processes have a much harder time ensuring consistency. If yours is one of those organizations where processes include a lot of human behavior, you might want to discuss approaches for preventing unwanted behavior. Many of these approaches would probably have been discussed already in the HR section. Behavior control approaches often include selection, employment testing, training, communication of performance standards, supervision, feedback, and recognition/reward systems. It is perfectly acceptable to refer back to these HR approaches as methods of preventive quality control.

Indicators for Question 6.2a(2)

- *Adequate sample sizes are used for testing to ensure overall product quality.*
- *Testing/inspection is performed frequently enough to detect possible problems.*
- *Automated equipment is used where possible to remove human error and judgment from inspections/tests.*
- *Inspectors/auditors are thoroughly trained and there are reliability checks on their work.*
- *Auditors/inspectors are objective and have no incentive to pass poor quality work.*
- *Auditors/inspectors are given proper authority to do their jobs.*
- *Testing/inspection methods are evaluated for effectiveness and efficiency and changed or improved as necessary.*
- *Auditing/inspection instruments/tools are calibrated frequently.*
- *Efforts have been made over the years to minimize inspection and testing by building in more prevention-based approaches.*
- *Outside audits/inspections are done, if appropriate, to supplement internal data.*
- *Evidence is shown of a prevention-based approach to ensuring product/service quality.*

AREA TO ADDRESS   [APPROACH, DEPLOYMENT]
6.2b. Work Process Improvement

HOW do you improve your work PROCESSES to achieve better PERFORMANCE, to reduce variability, to improve products and services, and to keep the PROCESSES current with business needs and directions? HOW are improvements and lessons learned shared with other organizational units and PROCESSES to drive organizational LEARNING and INNOVATION?

N1. To improve process performance (6.2b) and reduce variability, you might implement approaches such as a Lean Enterprise System, Six Sigma methodology, use of ISO 9000:2000 standards, the Plan-Do-Check-Act methodology, or other process improvement tools.

N2. The results of improvements in product and service performance should be reported in Item 7.1. All other work process performance results should be reported in Item 7.5.

What They're Looking for Here

The previous questions asked about how you measure, manage, and control your key processes to ensure that they are performed consistently. This final question in 6.2 asks about how you analyze and improve the processes. Previously, many companies taught their employees process analysis and problem-solving techniques and told all of them to form a team, find some process, and work on improving it. Some companies implementing "six sigma" and "lean enterprise" approaches still do the same thing. This is not what is looked for here. Trying to fix every process and having everyone work on process improvement teams is a ridiculous waste of time. Not every process needs improving, and no organization can afford to try to improve all of its processes.

The strategic plan should be the driver behind all process improvement activities. The strategic plan includes long- and short-term goals and objectives. The actions or strategies to accomplish these goals often involve new ways of getting work done. For example, if a major goal was to reduce the unit cost of service transactions by 20 percent, the process for performing those transactions would be analyzed to find ways to eliminate costs and do the work more efficiently. A big part of your answer to this final question should explain the link between strategic goals and process improvements. After you have established those links, and convinced the examiners that process improvement activities are very focused, you can explain how you go about analyzing and improving the processes.

There is no right answer or particular analysis/improvement model required by Baldrige. If your company has adopted the "six sigma" approach, that is great. Explain how it works and why this approach suits your company. If you don't use this approach and have your own home-grown model for process analysis and improvement, that is fine too. The key is to show that the approach is logical, systematic, and makes sense for the type of work you do. There are some organizations where variability in processes is a good thing. A work process such as teaching third graders to write in cursive, making a romantic comedy film, or designing a website all call for some degree of creativity, and there are many ways to do these tasks and get a quality output. An approach like "lean enterprise" or "six sigma" tends to work best in manufacturing companies that make many products per day.

This question also asks about how you keep your processes current with business needs and competitors. When one competitor makes a change to improve a process, this may set a new expectation in the minds of customers. For example, when the first rental car company pioneered the use of hand-held computers to check in rental car customers and get them a bill, this dramatically shortened the amount of time needed to return a car at the airport, and eliminated the need to wait in any lines. Not only did this improve the productivity of the return clerks, it set up a new expectation in the minds of the customer. The other rental car companies were quick to follow suit and use this technology to improve their car rental return process. While most processes get easier and more efficient with passing time, some get more complicated. Getting through security at the airport today takes much longer and is much more frustrating than before. There is also an expectation that passengers will be more thoroughly screened than before. Keeping your processes current with changing customer and business needs is something that will always be important to organizations. Your answer should indicate that you consider competitor performance, customer needs, changing economic and other external factors, technology, and a variety of sources of data to keep your processes current. An example or two will help add credibility to your response.

The final question here asks how you communicate process improvements to others in your organization. This was probably already addressed in the response to 5.1, which asks about knowledge management and communication of best practices. Some companies document process improvements in central databases that can be accessed by others. Other organizations take a more directed approach and implement new processes across the board when they have been proven in one part of the organization. Regardless of your approach, examiners want to make sure that there is a systematic approach for ensuring that improvements are not limited in their deployment. In large complex organizations, the left hand sometimes does not know what the right hand is doing. Where appropriate, improvements in processes from one unit or part of the organization need to be shared and implemented in others. Simply stating that this occurs is not enough. You must explain exactly how improvements are shared, and provide some examples to illustrate that this does occur.

Indicators for Question 6.2b

- *Evidence that process improvement activities are directly linked to goals and strategies outlined in the strategic plan.*

- *Use of a consistent model or approach for process analysis and improvement.*

- *Scope of process improvement activities shows focus on a few critical success factors rather than having everyone work on improving their processes.*

- *Teams or groups used to analyze and improve processes include members that are carefully selected for their expertise—having everyone participate in improvement teams is often a disaster.*

- *Deployment of a systematic process analysis and improvement model throughout all parts of the organization.*

- *Adequacy of training and coaching on use of process improvement model.*

- *Evidence that process improvement is not always a reaction to performance problems—a preventive approach is preferred.*

- *Use of outside data on technology, competitors, customer needs, and other factors to drive process improvement.*

- *Consideration of the interaction between processes when selecting one to improve.*

- *Appropriateness of process analysis/improvement model for the type and size of organization.*

- *Evidence that alternative models were considered before adopting an approach to process analysis/improvement.*

- *Scope and adequacy of examples presented to show improvements in processes.*

- *Link between process improvements and results shown in Category 7.*

- *Evidence that process improvements implemented in one part of the organization are systematically shared with others and implemented where appropriate.*

- *Systematic analysis of new and changing technology as a means for identifying process improvement opportunities.*

- *Number of different stimuli used as impetus for process improvement efforts.*

- *Use of competitor or benchmark data as stimuli for identifying opportunities for process improvement.*

- *Evidence that process analysis is used as a stimulus for process improvement.*

- *Breadth and scope of process improvements initiated via process analysis.*

Chapter

12

INTERPRETING THE CRITERIA FOR RESULTS (7)

OVERVIEW OF THE RESULTS CATEGORY

This seventh category, Business Results, is one where organizations are really put to the test. The previous six categories concentrate on processes and activities. A good writer may even make your approach and processes seem like they meet all the criteria in the first six categories, but this section (7) tells the true tale of the success (or lack thereof) of your performance improvement efforts. In this section, you must provide evidence that all of the processes and programs you employ have really worked to improve quality and overall performance in your organization.

The Baldrige Award Criteria define this category as follows:

> *The results Category examines your organization's performance and improvement in all key areas—product and service outcomes, customer-focused outcomes, financial and market outcomes, workforce-focused outcomes, process-effectiveness outcomes, and leadership outcomes. performance levels are examined relative to those of competitors and other organizations providing similar products and services. (p.31)*

This category is worth more points than any of the others (450 points) because it separates good organizations from mediocre ones. You might be able to talk about all the wonderful approaches you deploy in the previous sections, but this section is where you must prove their effectiveness. To receive a high score in this category, you need to show that your levels and trends in performance results separate you from your competitors and other comparative companies. Effective proposal writing will help get a higher score in other sections, but not here. The examiners are looking for data, not words.
The seventh and final category in the Baldrige criteria consists of six items:

7.1 Product and Service Outcomes (100 points)

7.2 Customer-Focused Outcomes (70 points)

7.3 Financial and Market Outcomes (70 points)

7.4 Workforce-focused Outcomes (70 points)

7.5 Process Effectiveness Results (70 points)

7.6 Leadership Outcomes (70 points)

As in the previous chapters, the information on the Examination Item appears in a shadowed box, and the Areas to Address appear in lighter shadowed boxes. The indicators for this chapter are a little different, because the criteria do not ask about your approaches or practices. The indicators in this chapter relate to the types of measures, levels, and trends with which positive results should be presented.

7.1 PRODUCT AND SERVICE OUTCOMES:
What are your product and service performance results?

RESUL TS
(100 PTS.)

Summarize your organization's KEY product and service PERFORMANCE RESULTS. SEGMENT your RESULTS by product and service types and groups, CUSTOMER groups, and market SEGMENTS, as appropriate. Include appropriate comparative data.

N1. Product and service results reported in this Item should relate to the key product, program, and service features identified as customer requirements or expectations in P.1b(2) based on information gathered in Items 3.1 and 3.2. The measures or indicators should address factors that affect customer preference, such as those included in P.1, Note 3 and Item 3.1, Note 3.

N2. For some nonprofit organizations, product or service performance measures might be mandated by your funding sources. These measures should be identified and reported in your response to this Item. For additional description of this Item, see page 49.

AREA TO ADDRESS

[RESULTS]

7.1a Product and Service RESULTS

What are your current LEVELS and TRENDS in KEYMEASURES or INDICATORS of product and service PERFORMANCE that are important to your CUSTOMERS? HOW do these RESULTS compare with the performance of your competitors and other organizations providing similar products and services?

What They're Looking for Here

This was a new question in 1999, when Baldrige was about quality. Its status has increased from a question in 2002 to a full item in 2003. In 2005, its status was further elevated by giving it more points than any other Result Item. I think it is a positive change that hard internal measures of product and service now have their own item because they are often predictors of customer satisfaction levels and their future loyalty. You will notice that the word "quality" is not used in the criteria here. The question asks about data on any product/service performance dimension that might be important to customer satisfaction. The types of metrics for which you provide data in this section should be consistent with your customer requirements research you described in 3.1.

The key here is to present data on metrics that are strongly linked to customer satisfaction. For example, FedEx tracks a metric each day called the Service Quality Index. It is a measure of the frequency and severity of the mistakes they make each day that impact how customers feel about the service. For example, losing a package completely might be weighted as a 10 because it is the worst mistake that could occur. Delivering a package an hour late might be weighted as a 1 because it is only a minor inconvenience to most customers. Another good example is a metric tracked by a major rental car company, which provides shuttle bus service at airport pick-up locations. Research showed that customers waiting for the company's bus got quite angry if the bus did not come quickly, especially if they saw a competitor's bus pass them twice while they were waiting.

These are great examples of the types of internal performance metrics that an organization might report in this section. Along with the usual graphs of your own and competitor performance, this section calls for some explanation. It may not be obvious to the examiner why you are tracking the measures for specific data presented in this section. You need to explain how and why these metrics were selected, and how they link to both customer satisfaction measures [7.2a(1)] and customer loyalty measures [7.2a(2)]. In fact, if you can show graphs that depict correlations or links between these and other measures, that will be sure to impress the examiners.

Indicators for Question 7.1

- *Number and breadth of metrics for which product/service performance data are provided in this section.*
- *Trends in product/service performance measures show excellent improvement over multiple years.*
- *Levels of performance are superior to industry averages and all major competitors.*
- *Product/service performance metrics selected are based upon thorough research, linking them to customer satisfaction and other important performance dimensions.*
- *Adverse indicators show both decreasing trends and levels that are better than relevant comparative data.*
- *Integrity of data on internal measures of product/service performance.*
- *Number of metrics in this section that can be linked to other metrics of customer satisfaction, loyalty, or even financial results.*

- *Strength of correlations shown will help improve the accuracy of business decision making.*
- *Breadth of data presented covers all major products/services and is segmented appropriately.*

7.2 CUSTOMER-FOCUSED OUTCOMES: RESUL TS
What are your customer-focused performance results? (70 PTS.)

Summarize your organization's KEY CUSTOMER-focused RESULTS, including CUSTOMER satisfaction and CUSTOMER perceived VALUE. SEGMENT your RESULTS by product and service types and groups, CUSTOMER groups, and market SEGMENTS as appropriate. Include appropriate comparative data.

N1. Customer satisfaction and dissatisfaction results reported in this Item should relate to the customer groups and market segments discussed in P.1b(2) and Item 3.1 and to the determination methods and data described in Item 3.2.

N2. Measures and indicators of customers' satisfaction with your products and services relative to customers' satisfaction with competitors might include objective information and data from your customers and from independent organizations.

AREA TO ADDRESS   [RESUL TS]

7.2a CUSTOMER-Focused RESULTS

(1) What are your current LEVELS and TRENDS in KEY MEASURES or INDICATORS of CUSTOMER satisfaction and dissatisfaction? How do these RESULTS compare with the customer satisfaction levels of your competitors and other organizations providing similar products and services?

What They're Looking for Here

As with any Result Item, levels and trends are the two most important dimensions of your performance. This is the area for which data should be reported that demonstrate how levels of customer satisfaction have improved over the last several years due to performance improvement efforts. This section should include graphs of customer satisfaction data for the different groups of customers you serve. Refer back to the guidelines included in Chapter 2 of this book for a discussion of how to prepare graphs and tables. Don't make the mistake some applicants have made and respond with a single graph of customer satisfaction data. Present several different graphs of customer satisfaction data from at least the past three years. Three data points do not establish much of a trend, so the more historical data you can present, the better.

In evaluating this section, the Baldrige examiners will be looking for several things. The first is the amount of data you present on customer satisfaction. Because they are constrained by the maximum of 50 pages for your entire application, some applicants devote only a couple of pages to this important Area to Address. Include as much data as you can, and don't be afraid to use several pages for this area. It is possible to fit as many as eight separate graphs on one page. Tables or charts also allow you to fit a great deal of data in a small space. (Make sure that your graphs and charts are readable, however.)

Two other related factors examined are the level of customer satisfaction you have achieved and the current level of performance in relation to past levels. If 80 percent of your customers are satisfied or very satisfied with your quality, a large number (20 percent) still remain unsatisfied. If only 50 percent were satisfied 3 years ago, you will receive some credit for a big improvement, but your overall levels of satisfaction are still low. Improvement is much more difficult when you are already doing well. It may take more effort and thus be more significant if you have raised customer satisfaction levels from 94 to 98 percent in 3 years. A trend showing steady improvement over the last 3 to 5 years is considered very positive.

The final factor examined in this Area to Address is the number of different indices and types of data you present on customer satisfaction. Different measures of customer satisfaction (or the same indices among different segments or groups of customers) should be presented. For example, you might present data on overall levels of satisfaction among new customers, existing customers, large company customers, small company customers, government customers, private sector customers, etc. Choose the breakdowns that make the most sense for your products/services and markets.

Obviously, not all of the indices mentioned regarding dissatisfaction will be relevant to your organization. You should respond to this section by presenting data you have for any indicators that are a good gauge of customers' dissatisfaction with your products and/or services. Present the data graphically and include at least 3 years of statistics. The number of different indices for which data are presented and the degree to which the data show a steadily decreasing trend are the factors that will be evaluated in your response to this section.

It is likely that not all of the results and trends will be entirely positive. Performance on one or more indicators of customer dissatisfaction may not show a consistent downward trend. It is important that you thoroughly explain each of these anomalies or adverse trends. A thorough explanation does not mean that blame should be placed elsewhere for the occurrence of the anomaly. It simply means that you can describe exactly why these phenomena occurred and explain the steps taken to prevent future lapses in performance.

It is important in your response for this Area that you compare your performance on several dimensions of customer satisfaction to several key competitors. The organizations you compare yourself to are also important. Comparing yourself to a world-class leader instead of local competitors obviously will earn you more points.

Indicators for Question 7.2a(1)

- *Presentation of a wide variety of customer satisfaction data.*
- *Number of different indices of customer satisfaction for which data are presented.*
- *Presentation of customer satisfaction data by customer or market group.*
- *Trend showing continual improvements over the last several years in all measures of customer satisfaction.*
- *Amount of historical data presented on levels of customer satisfaction.*
- *Overall levels of customer satisfaction (percentage of customers satisfied with service, etc.).*
- *Clarity of graphs and explanations of customer satisfaction data.*
- *Number and types of different breakdowns of customer satisfaction data.*
- *Number of different indices for which data are presented.*
- *Data are presented for all important adverse indices or measures of dissatisfaction in industry.*
- *All adverse indicators show a steady downward trend over the past 3 or more years.*
- *Minimum number of anomalies or positive trends in satisfaction/dissatisfaction indicators.*
- *Clear and complete explanations provided for all anomalies in data or positive trends in satisfaction/dissatisfaction indicators.*
- *Overall levels of performance on indicators of dissatisfaction.*
- *Number of different competitors to which comparisons are made.*
- *Number of different indices of customer satisfaction on which comparisons are made to the competition.*
- *Status/level of competitors (e.g., world-class leader in field) to which comparisons are made.*
- *Percentage of customer satisfaction indices on which applicant is superior to the competition.*
- *Applicant's superiority to competition in measures of customer satisfaction.*
- *Objectivity of data on how the applicant compares to competition.*
- *Extent to which competitors in all major markets and with all major products/services are used for comparison.*

> 7.2a(2) What are your current LEVELS and TRENDS in KEY MEASURES or INDICATORS of CUSTOMER-perceived VALUE, including CUSTOMER loyalty and retention, positive referral, and other aspects of building relationships with CUSTOMERS, as appropriate?

What They're Looking for Here

This question reflects the fact that this item has been broadened to include more than just customer satisfaction results. As I mentioned in section 3.2, a number of companies have found that improved customer satisfaction scores don't necessarily increase loyalty or predict future buying behavior. This section asks for data on hard measures that should link directly to financial results. The types of measures for which you provide data in this section should be consistent with those mentioned in sections 3.2b, 1.1, and 4.1. Some examples of important metrics that might be included here are:

- *Growth in business from preferred customers.*
- *Reduction in defecting or lost customers.*
- *Increased loyalty to your products/services.*
- *Customers giving your organization more business and giving less to competitors.*
- *Number and percentage of partnerships formed with key customers.*
- *Number and/or percentage of customers who will provide a positive referral.*
- *Percentage or money amount in new business that is based upon referrals from existing customers.*
- *Customer-perceived value data collected through surveys, focus groups, or other similar methods.*

Aside from the value perception data, most of the metrics in this section are what I would call "hard" measures because they are measures of actual customer behavior, not just their thoughts or opinions. The data you present in 7.2a(2) should correlate with the data presented in this section. If you can show increased customer satisfaction and value linked to future loyalty and increased spending, this will really impress the examiners. In fact, any sort of links between the soft and hard measures in this section will be impressive.

As with the previous section, it is important to show multiple years worth of data and to present as many sources of comparative data as you can. The data in this section tend to be weighted more heavily by examiners because hard measures of customer buying behavior are a much stronger indicator of their overall satisfaction than any survey or complaint metric.

Indicators for Question 7.2a(2)

- *Many different indicators of customer loyalty or retention for which data are presented.*
- *Data on customer loyalty are presented according to market segments identified in 3.1.*
- *Trends in loyalty data show impressive improvements over several years.*
- *Levels of customer loyalty and value perception are clearly superior to industry averages and major competitors.*
- *Adverse indicators such as losses of customers/defections show a decreasing trend and levels that are better than all major competitors.*
- *Breadth and integrity of comparative data that are presented.*
- *Extent to which correlations or links are shown between leading indicators of customer satisfaction shown in 7.1a(1) and lagging indicators of loyalty shown in this question [7.1a(2)].*
- *Number of different indices in this section for which correlations are shown to other metrics that relate to customer satisfaction or even other lagging indicators such as sales or profits.*
- *Data suggest that the organization has been careful to build loyalty from the "right" customers.*

7.3 FINANCIAL AND MARKET OUTCOMES:
What are your financial and market results? (70 pts.)

Summarize your organization's KEY financial and marketplace PERFORMANCE RESULTS by CUSTOMER or market segments, as appropriate. Include appropriate comparative data.

AREA TO ADDRESS   [RESULTS]

7.3a Financial and Market Results

(1) What are your current LEVELS and TRENDS in KEY MEASURES or INDICATORS of financial PERFORMANCE, including aggregate MEASURES of financial return and economic VALUE or budgetary MEASURES, as appropriate?

(2) What are your current LEVELS and TRENDS in KEY MEASURES or INDICATORS of marketplace PERFORMANCE, including market share or position, growth, and new markets entered, as appropriate?

N1. Responses to 7.3a(1) might include aggregate measures such as return on investment (ROI), asset utilization, operating margins, profitability,

Continued

profitability by market or customer segment, liquidity, debt-to-equity ratio, value added per employee, and financial activity measures. Measures should relate to the financial management approaches described in Item 6.2. For nonprofit organizations, additional measures might include performance to budget, reserve funds, cost avoidance or savings, administrative expenditures as a percentage of budget, and cost of fundraising versus funds raised.

N2. For nonprofit organizations, responses to 7.3a(2) might include measures of charitable donations or grants and the number of new programs or services offered.

What They're Looking for Here

This important section asks you to present your financial and marketplace results. Most organizations have no shortage of these types of data. The problem may lie in selecting the most important graphs to present, given the limited space you have in the application. You should present the overall financial indicators that are listed in your response to Item 4.1, which asks about the performance metrics in your company. If you mention that Return on Net Assets (RONA) is your primary financial statistic, you should present some data on RONA here. It is a good idea to present a mix of financial performance data that represent the past (profit, EBIT, ROI, etc.), the present (cash flow, money in booked orders, assets/liabilities), and the future (growth, money in outstanding proposals, money invested in R&D or new products/services). By presenting data on your financial performance from all three time perspectives, you give the examiners a good overall picture of your financial health.

It is important to keep in mind that the examiners are looking for evidence that your results are better than your competitors', and that you show a long history of good performance. Therefore, it is important to present data over multiple years. Getting comparative financial performance data on your competitors may be difficult, but this will help your score if your results show that you are clearly the industry leader.

This section is also used to present marketplace data, which might include market share, gains and losses of business, or other similar data. Again, comparative data are very important. One Baldrige applicant showed that its market share had been steadily increasing over the last 5 years, in a flat market, which meant that competitors' share of the market was being lost to the applicant's company. These kinds of data will be very impressive to the examiners. Make sure when you present data on marketplace results you indicate the source of any comparative data on your graphs. Using market data from an outside impartial source such as an industry trade association will give the presentation more credibility than data you collected yourself.

Some marketplace data may actually belong better in section 7.2. For example, gains and losses of key customers might be a very good hard measure of customer satisfaction. Another one, used by IBM, that could go either in 7.2 or 7.3, is increases or decreases in revenue from existing customers from year to year. You decide where to present the data, keeping in mind that both sections should include about equal amounts of data, and that these two Areas to Address in Category 7 are worth 15 percent of the points.

Indicators for Questions 7.3a(1) and 7.3a(2)

- *Presentation of financial results shows levels that are clearly superior to major competitors and industry averages.*

- *Data are presented on all major financial indices listed in section 4.1 of the application.*

- *Financial performance data include a good mix of indicators of past, present, and future financial health.*

- *Trends show continuous improvement over 3 or more years.*

- *Trends show better improvement rates than industry averages and/or competitors.*

- *Competitor data presented are actually the companies against which the applicant most often competes.*

- *Financial results represent the entire company's performance rather than that of a single unit or division.*

- *Financial results compare favorably to benchmark or world-class organizations in similar business.*

- *Sources of comparative data are credible.*

- *Market data show applicant's performance is clearly superior to that of all major competitors.*

- *Trends in market share and other similar metrics show excellent trends over time.*

- *Trends in market share growth are superior to industry averages and competitors' trends.*

- *Length of time during which levels and trends in financial and market performance are superior to industry averages and performance of major competitors*

7.4 WORKFORCE-FOCUSED OUTCOMES: RESULTS
What are your workforce-focused performance results? (70 pts.)

Summarize your organization's KEY WORKFORCE-FOCUSED RESULTS for WORKFORCE ENGAGEMENT and for your WORKFORCE environment. SEGMENT your RESULTS to address the DIVERSITY of your WORKFORCE and to address your WORKFORCE groups and SEGMENTS, as appropriate. Include appropriate comparative data.

AREA TO ADDRESS   [RESULTS]
7.4a. Workforce RESULTS

(1) What are your current LEVELS and TRENDS in KEY MEASURES or INDICATORS of WORKFORCE ENGAGEMENT, WORKFORCE satisfaction, and the development of your WORKFORCE, including leaders?

N1. Results reported in this Item should relate to processes described in Category 5. Your results should be responsive to key work process needs described in Category 6 and to your organization's action plans and human resource plans described in Item 2.2.

N2. Responses to 7.4a(1) should include measures and indicators identified in response to 5.1c(1).

N3. Nonprofit organizations that rely on volunteers should include results for their volunteer workforce, as appropriate.

What They're Looking for Here

This first question asks you to present data on key measures of employee or workforce engagement or commitment. These measures should have been identified in Category 5 of your application. Common metrics that are reported on in this section include:

- *Satisfaction/engagement surveys*
- *Focus group data*
- *Complaints/grievances*
- *New employees referred by existing employees*

- *Hours worked/overtime*
- *Percentage of time spent in meetings*
- *Absenteeism*
- *Turnover*
- *Requests for transfer in and out*
- *Training hours per employee*
- *Training test scores*
- *Completion of objectives in individual development plans*
- *Training/development dollars/total payroll*
- *Openings filled with internal versus external personnel*

As with all of Section 7, it is important that you show trends over multiple years, and relevant comparative data. It will be hard to assess the level of performance of your HR results unless you have data on the same measures from other organizations that are similar to your own.

Indicators for Question 7.4a(1)

- *Data are presented for all important workforce engagement/satisfaction and development metrics identified in 5.1.*
- *Trends show dramatic improvements over the last few years, or high levels of performance that have been maintained.*
- *Levels of performance on important metrics are superior to industry averages, competitors, and other relevant comparisons.*
- *Breadth and scope of data on workforce engagement, satisfaction, and development as appropriate.*
- *Results presented are a good mix of process or activity measures and output/outcome metrics.*
- *Correlations have been demonstrated between results in this section and those in other sections such as Customer Focus Results, (7.2), Financial and Market Results (7.3), and Process Effectiveness Results (7.5).*
- *Strength of correlations can be used for practical business planning and decision making.*
- *Negative trends or anomalies in the data are adequately explained.*
- *Results show that performance system changes like job redesign, teams, suggestion systems, compensation, recognition, and other approaches actually lead to improvements in financial and operational performance, or have positive impact on important measures on the company's performance metrics.*

> 7.4a(2) What are your current LEVELS and TRENDS in KEY MEASURES of
> WORKFORCE CAPABILITYand CAPACITY, including staffing levels, retention, and
> appropriate skills?

What They're Looking for Here

Results asked for in this question pertain to improving workforce capabilities through training and development. The more you can focus your results of training on learning outcomes rather than activities, the higher your score is likely to be. The note to this question suggests courses completed as a metric, but these types of "employee head count" data are not of much use. Rather, provide data that show the effectiveness of your employee training and development activities. These measures should be the same as those described in section 5.2 in the question that asked about how you evaluate your training and development (5.2.a[6]). Some of the graphs you might present in this section are:

- *Training evaluation scores from attendees.*

- *Test scores (performance and paper/pencil tests).*

- *Cycle time reduction in learning curve for new employees or employees promoted to a new position.*

- *Job behavior measures before and after training.*

- *Improvement in outcome measures such as accidents, sales, productivity, etc., attributable to training.*

- *Training cost per employee compared to history and competitors/benchmarks.*

- *Percentage of employees cross-trained to perform different jobs/tasks.*

- *Professional certifications and degrees.*

- *Percentage of employees pursuing educational opportunities.*

- *Money spent on training per employee compared to other organizations and benchmarks.*

Data included here might also be measures of employee development, cross-training, suggestions, and so forth. Essentially, the data on employee education and training from the metrics defined in section 5.1b would also go in this section.

This question also asks for performance data on workforce capacity measures. For example, one applicant prepared a chart that showed workload over the last 5 years, along with workforce capacity, to show that they have been narrowing the gap through selective hiring and training. You might also choose top present data on measures like offer to acceptance ratios, number of new hires for targeted job skills, and retention of employees with key skills. The idea is to present data that shows your organization is measuring and managing the intellectual capital needed for its current and future work.

Indicators for Question 7.4a(2)

- *Number and breadth of indicators for which data are presented on employee process improvement activities are appropriate.*
- *Performance on outcome measures of employee suggestions/ideas is excellent.*
- *Employee involvement programs show impressive results in both activity measures and outcome performance.*
- *Results indicate that the applicant spends more money on training and development than its competitors.*
- *Levels and trends in employee satisfaction with training are outstanding.*
- *Training test scores show impressive levels and trends.*
- *Measures of employee behavior change after training demonstrate the effectiveness of the training.*
- *Trends and levels of employees pursuing additional education are positive and compare favorably to others in the industry and area.*
- *Results show improvement in key organizational performance measures (e.g., financial, productivity, quality, customer retention) that can be attributed to training.*
- *Clear correlations can be established between training and performance improvements.*
- *Data show excellent levels and trends in measures of workforce capacity versus workload volume and mix.*
- *Results show success in recruiting and hiring individuals with needed skills to fill capacity gaps.*
- *Results of headcount measures show that the organization is achieving targets or at least showing improvements in shrinking the gap.*
- *Results show good levels of retention of employees with targeted abilities/skills.*

7.4a(3) What are your current LEVELS and TRENDS in KEY MEASURES or INDICATORS of your WORKFORCE climate, including workplace health, safety, and security and Workforce services and benefits, as appropriate?

What They're Looking for Here

This question was new in 2007 and it seeks data on important measures of your culture or climate along with health and safety measures. Most organizations have data on employee safety, but it often consists of only lagging measures like number of lost-time accidents, or worker compensation costs. It is a good idea to present results of leading or predictive measures as well. These leading measures of safety might include metrics such as:

- *Safety training attendance*
- *Safety training test scores or pass/fail rates (better than attendance)*
- *Safety meetings held*
- *Safety issues identified and resolved*
- *Safety audit scores*
- *Near misses*
- *Safe or unsafe behavior measures*
- *Implementation of preventive actions*
- *Use of protective equipment/clothing*
- *External violations or audits*

This question also asks for data on your organizational culture or climate. In other words, how do you know that your organization really lives by the values it professes to stand for? Most organizations I've worked with have no data on this, yet claim that culture is vitally important. Organizational culture might include measures such as employee/supplier/customer perception surveys where people are asked about the real values or culture of the organization versus the ones that are on the wall plaque. You might also include specific measures linked to individual values. For example, an organization that has "diversity" as one of its values might include a wide variety of measures that show how it is performing on diversity. Exit interviews may also provide an excellent source of data on your culture if you can get people to really open up versus check a box on a form from HR. Negative measures might be appropriate to present here as well. For example, one company has a value of balancing work and personal life, but the employees explained to me that the real culture is: "If you don't come in on Saturday, don't bother coming in on Monday". A good measure for a company like this is to count cars in the parking lot on Saturday and Sunday, and after 5:00 during the week.

I don't want to get too prescriptive here, but the data you need to present should provide proof that the organization is improving its climate/culture, or maintaining what is already a very strong positive culture. The challenge with this data will be to find any comparative statistics from other organizations. Measures of culture or climate tend to vary considerably, so it may be very challenging to find comparative statistics.

This question also asks for data on employee health and security. The security measures should be similar to the examples I presented for safety and focus mostly on leading or preventive indicators such as training effectiveness, audits, and behavioral measures.

The same thing is true for employee health measures. These measures might include hard data on key statistics such as weight, blood pressure, cholesterol, and other health metrics. You might also include behavioral measures such as what kind of food people buy in the cafeteria, how many use the company gym, and other lifestyle measures. Lagging measures like how many people die at work or have serious medical problems like heart attack or stroke might also be good to include here. A major aerospace company I know of had an unusual number of vice presidents having heart attacks. This might be a warning sign of too much stress in the work environment.

The final type of data asked for in this question relates to the use of workforce benefits and services. The purpose of this data is to show that the array of benefits and services offered are actually used by your people, indicating that you have offered a proper variety of services. Measures might include factors such as:

- *Percentage or number of employees using facilities such as day care, gym, cafeteria, etc.*
- *Employee ratings or feedback on facilities and services*
- *Comparisons of your benefits and services to those of similar organizations*
- *Money spent on employee benefits and services compared to money spent by similar organizations or competitors*
- *Employee participation in organization-sponsored events and social activities*

Indicators for Question 7.4a(3)

- *Safety results show dramatic improvements and levels that are superior to other similar organizations and/or benchmarks.*
- *Programs or initiatives designed to improve safety show impressive results in both process/leading and outcome/lagging measures.*
- *Number of different graphs presented that show performance on different measures of employee safety.*
- *Integrity of safety metrics.*
- *Degree to which safety data represent all levels and types of employees and other members of the workforce.*
- *Correlations or links can be seen between leading and lagging safety data.*
- *Excellent trends and levels of key measures of employee health.*
- *Breadth and scope of employee health measures.*
- *Degree to which organization's efforts to improve workforce health can be seen clearly in graphs and charts presented.*
- *Use of valid comparative data on charts of safety, security, and employee health.*

- *Declines in performance on health, safety, and security have been analyzed and corrected.*
- *Number and validity of metrics presented on organization climate/culture.*
- *Measures of climate/culture show excellent levels and trends and can be compared to other similar organizations.*

7.5 PROCESS EFFECTIVENESS OUTCOMES: RESULTS
What are your organizational effectiveness results? (70 pts.)

Summarize your organization's KEY operational PERFORMANCE RESULTS that contribute to the improvement of organizational EFFECTIVENESS. SEGMENT your RESULTS by product and service types and groups and by market SEGMENTS, as appropriate. Include appropriate comparative data.

N1. Results reported in Item 7.5 should address your key operational requirements as presented in the Organizational Profile and in Items 6.1 and 6.2. Include results not reported in Items 7.1–7.4.

N2. Results reported in Item 7.5 should provide key information for analysis and review of your organizational performance (Item 4.1) and should provide the operational basis for product and service outcomes (Item 7.1), customer-focused results (Item 7.2), and financial and market results (Item 7.3).

N3. Appropriate measures and indicators of work system performance (7.5a[1]) might include audit, just-in-time delivery, and acceptance results for externally provided products, services, and processes; supplier and partner performance; product, service, and work system innovation rates and results; simplification of internal jobs and job classifications; work layout improvements; changing supervisory ratios; response times for emergency drills or exercises; and results for work relocation or contingency exercises.

AREA TO ADDRESS   [RESULTS]

7.5a a. PROCESS EFFECTIVENESS RESULTS

(1) What are your current LEVELS and TRENDS in KEY MEASURES or INDICATORS of the operational PERFORMANCE of your WORK SYSTEMS, including WORK SYSTEM and workplace preparedness for disasters or emergencies?

What They're Looking for Here

This new question is a little confusing, in that it sounds very similar to what is being asked for in the next question. The difference is that this question asks for two types of data: overall high level measures of how your work systems perform, and how you perform on measures of emergency preparedness. Recall, that a work system is made up of a number of processes or activities, all of which may not be done within your organization. For example, a car company might have an overall work system for selling cars that includes some processes done by the company, such as marketing and advertising, and financing, and other processes done by outside partners or dealers: selling new and used cars. This question asks for data on how the major work systems in your organization perform. Detailed measures of the individual processes within those work systems would get presented in 7.5(2). Obviously there should be links and consistency, and perhaps even some of the same metrics. For example, cycle time might be a good metric for the overall work system, as well as each process in that system. When preparing your response to this question it is important to present data on work systems associated with all parts of your organization, and all products and services. It is also important that you present performance data on some of your work systems that might be considered administrative or support.

This question also asks for data on emergency preparedness measures. These measures should have been identified in your answer to 6.1c. Here is where you present graphs showing your performance on these measures.

Indicators for Question 7.5.a (1)

- *Degree to which performance data are presented for all major work systems linked to all products/services.*

- *Validity of work system metrics and integrity of data collection methods.*

- *Degree to which work system metrics are linked to important product/service characteristics and customer requirements.*

- *Presentation of competitor or comparative data on work system charts.*

- *Data include measures of major administrative or support work systems such as information technology, sales, research and development, facilities, and human resources.*

- *Data are presented on how key partners and/or suppliers perform.*

- *Number of different measures for which data are presented on emergency preparedness.*

- *Degree to which all major types of emergencies or disasters discussed in 6.1c are represented with data here.*

7.5a(2) What are your current LEVELS and TRENDS in KEY MEASURES or INDICATORS of the operational PERFORMANCE of your KEY work PROCESSES, including PRODUCTIVITY, CYCLE TIME, and other appropriate MEASURES of PROCESS EFFECTIVENESS efficiency, and INNOVATION?

What They're Looking for Here

As I mentioned previously, this section is designed to give you a chance to report data on key measures of process performance. Most organizations have a number of processes with many unique measures, so there will not be room to present data on all measures for all processes. Therefore, it is important that you select process measures that pertain to many or even all processes, such as the suggestions in the criteria to report on factors such as cycle time and productivity. Other generic process measures might include:

- *Schedule performance (hitting deadlines)*
- *Project performance*
- *Innovation*
- *Process improvement cost savings*
- *New products/services*
- *Industry awards or recognition*

In addition to these output or outcome measures, this is the place to present results on the key process measures you identified in section 6.1. It is important to make sure that the process results link well to the output results. It is harder to get comparative or competitor data on process measures, but it is important to have something to compare these results to.

As explained in note 2 in this Item, it is important that the results presented here link back to other results presented in the section. The focus of these results in 7.5 is more internal to the organization. You should explain how these internal results correlate to external results such as customer loyalty, and profitability or market share.

What is asked for is operational or internal measures whose performance impacts customer satisfaction, financial performance, or other aspects of performance. For example, a key measure of service quality might be on-time delivery, for which you would present data here, even though performance on this measure clearly impacts overall customer satisfaction. You might also present data in this section on productivity (e.g., sales per employee). Performance on this metric would clearly have an impact on company profits or return on investment.

One effective method of presenting the data in this section is to begin with a matrix chart that lists the performance metrics for which you will present data in this section along the left side of the matrix and the overall measures of customer and shareholder/owner satisfaction along the top of the chart. Use the matrix to indicate the level of impact of the internal (7.5) metrics on the customer (7.2), product and service performance (7.1), and financial/marketplace (7.3) metrics.

The results you present in this section of your application should correspond to the operational indices that you stated you measured in section 1.1, and the measures on which you set goals as described in section 2.2. What is considered important about your response to this item is the scope and breadth of the data you present. You should present data for a variety of operational and financial measures. The key here is to select and present data for those measures that reflect overall company performance. An error that Baldrige applicants could make in this section (judging from errors made in similar sections in the past) is to present graphs showing only those indices that signal an improving trend. When examiners see this they tend to wonder what performance looks like on the other indices for which there are no graphs. When the criteria refer to "operational results," they are not asking about quality data. Operational measures typically fall into three categories:

- *Productivity*
- *Timeliness*
- *Quantity*

The examiners also want to see evidence that key measures of supplier performance have improved over the last few years. If you have over 500 suppliers, obviously you don't have room to present data on every one of them. What you might do is select the two or three that you conduct the most business with, and present graphs on their performance trends. You could then summarize results for other suppliers in a table or chart similar to the one that follows.

SUPPLIER PERFORMANCE DATA					
COMPANY	MEASURE	2004	2005	2006	2007
Canon	Photocopiers Uptime	82%	78%	88%	94%
Cleansweeps Janitorial	Cleanliness Ratings	3.4/5	3.7/5	4.3/5	4.6/5
ABC Office Supplies	On-time Deliveries	82%	88%	90%	90%

Your response for this area will be evaluated both on the amount of supplier data you present and the degree to which supplier performance shows a trend of continuous improvement. Where there have been drops in supplier results, you will be expected to provide explanations.

You also need to explain how your suppliers' performance compares to that of your competitors' suppliers, and/or to benchmark organizations. Begin your response for this section by explaining the bases for your comparisons. You should address such questions as:

- *How are competitors selected for comparison?*
- *How are suppliers for which comparative data are presented selected?*
- *How are benchmark organizations selected for examining supplier performance?*

After explaining how you select supplier data from competitors and benchmark organizations, you should present the comparative data. As in the other sections, it is a good idea to present supplier data using graphs. Your response will be judged according to the amount of data you present and the level of quality your suppliers achieve in relation to competitors' suppliers.

The criteria in this Area to Address also ask you to present data on how you have reduced costs or improved other measures of performance, working with suppliers or partners. For example, going with a single source supplier may have reduced your raw material costs by 5 percent over the last few years. Or, outsourcing your Information Technology function may have improved system uptime and saved hundreds of thousands of dollars. These types of data are important to present here, rather than in 7.3, which asks for financial results.

Read over the example indices listed in the criteria for types of indices that should be taken into account. A study that was done by the U.S. General Accounting Office on the impact of using the Baldrige criteria to improve organizational performance lists eight operating indices used to evaluate past Baldrige finalists:

- *Reliability*
- *Order processing time*
- *Product lead time*
- *Costs of quality*
- *Timeliness of delivery*
- *Errors or defects*
- *Inventory turnover*
- *Cost savings*

Data on all of these metrics could go in section 7.5. Data on product/service errors or defects are reported in 7.2. The other seven indices are all appropriate, however. I am not suggesting that you need to present data on these indices, only that these should be considered in determining what is appropriate for your company.

Another type of data that should be presented in this section is data on measures that are unique to your industry or your organization. These should be indices by which the company measures itself.

In order to determine how significant or insignificant your results are, you need to present data on competitors and industry averages. What is important about your response to this Area to Address is the extent to which several different comparative statistics are presented for each of the indices presented in 6.2a. A good way of presenting these data is to prepare a chart that lists the various performance indices along the left and performance of your company and several others in the remainder of the chart. (A portion of an example of such a chart is shown below.)

COMPARISON OF OPERATIONAL RESULTS					
MEASURES	OUR COMPANY	COMPETITOR A	COMPETITOR B	INDUSTRY BEST	BENCHMARK
Order Processing Time	8 days	14 days	11 days	6 days	3 days
Sales per Employee	$140,000 per employee	$113,000 per employee	$110,000 per employee	$150,000 per employee	N/A
% On-Time Delivery	96%	95%	88%	98%	N/A

Another way of presenting these data is to present graphs showing trends over the last 3 to 5 years in your performance as compared with competitors and others. The problem with using a matrix like the one shown above is that only one year's worth of data is presented. The examiners are interested in how your overall levels of results compare with competitors', but they are also interested in how your trends compare with others. If other companies have improved at about the same rate as you have, your positive trends will not be nearly as impressive. The sources of your data on competitors and other companies will also be questioned, so make sure that you explain where these data come from.

Obviously, what is important for this Area to Address is that your levels of performance are better than your major competitors', and in the best-case scenario, than industry leaders' and other benchmarks you use for improvement planning.

Indicators for Questions 7.5a(1)

- *Number of different performance metrics for which data are presented.*
- *Data are presented for all important performance measures, not just a few.*
- *Number of years' worth of historical data presented to show trends.*
- *Degree to which all indices show continuous and steady improvement.*

- *Amount of variability in performance.*

- *Measures include inputs, processes, and outputs (the scope should not be limited to outputs alone).*

- *Credibility and clarity of explanations for anomalies or adverse trends.*

- *Evidence that when adverse trends are the fault of the organization, the situations causing the problems have been thoroughly investigated and corrected (this should be indicated by level of performance following the adverse trend).*

- *Use of outside sources of data on competitors.*

- *Use of reliable and appropriate sources to gather data on competitors.*

- *Use of ethical and fair methods of gathering data on competitors.*

- *Number of different sources of competitor data.*

- *Number of different aspects of the business that are compared to competitors.*

- *Percentage of suppliers/partners for which performance data are presented.*

- *Trend showing continual improvement in supplier/partner performance over the last several years.*

- *Overall levels of supplier/partner performance are high.*

- *Percentage of suppliers/partners showing trend toward improved quality.*

- *Evidence to suggest that actions by applicant to help suppliers/partners improve their performance have resulted in improved performance.*

- *Objectivity and reliability of data presented on suppliers/partners.*

- *Percentage of suppliers/partners for which comparative data are presented.*

- *Importance of suppliers/partners for which comparative data are presented.*

- *Degree of difference between quality performance of applicant's suppliers/partners and that of competitors' suppliers/partners.*

- *Number or percentage of suppliers/partners for which the applicant's supplier performance is superior to competitors' suppliers.*

- *Trend of performance improvement in applicant's suppliers/partners as compared to competitor's suppliers.*

- *Levels and trends in company performance results attributed to supplier/partner performance.*

- *Number of different areas for which data are presented illustrating supplier/partner contribution to good company performance.*

- *Linkage of operational results to customer satisfaction and overall financial performance.*

- *Scope and breadth of indices for which operational and process data are presented.*

- *Correspondence between measures identified in other sections and data presented in 7.5.*

- *Extent to which positive trends are demonstrated in productivity, waste, cycle time, and other key operational measures.*

- *Presentation of enough data to establish trends (typically 3 to 5 years).*

- *Amount of improvement occurring over the last 3 to 5 years for key indices of operational performance.*

- *Extent to which indices are appropriate measures of overall company performance.*

- *Presentation of data on key process performance measures (see Items 6.1 and 6.2).*

- *Levels and trends in measures of environmental performance and other measures of public responsibility.*

- *Levels and trends in regulatory/compliance results with no significant adverse findings.*

- *Levels and trends of company/industry-specific performance measures.*

- *Levels of financial performance have significantly improved over the last 3 to 5 years.*

- *Percentage of indices for which competitor and industry-leader results data are presented.*

- *Competitors are the companies against which the applicant most often competes.*

- *Credibility of sources for competitor data and benchmark data.*

- *Extent to which data are presented for major competitors, industry leaders, and benchmarks.*

- *Extent to which current levels of performance by the applicant are better than all major competitors, industry leaders, and benchmarks.*

- *Extent to which positive trends exhibited by the applicant are significantly better than trends in competitor data.*

- *Length of time (number of years) during which the applicant's performance on company-specific measures is superior to the competition.*

7.6 LEADERSHIP OUTCOMES   RESULTS
What are your leadership results? (70 pts.)

Summarize your organization's KEY GOVERNANCE, SENIOR LEADERSHIP, and social responsibility RESULTS, including evidence of strategic plan accomplishments, ETHICAL BEHAVIOR, fiscal accounta-bility, legal compliance, social responsibility, and organizational citizenship. SEGMENT your RESULTS by organizational units, as appropriate. Include appropriate comparative data.

AREA TO ADDRESS   [RESULTS]

7.6a Leadership and Social Responsibility RESULTS

(1) What are your RESULTS for KEY MEASURES or INDICATORS of accomplishment of your organizational strategy and ACTION PLANS?

What They're Looking for Here

In the previous Areas to Address in this category, you are asked to present results that show how your organization performs its mission for its various stakeholders such as customers, employees, and shareholders. This question asks you to present results that show progress toward your vision. Your vision should have been outlined in the Organizational Profile section and elaborated on in Category 2, Strategic Planning. In the Strategic Planning category you should have articulated the major (two to five) key success factors or strategies that you plan on using to achieve the vision. For example, a company that was looking to dramatically increase market share as its vision, focused on brand recognition as one of its strategic success factors. You might begin your answer to this section by reiterating the vision and key strategies for achieving it, and then listing the relevant performance measures that relate to the strategies/success factors.

The remainder of the answer to this question should be graphs showing performance on these strategic measures. These measures might be of a variety of factors, including increased customer loyalty (7.2), improved quality (7.1), cost reduction (7.3), brand image (7.5), improvement in profit margin (7.3), recruiting of top talent (7.4), meeting environmental requirements (7.6), or other factors. Just about any type of result could be presented here. The key is that all these results are strategic in focus and relate to your vision for the future.

Because these measures might be unique to your organization and its strategy, it will probably be more difficult to obtain relevant comparative data. If you have none, make sure to at least show how your performance compares to goals or targets, and that you can show trends over several years.

The types of data you choose to report here can vary. For example, a financial services firm I worked with had a vision of being identified by *Fortune Magazine* as one of the 25 best companies to work for from an employee point of view. Consequently, the types of data the firm would report here in 7.6a(1) would be employee education/training, job growth, employee satisfaction, turnover, and other related HR metrics. Another company had a vision of significantly growing market share, so the measures it reported were acquisitions, market share, increases in business from existing customers, and other measures linked to growing market share. Another company I worked with had a major strategy to improve margins and profitability. This company had grown rapidly, had a major share of the market, but margins had eroded, and its overall vision was to become profitable again. In this example, financial results such as cost reduction and margin of growth would be reported here.

Whatever data you choose to present in this section, explain why these particular measures are reported here, and not in other sections, and explain the link back to the vision, goals, and strategy of the organization. Go back to sections 7.1–7.5 and put notes about missing graphs there, explaining that they are in this last section. This will prevent examiners from giving you a lower score because of missing data and then having to go back and change the score when they find the graphs here.

Indicators for Question 7.6a(1)

- *Data are presented for all key strategies linked to the vision.*
- *Performance shows results are at or above targets/goals on the most recent data point.*
- *Data are presented for multiple years.*
- *Trends show steady improvement or consistently high levels over several years.*
- *Graphs include relevant comparative data.*
- *Measures for which data are presented here are valid indicators of progress toward vision.*
- *All strategic or vision-related performance measures are reported here.*
- *Trends in strategic measures indicate that strategies are working.*
- *Targets for strategic measures are appropriate and linked to vision and strategic goals.*
- *Performance is approaching or exceeding targets.*

7.6a Leadership and Social Responisibility RESULTS

(2) What are your RESULTS for KEY MEASURES or INDICATORS of ETHICAL BEHAVIOR and of STAKEHOLDER trust in the SENIOR LEADERS and GOVERNANCE of your organization? What are your RESUL TS for KEY MEASURES or INDICATORS of breaches of ETHICAL BEHAVIOR ?

(3) What are your KEY current findings and TRENDS in KEY MEASURES or INDICATORS of fiscal accountability, both internal and external, as appropriate?

(4) What are your RESULTS for KEY MEASURES or INDICATORS of regulatory and legal compliance?

(5) What are your RESULTS for KEY MEASURES or INDICATORS of organizational citizenship in support of your KEY communities?

Continued

N1. Measures or indicators of strategy and action plan accomplishment (7.6a[1]) should address your strategic objectives and goals identified in 2.1b(1) and your action plan performance measures and projected performance identified in 2.2a(6) and 2.2b, respectively.

N2. For examples of measures of ethical behavior and stakeholder trust (7.6a[2]), see Item 1.2, Note 4.

N3. Responses to 7.6a(3) might include financial statement issues and risks, important internal and external auditor recommendations, and management's responses to these matters. For some nonprofit organizations, results of IRS 990 audits also might be included.

N4. Regulatory and legal compliance results (7.6a[4]) should address requirements described in 1.2b. Employee-related occupational health and safety results (e.g., OSHA-reportable incidents) should be reported in 7.4a(3).

N5. Organizational citizenship results (7.6a[5]) should address support of the key communities discussed in 1.2c.

What They're Looking for Here

Results relating to ethics, regulatory complaints, and social responsibility were asked for in the past as part of the Organizational Effectiveness results item, but have never had this much focus. Currently, these results are worth just as many points as all other types of results, including financial performance. In the last few years we have seen a number of huge corporations disappear or file for bankruptcy because of ethical problems. The criteria in section 1.2 ask about the organization's system for governance and social responsibility. In this final Item, you are expected to present results pertaining to these areas.

Question 7.6a(2) asks for results relating to ethics and stakeholder trust. Some of the possible measures for which you could provide data include:

- *Percentage of employees attending ethics training.*
- *Test scores from ethics training.*
- *Increases in screening done of job applicants for ethics/values.*
- *Trends in numbers of ethics violations reported on hotline.*
- *Trends in seriousness of ethics violations.*
- *Employees disciplined or fired for ethical violations.*

- *Trends in supplier performance on ethics measures.*
- *Employee awareness/knowledge of policies pertaining to ethics.*
- *Surveys indicating increasing trends in shareholder and other stakeholder trust.*

Question 7.6a(3) asks for data pertaining to fiscal accountability. Some of the measures for which you might present data include:

- *Trend in remediation of financial audit findings*
- *Reduction of debt*
- *Poorly performing business units sold or otherwise disposed of*
- *Trends in percentage of executive pay at risk*
- *Reduction in bonus payments for executives in poorly performing units*
- *Increase in level of oversight of financial data*

For many organizations, it will be tempting to present anecdotal or event data that describes procedures to improve fiscal accountability. Remember, words are not what are asked for here—examiners want to see data showing levels and trends of performance. Methods to improve fiscal accountability should be discussed in section 1.2, not here.

Question 7.6a(4) asks for results on regulatory and legal compliance measures. Avoid presenting data that show your performance on standards regulated by law. For example, one Baldrige applicant showed a chart indicating that the company had paid its taxes on time for the past seven years in a row. This sort of data is a waste of time. Rather, present data indicating a reduction of audit/inspection findings, reduction in the seriousness of findings, and proof that your organization goes beyond minimum requirements. Some examples might include a chart showing increased spending on research to investigate potential hazards associated with your products, the number of times your company led the industry in meeting new regulatory requirements, and where you stand relative to key competitors on regulatory performance measures. As with all data in this section, you must show trends over multiple years, and as many sources of comparative data as possible so examiners can evaluate your levels of performance.

Finally, question 7.6a(5) asks for results relating to corporate citizenship and community support. This type of data has been asked for in the criteria for many years. The key here is to present enough evidence to show that you stand apart from your competitors and other companies similar to yours in the community. For this reason it is vitally important to have comparative data to present. Again, events or stories or what you have done need not be described here. Examiners want to see data presented as levels and trends, not stories.

Indicators for Questions 7.6a(2), 7.6a(3), 7.6a(4), 7.6a(5)

- *Trends in measures of fiscal responsibility show improvements over several years.*

- *Measures of fiscal responsibility are objective and valid.*

- *Some external data are presented demonstrating excellent performance levels and trends in fiscal accountability.*

- *Data are presented that show improvements in stakeholder trust.*

- *Levels of stakeholder trust are superior to those of key competitors.*

- *Any declines in image or stakeholder trust have been quickly remediated and performance has improved.*

- *Results show a flawless trend and level of performance in regulatory/legal compliance.*

- *Data show that the company is one of the industry leaders in the area of regulatory compliance.*

- *Results show the effectiveness of any initiatives designed to improve performance in the areas of regulatory compliance.*

- *Performance data indicates that the organization leads the industry in community support and corporate citizenship.*

- *Comparative data show that the applicant is superior to major competitors in organizational citizenship and community support.*

- *Results are presented for all key governance/social responsibility metrics listed in sections 1.1 and 1.2.*

- *Performance data are presented that show the effectiveness of new or existing approaches for governance.*

Chapter

13

PREPARING FOR A SITE VISIT

Many organizations have done a fine job writing Baldrige or state award applications, and had many of their strengths turn to areas for improvement after the site visit. Organizations that receive a site visit should be congratulated because it signifies that the written application warranted more data collection by examiners. In the Baldrige process, you generally need about 500 to 600 points out of 1000 to receive a site visit. Some states such as Minnesota, perform site visits on all applicants; therefore, it is not an indication of "finalist" status as it is with the Baldrige. The purpose of this chapter is to let you know how to prepare for a site visit if you are an applicant for an award, as well as how to prepare and conduct a site visit if you are an examiner. The first portion of the chapter explains how to prepare for the examination, and the second section of this chapter presents tips for examiners on conducting a site visit.

PURPOSE OF THE SITE VISIT

In spite of what it might seem, Baldrige is not an essay contest. An effective proposal or application certainly helps, but does not ensure winning an award. Review of the written application is the first step in the assessment process. If the application includes enough strengths to convince a team of examiners that yours is a well-run organization, they will probably request a site visit. Unlike an audit, the purpose of a site visit is not to look for problems that weren't uncovered in the written application. Examiners are not trained to strictly look for negatives. The purpose of a site visit is to look for positive aspects that may not have been addressed in the application, as well as for weaknesses or parts of the company's systems that may not be as effective as they appeared in the written application. Many factors are difficult to assess by reading an application. For example, employee morale is something a team can assess after spending a few hours talking to a cross section of employees. The extent to which systematic processes have been implemented or deployed is also a major purpose of the site visit. With only 50 pages to tell your story, it is hard to provide enough detail on where your systems and approaches have been deployed.

The overall purpose of a site visit is to reveal the truth about the organization, and provide a thorough assessment by spending a few days talking to its people and examining its systems and approaches. While it may be possible to "snow" a team of examiners by writing a great application, it is impossible to fake a good site visit. The world-class companies stand out right away, and identifying companies that don't meet the Baldrige ideals becomes very easy after a few days at the company.

WITH WHOM WILL EXAMINERS WANT TO TALK?

Anyone they want to. Keep in mind that you don't control the agenda during the site visit, the examiners do. They tell you what sites they want to visit, which people they want to interview, and what documents they want to see. They know that your agenda is to receive a good report, or win an award, so they are leery of any suggestions about to whom they should talk, or which facilities ought to be visited. In general, you can count on the examiners talking to most if not all senior executives. The CEO or president typically knows more about the overall systems in the company than anybody, and is often the only one who truly sees the "big picture." Other members of the senior management team are also interviewed by examiners. Examiners will not only ask questions about the Leadership category, but tend to ask executives about issues that cut across all seven categories.

Examiners also like to talk with individual contributors or hourly employees. In particular, those that have a great deal of customer contact are often asked a lot of questions by examiners. When examiners talk to employees individually or in groups, they are often probing for deployment issues, testing how well the company has communicated its vision, values, and plans. They also talk to employees to discover how they feel about the company, workload, pay, and whether or not employees feel like valuable members of a team. Beginning below is a list of questions that examiners usually ask of executives, middle management, and individual contributors.

QUESTIONS TYPICALLY ASKED OF EXECUTIVES

- *What is your role in the company?*
- *What is the vision of the company for the next 5 or more years, and how do you communicate that vision to your people?*
- *How much time do you personally spend each month with customers, suppliers, and employees?*
- *How would you characterize your management style?*
- *Why is the company organized the way it is, and what data do you look at to tell you this is the ideal structure?*
- *What methods do you use to stay in touch with your business?*
- *How do you seek out growth or expansion opportunities for the company to ensure its future survival and success? Can you give some examples?*
- *How do you select members of your executive team, and what sort of traits do you look for in a good executive?*
- *How will you ensure that your company will continue to be successful once you have retired or moved on to other opportunities?*
- *Describe your leadership system.*
- *What are your most important key success factors?*
- *What is your system for ensuring ethical practices among all employees and other partners?*

- *How do you ensure the integrity of your financial results?*
- *How will you maintain excellence as your organization grows and perhaps becomes more diverse?*
- *How do you know that the leadership system and your individual behavior is effective? What metrics do you look at?*
- *Give me some examples illustrating how your leadership approach/system has changed or improved over the past few years.*

QUESTIONS TYPICALLY ASKED OF MIDDLE MANAGERS

- *Who are the customers of your organization/department?*
- *What is the mission or purpose of your organization/department?*
- *What are the most important requirements of each of your customers?*
- *What is the most important priority of senior management in the company?*
- *What are the key processes in your organization?*
- *What are the performance measures for your organization/department?*
- *How do these performance metrics relate to those of senior management?*
- *What targets have you set for each of the performance metrics?*
- *What are the strategies for reaching your goals/targets?*
- *Can you give some examples of new products or services that you have introduced in the past few years? Explain how successful they have been.*
- *How do you communicate your vision, mission, and plans to your staff?*
- *What methods do you use to stay in touch with the daily operation in your organization?*
- *How do you ensure that work is done consistently in your organization, and that your outputs are defect-free?*
- *How do you know that you are cost-competitive?*
- *How do you get promoted? What are the most important criteria?*
- *What is this company's biggest problem?*
- *Can you think of any reason why this company would not be a good role model for other companies around the world?*

QUESTIONS TYPICALLY ASKED OF EMPLOYEES

- *Who are your customers?*
- *What are the most important requirements of each of your customers?*
- *What are the major work processes in your area?*

- *How do you measure your performance?*
- *What are your individual goals or objectives?*
- *How do these relate to the department and company goals and objectives?*
- *What are the values of the company? Do they really live by these values or are they just words?*
- *What is the company's vision for the future?*
- *What can you do in your area to help the company achieve its vision?*
- *What kind of training do you receive?*
- *What are the most important priorities of management?*
- *How are you involved in helping the company improve performance? Can you give me some examples?*
- *How much authority do you have to make decisions and spend company money?*
- *Do you currently have more authority than in the past?*
- *Is this a good place to work? Why or why not?*
- *What gets rewarded or recognized in this company?*
- *How important is safety and employee well-being in the company?*

TYPICAL APPROACH/DEPLOYMENT SITE VISIT ISSUES BY CATEGORY

Along with the questions that are often asked of senior executives, middle managers, and employees, it is important to understand what examiners typically ask about in each of the six Baldrige categories concerned with approach/deployment issues. Following is a list of typical site visit issues by category. Of course, some of these issues may not apply to a given application. However, in my experience, most teams of examiners tend to look for many of the same site visit issues in most organizations. Those listed here are variables that are hard to evaluate strictly from the written application. Those that begin with the word "clarify" mean that the examiners need additional information on an approach or its deployment. When the word "verify" is used, the examiners are looking for evidence to substantiate a claim made in the written application. This generally means that they need more proof before they agree that it is a strength.

1. Leadership Site Visit Issues

- *Clarify what the company's leadership system is, and how it works to direct and control performance.*
- *Verify that senior executives are in touch with the business by spending adequate time with customers, suppliers/distributors, and employees.*

- *Clarify why the company is organized a certain way.*
- *Verify claims made about open communication and accessibility of senior management.*
- *Clarify roles and responsibilities of various layers of management in the company.*
- *Clarify the actions senior executives take to look for future opportunities for the company and ask for examples of how this has been done in the past.*
- *Verify that the behavior of senior executives is consistent with the company values.*
- *Verify that all senior executives engage in activities to keep them in touch with employees, customers, and key suppliers/partners.*
- *Clarify the metrics and methods used to evaluate the leadership system.*
- *Verify that improvements have been made over the years in the company's leadership system.*
- *Clarify any inconsistencies between executive compensation and the importance of nonfinancial factors such as employee satisfaction, customer satisfaction, and innovation/growth.*
- *Verify that all senior executives actually review the performance metrics outlined in section 4.1 on a regular basis, and use these data to assess company performance.*
- *Clarify the company's criteria for selecting charitable/community organizations to support.*
- *Verify that the company stands out as better than other companies their size for their support of community/charitable activities.*
- *Clarify what the company does to encourage employees at all levels to give back to the community or support charitable organizations.*
- *Verify the company's environmental record and look for evidence of any unethical behavior.*
- *Verify that there are no ethical, human relations, environmental, or other similar problems that might not make the company a good role model for the United States.*
- *Verify that the governance system is effective.*

2. Strategic Planning Site Visit Issues

- *Verify that the planning process described in the application is the one actually used.*
- *Clarify the specific data gathered during the situation analysis phase of the planning process.*
- *Clarify the difference between strategic planning and annual planning.*
- *Verify that plans address more than just financial and operational issues.*
- *Verify that the Baldrige assessment is a major input to the planning process and not a separate and distinct activity.*
- *Verify that the planning process is logical, efficient, and that plans are finalized in a short time frame each year.*
- *Clarify the company vision and the key success factors it will use to differentiate itself from major competitors.*

- *Clarify that the company has completely articulated its strategies.*
- *Verify that strategic planning is an integral part of running the business, as opposed to a separate activity done once a year to satisfy some corporate requirement.*
- *Verify that plans have been well communicated to all levels of employees, and that unit, department, or functional plans are well integrated with overall company plans.*
- *Verify that performance against targets or goals in the plan is reviewed on a regular basis.*
- *Verify that the strategic plan is a living document that is revised as company strategy might change.*
- *Clarify the metrics used to evaluate the planning process, and obtain specifics on how the process has improved over the past 3 to 5 years.*
- *Clarify the company's mission and vision if they are vague.*
- *Clarify the link between the performance measures outlined in section 4.1 and the targets or goals appearing in the strategic plan.*
- *Clarify the data that were used to set targets/goals.*
- *Clarify how the plans are communicated to all levels of employees.*
- *Clarify the HR plans and ask for an explanation of links between HR goals/strategies and overall company goals and strategies.*
- *Verify that the company has collected adequate data on the market, competitors, and other factors to prepare valid projections/forecasts of position in 3 to 5 years.*

3. Customer and Market Focus Site Visit Issues

- *Clarify what percentage of business comes from each major group of customers.*
- *Verify that market research methods described in the application are actually used.*
- *Clarify the thoroughness of methods used to gather data on customer requirements.*
- *Verify that important requirements have been defined for all major market segments.*
- *Verify that all major groups of customers and potential customers' needs have been researched.*
- *Verify that research on customer requirements is a major input to the new product/service development process. Ask for examples to illustrate how customer requirements are integrated into new product/service designs.*
- *Clarify how new or enhanced products/services have led to greater market share or customer loyalty.*
- *Clarify the metrics and methods used to evaluate market research techniques.*
- *Verify that improvements have been made in the methods for market research.*
- *Clarify the major points of interactions between customers and the organization.*
- *Verify that customer-contact employees are selected with care, trained well, paid well, and given the authority to quickly resolve customer concerns.*

- *Verify how easy it is to access the company by testing toll-free numbers or other methods used for customers to contact the organization.*
- *Clarify standards for customer service.*
- *Clarify efforts to build loyalty from the most important customers and ask about the effectiveness of these efforts.*
- *Verify that the complaint management process works as described in the application.*
- *Clarify how customer satisfaction is measured by reviewing instruments, data collection plans, and reports.*
- *Verify that customer satisfaction is measured for all types of customers.*
- *Verify that reliable data are collected on customer satisfaction levels of competitors and other comparative organizations.*
- *Clarify how customer satisfaction data are reviewed and analyzed on a regular basis.*

4. Measurement, Analysis, and Knowledge Site Visit Issues

- *Clarify the criteria used to select the metrics that appear on the company scorecard.*
- *Clarify the data collection methods and frequencies with which data are collected on each performance metric.*
- *Verify that the metrics listed in the application are actually reviewed by management on a regular basis and used to assess business performance.*
- *Verify link between key success factors and vision and performance metrics.*
- *Verify that performance data are easily accessible, clearly presented, and understood by employees.*
- *Clarify how performance metrics have been evaluated and improved over the past 3 to 5 years.*
- *Clarify how promotions and compensation are linked to the company performance metrics.*
- *Verify that business unit, facility, department, and functional performance metrics are well linked to overall company performance metrics.*
- *Clarify the criteria used to select competitors and other organizations against which to compare.*
- *Verify that databases on competitors are complete and up to date.*
- *Verify that data on competitors are used for goal setting and planning.*
- *Clarify the scope of any benchmarking efforts and ask about changes that have been implemented based upon benchmarking.*
- *Verify that comparative data are used to improve processes if claimed in the application.*
- *Verify that performance data are actually analyzed as opposed to simply reviewed once a month in meetings.*

- *Verify that correlations have actually been defined for key metrics such as customer satisfaction and employee satisfaction and/or customer satisfaction and financial results. Ask for copies of correlation studies or data.*
- *Verify that analysis approach described in written application is actually used at all levels of the organization.*
- *Verify that performance against targets or goals is reviewed on a regular basis, and that actions are taken or diagnoses performed when performance is not up to par.*
- *Verify that the company makes all major management and investment decisions by analyzing appropriate performance data. Ask for examples to illustrate deployment of this practice.*

5. Human Resource Focus Site Visit Issues

- *Clarify the company approach to recruiting and selection and look for links between selection criteria and values and the company vision for the future.*
- *Clarify the logic behind the company approach to designing jobs, and get them to explain how their approach is the most effective way of dividing work tasks.*
- *Clarify any inconsistencies with the company's values, stated direction/vision and their approach to work systems.*
- *Verify deployment of innovative work system practices such as self-directed teams, cross-functional work groups, etc.*
- *Clarify the amount of authority employees at each level have, and verify claims by talking to employees.*
- *Verify deployment of recognition programs, and ask employees about the fairness of the programs.*
- *Verify that the items/privileges given to recognize employees are, in fact, rewarding to them.*
- *Clarify the criteria for receiving various reward/recognition items.*
- *Clarify the link between performance and compensation.*
- *Verify deployment of performance-based pay across levels and functions in the organization.*
- *Clarify the link between performance measures identified in section 4.1 and reward/compensation to look for any disconnects.*
- *Verify that there are no inconsistencies between the company's desire for teamwork/cooperation and their performance appraisal, promotion, recognition, and compensation programs.*
- *Verify the effectiveness of any innovative work system approaches, such as 360° appraisal, self-directed work teams, knowledge-based pay, etc.*
- *Verify link between company strategic plans and training needs analysis approaches. Ask for examples that illustrate how key competencies are identified that will help the company achieve its vision.*

- *Verify deployment of systematic training needs analysis to all types of training.*
- *Verify that training is not used as a "band-aid" solution to all performance problems.*
- *Clarify the delivery methods used for various types of training.*
- *Verify that training evaluation data show effectiveness.*
- *Verify that training content and delivery methods are integrated with overall approach to work systems.*
- *Verify that appropriate input is sought from various sources in doing training needs analysis.*
- *Clarify methods used to ensure transfer of training and for rewarding use of skills learned in training back on the job.*
- *Verify that training is continuously evaluated and improved.*
- *Clarify the company's approaches to ensuring a safe work environment.*
- *Verify that there is as much emphasis on safety as is claimed in the application. Talk to hourly employees about this.*
- *Clarify the company's efforts to ensure employee wellness and check on deployment of programs, such as health club memberships or participation in weight loss or "stop smoking" programs.*
- *Verify that special services offered to employees are actually the ones they want, and that these services are used by the majority of employees.*
- *Verify that team-building activities are a positive/fun experience rather than a dull obligation that must be met to avoid appearing like one is not a team player. Talk to employees about how they feel about picnics, parties, and other similar events.*
- *Verify that the company really tries to delight employees.*
- *Verify data collection methods for measuring employee satisfaction by reviewing instruments and data collection procedures.*
- *Verify that executives review data on safety and employee satisfaction as often and with as much emphasis as they do financial and operational results.*
- *Verify that the company can demonstrate how changes in employee well-being and satisfaction are correlated to other key results such as customer satisfaction and financial performance.*

6. Process Management Site Visit Issues

- *Verify that market research data on customer requirements are suited to drive development of new products/services.*
- *Verify deployment of product/service development process to all new products/services.*
- *Clarify how new products/services are designed and how parameters are set to ensure that new products/services meet or exceed customer requirements.*
- *Verify market success of new/enhanced products and services.*

- *Clarify key value creation processes, metrics, standards, and control strategies.*
- *Verify that process metrics are correlated to important output metrics.*
- *Verify that standards or targets for process metrics are linked to research on customer requirements and correlations with output performance.*
- *Verify effectiveness of control strategies in eliminating or minimizing variability in processes.*
- *Clarify scope of process improvement efforts.*
- *Verify use of benchmarking, technology review, market research, competitor analysis and other data in process improvement efforts.*
- *Verify deployment of process improvement methodology across all projects.*
- *Verify deployment of process improvements across all locations, units, and functions as appropriate.*
- *Verify employee understanding of process analysis and improvement methodologies.*
- *Verify link between process improvement activities and company strategic plan.*
- *Verify that each support function has defined its customers and their most important priorities.*
- *Clarify how support functions deal with conflicts between various internal customers such as the corporation versus users of their services.*
- *Verify that each support process has done research to identify what services and products their internal/external customers really want them to produce/deliver.*
- *Clarify the key processes, metrics, standards, and control strategies for each major support department/function.*
- *Verify success of any innovations found in support areas.*
- *Verify effectiveness of approaches to control variability in support processes.*
- *Verify that support functions collect and use data on internal customer satisfaction.*
- *Clarify how the company identifies its key suppliers/partners.*
- *Clarify the criteria used to select various types of suppliers/partners, and ask for examples illustrating deployment of these criteria in the selection process.*
- *Clarify the company's approaches to partnering with proven suppliers/partners.*
- *Verify that the company has selected the right partners/suppliers by talking with employees who use the services/products provided by these firms.*
- *Verify that true partnerships exist with suppliers by reviewing contracts and partnership agreements and looking at the frequency with which proposals/bids are asked for.*
- *Verify evidence of a cooperative approach of working with suppliers versus an adversarial relationship.*
- *Verify use of supplier report cards or evaluation systems with all key suppliers.*

- *Clarify how the criteria for evaluating suppliers are linked to customer and internal performance requirements.*
- *Verify efforts to reduce internal inspection of supplier goods and services.*
- *Clarify approaches that have been used to simplify the procurement process.*

7. Results Site Visit Issues

Compared with approach/deployment items, results are fairly easy to evaluate by looking at the written application. Examiners do ask about results in the site visit, but they are mainly looking for data to support the validity and completeness of the graphs presented in section 7 of the application. For each major graph or summary of performance data appearing in section 7, examiners usually ask the following questions:

- *Can I see the raw data that were used to calculate this graph?*
- *What is the process/methodology used to collect these data?*
- *Can I see graphs of the subsidiary data that make up this index or overall performance data?*
- *How do I ensure that these data are reliable and consistently measured?*
- *What is the source of these data on industry averages, competitors, and benchmarks, and may I see those source documents?*
- *Can I see any missing years' worth of data that are not included on the graph in your application?*
- *Can I see the graphs of performance data you said you collected in section 4, 5, or 6, but you did not provide in the application?*
- *What happened on this graph that shows a performance spike (could be positive or negative), and what was learned from the analysis?*
- *Although almost 50 percent of the points in a Baldrige application focus on results, you will find that most of the site visit is spent concentrating on the approach/deployment issues.*

PREPARING FOR THE SITE VISIT

One of the keys to receiving an award is impressing the examiners during the site visit. Most winners have managed to "blow away" the examiners in the site visit, convincing them that the company is even better in reality than it is on paper. One of the most impressive factors for an examiner is consistency of deployment. I've heard a number of examiners exclaim how impressed they were when every employee they talked with knew the company vision, key success factors, customers, processes, and so forth. A number of companies have actually run through a few dress rehearsals for the site visit, drilling employees on the key questions I've listed.

Drilling Employees

Knowing what the examiners are going to ask up front doesn't really help unless employees know the appropriate answers. If you are really interested in winning, it might be worth the time to teach these questions and answers to all employees, and run them through practice drills to make sure they understand their answers. Pulling out a wallet card or crib sheet in a site visit interview kind of destroys your credibility. Therefore, it is important the employees learn to memorize the right answers. Is this ethical? Sure it is. Hopefully it will be of more benefit to the organization for every employee to know this information than simply to impress the Baldrige examiners. Many companies spend a lot of time and money teaching employees to understand their customers, and how their job fits in with the company's plans.

Training Executives and Managers

It is also important that executives and managers present consistent information to the examiners' questions. I've known a number of companies that fell down in this area because the executives used their own judgment on how to answer questions, all giving different answers to the same questions. This led the examiners to conclude that the executive team lacked a unified focus and did not really work well as a team. Training executives and managers is more of a challenge because they tend not to think that they need it. An approach I've seen that works well for them is to hire an outside consultant that is a trained examiner and have him or her drill the executives for practice. A debriefing session after this mock site visit can go a long way toward coaching them in the right responses. An outsider is often preferred for this task because of his or her ability to give honest and sometimes critical feedback to executives without fear of repercussion.

Preparing Documents for the Examiners

One organization at which I performed a site visit did a great job preparing materials for the examiners. They prepared seven "bankers boxes" of file folders, each labeled with the appropriate Baldrige category and item. In the folders were documents that answered many of our questions about site visit issues. In some cases, they went a little overboard since we only had time to review about 25 percent of what they put in the boxes. However, it saved the examiner team a great deal of time by having most of the documentation we would have requested already there for us. I would highly recommend this practice. It shows the examiners that you understand the type of information they will be requesting, and that you are considerate of maximizing their productivity while on site. Most site visits for state awards or internal company awards do not last 4 to 5 days. In the state of California, for example, we do many site visits in one day. Because of this limited time, it makes it even more important to make it easy for examiners to find the information they need without hunting for it.

I can't really tell you what should go into each of the 7 boxes or 20 file folders, but I can give you a list of the typical documents that examiners ask to see in most site visits. You can almost guarantee that these will be requested and reviewed:

- *Governance system.*
- *Market research data/reports.*
- *Strategic and annual plans.*
- *Monthly performance reports reviewed by executives.*
- *Process models/maps.*
- *Benchmarking studies.*
- *Reports on key competitors.*
- *Safety plans.*
- *Human resource plans.*
- *New product/service development process and related documentation.*
- *Supplier report cards.*
- *Surveys and other data collection instruments.*
- *Organization charts and job descriptions.*
- *Supplemental performance data not included in the application.*

GENERAL TIPS FOR DEALING WITH EXAMINERS DURING SITE VISITS

As I mentioned earlier, I've talked to many examiners who believe applicants have performed poorly in the site visit on the basis of how they appear to examiners. These tips are based on discussions with both examiners and applicants I've met with during the past 10 years of my experience.

- *Don't over-explain anything—answer questions with brief responses.*
- *Listen to the question and make sure you know what is being asked before you answer it.*
- *Do not attempt to be too friendly with examiners—they want to maintain a certain distance to ensure objectivity.*
- *Do not try to control the discussion.*
- *Do not offer gifts, privileges, or anything else that might be seen as attempted bribery.*
- *Do not ramble and tell war stories.*
- *Find out the time for the interview and stay within the designated time frame.*
- *Do not constantly change the schedule for interviews by examiners.*

- *Make sure that all of your key people are in town and accessible when the examiners visit.*
- *Be honest about skeletons in your closet that may be discovered later by reviewing records from regulatory agencies.*
- *Do not prepare a "dog and pony show" at the beginning of the site visit. This will be viewed negatively by most examiners.*
- *Find out the background and experience of each examiner so you know his or her experience base.*
- *Do not attempt to argue or defend your approach.*
- *Do not ask the examiner for feedback during the site visit (e.g., "Is that what you are looking for?").*

The Examiner's Point of View

Up to this point, I've been discussing how to prepare for a site visit if you are an applicant. Much of this information, such as the typical site visit issues, is also relevant to examiners but it is more aimed at the applicant. In this section, I'll discuss tips for an effective site visit for the examiner team.

Preparing the Site Visit Plan

Most teams of examiners who are new to the experience often over-plan for a site visit. Site visit issues ("verifies and clarifies") are listed during the course of the application review. This often results in a list of 100 or more issues per examiner. Considering that there are usually at least five examiners on a team, this can mean many site visit issues to check out during the visit. Most teams of examiners prioritize their site visit issues prior to arrival, making sure that they spend time on the most important issues. It will be impossible to check out 100 or more site visit issues in 3 to 4 days on site at an organization. Most teams narrow the list to about 25 to 40 critical site visit issues.

Answers given by applicants should address the overall purpose of an item, rather than a sub-issue. The criteria you should use in selecting the most important site visit issues are as follows:

- *The answers given during a site visit could make a major difference in an applicant's score.*
- *Focus on information that is difficult to assess from reading the application.*
- *Focus on issues that cut across more than one category.*
- *Verify something that is a major theme in the organization's strategy for differentiating itself from competitors.*
- *Verify the deployment of innovative or impressive approaches.*

ISSUE		
ITEM/ AREA	WHAT TO CLARIFY AND WHAT TO VERIFY.	PRIORITY
1.1	Verify senior executives spend an average of 1 day a month with customers	Low
1.1	Clarify roles and responsibilities of various levels of management	Low
1.2	Clarify how the company decides which charitable causes it supports	Low
2.1	Verify claims that planning process follows systematic model	Moderate
2.1	Verify thoroughness of SWOT analysis done as part of planning process	Low
2.1	Clarify difference between annual and strategic planning	Low
2.2	Verify that targets are set based on data	Moderate
2.2/4.1	Clarify company vision and key success factors and explain link to performance metrics	High
3.1	Verify that customer requirements have been defined for other three market segments not defined in application	Moderate
3.1/6.1	Verify that high priority customer requirements are integrated into new product designs	High

Figure 13.1:   **Prioritization of Site Visit Issues—Sample Worksheet**

The process for narrowing down site visit issues is to use team consensus, or voting by examiners. This is usually done without much argument. Arguments often arise among individual examiners who insert their own biases. For example, the engineers on the team always want to spend a lot of time on the process management and new product design issues. Or, the information technology examiners want to spend most of the time looking at the company's information systems. A good senior examiner will help to ensure that the site visit issues that make the short list are balanced. Figure 13.1 shows a sample format for prioritizing the site visit issues.

Once you have identified the most critical site visit issues, the team needs to prepare a plan, outlining where they will go to gather the information and who will gather it. An example format of a data collection worksheet is shown in Figure 13.2. Each examiner would have a different set of data collection worksheets. It is common practice to divide site visit issues among the examiners and often to pair up examiners on critical interviews.

EXAMINER: JOHN EXAMPLE				
Item/ Area	ISSUE What to clarify. What to verify.	DATA COLLECTION METHOD What to ask. What to review. Who to ask.	Schedule	Notes
2.1	Verify claims made that planning is done using systematic model	Interview Planning vice president	10:00–11:30	Evidence supports full use of process
		Review Strategic Plan, Business Unit Plans and Operating Plans	11:30–1:00	Some questions about use of process in business unit plans
		Interview Planning Committee	1:30–2:25	Approach sounds less structured than vice president suggests; keep original score of 40%

Figure 13.2:   **Sample Data Collection Worksheet**

Site Visit Data Collection Strategies

There are many different ways to collect data in a site visit, including:

- *Individual interviews*
- *Group interviews*
- *Review of documents*
- *Review of performance data*
- *Demonstrations*
- *Walking around*

It is important that you don't spend all of your time in individual interviews. In fact, these are probably the least efficient means of gathering data in a site visit. This is particularly true of executive interviews. Executives generally know the right answers and are very articulate and convincing in an interview. I have found that one of the best ways of gathering data in a site visit is wandering around and watching people as they work. You can tell a lot about an organization by just observing employees as they do their work. Demonstrations or work-throughs are also an effective technique for evaluating things like how user-friendly a system is. Make sure that your site visit time includes an hour or two of free time each day for each examiner. This free time might be spent doing walk-arounds or making last minute decisions to interview someone who was not on the original schedule.

Generic Site Visit Questions

Although it is important to come up with specific site visit issues, I find that a logical series of questions can be used to evaluate approach/deployment in any of the first six sections of the Baldrige criteria. I keep these questions on my clipboard during each site visit interview, and tend to ask them over and over for each category. The questions are:

- *How do you do this? What is the process?*
- *Why do you do it this way?*
- *Where is it done this way and where isn't it?*
- *How do you measure this process?*
- *What has been done to improve this process?*

These five questions address approach, deployment, and continuous improvement, which are the major issues addressed in Categories 1 through 6. They can be used when asking about leadership, planning, training, or process management.

When looking at results, questions always center around levels, trends, and variability in the data. When spikes or anomalies occur in performance data, it is important to understand why these occur and what has been done to reduce the variability of the performance.

Reaching Final Consensus After the Site Visit

One of the most challenging parts of the site visit is reaching final consensus on the findings. This tends to be much easier when everyone has reviewed the same written application. In the site visit, everyone has seen or heard different things. Consequently, you often get some very diverse opinions about whether or not to raise or lower the applicant's score on a given item. In the Baldrige process, your scores are not actually changed, but most state awards do involve modification of the scores based on site visit findings. I've participated on some site visit teams where each team member is responsible for one or two of the seven categories. These individuals are primarily responsible for gathering data on the category, and make the final decision in the consensus meeting if agreement cannot be reached in a reasonable period of time.

Chapter

14

USING A BALDRIGE ASSESSMENT AS A STRATEGIC PLANNING TOOL

ASSESSMENT ALTERNATIVES

The previous chapter presented details on how to audit your organization against the Baldrige criteria. This approach is very thorough, but many organizations don't have the resources to use it to the best effect. Most of the companies I've worked with in conducting Baldrige assessments over the past few years don't use the full-scale audit approach. Rather, a number of other basic methods are used. These are listed below in order of least to most objective and thorough, and of least to most expensive.

1. Survey based on the Baldrige criteria
2. Armchair assessment
3. Mock Baldrige application
4. Formal Baldrige or state-level application
5. Audit against the Baldrige criteria

1. Baldrige Survey—The simplest and least expensive method of establishing some baseline data on where you stand in your implementation of the Baldrige standards is to send out a survey to all or a sample of employees, having them rate the organization on how well it has implemented each of the items making up the Baldrige criteria. A large variety of surveys exist that may be used for this purpose.

Using such a survey, or similar ones available through management consulting firms, is the least expensive way of evaluating your own status. However, it is also the least reliable, regardless of which survey instrument you are using. The problem with any survey is that it is subjective. People responding to the survey don't usually have the "big picture" of what is happening in the company, and they often mark their responses to the survey items based upon limited and most recent experiences. I've administered Baldrige surveys to 100 or so people in a single organization and gotten scores that ranged from 250 to 800 out of a possible 1,000 points. Does this mean that the survey instrument is poor? Perhaps, but I believe that all Baldrige surveys are, at best, a very rough and rudimentary indicator. Considering the low cost of the survey, however, this tool does provide you with a basic idea of where you stand, without spending much money or time.

2. Armchair Assessment—The second approach is a good deal more thorough and more useful than a survey, without much added expense. I have used this approach with a number of large organizations and have talked to a number of others that use a variation on it. Here's how it works. A team of senior executives from the business unit or organization being assessed attend a two-day workshop to learn the Baldrige criteria and gain an understanding of how an assessment is done. Next, the executive team attends a one-day meeting where they begin to assess their own organization. During the meeting, a facilitator begins by reviewing the first Baldrige Examination item, explaining what it means. Next, the participants brainstorm a list of the organization's strengths and areas for improvement relating to that item. The pluses and minuses are listed by the facilitator on a flip chart. After listing a page or so of strengths and areas for improvements, the facilitator asks the group to suggest a percentage score in multiples of 10. The group discusses and reaches consensus on a percentage score, the facilitator writes it on the flip chart, and together they move on to the next item. This process continues until all 18 items have been completed. A time limit of 15 minutes is observed for discussing each item, so the meeting is very fast-moving. After listing comments and scoring each of the 18 Baldrige items, percentage scores are multiplied by the official point value of each item to compute the final score. The 19 flip chart pages are typed and become the complete assessment report. Total time commitment for the approach is 3 days.

While this approach is quick and relatively inexpensive, it does have some problems. First, the objectivity of the senior executives is not always what it should be. The executives sometimes find it easier to list the good things than to spend time thinking of areas for improvement. They also tend to give more credit for partial deployment of systems or approaches than a Baldrige examiner would. Executives also tend to score a little higher than a Baldrige examiner might. The personality of the CEO or the most senior executive in the meeting also can make this approach problematic. I've observed a few assessment meetings where the participants simply deferred to what the senior executives said and what he/she said the score was.

Even with its problems, this approach is much better than using any kind of survey. The assessment is more thorough; you end up with a page of strengths, areas for improvement, and a score on each of the 19 items; and executives buy in to the results of the assessment more readily because they did it. This approach will only work, however, if the senior executives are willing to devote 3 days for training and assessment. Executives in many organizations don't feel they need to be involved in such training or assessment and prefer to delegate this task to others. The Armchair Assessment will only work if you can get the senior executives to commit to it. The Armchair Assessment is appropriate for organizations whose overall score is 300 or less.

3. Mock Baldrige Application—This is by far the most commonly used approach for assessment against the Baldrige criteria. This approach has been or is currently being used by, among others, AT&T, Baxter Healthcare, Northrop, McDonnell Douglas, Roadway Express, Whirlpool, Cargill, Ericsson, Westinghouse, Johnson & Johnson, Appleton Papers, and StoraEnso. The approach involves having business units, facilities, or even departments in a company prepare their own application using the same format as the Baldrige application. Generally, all 19 items are required to be addressed and the applications are often about the same size (50 pages) as an official application. Applications are reviewed and individually scored by a team of examiners from other departments or units, who then get together to reach consensus on the final scores. Examiners are usually company employees who have been trained in a 2- to 4-day workshop. Some companies use outsiders to supplement their team of internal examiners, adding Baldrige consultants, customers, and suppliers, for example.

In some companies, such as Cargill, the examiners score the written applications and do site visits on the best (usually the top 25%–50%). Most organizations also have their own awards that they give out to the best performers. The major difference between the Armchair Assessment and the Mock Baldrige Application is that one always uses examiners from one business unit or department to evaluate another business unit or department. Some organizations have gotten senior executives involved as part of their team of examiners. Cargill, a major agricultural firm with 70,000 employees, has a team of about 120 examiners that includes many senior executives. Many executives and high-level managers in Ericsson also have spent at least one year serving as an examiner for their assessment. A side benefit of getting executives to be examiners is that they almost always come away from the experience as staunch believers in the value of the Baldrige criteria as a tool for running a better organization.

The advantage of this approach, over the previous two, then, is the objectivity and thoroughness of the assessment and feedback. The approach can give you the same level of analysis and feedback that a company would get by applying for the Baldrige Award. The approach also does a great deal to help move the organization toward being an excellent company. Examiners become internal experts on the Baldrige criteria and can help others to work toward satisfying the criteria. Another advantage is that you can get near-immediate feedback on your application and probe the examiners for details if the feedback is unclear. Examiners can provide recommendations about what the organization should do to improve the areas for improvement that were uncovered in the assessment.

The only real disadvantage of this approach is that it is much more expensive than the other two. You will recall from Chapter 3 that it takes a great deal of time to write an application. In this case, time will also need to be spent in training examiners, having them review and score the applications, and possibly go on site visits. Examiners in many companies that use this approach can be expected to spend the following amount of time on the activities listed:

- Attend examiner training   3   days
- Score written applications   2   days × 3 applications = 6 days
- Reach consensus on scores   0.5 day × 3 applications = 1.5 days
- Prepare and conduct site visit   5   days
- Prepare and present feedback report   2   days
                                        ─────────────────────────────────
                                        17.5 days

When you consider that some large companies have over 100 examiners, this can add up to a major investment. If you supplement your team of internal examiners with consultants or other outsiders, the cost can become even greater. However, this is a great developmental opportunity for potential future senior managers and executives. This approach is appropriate for organizations above 300 points that would benefit from some outside objective feedback.

4. Formal Baldrige or State Application—A fourth and less commonly used approach for assessment is to formally apply for the Baldrige or State Award to see where you stand. This strategy was used by a number of organizations that later went on to win the award. (They applied and failed to win at least once before finally winning the award.) The $6,000 it costs to apply for the award for a large organization is minimal compared to the value of the feedback received. For $6,000 ($3,000 for small companies) you get a team of six to eight official examiners who will individually score your application, reach consensus on your scores, and present you with a feedback report that gives you a page of strengths, areas for improvement, and scores for each of the 19 Baldrige items. If you are lucky enough to receive a site visit, a team of examiners will spend up to a week in your organization doing a further assessment. If you were to pay an outside consulting firm to conduct such an assessment, you would probably pay $25,000 or more. Applying for the Baldrige Award to receive feedback is perhaps one of the government's biggest bargains. State award programs offer most of the benefits of applying for Baldrige, and are even less expensive (usually $500–$2,000).

If formally applying for the award offers such advantages, why don't more companies do it? Besides the initial cost (relatively small though it may be), the disadvantages are as follows. First, there is the delay between the time you send in the application (May 27th) and the time you receive feedback (September or October). This means that you can't use the feedback for planning purposes until the following year. A second disadvantage is that the approach forces you to apply as an entire company, or at least its major business units; units or facilities that have fewer than 500 employees are not allowed to apply for the Baldrige Award. A third disadvantage is that you do not receive your final score—only ranges are provided. This makes it difficult to gauge the level of improvement each year.

Another problem is that you are not allowed to talk to anyone about your feedback. I know of one Baldrige applicant that received a feedback report that was extremely vague. One page had three positive comments, an area for improvement, and a score of 20 percent. When the organization called the Baldrige office and asked to speak to the examiners or someone who could explain their feedback and scores, they were informed that no one was allowed to talk to them about these matters. One final reason why applying for the award as an assessment method may not be a good idea is that a low score might have a negative impact on employee morale. Imagine how the results would play if you received a score of 175 out of 1,000 (when you may have been expecting around 600). Such results will be used as ammunition by those employees who believe total quality management is just another passing fad. Baldrige also does not provide you with an overall score, or scores for each of the 19 items.

A better alternative to actually applying for a Baldrige Award is to apply for one of the state-level Baldrige-based awards. Most states have their own award programs that follow the Baldrige criteria and application process. While the national award has received fewer applicants over the last few years, applications for state awards have risen dramatically. We had over 50 applicants for the California Award this year, as did North Carolina. State-level awards are typically easier to win and many (California, Arizona, and others) offer a three-level award program (gold, silver, bronze), like the Olympics, that ensures that most applicants receive some type of recognition. Contact the Baldrige office at NIST for more information on Baldrige-based awards in your state.

5. Audit against the Baldrige Criteria—The most thorough and most expensive way of evaluating your implementation of total quality management is to prepare and conduct an audit of the organization's practices and results based upon the Baldrige criteria. This involves developing a detailed audit plan, creating audit instruments, and spending many hours interviewing various levels of employees, reviewing quality data, and observing processes and practices. The advantages of this approach over the other four are its objectivity and the level of detailed feedback provided. The scope of the audit can vary considerably and can be tailored to the organization's resource constraints. Some large organizations devote thousands of hours to such audits and assign 10 to 20 employees to work full time for several months on the audit. Another organization I know of, assigned a task force of seven people, and each spent a total of about ten person-days on the audit.

The audit is very similar to the approach taken by the Baldrige examiners when they do a site visit. However, you don't need to prepare a mock or real Baldrige application to conduct a Baldrige audit. The audit instruments are developed using the Baldrige criteria and the assessments are done based upon interviews, observations, and reviews of data rather than by reading a 50-page summary of the organization's approach and results.

USING THE BALDRIGE ASSESSMENT TO DRIVE IMPROVEMENT

Getting assessed against the Baldrige criteria is the organizational equivalent of getting a three-day physical. The problem, however, is that many organizations have not figured out how to take the information from a Baldrige-style assessment and use it for improvement planning. An organization I'm familiar with has been doing Baldrige assessments of each of its business units for the last 7 years; each year teams of examiners spend a great deal of time on site visits to evaluate the organization's approaches, deployment, and results. Findings of the assessment are presented to senior management, and the examiners are thanked for doing such an honest and thorough evaluation. In 1991, when this was first done, each of the business units received a score of around 300 points out of a possible 1,000. In 1992, the same type of assessment was done on the same business units, and, once again, the organizations all received scores of around 300 points. Some areas were slightly better; some had gotten worse. In 1993, a team of examiners did the third Baldrige assessment, and the scores once again ended up being around 300. In 1997, the company has simply told its business units to do their own assessments using whatever process they think works best. In late 1997 the company was purchased by a bigger firm and no longer does Baldrige assessments.

The problem is that this company, like many others, had not figured out how to put teeth into the assessment and assure that areas for improvement end up getting addressed in the overall business plan of the organization. This is what I will attempt to provide guidance on here.

Trying to Fix Everything at the Same Time

One commonly used approach in trying to make improvements is to take each area identified in the Baldrige assessment as lacking and developing an action plan for addressing the problem. Committees and task forces are formed and hundreds of people are involved in trying to improve the organization's performance, often in more than 100 different areas. A year is spent and thousands of dollars in labor are expended working on the various improvement projects. The assessment is done again the following year, and, to everyone's surprise, the overall score does not improve much. The reason for the failure is that such an approach is too diluted, too uncoordinated, too lacking tie-in to the company's strategic business plan. Teams end up stepping on each others' toes, perhaps improving performance in one area only to make it worse in another.

A Smarter Approach—Selecting a Few Major Areas to Work on Improving

A better improvement planning approach is to prioritize the areas for improvement before proceeding to develop action plans. With this approach, you take the 120 or so areas for improvement from the Baldrige assessment and select the most important 10 to 20 to work on over the next year. Senior executives may assign a score to each area for improvement, using the following variables and scale:

- *IMPACT—To what extent will fixing this weakness impact our performance on key measures of quality, customer satisfaction, or financial performance? (1 = no impact; 10 = great impact on a number of performance measures.)*

- *URGENCY—To what extent do we have to address this weakness immediately? (1 = can be postponed for several years; 10 = this needs to be fixed now.)*

- *TREND—Is performance in this area currently getting worse, stable, or better? (1 = performance is improving rapidly; 10 = performance is getting worse all the time.)*

By adding the scores for each area for improvement as given by each member of the senior executive team, you should be able to list the 100 or so areas in order of their priority. You then take the top ten and develop action plans for improving performance in these areas. A project manager is assigned to each action plan, and specific tasks and deadlines are developed for each improvement project.

Linking a Baldrige Assessment with Your Strategic Business Plans

Back in Category 2 of the Baldrige criteria, I explained that an important part of strategic planning is doing a thorough situation analysis, where you assess strengths, weaknesses, opportunities, and threats. A Baldrige assessment is a large part of this SWOT analysis that a company should do each year. The Baldrige assessment focuses both on the internal and external environment, incorporating data from customers, suppliers, and key competitors. There are other factors that should be examined in detail as part of the SWOT analysis, however. Knowledge of the strategies and strengths and weaknesses of key competitors is crucial information for planning. The same is true of knowledge of changes in regulatory conditions or requirements.

At best, the Baldrige assessment is one of several inputs to the planning process. An organization should never develop a specific plan to address the weaknesses uncovered in a Baldrige assessment. While this is a practice I have often seen, I have never seen it work well. The Baldrige criteria are a set of generic guidelines that are important for all organizations to address. However, every weakness found in an assessment does not necessarily need to be corrected. Organizations always have constraints on their resources, and those resources should be put to use improving the aspects of their performance that are most needed at the current time. This might mean ignoring a number of the negative findings from a Baldrige assessment and putting them on the back burner to be addressed later.

Strategic Planning Model

The overall strategic planning model shown below is followed by a number of major companies and government organizations:

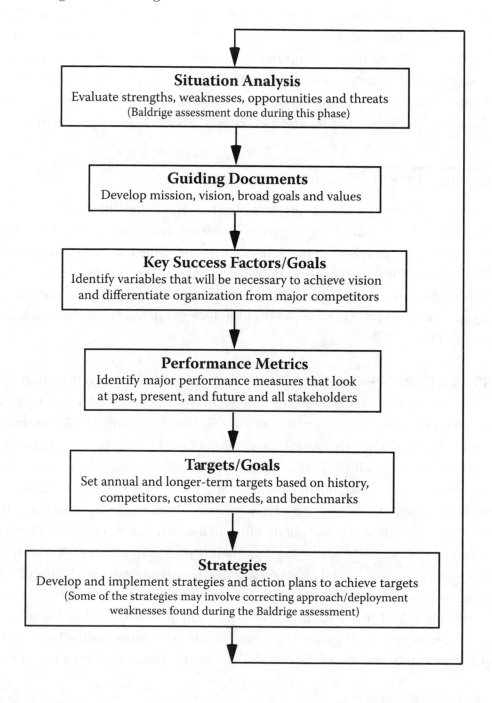

Situation Analysis
Evaluate strengths, weaknesses, opportunities and threats
(Baldrige assessment done during this phase)

Guiding Documents
Develop mission, vision, broad goals and values

Key Success Factors/Goals
Identify variables that will be necessary to achieve vision
and differentiate organization from major competitors

Performance Metrics
Identify major performance measures that look
at past, present, and future and all stakeholders

Targets/Goals
Set annual and longer-term targets based on history,
competitors, customer needs, and benchmarks

Strategies
Develop and implement strategies and action plans to achieve targets
(Some of the strategies may involve correcting approach/deployment
weaknesses found during the Baldrige assessment)

Achieving the targets set in the plan obviously requires a great deal of work, and plans are often revised as performance improves, priorities change, and new problems arise. The Baldrige assessment is useful at two points in the planning process. First, it is an important part of your situation analysis that occurs before you even begin developing a vision of where you want to go. The Baldrige assessment also becomes useful at the end of the planning process when you develop action plans or strategies to achieve your goals and targets. Weaknesses found in your approaches or deployment of those approaches from categories 1 to 6 in Baldrige may become improvement projects that are part of your strategic plan. The key is to make sure that the improvement projects or strategies selected will help the business get healthier. Forget focusing on improving your Baldrige score. If you make your company healthier, your Baldrige score will improve all on its own. Because almost half of the points in Baldrige focus on your business results, a higher Baldrige score will obviously be correlated with better company performance. For more detailed information on this approach to planning, consult my book, *Winning Score: How to Design and Implement Organizational Scorecards* (Productivity Press, 2000).

Breaking Out of the 400 to 500 Point Range

Just as most people who get annual physicals don't get much healthier the next year, most organizations don't get healthier as a result of Baldrige assessments. Once in a while you'll run across a company that is in so much trouble, the Baldrige looks like it might save them. These companies are certainly motivated to change because they sense that the end is near unless they do something dramatically different. The problem for these companies is that it is usually too late. They are so far in the hole that a long-term approach like Baldrige is too late.

In the 12 years I have been teaching organizations about the Baldrige criteria and how to use them for improvement, I have seen a few success stories. One such organization is the cellular phones division of Ericsson, Inc. Ericsson is one of the largest telecommunication companies in the world, with about 80,000 employees worldwide. About 6 years ago, their U.S. cellular phones division that manufactures cellular phones was in trouble. The parent company had been supporting them for years, and they had not made any money, or become a big player in the cellular phone business. They began looking at the Baldrige criteria due to urging from the corporate office in Sweden that required all Ericsson business units to evaluate themselves against their country's quality award criteria. Their initial score was quite low, as is typical of a business first being assessed. Many of the basic framework items were not even in place such as market research (3.1), a clear vision and strategic plan (2.2), and a balanced set of performance metrics (4.1). Based upon their initial assessment, their general manager worked with others in the business to develop a clear vision, key success factors, and a strategic plan that was communicated to each employee. Part of the longer-term vision was to achieve a Baldrige Award someday. In 1997, the division received the highest score of all Ericsson divisions in the United States on an internal Baldrige assessment. Their overall Baldrige score went from the low 200s to around 600 in about 4 years.

Another organization I worked with went on to be a Baldrige finalist in 3 years after receiving an initial score of around 250/1,000. How did these two organizations improve so much when most others did not? Focus. As a result of the Baldrige assessment, both companies came to the realization that they lacked focus. They were working on a variety of improvement initiatives, but lacked the fundamentals of a good business such as sound performance measures and an effective strategic plan. Another important characteristic of both companies is that their CEOs realized how Baldrige looks at all aspects of running a business, and made sure that necessary changes were made to improve the company's performance in areas where they were weak.

The Key to Success with Baldrige

The Baldrige criteria provide a set of general guidelines on how to cook, but you must design the menu, create the recipes, and develop the concept for your restaurant. Just as there is no one formula for a successful restaurant, there are many ways to achieve a good score from Baldrige. Employing planned systematic approaches throughout the organization and focusing on continuous improvement are the building blocks to the success of any organization. This book does not give you a formula for success. It helps you interpret the Baldrige criteria so that you can assess yourself and develop your own unique formula for success.

FURTHER READINGS

Alexander, Keith L. "Company Commitment Pays Off." USA Today, November 18, 1998, p. 5B.

Bemoski, Karen. "A Pat on the Back is Worth a Thousand Words." Quality Progress, March, 1994, pp. 51–54.

Brennen, Niall. Lessons Taught by Baldrige Winners. New York: The Conference Board, 1994.

Brewer, Bill. "Boeing Flies High." News for a Change, November 1999, pp. 1–12.

Brewer, Bill. "Xerox Documents Success." News For a Change, November, 1998, pp. 1–4.

Brown, Mark Graham. "Measuring Your Company Against the 1997 Baldrige Criteria." Journal for Quality and Participation, September, 1997.

——— Beyond the Balanced Scorecard: Improving Business Intelligence With Analytics. New York: Productivity Press, 2007.

——— Get It, Set It, Move It, Prove It: 60 Ways to Get Real Results in Your Organization. New York: Productivity Press, 1996.

——— Keeping Score: Using the Right Metrics to Drive World-Class Performance. New York: Productivity Press, 1996.

——— The Pocket Guide to the Baldrige Award Criteria, 13th ed. New York: Productivity Press, 2007.

——— Winning Score: How to Design and Implement Organizational Scorecards. New York: Productivity Press, 2000.

Brown, Mark Graham, Darcy Hitchcock, and Marsha Willard. Why TQM Fails and What to Do About It. Burr Ridge, IL: Irwin Professional Publishing, 1994.

Castañeda-Méndez, Kicab. The Baldrige Assessor's Workbook. New York: Quality Resources, 1997.

Conlin, Michelle. "Smashing the Clock." Business Week. December 11, 2006, pp. 60–68.

DeCarlo, Nell J., and Kent J. Sterett. "History of the Malcolm Baldrige National Quality Award." Quality Progress, March, 1990, pp. 41–50.

Escobedo, Patricia. "Malcolm Baldrige Award—Where is the Value?" Unpublished paper, 2004.

Fisher, Donald. The Simplified Baldrige Award Organization Assessment. New York: Lincoln-Bradley, 1993.

Garvin, David A. "How the Baldrige Award Really Works." Harvard Business Review, November/December, 1991, pp. 80–95.

Hardy, Quentin. "Motorola Broadsided by the Digital Era, Struggles for a Footing." Wall Street Journal, April 22, 1998, pp. A-1, A-12.

Hart, Christopher W.L., and Christopher E. Bogan. The Baldrige: What It Is, How It's Won, How to Use It to Improve Quality in Your Company. New York: McGraw-Hill, 1992.

Hemp, Paul, and Stewart, Thomas A. "Leading Change When Business is Good." *Harvard Business Review,* November, 2004, pp. 61-70.

Hertz, Harry S. "The Criteria: A Looking Glass to Americans' Understanding of Quality." Quality Progress, June 1997, pp. 46–48.

Jones, Del. "Teamwork Speeds Boeing Along." USA Today, November 18, 1998, p. 5B.

Reichheld, Frederick F. The Loyalty Effect—The Hidden Force Behind Growth, Profits, and Value. Cambridge, MA: Harvard Business School Press, 1996.

Rohan, Thomas M. "Do You Really Want a Baldrige?" Industry Week, April, 1991.

Rucci, Anthony J., Kirn, Steven P., and Quinn, Richard. "The Employee Service Profit Chain at Sears." Harvard Business Review, January/February, 1998, pp. 83–97.

Schaffer, Robert H., and Harvey A. Thomson. "Successful Change Programs Begin with Results." Harvard Business Review, January/February, 1992, pp. 80–89.

Sloan, Allen, "It's Not About Retailing." *Newsweek,* November 29, 2004, p. 41.

Stratton, Brad. "Goodbye ISO 9000: Welcome Back Baldrige Award." Quality Progress, August, 1994, p. 5.

U.S. General Accounting Office. Management Practices—U.S. Companies Improve Performance Through Quality Efforts, Publication GAO/NSIAD-91-190. Washington, D.C.: U.S. General Accounting Office, 1991.

Williams, Thomas A. "Do you Believe in Baldrige?" *Quality,* May, 2004, p.6.

Woodyard, Chris. "Engine Maker Never Stands Still." USA Today, November 18, 1998, p. 5B.

York, Kenneth M., and Miree, Cynthia E. "Causation or Covariation: An Empirical Re-examination of the Link Between TQM and Financial Performance." *Journal of Operations Management,* June, 2004, pp. 291-311.

Appendix

A

STATE AWARDS BASED ON THE BALDRIGE CRITERIA

ALABAMA

<u>State Award Program</u>

State Award Name: Alabama Quality Award
Award Office Address:
Alabama Productivity Center
Associate Director
249 Bidgood Hall
PO Box 870318
Tuscaloosa, AL 35487-0318
Tel: 205-348-8994
Fax: 205-348-9391
E-mail: <u>Linda@proctr.cba.ua.edu</u>
Web: <u>www.alabamaexcellence.com</u>
Award Categories: 1) Small Business; 2) Manufacturing; 3) Service (includes government); 4) Health Care; and 5) Education.

ALASKA

<u>No State Award Program in Place</u>

ARIZONA

<u>State Award Program</u>

State Award Name: Arizona's Pioneer and Governor's Award for Quality
Award Office Address:
Arizona Quality Alliance
Two North Central Avenue, Suite 2200
Phoenix, AZ 85004
Tel: 888-346-7768 or 602-364-7082
Fax: 602-364-7083
E-mail: <u>aqa@arizona-excellence.com</u>
Web: <u>http://www.arizona-excellence.com</u>
Award Categories: 1) Small (1–99); 2) Medium (100–499); and 3) Large (500+)
All sectors compete in the same categories. Sectors include private, public nonprofit (including education and health care), state and federal government.

ARKANSAS

<u>State Award Program</u>

State Award Name: Arkansas Institute for Performance Excellence
Award Office Address:
410 South Cross Street
Little Rock, AR 72201-3005
Tel: 800-447-9330 or 501-373-1300
Fax: 501-372-2722

E-mail: bharvel@arkansas-quality.org
Web: http://www.arkansas-quality.org
Award Categories: Governor's Award, Achievement Award, Commitment Award, Challenge Award

CALIFORNIA

State and Senate Productivity Award
State Award Name: California Awards for Performance Excellence
Award Office Address:
California Council for Excellence
PO Box 1235
Poway, CA 92074-1235
Tel: 858-486-0400
Fax: 858-486-8595
E-mail: cce@calexcellence.org
Web: http://www.calexcellence.org
Award Categories: 3 Level Awards in Manufacturing, Service, Government, Education, Military, Health Care, Nonprofit.

COLORADO

Colorado Performance Excellence Award
Local Award Program
Local Award Name: Excellence in Customer Service
Award Office Address:
3515 S Tamarac Drive, Suite 200
Denver, CO 80237-1430
Tel: 303-893-2739
Fax: 720-859-1353
E-mail: tmmauro@coloradoexcellence.org
Web: www.coloradoexcellence.org
Award Categories: 1) Small (1–20 employees); 2) Mid-size (21–50 employees); and 3) Large (251 employees or more).

CONNECTICUT

State Award Programs
State Award Name: Connecticut Award for Excellence
Award Office Address:
CSU Systems Office
39 Woodland Street
Hartford, CT 06105-2337
Tel: 860-493-0053
E-mail: Michael.Rose@po.state.ct.us

Award Categories: 1) Business (Service and Manufacturing); 2) Education (K–12 and Colleges); 3) Government (State and Local); and 4) Health Care. Within each sector, the Award categories are subdivided into small/medium (300 or less) and large (300+) organizations.

State Award Name: Connecticut Quality Improvement Award
Award Office Address:
P.O. Box 1396
Stamford, CT 06904-1396
Tel: 203-322-9534
Fax: 203-329-2465
E-mail: Cqia@aol.com
Web: http://www.ctqualityaward.org
Award Categories: Small (1–100); Medium (101–500; and Large (5001)

DELAWARE

State Award Program
State Award Name: Delaware Quality Award
Award Office Address:
John Riabov, Executive Director
Delaware Alliance for Excellence
13 East 8th St.
Wilmington, DE 19801
Tel: 302-571-5233
Fax: 302-571-5666
E-mail: jriabov@udel.edu
or
Mica Corradin, Program Manager
Professional and Continuing Studies
UD Downtown Center
13 East 8th Street (8th and King Streets)
Wilmington, DE 19801
Tel: 302-571-5239
Fax: 302-571-5666
E-mail: business-mgmt@udel.edu
Web: www.udel.edu/DQA
Award Categories: 1) Manufacturing (large, small—2 awards each);
2) nonmanufacturing (large, small—2 awards each); and 3) Not-for-Profit
(one size category—2 possible awards)

FLORIDA

State Award Program
State Award Name: Governor's Sterling Award

Award Office Address:
Florida Sterling Council
Post Office Box 13907
Tallahassee, FL 32317-3907
Tel: 850-922-5316
Fax: 850-488-7579
E-mail: jsherlock@floridasterling.com
Web: http://www.floridasterling.com
Award Categories: (None)

GEORGIA

<u>State Award Program</u>
State Award Name: Georgia Oglethorpe Award
Award Office Address:
148 International Blvd., Suite 650
Atlanta, GA 30303-1751
Tel: 404-232-3808
Fax: 404-232-3771
E-mail: goap@mindspring.com
Web: www.georgiaOglethorpe.org
Award Categories: Large Business—more than 200 employees; Small/Medium Business—up to 200 total employees; Large Industry—more than 200 employees; Small/Medium Industry—up to 200 employees; Government; Education; Health Care; and Not-for-Profit

HAWAII

<u>State Award Program</u>
State Award Name: The Hawaii State Award of Excellence
Award Office Address:
Hawaii SBDC Oahu Center
1041 Nuuanu Avenue, Suite A
Honolulu, HI 96817
Tel: 808-258-7662
Fax: 808-593-6466
E-mail: rona@aloha.net
Web: (None)
Award Categories: Business; Government; Military; Health; Education; and Not-for-Profit

IDAHO

<u>State Award Program</u>
State Award Name: Idaho Quality Award for Performance Excellence

Award Office Address:
Idaho Quality Award
Idaho Department of Commerce
700 West State Street
Boise, ID 83720
Tel: 208-334-2470
Fax: 208-334-2631
E-mail: clong@idoc.state.id.us
Web: http://www.idahoworks.com
Award Categories: Marketplace, Workplace, or Community, Quality
Management System

ILLINOIS

State Award Program

State Award Name: Lincoln Awards for Performance Excellence
Award Office Address:
The Lincoln Foundation for Business Excellence
1415 West Diehl Road
Mail Stop 514
Naperville, IL 60563
Tel: 630-637-1595
Fax: 630-579-1620
E-mail: info@lincolnaward.org
Web: http://www.lincolnaward.org
Award Categories: 1) Education; 2) Government; 3) Health Care; 4) Industry, and
5) Service

INDIANA

State Award Program

State Award Name: BKD Indiana Excellence Awards
Award Office Address:
BKD IN Quality Improvement Awards
201 N. Illinois Street Suite 700
P.O. Box 44998
Indianapolis, IN 46244-0998
Tel: 317-383-4000, 888-476-7258
Fax: 317-383-4200
E-mail: excellence@indianabusiness.com
Web: http://www.indianabusiness.com/quality
Award Categories: One category includes all for-profit and not-for-profit organizations

IOWA

<u>State Award Program</u>

State Award Name: Iowa Recognitive for Performance Excellence
Award Office Address:
Iowa Quality Center
3375 Armar Drive
Marion, IA 52302
Tel: 319-398-7101
Fax: 319-398-5698
E-mail: gnesteby@wqc.org, or info@iowaqc.org
Web: www.iowaqc.org
Award Categories: Gold, Silver, Bronze recognition levels

KANSAS

<u>State Award Program</u>

State Award Name: Kansas Award for Excellence
Award Office Address:
Kansas Center for Performance Excellence
Fort Hayes State University
600 Park Street
Hayes, KS 67601-4099
Tel: 800-743-6767, 785-234-6351
Fax: 785-234-8777
E-mail: mmwilson2@fhsu.edu
Web: www.kansasexcellence.org
Award Categories: (None)

KENTUCKY

<u>State Award Program</u>

State Award Name: Commonwealth of Kentucky Quality Award
Award Office Address:
Kentucky Center for Performance Excellence
2201 Broadhead Place
Lexington, KY 40515
Tel: 800-900-3360 or 859-245-9257
Fax:
E-mail: info@kycpe.org
Web: http://www.kycpe.org
Award Categories: Manufacturing Companies (large and small); Service Organizations; Educational Institutions, and in 1998; Health Care and Government Organizations.

LOUISIANA

State Award Program

State Award Name: Louisiana Performance Excellence Award
Award Office Address:
Louisiana Quality Foundation
c/o Louisiana Productivity Center
PO Box 44172
Lafayette, LA 70504-4172
Tel: 337-482-6422
Fax: 337-262-5472
E-mail: cdupuy@louisiana.edu
Web: http://www.laqualityaward.com
Award Categories: Manufacturing, Service; Health Care, Education, and Public Sector

MAINE

State Award Program

State Award Name: Margaret Chase Smith Maine State Quality Award
Award Office Address:
Margaret Chase Smith Quality Association
7 University Drive
Augusta, ME 04330-9412
ATTN: Andrea Jandebeur, Program Administrator
Tel: 207-621-1988
Fax: 207-282-6081
E-mail: mqc@gwi.net
Web: http://www.maine-quality.org/awards program.html
Award Categories: 1 and 2) Large Manufacturing and Large Service (100 or more employees); 3 and 4) Small Manufacturing and Small Service (fewer than 100 employees); and 5) Nonprofit (no size qualifications)

MARYLAND

State Award Programs

State Award Name: Maryland Performance Excellence Award and the Maryland Senate Productivity Award
Award Office Address:
Maryland Performance Excellence Award Program
3114 Potomac Bldg, 092
University of Maryland
College Park, MD 20742-3415
Tel: 301-405-7173
Fax: 301-403-4105
E-mail: martys@umd.edu
Web: www.mpea.umd.edu

Award Categories: Gold, Silver and Bronze; U.S. Senate Productivity Award; 1) Manufacturing; 2) Service; and 3) Public Sector/Nonprofit

MASSACHUSETTS

<u>State Award Programs</u>

State Award Name: Massachusetts Performance Excellence Award
Award Office Address:
Perry Jewell
President and Executive Director
MassExcellence, c/o Massachusetts Council for Quality, Inc., Center for Industrial Competitiveness
600 Suffolk Street (5th floor)
Lowell, MA 01854
Tel: 978-934-2733
Fax: 978-934-4035
E-mail: info@massexcellence.com
Web: www.massexcellence.com

Local Award Name: Pioneer Valley Business Excellence Award
Award Office Address:
Jeanette Jez
Executive Director
The Springfield Area Council for Excellence (SPACE)
1441 Main Street, 1st Floor, Banknorth Building
Springfield, MA 01103
Tel: 413-755-1300
Fax: 413-731-8530
E-mail: info@spaceforexcellence.org
Web: www.spaceforexcellence.org

MICHIGAN

<u>State Award Program</u>

State Award Name: Michigan Quality Leadership Award
Award Office Address:
Geri Markley
President, Michigan Quality Council
3601 Plymouth Road
Ann Arbor, MI 48105-2659
Tel: 734-929-9124
Fax: 734-332-8918
E-mail: info@michiganquality.org
Web: http://www.michiganquality.org/
Award Categories: Business, Health Care; Education

MINNESOTA

<u>State Award Program</u>

State Award Name: Minnesota Quality Award
Award Office Address:
Kathryn Mackin
Minnesota Council for Quality
PMB 156
13033 Ridgedale Drive
Minnetonka, MN 55305-1807
Tel: 612-462-3577
Fax: 763-476-1614
E-mail: info@councilforquality.org
Web: www.councilforquality.org
Award Categories: Education, Government, Health Care, Manufacturing, Service, and Nonprofit

MISSISSIPPI

<u>State Award Program</u>

State Award Name: Mississippi Quality Award
Award Office Address:
Duane Hamill
Director
Mississippi Quality Award
State Board for Junior & Comm. College
3825 Ridgewood Road
Jackson, MS 39211
Tel: 601-432-6349
Fax: 601-432-6363
E-mail: dhamill@sbcjc.cc.ms.us
Web: http://www.sbcjc.cc.ms.us/mqa.html

MISSOURI

<u>State Award Program</u>

State Award Name: Missouri Quality Award
Award Office Address:
Excellence in Missouri Foundation
205 Jefferson St., 14th Floor
P.O. Box 1085
Jefferson City, MO 65101
Tel: 573-526-1725
Fax: 573-526-1729

E-mail: brenda.hatfield@mqa.mo.gov
Web: http://www.mqa.org
Award Categories: Manufacturing, Service, Education, Health Care, Public Sector, (nonprofit in all of above categories). Awards may be presented in the following size classes by number of employees; Small 5 0–99, Medium 5 100–499, Large 5 5001 employees.

MONTANA

No State Award Program in Place

NEBRASKA

State Award Program
State Award Name: The Edgerton Quality Award
Award Office Address:
301 Centennial Mall South
P.O. Box 94666
Lincoln, NE 68509-4666
Tel: 402-471-3745or 800-426-6505
Fax: (402) 471-3778
E-mail: edgerton@neded.org
Web: http://assist.neded.org/edgerton
Award Categories: Edgerton Award of Commitment, Edgerton Award of Progress, Edgerton Award of Excellence

NEVADA

State Award Program
State Award Name: Nevada Governor's Awards for Performance Excellence
Award Office Address:
Board of Directors
Nevada Governor's Award for Performance Excellence
4132 S. Rainbow, #394
Las Vegas, NV 89103-3106
Tel: 702-451-8015
Fax:
E-mail: richalons@cox.net
Web: www.nvqa.org
Award Categories: Business, Health Care, Education, The Nevada Awards for Quality Leadership, Customer Service Excellence, Community Support, and Workplace Development

NEW HAMPSHIRE

<u>State Award Program</u>

State Award Name: Granite State Quality Award
Award Office Address:
Granite State Quality Council
PO Box 29
Manchester, NH 03105-0029
Tel: 603-223-1312
Fax: 603-223-1299
E-mail: info@GSQC.COM
Web: http://www.gsqc.com
Award Categories: 1) Service: Small (,200 employees) and Large (200 employees); and 2) Manufacturing (Small and Large). Health, education, not-for-profit, and small businesses are eligible under either of the two categories.

NEW JERSEY

<u>State Award Program</u>

State Award Name: NJ Governor's Award for Performance Excellence
Award Office Address:
Mary G. Roebling Building
20 West State Street, 12th Floor
P.O. Box 827
Trenton, NJ 08625-0827
Tel: 609-777-0940
Fax: 609-777-2798
E-mail: qnj@qnj.com
Web: http://www.qnj.org
Award Categories: Business; Governmental; Education; Health Care.

NEW MEXICO

<u>State Award Program</u>

State Award Name: New Mexico Quality Awards
Award Office Address:
Quality New Mexico
500 4th St. NW, Suite 215
Albuquerque, NM 87102
Tel: 505-944-2001
Fax: 505-944-2002
E-mail: qnm@quality-newmexico.org
Web: http://www.qualitynewmexico.org
Award Categories: Zia Award, Roadrunner Recognition-Progress, and Pinon Recognition

NEW YORK

State Award Program

State Award Name: The Governor's Award for Excellence
Award Office Address:
The Empire State Advantage: Excellence at Work
16 Computer Drive West, Suite 107
Albany, NY 12205
Tel: 518-482-1747
Fax: 518-482-2231
E-mail: esanewyork@aol.com
Web: www.empireadvantage.org
Award Categories: For-profit and Not-for-Profit Sectors; Private; Government; Education; and Health Care

NORTH CAROLINA

State Award Name: North Carolina Awards for Excellence
Award Office Address:
Wayne Tindle
NCAfE Program Director
NC State University Industrial Extension Service
Campus Box 7902
Raleigh, NC 27695-7902
Tel: 1-800-227-0264
Fax:
E-mail: ies_services@ncsu.edu
Web: www.ies.ncsu.edu/ncafe

NORTH DAKOTA

No State Award Program in Place

OHIO

State Award Program

State Award Name: Ohio Award for Excellence
Award Office Address:
Ohio Partnership for Excellence
829 Bethel Road
PMB #212
Columbus, OH 43214
Tel: 614-441-8337
Fax: 614-515-4771

E-mail: info@ partnershipohio.org
Web: www.partnershipohio.org
Award Categories: Business; Education; Government; Health Care; and Not-for-Profit.
Bronze, Silver, Gold or Platinum

OKLAHOMA

State Award Program

State Award Name: Oklahoma Quality Award
Award Office Address:
OK Quality Award Foundation
900 North Stiles
PO Box 26980
Oklahoma City, OK 73126-0980
Tel: 405-815-5295
Fax: 405-815-5205
E-mail: Mike.Strong@oklahomaquality.org
Web: www.oklahomaquality.com
Award Categories: Manufacturing; Service; Health Care; Education; Government:
1) Small (,50), 2) Medium (51–250), and 3) Large (2511)

OREGON

State Award Program

State Award Name: Oregon Excellence Awards
Award Office Address:
PO Box 13758
Portland, OR 13758
Tel: 503-475-6503
Fax: 503-614-6393
E-mail: ope@ope.com
Web: http://www.oregonexcellence.org
Award Categories: (None)

PENNSYLVANIA

No State Award Program in Place
Local Award Programs

Local Award Name: Lehigh Valley Community Quality Award
Award Office Address:
Manufacturers' Resource Center
125 Goodman Drive
Bethlehem, PA 18015-3715
Tel: 610-758-4596 or 800-343-6732
Fax: 610-758-4716

E-mail: tony@net.bfp.org
Web: (None)
Award Categories: Manufacturing; Service; Nonprofit; Health Care; Education; Finance; Government; Retail; and Other

Local Award Name: Lancaster Chamber of Commerce Business Excellence Award
Award Office Address:
Sandi Thompson
Program Director
Lancaster Chamber Performance Excellence Award
The Lancaster Chamber of Commerce & Industry
P.O. Box 1558
Lancaster, PA 17608-1558
Tel: 717-397-4049
Fax: 717-293-3159
E-mail: sthmpso@lcci.com
Web: http://www.lcci.com
Award Categories: (None)

RHODE ISLAND

State Award Program
State Award Name: Rhode Island Quality Award
Award Office Address:
Brian Knight
P.O. Box 6766
10 Abbott Park Place
Providence, RI 02940
Tel: 401-459-4914
Fax: 401-528-1976
E-mail: bknight@ricpe.org
Web: www.ricpe.org
Award Categories: Manufacturing; Service; Health Care; Government (state); and Not-for-Profit. U.S. government and trade associations are not eligible.

SOUTH CAROLINA

State Award Program
State Award Name: South Carolina's Governor's Quality Award
Award Office Address:
South Carolina Quality Forum
University of South Carolina Upstate
800 University Way
Spartanburg, SC 29303
Tel: 864-503-5990/888-231-0578
Fax: 864-503-5583

E-mail: jreeves@uscupstate.edu
Web: www.scquality.com
Award Categories: Business, Education, Healthcare, Government

SOUTH DAKOTA

State Award Program

State Award Name: South Dakota Business Excellence Awards
Award Office Address:
South Dakota Chamber of Commerce and Industry
P.O. Box 190
Pierre, SD 57501-0190
Tel: 605-224-6161
Fax: 605-224-7198
E-mail: (None)
Web: www.sdchamber.biz
Award Categories: Any private-sector, nongovernment, for-profit business

TENNESSEE

State Award Programs

State Award Name: Tennessee Center for Performance Excellence
Award Office Address:
Kathryn S. Rawls, President/CEO
Tennessee Center for Performance Excellence
2525 Perimeter Place Drive, Suite 122
Nashville, TN 37214-3773
Tel: 800-453-6474 or 615-889-8323
Fax: 615-889-8325
E-mail: contact@tncpe.org
Web: http://www.tncpe.org
Award Categories: Any public or private organization

Local Award Programs

Local Award Name: Greater Memphis Association for Quality
Award Office Address:
Jennifer McNary
Executive Director
Greater Memphis Association for Quality
The University of Memphis
213 Alumni Center
Memphs, TN 38152-3750
Tel: 901-678-4268
Fax: 901-678-4301

E-mail: jmmcnary@memphis.edu
Web: www.gmaq.org

Local Award Name: Quality Cup Team Award
Award Office Address:
Dr. Donald C. Fisher
Executive Director
MSQPC—The Quality Center
22 N. Front St., Suite 200
Memphis, TN 38103
Tel: 901-543-3551
Fax: 901-543-3510
E-mail: ldale@memphischamber.com
Web: www.msqpc.com

TEXAS

State Award Program
State Award Name: Texas Award for Performance Excellence
Award Office Address:
Quality Texas Foundation
1402 Corinth, Suite 2004
Dallas, TX 75215
Tel: 214-565-8550
Fax: 214-565-9082
E-mail: quality-info@texas-quality.org, or jwestbrook@texas-quality.org
Web: http://www.texas-quality.org
Award Categories: 1) Manufacturing; 2) Service; 3) Small Business (less than 100 employees); 4) Public Sector; 5) Education; and Health Care

Local Award Programs
Local Award Name: Central Texas Regional Performance Excellence Award
Award Office Address:
Gail Bickling
Program Manager
The University of Texas at Austin
P.O. Box 7518
Austin, TX 78713-7518
Tel: 512-232-9530
Fax: 512-232-6126
E-mail: bickling@mail.utexas.edu
Web: www.utexas.edu/cee/cpe

UTAH

State Award Program

State Award Name: Utah Quality Awards
Award Office Address:
Utah Quality Council
P.O. Box 271367
Salt Lake City, UT 84127-1367
Tel: 801-825-3336
Fax: 801-825-3337
E-mail: uqc@utahqualityaward.org
Web: www.utahqualityaward.org
Award Categories: 1) Manufacturing (organizations that produce, process, or assemble products); 2) Service/Nonprofit (for profit or nonprofit organizations that provide services); 3) Education (institutions that are degree granting or credit giving, according to Utah law); and 4) Government (federal, state, or local.) Each of these categories has these groupings: a) Large, b) Medium, and c) Small.

VERMONT

State Award Program

State Award Name: Vermont Performance Excellence Awards
Award Office Address:
Gerald Brown
President
Vermont Council for Quality
480 Hercules Drive
Colchester, VT 05446
Tel: 802-655-1910
Fax: 802-655-1932
E-mail: laurie@performanceexcellence.com
Web: www.vermontquality.org

VIRGINIA

State Award Program

State Award Name: U.S. Senate Productivity and Quality Award for VA
Award Office Address:
PO Box 6099
Suffolk, VA 23433
Tel: 757-523-6762
Fax: 757-523-6030
E-mail: director@spqa-va.org, or chair@spqa-va.org
Web: www.spqa-va.org
Award Categories: Private Sector Manufacturing; Private Sector Service; Public Sector State and Federal Agencies; and Public Sector Local Agencies

WASHINGTON

State Award Program

State Award Name: Washington State Quality Award
Award Office Address:
Jennifer Sprecher
Executive Director
Washington State Quality Award Program
P.O. Box 609
Keyport, WA 98345
Tel: 800-517-8264 or 360-697-2444
Fax: 360-394-2445
E-mail: wsqa@wsqa.net
Web: http://www.wsqa.net
Award Categories: 1) Government; 2) Private; 3) Not for Profit; 4) Education.
(All categories are further divided by large (2011 employees) and small (less than 201 employees).

WEST VIRGINIA

No State Award Program in Place

WISCONSIN

State Award Program

State Award Name: Wisconsin Forward Award
Award Office Address:
Elizabeth Menzer
Executive Director
Wisconsin Forward Award, Inc.
2909 Landmark Place, Suite 110
Madison, WI 53713
Tel: 608-663-5300
Fax: 608-663-5302
E-mail: menzer@forwardaward.org
Web: http://www.forwardaward.org
Award Categories: All eligible

WYOMING

No State Award Program in Place